# *Way Out* WEST

## JANE & MICHAEL STERN

FIRST EDITION

*Designed by Charles Kreloff*

Library of Congress Cataloging-in-Publication Data
Stern, Jane.
Way out west / by Jane & Michael Stern.—1st ed.
      p.      cm.
Includes index.
ISBN 0-06-016873-0
1. Popular culture—West (U.S.)    2. West (U.S.)—
Social life and customs.    I. Stern, Michael, 1946- .
II. Title.
F596.S844 1993
978—dc20                                        92-56223

93 94 95 96 97 ❖/RRD 10 9 8 7 6 5 4 3 2 1

**To Gus**
**True to the end of the trail**

# CONTENTS

# ACKNOWLEDGMENTS

This book was a special pleasure to write because we met so many good people along the way. In particular, we want to acknowledge the help and inspiration of:

Donna Bachman of the Wyoming State Museum for finding us such beautiful photos of fancy saddles;

Tyler Beard—Comanche, Texas's oracle of cowboy boots—for his good advice;

Scott Binning for his hospitality at Cheyenne Frontier Days;

Baxter Black for wise suggestions, permission to reprint his poem, "The Oyster," and for being such a nice guy as well as an inspiring artist;

Cheryl Blevins for helping us find out about Mesilla, New Mexico;

Paul Bosland for an enlightening tour of the chile fields of Hatch and a delicious trip to Chope's cafe;

Paula West Chavoya of the Wyoming State Museum for helping us find fabulous pictures of pioneer cowgirls;

Richard Collier for his photos of Don King and Verlane DesGrange's saddles;

Chuck and Barbara Cooper of Rancho for being just about the most hospitable folks we know—allowing us to photograph their incomparable inventory of Western collectibles and generally making us feel at home whenever we visit Santa Fe;

Cecil Cornish for the loan of his photos and his nearly irresistible encouragement for us to join him on a trail drive in Oklahoma;

Debbie Cox, Bob and Marianne Kapoun of the Rainbow Man for their help and hospitality in allowing us to photograph some of their dazzling collection;

Verlane DesGrange for pictures of the beautiful saddles she makes;

Dave DeWitt for a four-star tour of the fiery foods of Albuquerque;

Dickinson Cattle Company for giving us so much information about longhorn cattle, and for going the extra 2000+ miles to get a stunning skull to us from Colorado;

Bo and Jim at East-West traders on Canyon Road for permission to photograph some of the beautiful things they have in their store;

Judy Ebbinghouse and Bobby Morean of Santacafe, where we enjoyed so many memorable meals;

Steve Fleming for help in our research about rodeo, and for the loan of some great action photos;

Liliane Francuz of the Wyoming Arts Council for tracking down photos of well-dressed horses;

Michael Friedman of the Friedman Gallery for opening the door to the world of Western collectibles;

Betsy Houlihan of the Millicent Rogers Museum, which supplied us with photos and precious information about Miss Rogers and her times;

Robert N. Gray, author of the rousing *Mr. Rodeo, Himself,* for helping us find Cecil Cornish;

Alden Hamblin for his fine dinosaur photos from the Utah Field House;

Wendy Lane for giving us run of her delectable store, Back to the Ranch, where we photographed boots, hats, and Westernalia;

Gary and Sandie Leffew for being our pals in Cheyenne and Santa Maria, and for giving us a true World Champion's view of rodeo;

Ron Linton for letting us photograph his father's fantastic boots at his store P.T. Crow in Albuquerque;

Belva Lowery for permission to reprint her poem, "Rhythm of the Rodeo," and for taking time to reminisce about Nebraska's Big Rodeo on our behalf;

Howard and Ron Mandelbaum and the rest of the staff at Photofest for helping us zero in on some marvelous pictures of movie cowboys;

Alan Manley for locating some of his father's priceless Sonora Desert dude ranch photos;

Wallace McRae for directing us to his poem "Ol' Proc," and for permission to reprint it;

Kathryn Wiese Morton of the University of Kansas Museum of Natural History for the full story of Comanche, the war horse;

Marilyn Peil, who guided us through the magnificent archives of the National Cowboy Hall of Fame and helped us locate so many of the classic pictures in this book;

Dickie Pfaelzer—the best-dressed woman in Santa Fe—for an unforgettable lunch at the Palace;

George Pitman, whose generous help supplying pictures and information about Bohlin saddles and fine Western wear has been indispensable, and whose enthusiasm for the West is positively contagious;

John Porto and Karen Rue of High Lonesome Stables for their skill and patience teaching us horsemanship, and Clyde, Bonnie, Pepper, and Traveler for *their* patience when we were greenhorns on their backs;

Don Preziosi, who, as usual, supplied some stunning post-card images;

Dusty Rogers, Roy Rogers, and Dale Evans, for their hospitality and willingness to help;

Joanna and Bill Seitz, whose friendly shop, J. Seitz, provides a satisfying regular Western fix close to home;

Lindee Shaw for sharing her research and enthusiasm regarding the history of fiesta fashion;

Denny Shewell of Tonto Rim for expert advice and permission to reprint his hat crease chart;

Jim Shoulders, rodeo's greatest champion, for sitting down and giving us just about the most entertaining and informative interview we've ever conducted;

The Sparks—Ron and Marcia and Marie—for a first-class tour of Tucson's high spots in their impeccable Checker car, and also for the loan of some eye-boggling Western neckties, and for sharing with us their all-around outstanding good taste;

Janice M. Stengel of the Estate of Clifford P. Westermeier for permission to reprint a verse from Mr. Westermeier's *Man, Beast, Dust;*

Dana Sullivant, for her open-door policy at the National Cowboy Hall of Fame.

Greg Tuza of Wrangler for some fine photographs of spokesman Jim Shoulders.

Thanks especially to the gang at the HarperCollins spread: Bill Shinker and Susan Moldow, the Roy Rogers and Dale Evans of publishing; Rick Kot, our editor, and Susan Friedland, who helped bring this book home; Joseph Montebello, top hand in the design corral; Charles Kreloff and Jessica Shatan, who made *Way Out West* plumb beautiful; and Jennifer Griffin and Sheila Gillooly, all-around cowgirls. Thanks also to our sharp-shootin' agent, Binky Urban.

# INTRODUCTION

Four years ago we made a trip to New Mexico on assignment for the *New Yorker* magazine. Although our work had taken us around the world, it had been a while since we had spent much time in the West. We had relished traveling there while working on our first book, *Trucker: A Portrait of the Last American Cowboy* (1976), and feasting on chili con carne along the road in the years since, but this trip was different. Rambling up along the Rio Grande, we were overwhelmed by a sense of déjà vu. Cowboy hats and sharp-toed boots everywhere; a hand-tooled Western saddle on a pinto pony; a red mesa set against a turquoise sky; a thorny prickly pear cactus:

these images exercised a strange psychic pull. They were more familiar than they should have been, considering that we have lived in the East most of our lives. After several return trips, we began to make sense of our feelings. We realized that the West is a land of extraordinarily potent icons and images, images that express this nation's very soul and character: the saga of the frontier, the promise of big skies and wide-open spaces, the land—as Navajos call it—of "time enough and room enough."

The West is America's national mythology. Its story is the greatest romantic fable this country has produced, and it belongs to all of us. There is a little bit of cowboy and cowgirl in nearly everyone. It's in those who wear

suits and ties instead of chaps and boots, and it's in those who spend their days staring at the screen of a computer terminal instead of at the broad horizon. Can there be a soul so calloused by modern life that he or she doesn't thrill to the sight of a magnificent palomino rearing up, to the sorrowful sound of a lonesome cowboy song, or to the inviting smell of bacon sizzling in a skillet over the morning campfire?

Like so many other pilgrims who have gone West, we were smitten after that trip four years ago, and we have spent the time since traveling there at every opportunity and researching it in between. Wherever we explored and whatever adventures we had, we found the same feelings washing over us: that we had been there before, and the land was part of us. We have made our living writing about America for some twenty years now, and there isn't a part of the country we don't enjoy, yet we have never felt so passionate about a region as we do about the West.

As our own library of Western books grew, we realized that people have written about every aspect of the region's history, all about its natural wonders, and about the newly popular "Western style." As much as we savored all these kinds of books over the years, none quite evoked the West that spoke to us or, we suspected, to the many travelers who go there and feel as we did: inspired. We knew we had to write a book about the West. Our goal when we conceived it was to try to capture the distinct magic of the region, which includes fact and tall tales, history and entertainment.

Many of us first fell in love with the West thanks to cowboy stars like Roy Rogers and Dale Evans, Hopalong Cassidy, and Gene Autry. As children, we pleaded with our parents to buy us their official lunchboxes, toy pistols, and horse-shaped night lights so we could drift off to sleep dreaming that we, too, owned a beautiful steed with a silver saddle, then go to school the next day pretending our soggy egg salad sandwiches were actually authentic cowboy vittles prepared by some grizzle-cheeked chuck wagon cook.

The glory of the West was a dream shared by generations of children who knew cowboys as men who galloped off into the sunset after they made the world a better place to live. Gene Autry at one time even published "The Ten Commandments of a Cowboy" for his legions of young fans; it was a code of virtuous behavior in which a cowboy pledged never to cheat, lie, or hurt anyone, to be a patriot, and to help people in distress. In emulation of their heroes, scores of "little partners"

mounted the backs of broomstick ponies and promised to be brave and true, to love their horses and respect their teachers and their parents.

As we planned this book, we considered the fact that much of what people love about the West has been filtered through popular culture, which tends to romanticize it. Life in the real West was very different from the shimmering yarns it has inspired. For the most part, the frontier was brutal and without much glamour. The cowboys' actual job was to move huge, recalcitrant herds of livestock from one place to another, for which they received subsistence wages. The region's settlers and pioneers faced stupendous hardships on the frontier, and most of them did so without a trick horse and shiny saddle, without flamboyant chaps and Stetson hats and blazing six-guns. As hard as life was for these white pathfinders, it was worse for the Native Americans who were the region's original occupants. The holocaust visited upon them by the opening of the West was anything but a romantic tale; and the legacy of what happened to them is still an open wound.

The image of the cowboy, and the mythology of the West in general, began veering away from reality more than a century ago—in dime novels, Wild West shows, and rodeos. By the time historian Frederick Jackson Turner declared the frontier closed, in 1893, the West had already become a great folk tale, and just after the turn of the century, as the movie business got underway—not coincidentally, in the West—Westerns soon became this nation's favorite kind of entertainment, containing adventure, moral lessons, history, pretty cowgirls, and handsome cowboys. Many of the region's real problems were incorporated into movie mythology (cowboys vs. Indians, sodbusters vs. cattlemen), but for the most part, the blunt and painful truths of history have had little bearing on the West of the imagination. That West, the West of song and poem and paintings and movies and romantic fantasies, may contain man's darker nature, but it is unspoiled by despair. It is that West we decided to make the subject of *Way Out West*—the West of cowboys in silver spurs singing "Whoopee ti-yi-yo," of smoke curling up above Sioux tepee encampments in the Badlands, of Roy and Dale's "Happy Trails."

What we wound up with is a love poem to a region that continues to hold the world in its thrall. This is a book about the allure of the West, about a unique culture and way of life that has immense power to inspire those it touches. The heyday of America's infatuation with the West was the middle of the twentieth century, when dude ranches were in style, when cowboy movies flourished on the silver screen and TV cowboys enchanted millions of children, when Route 66 was still a place to get your kicks, and when the *Super Chief* rocketed toward the sunset with its promise of adventure. Of course, the mythology goes back at least to *Last of the Mohicans* and Longfellow's "Song of Hiawatha," as well as to the romantic paintings of George Catlin, and it continues into the present day, as seen in such pop-culture phenomena as *Lonesome Dove* and *Dances with Wolves,* and in the popularity of Western style in country music.

If the time frame of *Way Out West* is far-flung, the geography is spacious, too. Exactly where, you ask, is the West we're writing about? It is wherever the mythology fits. Texas and Oklahoma, of course, and New Mexico and Arizona and Colorado, and the High Plains, and California and the Pacific Northwest, and even the Midlands and the prairie: all play a part in that great collective saga. Of the many books we have enjoyed about the West, a particular favorite is a slender red volume written in 1936 by Oren Arnold, and titled *Wonders of the West,* filled with awe and admiration. Its frontispiece is a lithograph of Enchanted Mesa, followed by these wise words: *"The truth is that nobody knows exactly where the West begins. The West is as much a state of mind as of geography."*

We would like *Way Out West* to serve as a wonder book for our readers, just as *Wonders of the West* did for people half a century ago. In eight chapters we have tried to define the classic elements of the West of the imagination: the cowboy ideal and the image of the Indian, funky roadside attractions and great sleeves-up food along the way, heroic horses and legendary longhorns, fabulous Western fashions and the thrills of rodeo life. Of course, we had to include a great big shopping directory at the end, because if you are anything like us, you will be inspired to run right out and buy the best Western stuff around.

So, saddle up: we aim to show you how to rope like a cowboy, how to identify a horned toad, and how to cook a crisp chicken-fried steak. We'll show you how to pleat a Navajo broomstick skirt and spot the difference between an Idaho cowboy and a Texas cowboy by the crease of his hat, how to select the best turquoise jewelry in a trading post, and how to ride a bucking bronco. To welcome you on the journey, we'd like to share these final words from *Wonders of the West:* "One book can do little more than give you a taste of it, but maybe it will be a pleasant taste. Get your cowboy hat and swing on your saddlebags: let's be riding down some Western trails."

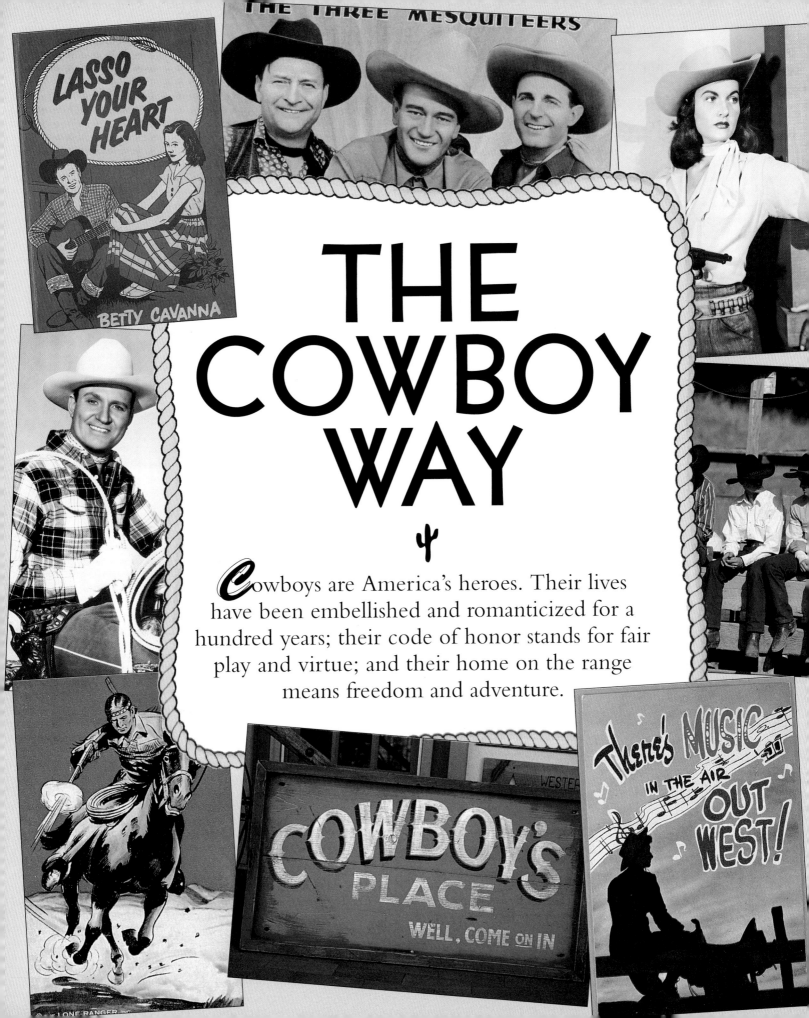

# THE COWBOY WAY

❦

$\mathscr{C}$owboys are America's heroes. Their lives have been embellished and romanticized for a hundred years; their code of honor stands for fair play and virtue; and their home on the range means freedom and adventure.

LASSO YOUR HEART

BETTY CAVANNA

THE THREE MESQUITEERS

COWBOY'S PLACE

WELL, COME ON IN

There's MUSIC IN THE AIR OUT WEST!

# *The* COWBOY IDEAL

Oh, to be a cowboy! To ride the high lonesome, to strum a guitar with good companions, to eat chili and sourdough biscuits from a tin plate, and to sleep at night under a million stars by the crackle of a campfire as coyotes wail their desert serenade! To be a cowboy is a dream that is simply bliss, American-style.

The cowboy ideal is a huge myth, one that contains the reality of life on the range, but has also unfurled way beyond plain facts. Most men who originally defined the cowboy way of life were underpaid, overworked laborers. Their heyday lasted hardly more than twenty-five years when, soon after the Civil War, they made their mark in American history—and eventually captured the imagination of the world—by signing on to make the long cattle drives from Texas to the railheads of Kansas. Historians estimate there weren't more than forty thousand of them altogether, and they were a motley bunch: rootless war orphans, maverick Texas Rangers, itinerants looking for a better life, a fair number of displaced Mexicans, and as many as five thousand freed slaves.

To be a cowboy in 1865 had little honor or romance about it, and Texas "cow-boys" weren't thought of as any

Opposite: *Charles Starrett, one of the brave cowboy heroes of the 1930s and 1940s. He was chivalrous to ladies and kind to boys and girls who admired him.*

better than the pig-boys and turkey-boys who moved livestock for a living in other parts of the country. The word *cow-boy* itself had been used as early as the 1640s to refer to Irish prisoners of war who had been shipped to the American colonies to work on cattle ranches; it was also the term applied to cattle thieves in Westchester County, New York, during the Revolutionary War.

Wherever the term originated, cowboys would become forever linked to the West, and regardless of the hard realities of their profession, their legend became an inspiration for generations and remains potent today. The transformation of the image of the cowboy from a hired man to a national ideal began in the 1880s, when artists and writers and showmen, and cowboys themselves, began to believe that the frontier was vanishing; out of that sense of loss came a yearning to preserve the cowboy's life as a sterling example of liberty and self-reliance.

In magazines and dime novels about the frontier, in literary works like Stephen Crane's "The Bride Comes to Yellow Sky," and in Theodore Roosevelt's *Ranch Life and the Hunting Trail,* the West took on a gleam as the land of adventure where cowboys rode free. (Roosevelt was known to invite High Plains cowboys to the White House for dinner

Left: *William S. Hart, toting Peacemakers he got from real Wild West gunslingers.* Right: *Tom Mix, the original hero in a white hat.*

alongside government dignitaries and ambassadors.) In paintings and sculptures by Frederic Remington and Charles M. Russell, and in the magical photographs of Edward S. Curtis, the world learned to see the West as a charmed place where heroes dwelled. Owen Wister's popular novel *The Virginian,* (1902) crystallized the image of the cowboy as a gun-totin' buckaroo who lived by a code of honor as chivalric as a knight of yore, and it helped make cowboys seem familiar even to those who never set foot in the land of tumbling tumbleweeds. At the same time, Wild West shows and rodeos were transforming the cowboy's mundane job into a pageant of show-business thrills. Ultimately, movies, popular songs, and television created a hero that was true of heart, brave of deed, and clean of mind. In place of real cowboys, most of whom spent their lives eking out a living, came the mythic cowboy— a square-jawed man with jingling spurs and a white ten-gallon hat, who gallops on a golden palomino through America's imagination.

It was not easy or natural at first to regard cowboys as honorable. Although the Republic of Texas had put one on its two-dollar bill as early as 1841, most people after the Civil War, especially people in the North, thought of them as disreputable sorts of men on the wrong side of the law. They were impugned (to a degree, correctly) as draft-dodgers or border-state saboteurs, young delinquents who ran away from home in the East, and shiftless drifters unwilling to take a steady job. In 1881, President

Chester A. Arthur warned Congress about "armed desperadoes known as 'Cowboys'" in the Arizona Territory; the following year the *Cheyenne* [Wyoming] *Daily Leader* reprinted an article from the *Providence Journal* describing the typical Western cowboy as "foulmouthed, blasphemous, drunken, lecherous, utterly corrupt."

The year after the *Daily Leader* excoriated cowboys, Buffalo Bill Cody organized his first Wild West show, in Nebraska. While the Wild West had already become something of a national obsession (via dime novels and sensationalized magazines), Cody originally had no intention of making heroes out of the ragged cowboys of the range. To ennoble a cowboy in a theatrical production verged on scandal, like putting a tramp or a derelict on stage. In Cody's first "Old Glory Blowout," as his show was called, the role of cowboys was minimal, and was restricted to providing some Western color, like clowns on horseback, by doing trick riding and roping. They were nothing like the majestic figure of Cody himself, who had the far more exalted title of Army scout.

Two years later, Cody conceived of a way to clean up the image of cowboys and transform them into knights of the prairie by adding a featured player to the show named Buck Taylor, billed in advertisements as King of the Cowboys. Originally from Texas, Taylor was a master shot and trick roper, but as William W. Savage, Jr., wrote in his book *The Cowboy Hero,* "Cody had no easy chore to make Buck Taylor palatable, but he did it, and the salesmanship was something for any entrepreneur to envy."

The tactic Cody used was to pull at his audience's

*Roy Rogers and Dale Evans.*

heartstrings. His Wild West show programs described Buck Taylor as a brave orphan boy who grew up in Texas cattle country "with privations, hardship, and danger . . . excitements and adventure." According to Taylor's official biography, he was far from a saddle tramp; in fact he had grown up to become an incorruptible man of the West, a cowboy who had vowed to fight any man or animal for the betterment of the human race. This giant among men, big in deed and in heart, was humble, too: audiences were assured that he was "amiable as a child."

The newly formulated cowboy hero found eager believers. In his book *Cowboy Culture* David Dary told about an 1885 Wyoming newspaper story alerting readers that two Eastern detectives were coming West on the trail of an eleven-year-old boy, son of a wealthy banker, who had run away from home after reading a dime novel about a cowboy who solved a murder mystery. The boy had retrieved twenty dollars in dimes and quarters from his toy bank, packed some clothes, and supposedly scribbled a farewell note to his parents saying, "I'm goin' West to be a cowboy detective," then climbed out his window and headed for Wyoming.

For many years after Buck Taylor made American children (and adults) swoon with admiration, it was common for cowboy heroes in dime novels, then in movies, to be bad guys—legacy of the original cowboy reputation—but bad guys who, when faced with a moral dilemma, revealed a righteous soul. Broncho Billy, the first cowboy movie star, often played an outlaw who redeemed himself by saving a girl, a baby, a nice young family, or a whole town. Part of the charm of the cowboy ideal has always been the chance to start fresh and leave a checkered past behind. Many of America's favorite cowboys, from Broncho Billy in *Broncho Billy's Redemption* to *Shane* to Clint Eastwood in *Unforgiven,* have done things that shame them, but they are men of real character: they walk straight and tall and are every bit as gallant to women and kind to children as they are merciless to wrong-doers.

William S. Hart, the biggest Western movie star of the 'teens, was often cast as a bad guy who is reformed by a good woman's love. When Hart's 1925 movie *Tumbleweeds* was rereleased in 1939 he added a prologue in which he told his audience about the sheer joy of playing a cowboy, his words conjuring up exhilarating scenes of him riding his faithful horse, Fritz, through the sagebrush on a rousing cowboy quest:

> *The rush of the wind that cuts your face . . . the pounding hooves of the pursuing posse. Out there in front a fallen tree trunk that spans a yawning chasm,*

# Gene Autry's Ten Commandments of a Cowboy

He Must Not Take Unfair Advantage of an Enemy.

He Must Never Go Back on His Word.

He Must Always Tell the Truth.

He Must Be Gentle with Children, Elderly People, and Animals.

He Must Not Possess Racially or Religiously Intolerant Ideas.

He Must Help People in Distress.

He Must Be a Good Worker.

He Must Respect Women, Parents, and His Nation's Laws.

He Must Neither Drink or Smoke.

He Must Be a Patriot.

Gene Autry

**Gene Autry**
COWBOY BOOTS
Styled by Gene Autry exclusively
for
GRAHAM BROWN SHOE COMPANY

For the
Young
Cowpokes . . .

**BOYS!**
**GIRLS!**

Get this newest
Gene Autry designed
merchandise—available
now at your local stores*

*If your local dealer does not carry this merchandise,
he can obtain same by writing the Mitchell J. Hamilburg
Agency, 8778 Sunset Blvd., Hollywood 46, California

*Gene Autry, who started his career on the radio as "Oklahoma's Yodeling Cowboy," established the highest standards of conduct for movie buckaroos and encouraged his young fans to behave likewise. An astute businessman, he also pioneered merchandising tie-ins.*

*with a noble animal under you that takes it in the same low, ground-eating gallop. The harmless shots of the baffled ones that remain behind, and then the clouds of dust through which comes the faint voice of the director—"Ok, Bill, ok. Glad you made it. Great stuff, Bill, great stuff. . . ." Oh, the thrill of it all!*

Tom Mix, a cinema contemporary of Hart's whose movie career lasted into the early 1930s, polished the cowboy ideal to an even brighter luster. He was no severe enforcer of virtue, nor was he a bad guy with a heart of gold; rather, he was pure delight and frolic, the man in the white hat, always on the right side of the law. In his own words, "I ride into a place owning my own horse, saddle, and bridle. It isn't my quarrel, but I get into trouble doing the right thing for somebody else. When it's all ironed out, I never get any money reward." Mix's movies were less about morality than adventure, and they were loaded with fistfights, slapstick stunts, fair ladies (with whom he seldom rode off into the sunset, to the relief of his adolescent fans), and, best of all, Mix's trick horse, Tony. Tony was nearly as popular a star as Mix himself, and like his rider, he had many a flirtation (with comely colts), he rescued people in

distress, and he frequently got the big close-up at the end.

Some movie critics assumed that talking pictures would mean the end of the cowboy star, whose virtuous character was seen as an oldfangled legacy of Victorian times. In fact, Western-movie historians George N. Fenin and William K. Everson report that, in 1929, *Photoplay* declared the Western genre dead, and its mounted knight-errant an out-of-date relic in a new age of air travel. "Lindbergh has put the cowboy into discard as a type of national hero," the editorial announced. "Tom Mix, Hoot Gibson, and Ken Maynard must swap horses for aeroplanes or go to the old actors' home."

But cowboy heroes did not disappear: They modernized. Starting in the 1930s many Westerns were set, somewhat incongruously, in the present day, allowing them to feature not only horse chases and gunfights, but car chases and airplane chases, too. In Gene Autry's contemporary *Western Jamboree* (1938) the bad guys are helium bandits; in *The Old Barn Dance* (1938), they are crooked tractor salesmen. A former radio star, Autry became the movies' first successful singing cowboy, and the thirties' quintessential B-movie headliner. (John Wayne actually

*1940: America's Cowboy Swing Band, Pals of the Range ("Now available for your theater, nite club, lodge, Grange hall, or school!").*

preceded Autry as a cowboy vocalist, playing a gunslinging hombre called "Singin' Sandy" in Lone Star Studio pictures between 1933 and 1935. Sandy warbled a dirge at his opponent as they walked toward each other before a shoot-out, but Wayne's voice—which was actually dubbed by a little-known singing cowboy named Smith Ballew—did not impress audiences.)

Gene Autry played his guitar as handily as he shot his gun, and his adventures in the modern West elevated cowboy honor to heights even Tom Mix couldn't have imagined. He lived on a "Radio Ranch," and he portrayed a cowboy (named Gene Autry) who was a polite, patriotic, well-groomed gentleman on a polite, patriotic, well-groomed horse (named Champion). He spent little time in barroom shoot-outs; he was too busy raising money for crippled kids, showing wayward juveniles the difference between right and wrong, or saving a pretty girl (usually June Storey) trapped on a runaway buckboard. Autry galloped through a sunny Western world where cheaters always got what they deserved, honesty was rewarded, and life was one neat adventure after another. Shortly after he became a movie star, he conceived "The Ten Commandments of a Cowboy," which was distributed in theaters, in schools, and in churches. It told children how to live up to the cowboy ideal.

Gene Autry was such a big success that his studio, Republic, added another singing cowboy to its roster: Roy Rogers. Rogers had played a few bit parts in Westerns, including Gene Autry's *The Old Corral* (1936), in which he was forced to sing a song at gunpoint, and after Gene Autry joined the Army in 1942, Republic declared Roy Rogers King of the Cowboys. Roy was a fitting heir to the silver saddle, and he reigned as America's favorite buckaroo well into the 1950s. In movies, then on televi-

sion, and in personal appearances as well, Roy and his wife, Dale Evans, were the personification of wholesome family values, cowboy-style. He was handsome, she was pretty, they wore some of the flashiest duds in the West, they had a passel of happy kids, and they rode a pair of gorgeous, high-stepping steeds— Trigger and Buttermilk.

Gene Autry and Roy Rogers and Dale Evans inspired literally dozens of cactus crooners in movies of the 1930s and 1940s. They included Tex Ritter, Jimmy Wakely, Monte Hale, Rex Allen, and even grand-opera singer Fred Scott, who made the leap from *Salome* to *Romance Rides the Range* in 1936 and followed with some two dozen

Above: *R. E. Madsen—height 7 feet 6, weight 230, "Every inch American."* Right: *Jack Dalton, singing cowboy of Boston's WBZ, with his horse Prince in 1942.*

# The Code of the West

As far as valuable life lessons go, the American cowboy probably knows more about making it in this world than all the self-help psychologists who have ever been on "Oprah." We therefore present here our own version of The Code of the West, drawn from many different cowboy codes, including those in Owen Wister's novel *The Virginian*, David Dary's *Cowboy Culture*, "The Cowman's Code of Ethics" from the *1949 Brand Book*, Philip Ashton Rollins's *The Cowboy* (1922), as well as the lessons taught by Will James stories, Roy Rogers, Gene Autry, and Hopalong Cassidy. We can't promise that adhering to The Code will make you rich, thin, successful, or even happy, but we can almost guarantee that you will never be shot dead for cattle rustling.

1. Never pass anyone on the trail without saying "Howdy." When approaching someone from behind, give a loud greeting before you get within pistol-shot. Proper hailing phrases, according to *The Cowboy* (1922), are "Hulloa, stranger" and "Whoo-up, whoo-up, whoo-pee."

2. Don't wave at a man on a horse. It might spook the horse and the man will think you are an idiot. (A nod is the proper greeting.)

3. After you pass someone on the trail, don't look back at him. It implies you don't trust him.

4. Riding another man's horse without his permission is nearly as bad as making love to his wife. Never even *bother* another man's horse.

5. Never shoot an unarmed man. Never shoot a woman at all.

6. A cowboy is pleasant even when out of sorts. Complaining is what quitters do, and cowboys hate quitters.

7. Always be courageous. Cowards aren't tolerated in any outfit worth its salt.

8. A cowboy always helps someone in need, even a stranger or an enemy.

9. When you leave town after a weekend of carousing, it's perfectly all right to shoot your six-guns into the air, whoop like crazy, and ride your horse as fast as you can. This is called "hurrahing" a town.

10. A horse thief may be hung peremptorily.

11. Never try on another man's cowboy hat.

12. Never wake another man by shaking or touching him: He might wake up suddenly and shoot you.

13. Real cowboys are modest. A braggart who is "all gurgle and no guts" is not tolerated. A cowboy doesn't talk much; he saves his breath for breathing.

14. No matter how weary and hungry you are after a long day in the saddle, always tend to your horse's needs before your own, and get your horse some feed before you eat.

15. Cuss all you want . . . but only around men, horses, and cows.

LIFE AMONG THE COWBOYS,

ENJOYING THEIR RACES AND CONTESTS AND GIVING WONDERFUL EXHIBITIONS OF DEXTERITY ON THEIR MOUNTS.

singing-cowboy pictures, teamed with Al "Fuzzy" St. John as his comic foil. A few years later, Fuzzy once again served as funny sidekick to another former opera singer, George Houston, who became the Lone Rider in eleven low-budget movies made in 1941 and 1942. Most of the singing-cowboy pictures of the late 1930s and early 1940s were made with little regard for their story lines; the point was to intersperse song and action. In his book *The Singing Cowboys* David Rothel recalls a Bob Baker musical oater called *Phantom Stagecoach* (1939) in which Baker and his sidekick are camping out at night and suddenly hear a sneeze from somewhere in the brush. Apparently, the screenwriter forgot to think of an explanation for the sound: Baker and his partner simply say, "Let's get out of here!," saddle their horses, and ride away. The sneeze remains an enigma. One thing was consistent in these movies, though: every singing cowboy was a good guy. He worked tirelessly to make the frontier safe from desperadoes, but still he managed to make the cowboy's life seem as much fun as a gambol at summer camp.

In 1936, at the height of the singing-cowboy era, Oren Arnold wrote a book called *Wonders of the West*. It is hard to imagine any young boy or girl reading the following lines and remaining content to eat oatmeal in Mom's kitchen, wear a drab school uniform, or do homework at night in a stuffy bedroom:

*Let the cowboy continue to gallop through the sagebrush and mesquite on a paint horse, popping his pistol and shouting "yip-EEE" at the fleeing Indians or desperados. Let him wear a ten-gallon hat, a great neckerchief of silk, a shirt louder than a Rio Grande sunset, chaps of rawhide, shining boots, and musical spurs. Let his hips sag under the weight of six-shooters. Let him have a strong chin and a pleasing drawl. Let him be gallant to ladies. In emergencies let him always come through capable and modest. Keep him, keep him forever: next to the wild Indian he is our most interesting American citizen.*

Paeans such as this created a powerful hankering among adults as well as children to experience the cowboy's life firsthand. Dude ranches evolved to give city folks a taste of life on the open range. They had existed as far back as the 1880s, but it was in the 1920s and 1930s, thanks to cowboy movies and popular Western

songs, as well as to the romance cultivated in advertisements for the Santa Fe rail line, that dude ranches became a national passion. The Dude Rancher's Association was formed in 1926, with these words as its purpose:

*The heritage of the old-time West has been handed down to the dude rancher. His now is the responsibility to keep forever fanning those few sparks and embers still left, and thus keep alive the memory of those traditions that made this country what it was.*

By 1940 there were more than fifty dude ranches in the Tucson valley alone. In 1943, at the height of World War II, the *Arizona Daily Star* praised dude ranches as "a very definite contribution to the nation's war effort as a means of keeping fit many valuable men." In her book *Another Tucson* Bonnie Henry noted that they were mostly for the very rich, costing from ten to twenty dollars per day, "including three squares and all the horseback riding your bottom could take. Most folks stayed at least a month, some stayed all winter."

Whereas the earliest dude ranches had been little more than hunting and fishing camps with wilderness accommodations, lumpy mattresses, and gruesome food, by the time *Whoopee!* went from Broadway to the movies in 1930 (set on the Bar M Ranch in Arizona, in Technicolor, with Busby Berkeley dance numbers), the popular image of the tenderfoot's life Out West was one of song, merriment, and cowboy-and-Indian fun with all the amenities. Dude ranch guests woke at dawn to breakfasts of flapjacks with molasses syrup, rashers of thick-cut bacon, fried potatoes, eggs in a

*Las Vegas originally drew tourists because of its Wild West theme, which is still reflected in neon signs along Glitter Gulch.*

skillet, sourdough biscuits, and strong brewed coffee. They ate off Wallace Rodeo Pattern china in a colorful ranch house with a blazing fireplace, or possibly sitting on a blanket or at a calico-covered picnic table in the great outdoors. "Cookie" always offered seconds, and the cheerful ranch owners promised all their visitors that a few hours of trail rides through the cool of the desert morning would put roses in the cheeks of even the most wan urbanite.

A dude for a day filled his or her time with horseback rides on scenic trails, fishing in well-stocked streams, watching demonstrations of fancy roping and trick riding by ranch employees, visits to nearby Indian sites, joining sing-alongs by the light of the moon, and taking mid-night hay rides. There was even the occasional fashion show to highlight the latest in fancy-pants ranch attire. In the evening, guests might gather in the lodge room, swapping stories with cowboys ensconced on manly fur-niture crafted by designer Thomas Molesworth from lodgepoles, bright red leather, and colorful Chimayo weavings. The cowboys with whom guests mingled were selected not only for their skills, but for their charm and colorful personalities. The problem was that it was diffi-cult to find a lot of real cowboys with these attributes; so, according to Lawrence R. Borne's *Dude Ranching: A Complete History,* many ranch owners recruited former guests to play the part of cowboys. These ex-city slickers had learned to walk and talk just like cowboys, and they dressed the part to their eyeteeth, but they were far more mannerly than the real McCoy, and less likely to cuss out a guest or get into a brawl. "Joke if you will," one dude ranch manager said, "but there is a real future here for a cowhand who can ride, play the guitar, and still smell nice."

It was the job of a dude ranch manager to make sure guests had the ideal cowboy experience with none of a

Opposite: *Dude ranchers enjoy a singalong outside Tucson.* Right: *Eleanor and Harry Smythe's Buck Lake Ranch was in Angola, Indiana.*

real cowboy's hardships or difficulties. So instead of the spirited mounts preferred by working cowboys, "dude horses" were selected for their stolid temperaments and gentle ways. Bunkhouses were equipped with soft beds that had embroidered spreads with designs of ranch brands or majestic chenille cactus plants, and festive Indian rugs were scattered on the wood-plank floors. Real wranglers did the dirty work with the livestock, but they were customarily kept far away from the guests, so as not to spoil the illusion.

Still, seeing genuine cowboys and being close to them was one of the principal attractions of a dude ranch, and for some guests, the allure became irresistible. Lawrence R. Borne recounted that:

> Some of the women who went west were enthralled with cowboys and brought a huge dose of romantic fantasy with them. Sometimes when an enthralled female met the irresistible cowboy, marriage was the result. It is a little difficult to envision a rich, "proper" girl from the East marrying a rough, footloose cowhand, but many people mentioned such matches. Some of these couples returned to the East; others remained in the West. There were many cases of young girls who tired of the formality and restrictions of their eastern lives, journeyed to ranches, married cowboys, and settled down to become ranch wives in Wyoming and Montana.

The cowboy ideal has endured for decades, upheld by such movie greats as William Boyd, who immortalized Hopalong Cassidy, and John Wayne, who came to symbolize the ultimate cowboy hero. Television brought a spate of cowboys into American homes: first, former movie heroes Gene Autry and Roy Rogers, whose TV ranches were a children's delight, and Hoppy, whose sixty-six feature films were edited into episodes for TV and became the new medium's first successful action series. The small screen introduced Marshal Matt Dillon, star of "Gunsmoke," the longest-running prime-time series ever (1955–75, on the radio before that from 1952), who each week transported viewers back to a dusty Dodge City where bad men drew fast (but never fast enough) and where Miss Kitty, Chester, Doc, and Ma Smalley felt like neighbors. In "Gunsmoke," as well as in such movies as *Shane* (1954) and *The Magnificent Seven* (1960), the 1950s cowboy ideal was a man who could outdraw any foe: a gunslinger more than a cattle-puncher.

*Outdoor fun in the Sonora Desert, as envisioned by Arizona tourist authorities, circa 1960.*

Some of the small screen's top guns included Palladin (Richard Boone), the mysterious man-in-black hero of "Have Gun, Will Travel" (1957–63); "The Rifleman" (1958–63), which starred Chuck Connors as a homesteader who could fire his customized Winchester as fast as a machine gun; and "Yancy Derringer" (1958–59), who almost always got himself out of a tight squeeze with a hidden pocket pistol. The exception to the quick-draw ideal of the time was "Maverick" (1957–62), which became a beloved TV Western because it went against the norm; its hero (James Garner) was much better with his wits than with his shooting iron.

There aren't as many Western heroes on TV or in the movies anymore, but the appeal of the cowboy life continues to thrive in a more congenial and adult medium: cowboy poetry. Western ranch hands and balladeers have been writing and singing about the life they love since the frontier began to seem like a lost ideal a hundred years ago, but

*Johnny Mack Brown, Western movie star from 1933 to 1950. "Ride 'em Cowboy!" says the back of this souvenir picture. "And the villains had better keep out of his way!"*

for most of this century, genuine cowboy poets were obscured by movies, TV, and songs that romanticized and commercialized their lives. Hal Cannon of the Western Folklife Center wrote in his introduction to *New Cowboy Poetry* (1989) that a resurgence of cowboy poets began in 1985, distinguished by the new poets' strong sense of the West as a special part of America. They have performed not only in the traditional poets' venues of church socials, cattlemen's dinners, and country fairs but also at national and regional poetry gatherings, on network TV talk shows, on videotape, and radio.

Such poets as Waddie Mitchell, Baxter Black, and Wallace McRae honor the cowboy life in a charismatic way that earns them legions of loyal fans, and not only in the West. When they read their poems at the Elko Cowboy Poetry gathering or the Best of the West Festival in Scottsdale, Arizona, these men fully play their part as bards of the frontier: some with well-waxed mustaches, nearly all dressed in old-fashioned cowboy hats, bib-fronted shirts, and boots. They talk about the life of the cowboy, then and now, sometimes contrasting that life to Eastern ways, but more often simply celebrating it as a kind of privileged existence. Many of these poets are real-life ranchers, and their poems, with such titles as "Alkali Pete Hits Town" (T. J. McCoy), "The Last Buckaroo" (Dick Gibford), "The Big High and Lonesome" (Baxter Black), and "Hat Etiquette" (Wallace McRae), are frequently reminiscent of old ballads—mournful, bawdy, wily, and sentimental, but also sometimes as barbed as an old barrel cactus.

Some cowboy poetry readings are held as part of festivals organized to celebrate the cowboy ideal in all its aspects. Year round throughout the West, there are weekend gatherings that include auctions of cowboy collectibles (old saddles, guns and gunbelts, chaps, etc.), chili cook-offs, Texas two-step contests, fast-draw shoot-outs (against a stopwatch), boot-making demonstrations, and songfests. The biggest rodeos in North America often include many such events, and they attract cowboy admirers from all over America and the world. Cheyenne, Wyoming, for example, goes cowboy crazy each July, as it has done every year since its Frontier Days celebration and rodeo began in 1897. The windows of stores are soap-painted with images of bucking horses and their bow-legged riders and splashed with such slogans as "Howdy, Pardner!" and "Yippie Ki Yea!" Truck stops on the outskirts of town sell buckskin chaps and vests designed to fit ages two to six; streets are crowded with tourists shopping in Western-wear stores (open late each night), including

some buckaroos from Japan and Europe who speak no English, trying on ten-gallon hats, and staggering along the sidewalks in newly purchased high-heel cowboy boots. Local restaurants push buffalo burgers and Rocky Mountain oysters (deep-fried bull's testicles), and mock gunfights, featuring local businessmen dressed like Billy the Kid and Butch and Sundance, are fought twice daily in the town square.

The West has become the trendiest place for stylish Americans to have a second home, whether a ranch in Montana or an adobe hacienda outside Santa Fe, but playing cowboy is every bit as much a passion in other countries. *The Japanese Version,* a documentary film made in 1990, showed "cowboy bars" in Tokyo where local businessmen dress in full broncobuster regalia and spend their evenings sucking long-necks and phonetically singing the lyrics to the theme from the TV show "Rawhide." In Paris, you can shop for El Paso–made boots, Brushpopper shirts, and Stetson hats in a store called Cowboy Dreams, where the motto is, *Un coin de Texas à Paris.* The Winter 1993 edition of *Cowboy Magazine* (published in Colorado) contained an article by Josephine Spruijt of the Netherlands called "Continental Cowboys," in which Ms. Spruijt told about "The Future Guys Saloon" in Holland, where weekend cowboys go to drink

*"Cowboy's Prayer" was written in 1906 by South Dakota poet Badger Clark, author of "Sun and Saddle Leather."*

tequila and Mexican beer and dance to country-western music:

> *Every Friday, after work, they change their clothes and personalities and become their own fantasy. People introduce themselves as Red Fox, Jeremiah, Sheriff Madison, or Deputy John. They chew tobacco and live, talk and dress like any man who lived in the wild West. They are not kidding! . . . They are so serious that it's wise for outsiders not to try to make fun of them in their presence. They could lynch you!*

In 1992 the *New York Times* ran a story titled "At Euro Disney, Mickey Mouse Takes a Back Seat." The star of the show, Anna Kisselgoff wrote, was not Disney's mouse; it was America's cowboy, as featured in a theatrical re-creation of Buffalo Bill's Wild West show. "Even the glum Italians sitting next to me got excited," she wrote, describing how everyone in the audience put on straw facsimiles of cowboy hats and ate "on-the-range vittles" including corn on the cob and sausage served in bent tin dishes.

Fortunately, no one needs to take a trip to Euro Disney to get in the spirit of the American West. Nor do you need a big ranch in Montana, or even a ten-gallon hat and boots to be a cowboy (although the hat and boots really do help). As any cowboy hero, from Roy Rogers to Baxter Black, can tell you, being a cowboy is all a matter of how you think and act.

# *Cowboy* SIDEKICKS

In Westerns, nearly every handsome hero needs a cantankerous old man as his companion (like Gabby Hayes). If not that, then a fat, silly one (like Smiley Burnette), or a dopey, well-meaning one (like Sterling Holloway), or a strangely behaved ethnic one (like Tonto); or one who limps (like Chester), or at least one who is always getting into a mess that the hero gets him out of (like Andy Devine).

Sidekicks might be annoying and troublesome to just about everyone in town, but the man they hang around with knows they are good at heart. Very often they are pariahs whom no one else will be friends with because they used to have a drinking problem, because they don't shave and smell bad, because they're moochers, or simply because they're different. But a real cowboy hero has a noble perspective on human nature and sees beyond all such superficial shortcomings to become a true friend to his inferior companion. Besides, on those rare occasions when a cowboy hero is in trouble, it is often his sidekick who helps him out—never by dint of fists or straight shooting (which are too assertive for a sidekick), but stealthily, perhaps by masquerading as a mule or hiding in a keg of rum,

Left: *Gabby Hayes.*
Right: *Walter Brennan.*

Above: *Fuzzy St. John with Buster Crabbe.* Top right: *Smiley Burnette.* Right: *Andy Devine.*

or by otherwise taking advantage of his hopelessly second-rate stature to sneak past the bad guys and help his friend.

The king of sidekicks was George Hayes, who had made a fortune as an actor playing all sorts of roles on stage and in movies in the 1920s, after which he retired. However, he lost his money in the stock market crash of 1929, so he was forced to return to the screen to earn a living. At first Hayes played bad guys in cowboy movies, but in 1936 he hit his stride as "Windy Halliday," Hopalong Cassidy's colorful, irritable sidekick, whom he played until 1939, when he became Roy Rogers's sidekick, Gabby, a role he also played alongside leading man Bill Elliott. The definitive sidekick, Gabby Hayes—who in real life was a well-read,

art) in *The Far Country* (1955), and a crabby, toothless, lame sheriff's helper (in the company of John Wayne) in *Rio Bravo* (1959). In all three films, Brennan made a fetish of how he brewed his coffee.

The other basic types of sidekicks include:

## MEN OF GIRTH

The two best-known portly sidekicks were Smiley Burnette, who rode alongside Gene Autry in eighty-one films (and then played railroad engineer Charley Pratt in TV's "Petticoat Junction") and Andy Devine, who appeared as the always-hungry stage driver in *Stagecoach* (1939) and whose signature line as Jingles B. Jones in TV's "Wild Bill Hickok" (1951–58) was "Wait for me, Wild Bill!" One of the oddest fat sidekicks was Oliver Hardy in a raccoon-skin cap—John Wayne's comrade in *The Fighting Kentuckian* (1949).

## MEN OF COLOR

The wisest of all sidekicks was the Lone Ranger's Tonto (Jay Silverheels, a Canadian Mohawk Indian born "Harold J. Smith"), who was motion pictures' foremost speaker of "Injun dialect"—a language limited to nouns, adjectives, and simple verbs accompanied by expressive grunts, but devoid of articles, prepositions, and all nominative pronouns, i.e.: "Ummmm . . . Him big chief all Comanches." One of the most memorable ethnic partners was Leo Carillo, who played the Cisco Kid's merry, skirt-chasing amigo, Pancho; of him, Duncan Renaldo (who played the Kid) said,

*Pahoo Ka-Ta-Wa (X Brands) helps Yancy Derringer (Jock Mahoney) make time with a pretty lady.*

cultured man of the world—was an ornery, mush-mouthed, toothless cuss who frequently expressed his convictions by appending statements with the phrase, "Yer dern tootin'!"

The majority of sidekicks were bewhiskered coots of the Gabby Hayes school, foremost among them Andy Clyde, who played California Carlson, Hoppy's pal, in the 1940s; Al "Fuzzy" St. John, who played Fuzzy Q. Jones alongside nearly every big cowboy star in the 1940s; and Walter Brennan, who played John Wayne's companion in *Red River* (1948), a crabby, toothless, lame prospector (in the company of Jimmy Stew-

*Leo Carillo as Pancho, partner of the Cisco Kid.*

Above: *Robert (then known as Bobby) Blake as Little Beaver. Right: Jay Silverheels as Tonto, with Silver and Clayton Moore (the Lone Ranger).*

"His accent was so exaggerated that when we finished a picture, no one in the cast or crew could talk normal English any more." A few notable non-Caucasian sidekicks were Robert Blake as Little Beaver, the juvenile Native American chum of Bill Elliott (as Red Ryder) in the 1940s; Woody Strode as Pompey, John Wayne's African-American confidant in *The Man Who Shot Liberty Valance* (1962); and X Brands as Pahoo Ka-Ta-Wah (Pawnee for "wolf who stands in water"), the stealthy companion of TV's Yancy Derringer (1958–59). Pahoo carried a double-barreled shotgun and was always ready to slip Mr. Derringer a Bowie knife in emergencies; Pahoo was also apparently a mute.

## THE PHYSICALLY CHALLENGED

Handicapped sidekicks (not counting minor afflictions like lack of teeth) include John "Fuzzy" Knight, whose stutter and hyperthyroid eyeballs made him a comic foil for many leading men from the 1930s into the 1950s; Gene Sheldon as Bernardo, Zorro's mute manservant (and the only person other than Zorro's father who knew his real identity) in the TV series of 1957–59; and Dennis Weaver, whose game leg in "Gunsmoke" seemed to be at least part of the source of his irascible nature as Matt Dillon's deputy, Chester B. Goode.

# *Cowboy* SKILLS

## HOW TO RIDE LIKE A COWBOY

First, select a proper Western mount: preferably a fast, stocky quarter horse; a white-maned palomino; a paint (also called a pinto) with great red or brown splotches over gray or white; or an Appaloosa with leopard spots. Make sure he isn't "broke down," meaning poorly treated, badly ridden, or improperly shod; you don't want a ewe-necked broom tail (that's a sway-necked horse of undeterminate breeding) or a stargazer (who points his nose too high) or a jug-headed, tucked-up cayuse that other cowboys will refer to as buzzard bait. Look for one with sloping shoulders (an easier ride), short back and an intelligent look to his eyes.

Saddle him with a nice, roomy Western saddle, one with a low cantle (that's the back) so you can get on and off in a hurry and a saddle horn to grip when mounting . . . although some cowboys ignore the horn and prefer to grab the horse's mane instead. Unlike a stingy Eastern saddle that resembles a flat leather pancake way up on a horse's back, a cowboy saddle ought to be as comfortable as an easy chair. It will weigh thirty to fifty pounds, or if it's a fancy parade saddle festooned with silver trim and draped with hand-tooled saddlebags and hooded stirrups known as tapaderos, it can weigh

*Bob Steele was one of the best genuine horsemen among cowboy movie stars in the 1930s.*

23

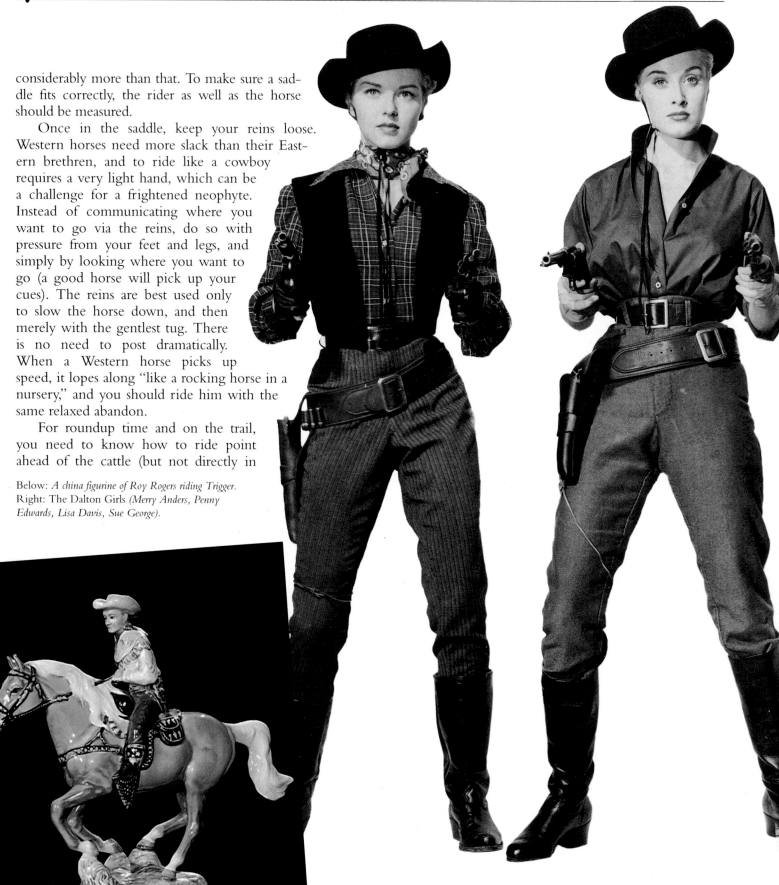

considerably more than that. To make sure a saddle fits correctly, the rider as well as the horse should be measured.

Once in the saddle, keep your reins loose. Western horses need more slack than their Eastern brethren, and to ride like a cowboy requires a very light hand, which can be a challenge for a frightened neophyte. Instead of communicating where you want to go via the reins, do so with pressure from your feet and legs, and simply by looking where you want to go (a good horse will pick up your cues). The reins are best used only to slow the horse down, and then merely with the gentlest tug. There is no need to post dramatically. When a Western horse picks up speed, it lopes along "like a rocking horse in a nursery," and you should ride him with the same relaxed abandon.

For roundup time and on the trail, you need to know how to ride point ahead of the cattle (but not directly in

Below: *A china figurine of Roy Rogers riding Trigger.*
Right: The Dalton Girls *(Merry Anders, Penny Edwards, Lisa Davis, Sue George).*

front, which makes them nervous) so you can keep your herd going where it is supposed to go, how to flank a herd so cattle don't stray (and to catch those who do), and how to eat dust if you are unlucky enough to be stationed at the back tending to stragglers. A real good cowboy also knows how to ride in such a way that he can halt a stampede—by galloping out in front of the runaway cattle and steering them into a circle, called a mill, so they run back into the rear of the herd and wind to a stop. Contrary to movie lore, shooting in front of a stampede is unlikely to stop it; in fact, it will probably agitate the cattle further.

## HOW TO SHOOT LIKE A COWBOY

To be a cowboy without a gun is like watching TV without remote control: it can be done, but you feel at the mercy of whatever comes your way. In an untamed land where the trail boys from Texas faced homicidal road gangs, thugs in the Kansas boomtowns, crooked marshals with shotguns, posses of vigilantes with a noose for anyone they thought misbehaved, and cattle barons' hired killers, "Judge Colt and his jury of six" were the only law a lonesome cowboy could

A GOOD SIGHT

Above: *This sharpshooting lass with her still-warm Colt .45 is the subject of a painting discovered in an Iowa flea market. Opposite: Alan Ladd wielded two shooting irons in Whispering Smith (1948). Opposite, far right: A 5'4" fiberglass Peacemaker is admired by a young lad at a roadside attraction in Alpine, California.*

depend on. Besides your horse, your gun just might be your only real friend.

In the lore of the West, gunfighting is as vital a skill as horseback riding. In fact, the basic business of a cowboy—herding cows—doesn't really require much firepower. But if you want to be a mythical American cowboy, you need to be able to outdraw and outshoot anyone who means you harm. You have to be quick enough to use rapid fire to make a tin can dance, or—if you're a nasty sort—make a tinhorn dance, by shooting at the tinhorn's toes. You'll want to plug a silver dollar if

someone throws it in the air, and you should be able to fell pursuers by shooting backward while galloping through sagebrush on your stallion.

The cowboy gun nonpareil—in the real West as well as in movies—was the Colt .45, patented in 1872 by Samuel Colt and designated the New Model Army revolver, then the Peacemaker (a version of which remains in production today). Bat Masterson ordered eight Peacemakers in various barrel lengths and with custom sights, nickel finish, and pearl handles; novelist Ned Buntline gave one with a foot-long barrel, known as the Buntline Special, to Wyatt

Earp (which Earp used mostly to clobber people on the head). Although one nickname for the Colt was the equalizer, gunfighters found ways of fine-tuning theirs to work even better. The mainspring was replaced with a tempered version that made the gun easier to cock (and—in movies only—to fan, meaning to hold the trigger back and whack the hammer spur repeatedly, sending a whole cylinder load of bullets flying in a flash); the notches in the hammer were filed, eliminating the half-cocked safety position and creating an easy let-off, known—with great dread to anyone downsight—as a hair trigger.

Most fictional cowboys brandish their .45s with the speed of a prestidigitator. Instead of simply pulling the gun from the holster and pointing it, they pull it out and set it twirling, winding up with the business end pointing in the right direction, hammer cocked, and finger on the trigger. This flourish is known as the Curly Bill Spin,

named for William (Curly Bill) Brocius, of Tombstone, Arizona, who first used it in 1880 to get the drop on a marshal who thought Curly Bill was handing him the gun butt-first to surrender.

Quick-draw has always been a Western movie obsession, especially since *The Gunfighter* (1950). Cowboy movie heroes are so fast that they can plug a foe even if the foe goes for his gun first. In fact, the whole idea of letting an opponent draw, then pulling your gun out and shooting him before he gets a shot off, was a strategy that likely never occurred to any shootists in the real West. Virtually every famous victim of frontier gunplay, including Jesse James, Billy the Kid, and Wild Bill Hickok, got shot because someone ambushed him, from behind or in the dark, never giving him a chance. Quick-draw is a showman's trick, usually accomplished by fast editing, not fast reflexes.

# HOW TO ROPE LIKE A COWBOY

There isn't a more appreciated skill on a ranch than roping, and the art of trick roping elevated this workaday craft to prime cowboy entertainment.

Roping is necessary to catch calves for branding, or to lasso a steer in need of medical help. In addition to being accurate, a good roper must be fast. A nimble cutting horse will quickly detach a cow from the herd, but it takes an artful cowboy in the saddle to whirl a rope in the air until it dilates to a big round loop, then send it circling out over the head of or around the legs of a running cow. A really top hand knows how to throw a *mangana,* which is an underhand toss that catches the front feet of a running cow, or he can throw a big Blocker loop around a cow's shoulders, or a *peal,* which means a

rope that catches each of an animal's hind legs in one loop of a figure 8.

Out West, a throwing rope is called a lariat, from the Spanish *la reata,* the rope Mexican vaqueros carried on their saddles. (*Lazo,* the Spanish word for slipknot, became lasso.) Lariats used by working cowboys can be more than twenty-five feet long, but the ones used for trick roping are traditionally about fourteen feet. The "honda" is the eye that the rope is threaded through to form the circle. Centrifugal force is what keeps the lasso in a circle as it spins, and the most important thing is to get it spinning as soon as it leaves your hands. Little loops are easier to spin than big ones. The rope itself has to be of a slicker material than ordinary rough hemp, which will stick to itself when twirled.

Thread the rope through the honda until you have a loop about three feet across. Hold the loop with the fingers of your left hand about a foot and a half from the honda. Use your right hand to secure the remaining

Below: *Will Rogers made roping popular entertainment in the 1920s.* Opposite: *Monte Montana on his trick horse Rex. As a publicity stunt, Monte once rode to the steps of the Capitol in Washington, D.C., and lassoed President Dwight D. Eisenhower as Vice President Nixon looked on.*

McLAUGHLIN BROS TRICK ROPERS
GENE 4 YEARS OLD DON. 6
(DOUBLEDAY)

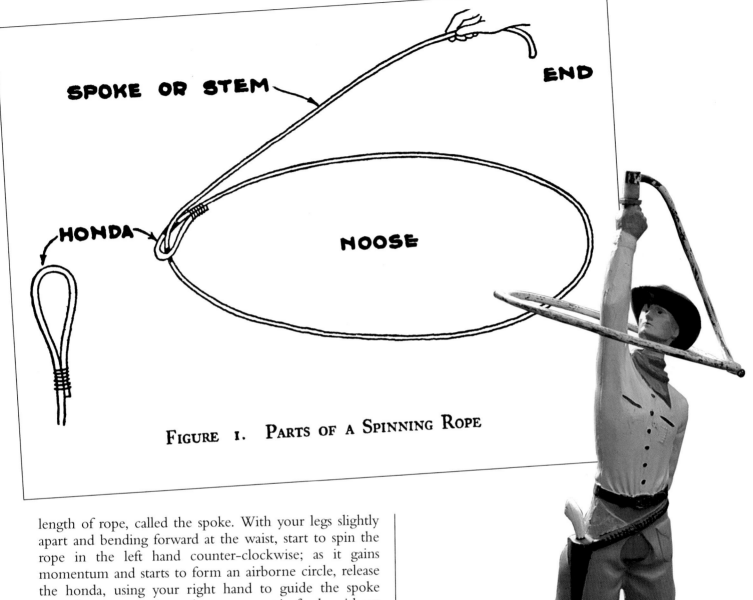

SPOKE OR STEM

END

HONDA

NOOSE

FIGURE 1. PARTS OF A SPINNING ROPE

length of rope, called the spoke. With your legs slightly apart and bending forward at the waist, start to spin the rope in the left hand counter-clockwise; as it gains momentum and starts to form an airborne circle, release the honda, using your right hand to guide the spoke away from your body so the rope can spin freely without getting snagged on you or your clothing.

One nice thing about roping is that cowgirls can do it as well as cowboys; it is an equal-opportunity sport. With a little practice, women can do the basic Wedding Ring Loop, the Big Loop (a huge Wedding Ring), and perhaps even the Skip—roping's crowning feat of skill—in which an eight-foot loop is set twirling in a zigzag from side to side, using quick wrist strokes to whip it into a perfect whirling circle, taller than a person, through which the twirler leaps, left and right, as it spins like a giant hemp corkscrew.

In 1928, one of roping's all-time greats, Chester Byers, wrote a book, *Roping,* in which he introduced readers to Elsie Janis, a pretty young woman who cheerfully admitted to suffering a case of "lariatitis"— being in

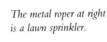

*The metal roper at right is a lawn sprinkler.*

FIGURE 46. WAVING THE FLAG

Fancy rope-spinning was first performed for the public in the 1880s by Vincenzo Orapeza, a Mexican vaquero with Buffalo Bill's Wild West show. Orapeza was a catch-roper, but he festooned his act with twirling tricks, and they were such a crowd-pleaser that they became an act unto themselves. Will Rogers learned from Orapeza; in 1904 he began as a roper known as "The Cherokee Kid" with Texas Jack's Wild West show. The following year, performing with the Mulhall Wild West show in Madison Square Garden, he became a hero when he lassoed a steer that ran wild into grandstands. By the end of the 'teens, Rogers was alternating between rope antics and jokes on stage, and in 1922 he produced and starred in *The Ropin' Fool,* a short movie containing fifty-three rope-spinning tricks. Fancy roping became as much a part of most

Above: *"Waving the flag" is an especially impressive trick if the roper's right hand holds a battery connected to flashing red, white, and blue bulbs attached to the noose and spoke.*

love with roping. She offered these words of encouragement to other ladies who want to give it a try:

*Don't start in the drawing room . . . unless it is someone else's house.*

*Don't wear a dress for which you have any future plans.*

*Don't get discouraged if you nearly hang yourself. Be glad you didn't succeed in doing so.*

*Don't expect to do Will Rogers' act the first week. It took me two months and I'm fairly quick at grabbing other people's stuff.*

show-business cowboys' repertoire as sharpshooting and trick riding.

## HOW TO IDENTIFY BRANDS LIKE A COWBOY

A brand is a bald keloid scar seared into the hide of a horse or cow signifying that the animal belongs to someone. Because brands are proof positive of ownership in the West, they also appear on ranch house gates, saddles, boots, checkbook covers, horse trailers, and steaks sizzling on an outdoor grill (the latter feat accomplished with a mini branding iron available from stores like Neiman-Marcus).

Originally brands were made with straight pokers, heated until red hot and drawn across the flesh of an animal to write a mark, such as the owner's initials. These were known as running brands, but because they were fairly crude and blurry, it was all too easy for rustlers to alter them to what was known as a slow brand—one not registered with the county cattlemen's association. Running brands were replaced with stamping irons, which burn an exact design into the animal's hide, and are more difficult to alter.

A maverick is a cow without a brand, named for Texan Samuel Maverick, a lawyer who in 1845 received four hundred head of cattle as settlement of a debt. Maverick had little interest in raising cattle, so he let them wander free and unbranded on Matagorda Island, from which, at low tide, some of them wandered onto the mainland. When other ranchers saw an unbranded cow wandering

*The back of this postcard says, "If you want to enjoy Arizona, Dude, go and be wrangled."*

along, they assumed it was one of Maverick's. Charles Siringo, the first cowboy autobiographer, reminisced in 1885 that Maverick was "a chickenhearted old rooster [who] went on claiming everything that wore slick ears." ("Slick ears" means ears that haven't been bobbed: see below.) Maverick sold his cattle holdings in 1856, but the name endured to describe a cow (or person) who doesn't wear a brand.

Spring roundup is branding time. In the days when the range was unbroken by fences and barbed wire, all the cows with newborn calves were cut from their herd and driven in to camp. These sessions were often communal affairs and included cows of many different ranchers, wearing different brands, so the roper who brought cows in called out the mother's brand to the iron man, and the iron man selected the proper ranch's stamping iron from his coals. To brand a calf, it must be lassoed and flanked (thrown onto its side), and held down. The calf bawls, its mother bellows, and the branding iron sizzles when it hits the critter's rump.

The air fills with the smell of singed hair and burning flesh.

The application of the brand is a short ceremony done with an iron hot enough to leave a scab, but not so hot that it damages the hide. At the same time a male calf is branded, it is also castrated, which requires little more than a quick slit of the scrotum with a pocketknife. In addition, a distinctive notch, known as a bob, will likely be cut in the calf's ear to match its mother's notch—additional means of identification. The most famous notch, known as the jingle bob, was Texan John Chisum's: ear split in such a way that the top half stood up, but the bottom half dangled, like the jangler on a spur.

The entire process—branding, castration, and ear-notching—takes less then a minute per animal. At the end of a long day at roundup time, cowboys gather around the campfire and enjoy a tasty lagniappe of their trade—supper of freshly amputated, skillet-cooked calf fries.

*A well-muscled cowpony with a Triple-V brand.*

# How to Read a Brand

**B**rands are like hieroglyphics; and the meaning of certain symbols varies from region to region, but there are some rules that almost always apply to reading them.

They are read left to right, top to bottom, and from the outside in.

A short horizontal rail is called a bar, a long one is a rail. A letter on its side is called *lazy*. A quarter-circle underneath another symbol is called a *rocker*. A roof above a letter is a *rafter*. Here are some classic Western brands:

LAZY M

M BAR J

ROCKING A

FLYING U

RAFTER O

RAFTER HOLE RAIL

RUNNING M

WALKING X

TUMBLING Y

SEVEN UP

TURKEY TRACK

Branding Time On The Range

TX12

# HOW TO DANCE LIKE A COWBOY

"The Cowboy Dance is the true folk dance of the last American frontier," Lloyd Shaw wrote to introduce his book *Cowboy Dances* in 1936. "To laugh and play together, stimulated by the rhythm of good folk music: The Western Cowboy Dance offers a perfect opportunity for this." Mr. Shaw's enthusiastic volume contains seventy-five variations of such revelry, from basic do-si-do square dance steps ("Right and Left Through and Swing that Girl Behind You") to elaborate variations including "Cheat and Swing," "Don't You Touch Her," and "Buffaloes and Injuns." Some were group steps for squares, circles, and lines; others emphasized what you did with a partner.

Dancing to a fiddle and a caller has always been wholesome fun—for barn raisings, weddings, and town celebrations—but there is another kind of cowboy dancing, and it is a lot more racy. Joseph McCoy, the beef dealer who made Abilene a cattle town in the 1860s, wrote about the scene at the dance hall in one of the town's saloons:

> *The cow-boy enters the dance with a peculiar zest . . . with the front of his sombrero lifted at an angle of fully forty-five degrees; his huge spurs jingling at every step or notion; his revolvers flapping up and down like a retreating sheep's tail; his eyes lit up with excitement, liquor, and lust; he plunges in and "hoes it down" at a terrible rate.*

Western writer Oren Arnold wrote an essay called "The Honkytonkers" in which he said that such dancing was frequently a prelude to illicit sex in the Old West, and it took place in brothels that were equipped with tiny rooms called cribs, where cowboys and "soiled doves" (also known as "nymphs du prairie") had their brief assignations: "For the younger men and shy ones, dancing might precede cribbing. But it was not a stately cotillion of a Waldorf ballroom. It was quick-tempo'd chest-to-bust dance plus the bumps and grinds still favored in our modern burlesques." After a few minutes of honky-tonkin' on the dance floor, most couples beat a hasty retreat for a few moments of privacy in a crib.

There are still honky-tonks all over the West, and cowboys still go there to dance like crazy, and to get lucky (although none that we know are equipped with on-premises cribs). Billy Bob's in Fort Worth, which owner Billy Bob Barnett called "a monument to the real cowboy," is so big that live bulls are brought inside for daredevils to try and ride, and musicians are driven by limo from their dressing room to one of the club's several stages. Gilley's in Pasedena, outside Houston, is the most famous honky-tonk on earth and the place where the fad for mechanical bull riding began (and where *Urban Cowboy* was filmed). On a good night, five thousand Gilleyrats crowd into the cavernous club to drink beer (by the long-neck bottle), to search for love and for devilment, and to dance to the music of Willie, Waylon, Billy Ray, Randy, and Travis.

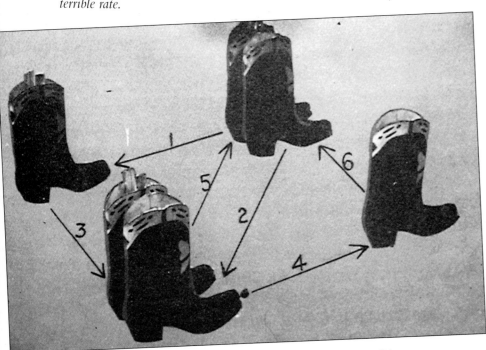

*Left: Box step instructions from the 1936 book* Cowboy Dances. *Right: You don't have to go to a nightclub to dance like a cowboy. A stack of 78 rpm records seems to have provided this curiously dressed couple all the atmosphere they need.*

To dance cowboy dances, cowboy attire is mandatory. In some circles, it might be impolite to wear a hat indoors, or jeans and pointy boots to a social event, but for a man or woman to go out dancing cowboy-style *without* a nice pair of boots, or to even consider removing one's hat (except to wipe one's brow) would be as weird as going to a baseball game wearing a tuxedo and a top hat. Other vital articles of attire for men and women on the dance floor are a wide belt with a big buckle (and pants with belt loops big enough for a partner to insert a thumb and hang there while slow dancing) and a loud, tight-tailored shirt with pearl snap-buttons. Men almost always wear their jeans outside their boots; it is more common for women to tuck their jeans inside their boot tops, showing off their fancy stitching, or to wear a skirt with a hem that flies wild when they twirl. Whereas a man's hat is usually white, black, gray, or brown, women sometimes wear them in pastel colors, and with bands of fluffy feathers. Women also favor earrings with a Western motif, such as silver coyotes, cactus plants, or armadillos.

The dances cowboys and cowgirls do are as varied as the Boot-Scootin' Boogie, the Tush-Push, the Achy-Breaky, the La Doux Shuffle, and even one called the Country Lambada, but nearly all are variations of the classics: the Texas two-step and the Cotton-Eyed Joe, the former done in a group of six or more who form a wagon-wheel shape on the floor, the latter a stately stroll with a partner around the room. As dancers, most cowboys are fairly formal: there is no fanny-shaking or wild spasms of the type favored in discos. Cowboys stand up straight when they dance, and lead their partners with dignity. Even when they break away to do a bit of fancy footwork reminiscent of a Scottish reel or an Irish jig, they let their legs and feet do all the talking; above the beltline, a cowboy always maintains his purposeful masculine demeanor.

# *King of the Cowboys?:* HOPPY vs. ROY

*William Boyd as Hopalong Cassidy.*

*Roy Rogers.*

**R**oy Rogers is a real man who played a cowboy named Roy Rogers. Hopalong Cassidy is a fictional hero who was played by William Boyd. Real or imaginary, Roy and Hoppy were the two top kiddie heroes in America in movies, in personal appearances, and on television from the 1940s into the 1950s:

To help you, the reader, decide once and for all who should wear the ten-gallon crown as King of the Cowboys, we present the following facts:

## HOPALONG CASSIDY, AS PLAYED BY WILLIAM BOYD

**Real Name:** William Boyd

**Hoppy's Real Name:** In the Clarence E. Mulford novels on which the character was based, he was called Hop-A-Long because of a game leg.

**Birthplace (Boyd):** Hendrysburg, Ohio

**Birthplace (Hoppy):** Texas

**Original Ambition (Boyd):** To be a lumberjack or automobile salesman

*William Boyd believed it was his duty to strengthen the fiber of American youth, with whom Time described him having a "semi-mystical relationship."*

HOPALONG CASSIDY
Around every corner, a cattle rustler.
*(National Affairs)*

**Original Ambition (Hoppy):** Hop-A-Long Cassidy, as created by Clarence Mulford, was the sidekick of a hero named Buck Peters. Hoppy was a foul-mouthed ruffian with no ambition whatever. When author Clarence Mulford went to his first Hopalong Cassidy movie and saw how drastically his character had been sanitized, he fainted from shock.

**Number of Western Movies:** 66

**Exceptional Talents:** Certainly not riding. When William Boyd first took the role of Hoppy, he was terrified of horses.

**Love Interest:** Hopalong Cassidy was a bachelor, and never kissed a girl on screen. William Boyd was married four times.

**Horse:** Topper, a magnificent white steed decked out in a black-and-silver parade saddle and bridle. Handsome though he was, Topper never shared top billing with Hoppy, as Trigger did with Roy.

**Sidekicks:** Gabby Hayes, Johnny Nelson (the latter originally played by Jimmy Ellison)

**Fictional Ranch:** The Bar-20

**Official Title:** None

**Merchandising Spin-offs:** In 1950 Hoppy wallpaper outsold any other design in the U.S.A. That same year, American clothing manufacturers *ran out* of black dye because so many kiddie fans wanted black shirts and pants and pajamas that looked like Hoppy's outfits. Other products included Hopalong Cassidy hair cream, a Hoppy bike with handlebars shaped like steer horns, Hoppy peanut butter, Hoppy watches, Hoppy potato chips, etc. In 1950 *Time* magazine called Hoppymania "one of the most amazing jackpots in the history of the entertainment industry"; 108 licensed manufacturers sold $70 million worth of Hoppy products that year to TV viewers whom *Time* called "electronic slaves."

**Hobbies:** None reported for the fictional Hoppy, except spitting tobacco juice accurately. William Boyd, before he assumed the cowboy role, was famous in Hollywood for his strictly adult hobbies. He liked to drink, he liked pretty women, and he once bought a yacht on the spur of the moment because everyone at a rowdy party he was at felt like going for a boat ride.

**Shooting Ability:** Always got his man by fast-drawing from a double-holstered black and silver buscadero gun belt, wielding two pearl-handled .45s.

**Wardrobe:** On TV and in movies, Hoppy appeared to dress all in black, a startling fashion statement for a good guy. His outfit included a big-brimmed and tall-crowned Stetson, a neckerchief with its ends threaded through a silver longhorn steerhead slide, tight shirt, tight trousers, and high black boots, with white piping around the top, into which he tucked the cuffs of his pants. Curiously, Hoppy's outfit wasn't really black at all. It was navy blue, but in black-and-white, the color didn't show.

**Fans:** Hoppy's fan mail was equally divided between girls and boys. A 1943 press release said "The West and Midwest like him because he presents a true picture of a cowboy without strumming a guitar or singing serenades, and he shows he can really handle horses. The East likes him because he speaks good English in the American vernacular without drawling or striving for phony Western effect." Boyd's allegiance to his fans, whom he called "my friends," was such that he refused to permit any license for bubble gum (bad for his friends' teeth) or toys with pointed tops (too dangerous). At parades his saddlebags were jammed with good-luck tokens he threw to the crowd. He once punched a department store manager in the nose when the man insisted that Hoppy's friends had to buy something before they could shake his hand.

**Most Unusual Compliment:** During World War II, newspapers lauded William Boyd for his patriotism. In response to government requests for dimouts (so enemy bombers couldn't find a target), he announced he would no longer shoot night scenes for his movies. Henceforth, all his battles would be fought in broad daylight. One article (sent out by his studio) concluded, "Hoppy is a dauntless soul and his brilliance will shine even more brightly under the rays of the sun."

**How Life Follows Art:** Before he took on the role of Hopalong Cassidy, William Boyd was an actor with a wicked reputation as a boozer and hell raiser. His career had foundered because producers were afraid to hire him. But when he landed the role of Hoppy in 1935 he became so inspired by the fictional cowboy's good behavior that for the rest of his life he never drank anything stronger than white wine, he quit smoking, he stopped going to wild parties, and he stayed faithful to his fourth and final wife from his marriage to her in 1937 to his death in 1972.

**Quote:** "When you've got parents saying what a wonderful guy Hoppy is, what the hell do you do? You've got to be a wonderful guy."

# ROY ROGERS

**Real Name:** Leonard Franklin Slye

**Birthplace:** Duck Run, Ohio

**Original Ambition:** To be a dentist

**Number of Western Movies:** 87

**Exceptional Talents:** Actor and singer, yodeler, square dance caller, guitar and mandolin player

**Love Interest:** Dale Evans (wife in real life)

**Horse:** Trigger, billed as "The Smartest Horse in the Movies." Trigger's talents included the ability to count to 25, do simple subtraction and multiplication, write his "X" in a hotel register, and drink milk out of a bottle without human help. Trigger is now mounted, rearing up for all eternity, at the Roy Rogers and Dale Evans Museum in Victorville, California.

**Sidekicks:** George "Gabby" Hayes, Pat Brady, Andy Devine

**Fictional Ranch Name:** Double R Bar

Roy Rogers

KF 40

Rep. Pict.

**Official Title:** "King of the Cowboys," awarded him by his studio, Republic Pictures, when Gene Autry joined the Army

**Merchandising Spin-offs:** Roy Rogers Tuck-A-Way Gun, Roy Rogers Signal Siren Flashlight, Roy Rogers Chow Wagon Lunchbox, Roy Rogers Happy Trails Plaster Lamp, Trigger and Roy Slip-On Boots, Roy Rogers and Trigger Toy Guitar, et cetera. More recently: Roy Rogers Restaurants (franchised by Marriott Corp.), Roy Rogers and Dale Evans Happy Trails Resorts

**Hobbies:** Raising chickens and homing pigeons, watching the TV soap opera "Guiding Light," throwing darts, fishing, shooting, and cooking his longtime specialty—an omelet made from onions, catsup, cream, and eggs

**Shooting Ability:** Mastered quick-draw for the movies, but told *Life* magazine he is better with a slingshot

**Wardrobe:** One of the great Western fashion plates of all time. Roy favored plaid or fringed shirts with embroidered yokes, a colorful silk scarf fastened with a monogrammed silver slide, a white Stetson hat of relatively modest proportions, fancy boots with flamboyant designs, and a hand-tooled gun belt with a single holster, festooned with silver dots and conchos.

**Fans:** In 1942, Roy was getting a thousand letters a day. Today his fans include former President and Mrs. Reagan, former President Bush, Randy Travis, Clint Black, and Billy Graham.

**Most Unusual Compliment:** Louella Parsons once said of Roy, as he walked in front of her into a banquet at a Hollywood hotel: "There goes the handsomest behind I ever saw in my life."

**How Life Follows Art:** Roy Rogers and Dale Evans are as much paragons of cowboy virtue off screen as on. In addition to four children from their previous marriages, together they adopted four children and one foster child of various ethnic origins. Their humanitarian work on behalf of children has earned them untold numbers of honors and awards, and they have served as co-chairmen of the National Committee for the Prevention of Child Abuse. One person close to them said, "Throughout their careers, Roy Rogers and Dale Evans have represented honesty, decency, and faith in God and Country."

**Quote:** "When I die you can skin me and put me on top of Trigger, and I'll be happy."

*The lunch box opposite at far left commands several hundred dollars in today's Western memorabilia market.*

# *John* WAYNE

ohn Wayne, an actor, was the greatest cowboy America ever produced. His career spanned almost half a century, and he made over two hundred pictures, nearly ninety of them Westerns. During that time, Hollywood's West went through many transformations. When Wayne first strapped on a shooting iron and hit the trail in *The Big Trail* (1930), Tom Mix was the reigning ideal, bedizened in conchos and silver spurs and always fighting on the side of justice; Wayne's final shoot-out, in *The Shootist* (1976), came at a time when Westerns already had been declared dead, and the top box office buckaroo was Clint Eastwood as the Man with No Name—a cynical assassin in need of a bath and a shave. Westerns changed; movies changed; America changed; but through it all, John Wayne remained remarkably the same.

There was no one else in his league, and he was not like any other screen cowboy: never a fashion plate or a cold-blooded killer, and very different

from the saintly superstars who appealed primarily to kids, such as Hoppy, Gene, and Roy. In his finest roles, John Wayne was an adult's hero—an imperfect idol who was gallant and strong, who wrestled with serious moral issues and with the dilemmas of the real American frontier, and who, in film critic Gene Siskel's words, "inspired grown men to curl up in his arms and ask about the Old West."

Wayne rarely played the same role (in the 1930s he was one of the Three Mesquiteers in a handful of films and played a tuneful buckaroo named Singin' Sandy in a series of low-budget oaters; at the end of his career, he was Sheriff Rooster Cogburn twice); in various Westerns he appeared as a cowboy, a gunman, a soldier, a rancher, a sheriff, and a fugitive; he fought on both sides of the law; he helped settle the West and he was a victim of its settlement. One thing was constant about him: John Wayne always played an honorable man who rode tall in the saddle; audiences knew they could depend on him to never let them down.

*John Wayne, 1965.*
Opposite: *1930.*

After his first starring role, in Raoul Walsh's *The Big Trail,* which was a big-budget dud, Wayne got stereotyped in the 1930s as a low-budget cowboy, in a decade when Westerns were considered second-class projects in Hollywood. Director John Ford revived the Western as an A-picture, and John Wayne's career, too, with *Stagecoach* (1939), in which Wayne, playing a boyish outlaw (he was actually thirty-two, but seems ten years younger in the role) gave a riveting performance as the Ringo Kid—a gunslinger bent on vengeance, but with a good heart and a rigorous code of honor.

After World War II, he became a superstar, and a symbol of American character around the world, mostly because of the roles he played in cowboy movies directed by Howard Hawks and John Ford. Hawks's *Red River* (1948), about the first cattle drive up the Chisholm Trail, gave Wayne one of the meatiest roles of his career—a dauntless cattleman whose iron will verges on affliction. Playing an older man, Wayne amplified his righteous screen image in this picture until it assumed the strength of a force of nature. The fact that *Red River* was based on one of the most inspiring events in real Western history made it all the more convincing and gave its flawed hero a patriotic radiance. He later established himself as a virtuoso gunfighter in a trio of masterful Hawks films, *Rio Bravo* (1959), *El Dorado* (1967), and *Rio Lobo* (1971), in which he added humor and even a measure of self-parody to his cowboy image . . . but was never less than totally professional.

It was in John Ford's epic cavalry trilogy—*Fort Apache* (1948), *She Wore a Yellow Ribbon* (1949), and *Rio Grande* (1950)—that John Wayne became the movies' sturdiest pillar of morality. All three pictures were filmed in Monument Valley, a stately range of rock monoliths that seemed an ideal geological foil for his role as a noble sol-

dier. In the first two of the cavalry films, in which he struggles against more reckless officers' inclination to kill Indians, he played his part with a rich ambivalence: a character with a ramrod spine who would never shirk his duty, yet who was profoundly grieved by his duty to "civilize" the West. Similarly, in Ford's melancholy *The Man Who Shot Liberty Valance* (1962), about the coming of law and order to the wilderness, Wayne plays a cowboy who sees himself become obsolete. In these John Ford films, John Wayne became the consummate Western hero: a man with a screen image big enough to contain the full heroics of the cowboy myth as well as the disturbing historical realities that sometimes contradict that myth.

The friction between the West's splendor and its savagery was particularly stunning in *The Searchers* (1956), which its director, John Ford, called a "psychological epic." Filmed mostly in Monument Valley, in VistaVision ("motion picture high fidelity") by Winton C. Hoch, the movie has an exquisite clarity that makes John Wayne appear etched into a Western Valhalla. He plays a drifter, perhaps an outlaw, who sets out on what seems like a chivalrous quest to find a niece kidnapped by Comanches. But his monomaniacal hatred careens toward insanity, and when he suddenly begins shooting buffalo in order to deprive the Indians of food, then later scalps his nemesis, the spiteful glint in his eyes is truly horrifying, and a good example of John Wayne's talent for encompassing heroism and ferocity in a single, enigmatic character. At the end of the picture, he stands alone, then turns and walks away, a friendless wanderer in a windswept landscape, a mythic figure and a mournful one—perhaps the single most resonant image of the American cowboy ever put on screen.

# *Ol*
# PROC

**W**allace McRae runs a cattle ranch in Montana. He has written poetry since the 1960s and has read his poems at the Elko, Nevada, Cowboy Poetry Gathering, on a syndicated television program titled "The West," and at the National Cowboy Hall of Fame in Oklahoma City. During the 1992 Presidential campaign, candidate Bill Clinton said that McRae was one of his favorite contemporary American writers.

We asked him for permission to reprint his most famous poem, "Reincarnation," but he felt it had been overdone and therefore directed us to one of his personal favorites, "Ol' Proc," in his book *Cowboy Curmudgeon and Other Poems.* We're glad he did. "Ol' Proc" isn't as funny as "Reincarnation," but it gives a brimful measure of the cowboy state of mind.

*Wallace McRae, photographed by Robert Landau.*

# OL' PROC

Old-timers in the neighborhood
Would bandy words on who was good
At puncher jobs for hours on end when I was just a kid.
They'd get wall-eyed 'n paw and bawl
And swear, "By damn I knowed 'em all.
If'n Josh he wasn't best trailhand, I'll eat my beaver lid!"

"Down and dirty, I'm the dealer.
Old Bob Seward? Best damn peeler
Ever snapped a bronc out, jist give me one he broke."
"Give, you say? That's what I heard.
You're right that Bob's a tough ol' bird.
But better practice cactus pickin' and work on your spur stroke.

Cain't stay astraddle one of his'n
When he pops the plug and goes t'fizzin'
She'll be adios caballo and howdy to the nurse."
They'd move from bickering bronc peelers
To rawhide hands 'n fancy heelers.
"Red Carlin?" "Young Mac Philbrick?" They'd testify
    and curse.

They'd analyze Link Taylor's cuttin':
"His bag-splittin' way of calf denuttin'
Is pure askin' for trouble, 'sides he don't cut by the sign."
"You cut your calves by the moon?
Keep on night brandin' and pretty soon
The sheriff'll change yer address and you'll be twistin' hair
    and twine."

On they'd rave and postulate
'Bout who was fair 'n who was great.
As they scratched brands in the hot dust, I'd never say a word.
But in their jousting verbal battle,
Among the boasts and barbs and prattle,
I sat in youthful judgement as they sorted out the herd.

So I came to early understand
The names of every good top hand.
In my scope of country, from hearing tough hands talk.
But when they'd crow and blow and boast
The one name that came up the most
Was a wily wild horse runner they simply called "ol' Proc."

"You boys jist start 'em. I'll stop 'em,"
Old Proc'd say and then he'd chop 'em
Off at some escape route. He'd wheel 'n bring them in.

"Proc thinks horse," I heard them say,
And finally there came the day
That I would get to meet this fabled mounted paladin.

My mother's father, John McKay,
Up and said one fine spring day
While I was staying with them, "Minnie get your bonnet."
"Let's go up by the Castle Rock
'N see some country, visit Proc.
If you're late, I'll be upset. You can bet your life upon it."

He never paused for her reply.
My grandma fussed around and I
Asked grandpa, "Is he the wild horse man?" "That's him,"
    my grandpa said.
As we ricocheted and bounced our way
In a tobacco-stained green Chevrolet
My grandpa told "Proc stories" and chewed and spit and sped.

From all the tales Grandpa told me
I felt like an authority
On this ranahan, Joe Proctor, who came north with Texas cattle.
His wife had been the JO cook.
But Proc had sparked and won and took
Her for his bride. They fought and won the homestead battle.

I couldn't wait to meet Mr. Proc,
Whose peers all praised his way with stock.
But when his calloused hand gripped mine, surprise hit me
    in waves.
Those old cowboys who cut no slack
Deemed it unimportant Proc was black,
And wasn't worth a mention that Joe Proctor's folks were slaves.

# Singing
# COWBOYS

**7**he idea of a singing cowboy anywhere other than in Nashville or a Hollywood movie seems at least a little farfetched, but in fact real cowboys did sing—maybe to calm down skittish cattle, but more likely to alleviate their boredom in the saddle and to romanticize their lives.

*Songs of the Cowboys,* by Jack Thorp, a former New Yorker who became a wrangler at the Bar W Ranch in New Mexico, was published in 1908 after Thorp spent more than ten years gathering verses from cowboys he met along the trail. Thorp later observed, "I never did hear a cowboy with a real good voice; if he had one to start with, he always lost it bawling at the cattle, or sleeping out in the open, or tellin' the judge he didn't steal that horse."

Modern singing cowboys continue to honor and embellish the cowboy ideal. Such prodigious talents as Ian Tyson, Red Steagall, Fletcher Jowers, Sons of the San Joaquin, and Michael Martin Murphey are known to their fans as cowboy-western singers, NOT country-western; their recordings of classic range songs as well as original odes to frontier life are treasured by buckaroos from coast to coast, and their talents are lovingly documented three times a year in the vastly entertaining periodical *Song of the West* (see page 385). In the last few years Michael Martin Murphey has gone beyond the microphone

BIG
COLORING and

Rex Allen

KF 47                                    Rep. Pict.

Of the gray coyotes
To him are a glad refrain.

And his jolly songs
Speed him along
As he thinks of the little gal
With golden hair
Who is waiting there
At the bars of the home corral.

For a kingly crown
In the noisy town
His saddle he wouldn't change;
No life so free
As the life we see
'Way out on the Yaso range.

His eyes are bright
And his heart as light
As the smoke of his cigarette;
There's never a care
For his soul to bear,
No trouble to make him fret.

The rapid beat
Of his bronco's feet,
On the sod as he speeds along,
Keeps living time
To the ringing rhyme
Of his rollicking cowboy's song.

Hike it, cowboys,
For the range away
On the back of a bronc of steel,
With a careless flirt
Of the raw-hide quirt
And the dig of a roweled heel.

to produce "West Fests"—big festivals of cowboy-themed art, dance, fun, and continuous music.

Thorp said that he heard a wrangler named Spence sing this song at a round-up at Seven Lakes, New Mexico:

## THE COWBOY'S LIFE

The bawl of a steer
To a cowboy's ear
Is music of sweetest strain;
And the yelping notes

The winds may blow
And the thunder growl
Or the breeze may safely moan;
A cowboy's life
Is a royal life,
His saddle his kingly throne.

Saddle up, boys,
For the work is play
When love's in the cowboy's eyes,
When his heart is light
As the clouds of white
That swim in the summer skies.

This classic cowboy ballad, about a trail drive up into the High Plains, was described by Arlene Hodapp, in an article about "Songs of the Cowboys" (*Yippy Yi Yea* magazine, Summer 1992) as having a rhythm like the gait of a loping horse. Ms. Hodapp suggested that it was probably composed by someone sitting in the saddle.

## GIT ALONG, LITTLE DOGIES

*As I was a-walking one morning for*
*    pleasure,*
*I spied a cowpuncher a-riding along.*
*His hat was throwed back and his spurs*
*    was a-jingling,*
*As he approach'd me was a-singing*
*    this song.*

*"Whoopee ti-yi-yo, git along,*
*    little dogies,*
*It's your misfortune and none of*
*    my own.*
*Whoopee ti-yi-yo, git along*
*    little dogies,*
*For you know Wyoming will*
*    be your new home.*

*"Early in the spring we*
*    round up the dogies,*
*Mark and brand them and*
*    bob off their tails;*
*Round up our horses, load up*
*    the chuck-wagon,*
*Then throw the dogies upon*
*    the North trail."*

Opposite: *Rex Allen.* Below: *Curly Fox and Texas Ruby. Curly started his career in Tennessee with The Skillet Lickers. Ruby was known as the Sophie Tucker of cowgirl singers.*

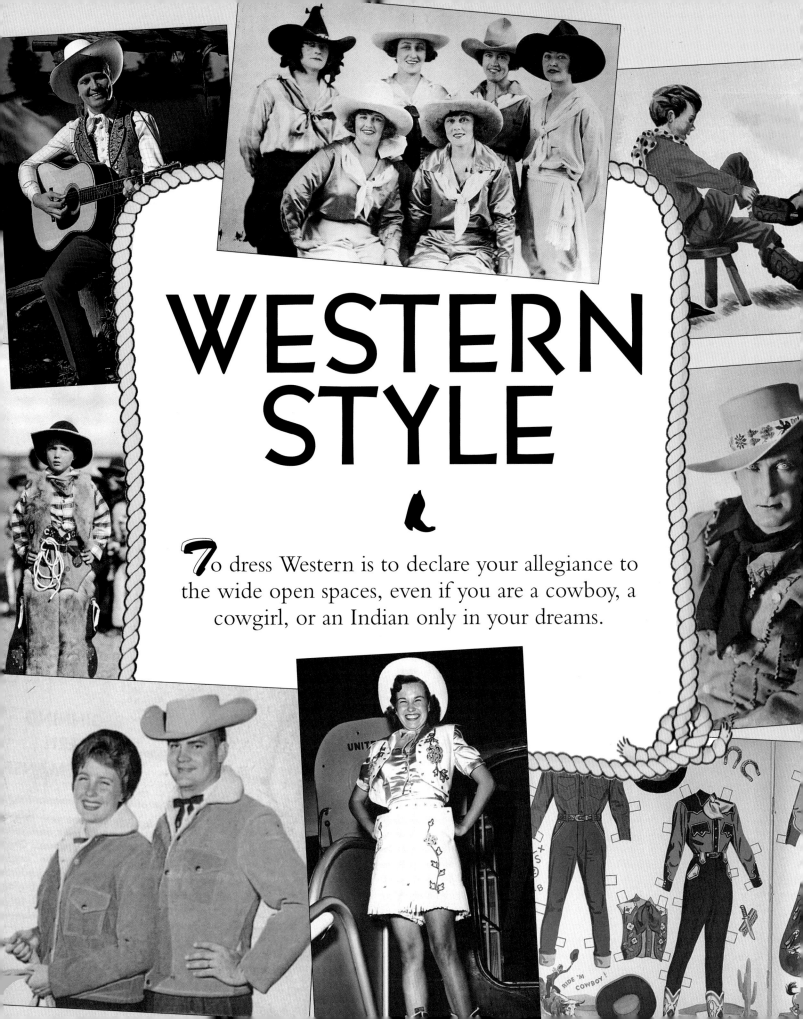

# WESTERN STYLE

**T**o dress Western is to declare your allegiance to the wide open spaces, even if you are a cowboy, a cowgirl, or an Indian only in your dreams.

# *Rhinestone* COWBOYS AND COWGIRLS

*The fringed leathern chaparreros, the cartridge belt, the flannel shirt, the knotted scarf at the neck . . . Worn by this man now standing at her door, they seemed to radiate romance.*

—Owen Wister in *The Virginian* (1902)

n 1882 Oscar Wilde toured the West delivering lectures that included advice to frontiersmen about how to dress fashionably. Historian Dee Brown reports that as Wilde traveled to mining camps and outposts, the famous fop bought himself a Stetson hat and corduroy pants, then a buckaroo neckerchief and high-heeled boots. By the time his tour was finished, Wilde had given up his knee britches and lace cuffs and adopted an outfit every bit as flamboyant—the clothes of an American cowboy. Western style is simply irresistible.

Cowboy fashions began as work clothes. In some sense, they still are. Tight-fitting jeans, boots with underslung high heels, leather chaps, a billowy neckerchief, and a broad-brimmed hat are all useful garments if you make your living herding cows on horseback. But a remarkable thing has happened in the last hundred or so years: these clothes that were originally developed for the dirty tasks of cowboying have become the epitome of American fashion, and an inspiration to people around

Right: *Hollywood cowboy Ken Maynard—shy, kindly, a great horseman, and always well dressed.* Opposite: *Cowgirl Dolly Eskew.*

the world who wear them just for fun. "Western wear," Stanley Marcus (of Neiman–Marcus stores) wrote, "has undoubtedly been America's single greatest contribution to world fashion."

You don't have to be a buckaroo to enjoy the bravura of pointy-toed footwear, a pearl-button plaid shirt, or a steer-head bolo for your scarf; these are apparel that give everyone the opportunity to wrap him- or herself in the pleasure of a cowboy fantasy. For dudes who don't know the croup of a horse from its withers, as well as for urban and suburban cowboys, rodeo stars, and genuine ranch hands, sagebrush style is a marvelous costume. Practical though it may be, for many people the point of wearing it is simply to look sharp and to enjoy the hard-riding, straight-shooting, hell-bent-for-leather implications of the guise.

*Bronc rider Marge Greenough, photographed at her ranch in Red Lodge, Montana. Below right: Buffalo Bill in buckskin.*

The thrill of cowboy clothing set the tone of *The Book of Cowboys* (1936), written and illustrated by Holling C. Hollings as a child's introduction to the cowboy way of life. Hollings tells of the adventures of a young brother and sister from New York City who travel to visit their uncle Harry on his ranch in New Mexico one summer.

They arrive by train, and after they are refreshed by a brisk shower of icy mountain water, Uncle Harry brings the city kids two wooden chests, each filled with a new wardrobe of cowboy clothes for them to wear.

*On top were the shirts, one green and one blue. Then came, one after the other, silk scarves, cowboy cuffs, felt sombreros, blue overalls, brown leather chaps with gleaming silver conchas down the side flaps; and at the bottoms of the chests were black cowboy boots, neatly stitched in leaf designs, and with high heels.*

Left: *The largest couple in America, Mr. and Mrs. Fischer, wore matching Western outfits. Mr. Fischer's boots were size 16, but his hat was a mere 7⅝. Below: Bronc rider Prairie Rose Henderson, one of rodeo's first female headliners.*

*Manly duds (clockwise from opposite, far left): Duncan Renaldo as The Cisco Kid; Michael Yager, bull rider; movie cowboy Ken Roberts; a card entitling a little boy to a free gift; a rodeo bull rider surveys the chutes before showtime.*

*Happy Birthday*

LEGGETT'S

*Boys' Department*

The frontier really did have its share of showy dressers. Wild Bill Hickok was known for his long hair and embellished buckskin clothes; Bat Masterson was famously well groomed; and photographers throughout the Old West kept fancy outfits in their studio so cowboys could wear something better than their trail clothes when they came to town and decided to have their picture taken. In fact, many real working cowboys, especially those who rode the range as the cowboy myth began to proliferate after the era of the great trail drives, seemed to be extraordinarily fashion-conscious. In his book *Forty Years on the Frontier*, rancher Granville Stuart described some of the hands he had employed in the 1880s as men who

> took great pride in their personal appearance and in their trappings [which] consisted of a fine saddle, silver mounted bridle, pearl-handled six-shooter, latest model cartridge belt with silver buckle, silver spurs . . . and a fancy hatband often made from the dressed skin of a diamond rattlesnake. They wore expensive stiff-brimmed light felt hats with brilliantly colored handkerchiefs knotted about their necks, light colored shirts and exquisitely fitted high-heeled riding boots.

Despite some cowboys' taste for such fine regalia, few people considered cowboy attire stylish until Buffalo Bill Cody elevated frontier trappings into showy glad rags. Cody had originally made a name for himself as the ultimate Westerner, thanks not only to his real exploits, but to dime novels that dramatized them and to plays he starred in with such titles as *Knights of the Plains*, *Saved from the Sioux*, and *From Noose to Neck*. In these melodramas, Cody played himself—frontier scout supreme, dressed to the nines in an extravagant version of his real scout apparel, including ornamental beads and flowing fringed buckskin and a deep-crown John B. Stetson hat. Starting in the 1880s his Wild West shows exaggerated cowboy wear the same way, and made cowboys into icons whose adornments evoked romantic images of a dashing life on the Plains. He outfitted his rough riders in fabulous ornamental versions of working cowhand attire, including silver conchas for their chaps, ornate belt buckles, vests with resplendent beadwork, and wide-placket shirts with glittering buttons.

Wild West shows transformed the popular image of the cowboy from a laborer in work clothes to a knight of the Plains in resplendent livery; movies embellished that image, helping make cowboys into the best-dressed heroes of American folklore. From Roy Rogers in fringe

to Clint Eastwood as the Man with No Name in serape and hip-hugger bell-bottom pants, cowboys on the screen have offered up a wide range of inspiring styles for audiences to admire, and to a degree, imitate.

Curiously, the earliest cowboy movies did not trade on the flamboyant look of Wild West show performers. Movies were a novel medium when the West was still only recent history; cinema's ability to *document* reality

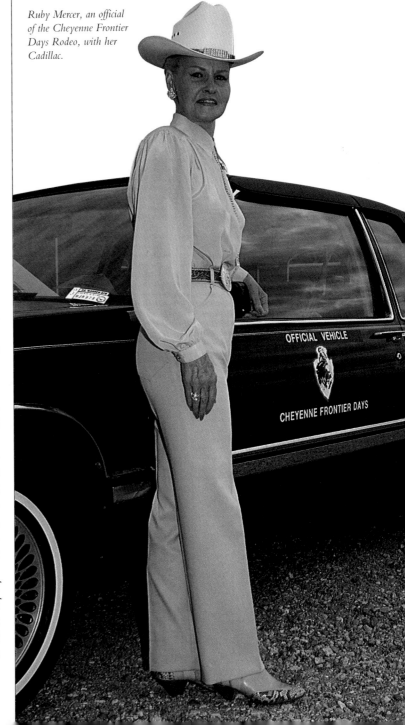

*Ruby Mercer, an official of the Cheyenne Frontier Days Rodeo, with her Cadillac.*

was applied to the West. *The Great Train Robbery* of 1903, for example, was inspired by a real heist in Wyoming only three years before by The Wild Bunch (although it was filmed in New Jersey), and the gunmen it depicts are anything but dandies. The plots of Westerns made by D. W. Griffith and William S. Hart may have been florid Victorian melodramas, but their vision of the West had an almost realistic quality, and the clothes worn by cowboys in their sagas tended to be dusty and drab. Hart actually wore gun belts and guns that he had gotten from Wyatt Earp, Bat Masterson, and other surviving lawmen (and some outlaws), and he never appeared without a thick sash wrapped around his waist beneath his gun belt: the sash was a common garment among real cowboys, who used it like a pigging string, to tie the legs of cattle they had wrestled to the ground.

Tom Mix was the original fashion king of cowboy movies. He began his career as a performer with the 101 Ranch Wild West show, and although his first movies, starting in 1909, followed the early Western's convention of stark and realistic costumes, he soon developed a style of outlandish attire that film historians George N. Fenin and William K. Everson called a "circus" approach to dress. Derived from his experience as a showman, he wore a uniform that was a delirious impression of cowboy style as the height of masculine glamour: huge high hat, embroidered shirt, riding britches embellished with gold braid, boots hand-carved in intricate floral and Wild West designs, big silver spurs attached with concha-crusted strips of leather, and the finest leather gun rig money could buy to hold his nickel-plated Peacemakers. (As an alternate to his leather gun belt, he had a horsehair belt with diamond buckle and the inscription *Tom Mix, America's Champion Cowboy*.) Mix inspired generations of Hollywood cowboys who came after him; his influence has reverberated through not only movies but also the attire of rodeo, Saturday-night honky-tonks, and country music.

Tom Mix and the box office broncsters who came after him set lofty sartorial standards for cowboys on the screen; but there were also plenty of cowgirls, starting with Ruth Roland in the silent era, who established their own opu-

*Hollywood cowgirls, including Joan Crawford (opposite, far left), Jean Arthur (opposite, above right). Right: The most famous name in Western wear before Nudie of Hollywood.*

lent tradition of ecstatic Western wear. Ms. Roland, known in the 1920s as the Queen of the Western Serials, wore a giant felt hat, a checked shirt with a sweeping bandanna, and full leather batwing chaps with *RRR*, her initials, emblazoned in contrasting colors down the side.

The influence of movie cowgirls was abetted by the popularity of dude ranching. After all, the point of a dude ranch for most people who began vacationing at them in the 1920s and 1930s was to play cowboy, and what better way to do that than to dress like one? In his book *Dude Ranching*, Lawrence R. Borne included this description of a couple of guests at a dude ranch in 1920: "One wore lavender angora chaps, the other bright orange, and each sported a tremendous beaver sombrero and wore a gaudy scarf knotted jauntily about his throat." Twenty years later, Western fashion was still making news, and *Life* magazine announced, "Dude girls of the West are taking to nifty riding clothes with fancy skirts and pants." *Life*'s story showed a comely cowgirl model walking through a corral in skin-tight "frontier pants" made of light blue suede with white lacing along the side. Another cowgirl leaned against a split-rail fence, wearing a black divided skirt and bolero, both decorated with white suede scrolls and fringes, along with a fancy silver-stud belt. "Even the least dressy girls wear big, round hats and fancy cowgirl boots," *Life* noted.

Movie magazines from the golden age of the serial Western, from the 1930s into the 1950s, are replete with breathless stories that feature current cowgirl actresses modeling the latest in fringed buckskin skirts, colorful neckerchiefs, and ladies' riding boots—either at a dude ranch or on their own spread. These women helped give

Western style a strong appeal to people in the audience who weren't themselves movie stars or even dude ranch types, but who definitely might want to emulate a cowgirl they admired.

In November 1950, *Movie Thrills* magazine featured an article titled "Weekend Cowgirl" about TV actress Roberta Quinlan, "star of NBC's 'Mohawk Showroom,'" who with her husband, Jack, and her French poodle, Bonga, was heading for East Jewitt, New York, high in the Catskill mountains, to the Timberlane Dude Ranch. Pictures showed Roberta on horseback shooting her two six-guns, relaxing after a huge steak dinner typical of the cowboy life, and wearing ensembles of lovely cowboy clothes, including a hat with a whipstitched brim, deep-cuffed Levi's, and a jaunty plaid shirt. Only two months earlier, *Movie Thrills* had done a similar story about Ruth Roman, this one titled "Ranch Vacation Bound," that showed the actress "in a Western mood" wearing a fringed and beaded Indian jacket in soft honeysuckle suede, canary yellow shantung skirt, and brown jodhpurs.

Now that high-fashion cowboy movies are passé, rodeo is the best place to see Western style in its fullest glory. Like cowboy movies, rodeo descended from the Wild West shows, and although many of its participants are working ranch hands, everybody understands that the events in the arena are supposed to look like a cowboy-gone-to-heaven jubilee. (At the Cheyenne Frontier Days rodeo, for example, all members of the press are required to wear a full complement of boots, hats, jeans, and cowboy shirts buttoned at the wrist.) In his rodeo history *Man, Beast, Dust* (1947), Clifford P. Westermeier wrote that flashy clothes were worn by rodeo hands mostly "for the purpose of giving the dudes a thrill"; nonetheless, he acknowledged that the costume typical of cowboys, even when they weren't showing off, was indeed some-

thing to behold: "The cowboy is clothes-conscious and he certainly wears one of the most extreme styles of garb that has ever been devised for man. . . . It has a cut, a line, a texture, and a color that might be called a conservative-extremeness." Westermeier made particular mention of riveted jeans, with what he called "the Robin Hood effect"—worn so tight that "the belt is purely ornamental, but as for serving the purpose of keeping up their trousers, one can readily see from the fit that a surgical operation would be needed to remove them [from] these 'he men' of the West."

The most dramatically well-dressed rodeo hands were some of the sport's women in the 1920s and 1930s. Wearing huge angora chaps, ostrich plume skirts, or billowy satin bloomers and boots embossed with bright red hearts, trailing colored streamers from their gauntlets as they rode bucking broncs and wrestled steers, they dazzled audiences with their very presence as much as with their skills. Bernice Taylor, known as the Gardenia Lady for the white flower she kept in her hair during trick riding demonstrations, could swing under the neck of a horse while riding at full gallop. In her book *The Cowgirls* (1990) Joyce Gibson Roach wrote about another rodeo star named Kitty Canutt, who had a diamond set into the enamel of her front tooth. It created a dazzling visual effect when she smiled, especially under lights, and it was also useful to pawn whenever she needed money to enter a rodeo.

One of rodeo's greatest female performers, Tad Lucas, told Joyce Gibson Roach that until the 1930s, cowgirls—and cowboys, too—had to have their fancy clothes custom-made for them because no commercial tailor produced that kind of flamboyant Western wear. Many women sewed their own clothes; Hall-of-Famer Marge Greenough carried a small sewing machine along with her saddle and tack whenever she went on tour.

By the 1930s the fashion industry began responding to the popularity of cowboy movies and of such sensationally well-dressed heroes as Gene Autry and Roy Rogers. The Justin Boot company got its first lasts for women's sizes in 1936, which also happened to be the year of the Texas Centennial Celebration and the year Stanley Marcus later identified as the real beginning of America's love affair with Western style. Marcus also said that he believed that European designers first discovered

*Hostesses at the rodeo in Dallas, 1959.*

the magic of Western wear in 1949, when Jacques Fath, a French couturier, came to Dallas and was so impressed by the costumes he saw at a square dance that he and his wife bought outfits and staged a Western hoedown of their own at their château the following summer. Fath's August 1950 collection contained his own version of a cowboy shirt: satin, with rhinestone buttons.

Only a few years before Monsieur Fath saw the light in Dallas, Wrangler (then called Blue Bell) hired a Philadelphia tailor named Rodeo Ben to design Western-cut jeans for the mass market, based on the fancy cowboy attire for which Ben had become famous on the rodeo circuit. "He made the best," Rodeo champ Jim Shoulders recalled. "Even before I went to rodeo in New York, I knew that anybody who had himself a Rodeo Ben suit or even a Rodeo Ben pair of britches, why, he'd been winning something. It was a big deal." Wrangler gave every cowboy at the Madison Square Garden rodeo two pairs of their Rodeo Ben jeans, and in 1948 the company hired Jim Shoulders—who was on his way to becoming the winningest rodeo cowboy ever— to be its spokesman in national advertisements.

Rodeo Ben was one of a handful of tailors, including also Fay Ward ("The Best in Western Garb") of New York, Sing Kee of San Francisco, and Nathan Turk of Sherman

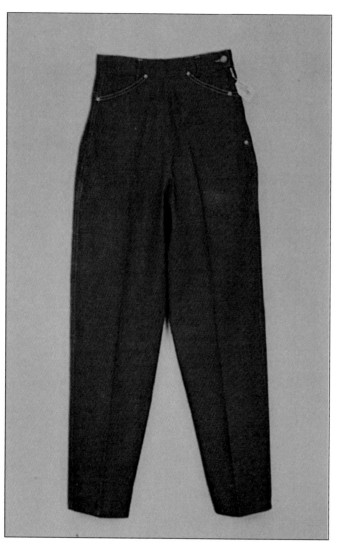

Oaks, whose reputations were based on their skills at producing luxurious, high-fashion cowboy attire. Clifford P. Westermeier described Ben's garments as being made of "the finest fabrics, shirts of whipcord, gabardine, serge, silk crepe, and silk satin of two weights. Suits are of worsted materials, cavalry twills and Bedford cords." In 1947, a fine Rodeo Ben shirt cost as much as one hundred dollars.

The most famous cowboy tailor of them all was a little man named Nudie. After starting his career in Brooklyn as a 112-pound small-time prizefighter known as "Battling Nudie Cohn," he came to Hollywood in 1918 in the hope of becoming a cowboy star. When that failed, he moved to Minnesota and opened "Nudie's for the Ladies," a business that specialized in G-strings for exotic dancers. Finally Nudie moved back West, where, in 1947, after apprenticing with Nathan Turk, he opened "Nudie's Rodeo Tailors." Five years later when country singer Lefty Frizzell needed a stage outfit, Nudie counseled him against wearing an ordinary suit like someone in the audience might wear, so he made Lefty something that would set him apart: a suit studded with rhinestones. This outfit made Nudie famous, and gave birth to the term "rhinestone cowboy."

Nudie became the world's largest outfitter of baroque Western wear (and more: he made Elvis's ten-thousand-dollar gold lamé suit in 1957). He had finally realized his dream of becoming a cowboy star, but in his own way. He was famous in the film community for going around town in a huge Stetson hat, gaudy gold rings that featured tiny diamond-bedecked saddles, and Western-cut suits embroidered with cactus and bucking bronc motifs in sparkling stones. Instead of riding a horse, Nudie drove a Pontiac convertible with steer horns on the front bumper and an array of decorative pistols, rifles, and chrome statues of cattle affixed to its hood and fenders. The car's interior featured a saddle for an armrest between the two front seats and hand-tooled leather everywhere, embedded with four hundred silver dollars. "Nudie the Tailor rides again!" *Newsweek* commented in 1971.

Owning a closet full of Nudie suits became de

rigueur for any cowboy movie star or singer. The most spectacular of Roy Rogers's and Gene Autry's outfits—the ones too gaudy for film, but perfect for personal appearances—were made by Nudie, and a host of civilians lined up to buy their own wondrous duds from the man who invented the rhinestone cowboy. Some of his more unusual custom orders included an entire wardrobe embroidered with poodles for the wife of a Houston oilman and a restaurant owner's suit that featured hand-stitched steaks appliquéd on the jacket and pants. Nudie has passed away, but his shop is still thriving in North Hollywood, and vintage clothes he made—worth fortunes to collectors—are on display in Western galleries from the Cowboy Hall of Fame in Oklahoma City to the Gene Autry Western Heritage Museum in Los Angeles.

Among the couturiers who apprenticed with Nudie, the greatest is Manuel Cuevas (who also happened to marry Nudie's daughter). Manuel is today the dean of Western fashion, and celebrities line up at his Nashville studio to be fitted in sequined, fancy-stitched attire or whatever Manuel deems best for their image (he insisted Johnny Cash wear black back in 1953). "Manuel is the King," Country star and cowboy clothes collector Marty Stuart declared. "I can't imagine my life without Manuel." If you want to join the likes of Elvis (Manuel invented his white jumpsuit), Dwight Yoakam (bolero jackets), Linda Ronstadt (embroidered Mexican dresses), and Bob Dylan (a $7,500 jacket made from a Chimayo blanket), you need to make an appointment; if Manuel can fit you in, you will get a handmade garment with a label that says Designed For [Your Name Here] by Manuel. If, on the other hand, you don't mind buying Manuel's spectacular duds off the shelf, we recommend a trip to Jane Smith of Santa Fe (see page 369), a wondrous Western-wear store that features ready-to-wear (also custom-made) Manuel garments with fringe and flash guaranteed to drop your jaw.

# Hollywood Fashion Plates: GENE AUTRY AND ROY ROGERS

You can argue about who were the toughest hombres ever on the silver screen (William S. Hart and Clint Eastwood?) or the fastest with a six-shooter (Alan Ladd as *Shane* and Gregory Peck as *The Gunfighter*?), but there can be little doubt as to who were the best-dressed: Gene Autry and Roy Rogers. This pair of sagebrush superstars, who would also be in the running for the nicest, cleanest-cut, and most patriotic of all screen Westerners, set the gold standard for splendor in the silver saddle.

We have met a few old-time ranch hands who, in a spirit of Western devilment, like to refer to Gene as "Gene Altarpiece" and Roy as "Roy Roget" (pronounced like the Frenchman who wrote the thesaurus) for the exorbitant way they dressed. Make no mistake about it: Their skin-tight gabardine extravaganzas, bedecked with swinging fringe and embroidered folderol, were definitely not designed for some dust-sucking wrangler to wear while branding a calf or breaking a

bronco. That was never the point: theirs were not supposed to be the clothes of working cowboys. They were cowboy superstars, and no real-life buckaroo ever sang as pretty or shot as straight as they, or had a horse that jumped through fiery hoops and walked around a corral on its hind legs. Gene and Roy were not cowboys, they were symbols of cowboys, and to play that part, they wore outfits designed to take their viewers' breath away.

Tom Mix, the jazz-age Western movie star, had set high standards in his romantic versions of cowboy clothes, and William Boyd as Hopalong Cassidy cut a dazzling figure in his sleek blue-black vestments, Bohlin belt, Hamley double-rig holsters, and checked scarf, but it wasn't until the heyday of musical Westerns that the Hollywood cowboy reached a kind of sartorial apotheosis, related to authentic working-cowboy gear only in the way a flag symbolizes a nation.

Gene Autry was the first to take cowboy style to its outer limit, and it wasn't only in the movies he made for

Republic Studios starting in 1934. In fact, his movie attire—usually featuring stark black shirts piped with gold braid on the pockets, collar, and placket—was generally quite subdued compared to what he wore for personal appearances and rodeo specialty acts he performed with Champion. Gene saved his fanciest movie duds for when the plot required them (at a hoedown, when he was performing a song). His most deluxe costumes in the early days, made by Nathan Turk and Rodeo Ben as well as now long-forgotten studio tailors, featured shirts with flower patterns, images of ducks fashioned from elaborate beadwork, or eagles spread across their backs, as well as some incredible hand-tooled leather vests. Nearly all of Gene Autry's most distinctive britches-and-shirt ensembles were edged with piping or glittering braid along the yoke, sleeves, and collar of the shirt, as well as on the seams of the pants, in a color that contrasted to the body of the garment.

He wore silver spurs, attached with silver-buckled straps, and his boots, crafted by the master bootmakers Lucchese and Justin, always featured decorative motifs in carved leather inlaid on the uppers: longhorn steer heads, butterflies, cactus roses, lone stars, and crescent moons. His hat was a Stetson, creased fore-to-aft lengthwise once on the top and once on each side. Today Western hatmakers still refer to this configu-

Top: *Gene Autry and his Independence Day shirt, 1940*. Bottom: *Roy Rogers and Dale Evans, circa 1965*.

ration as the Autry crease.

So his fans (mostly youngsters) could get in the spirit of the high-fashion West, Autry licensed his name for dozens of articles of child-sized clothing, including a 1941 "Official Gene Autry Ranch Outfit" that featured hat, shirt, vest, neckerchief, lariat, and a pair of chaps—one of which said *Gene,* the other *Autry.* There were Gene Autry guns and holsters, spurs, boots, and galoshes, as well as wristwatches ("Guaranteed watch for American Youth"), and even a Gene Autry Bicycle with a saddle for a seat, glass jewels on the frame, and a steer horn between the handlebars. In their book of cowboy collectibles, *Box-Office Buckaroos,* Robert Heide and John Gilman report that the bicycle is today the ultimate Gene Autry souvenir: apparently Gene felt foolish going on TV riding a bicycle instead of a horse, so the product was never publicized, and only a few thousand were made.

When Gene Autry went from Republic Studios to Columbia in 1974, he muted his famously loud screen image, and sometimes wore nothing fancier than blue jeans and a simple checked shirt unless the plot demanded he dress up for a fiesta; however, his wardrobe for personal appearances after the war grew even gaudier, thanks in part to Nudie of Hollywood, who sup-

Roy Rogers in THE GAY RANCHERO, a Republic picture.

plied Gene with showman's attire in hot pink and eye-popping green, bedecked in sequins that glittered in the lights of a night rodeo and in the noonday sun of a parade.

As King of the Cowboys starting in 1943, Roy Rogers wore the most flamboyant clothes of all, and his movies, made on bigger budgets than most Westerns, and in Trucolor starting with *Apache Rose* in 1947, featured dazzling production numbers built around duets by him and his wife, Dale Evans. "His pictures often looked more like a Romberg operetta than a story allegedly set in the West!" sniffed film historians George N. Fenin and William K. Everson. Roy was one of Nudie's best customers; that is where he bought many of his heavily embroidered and sequined dress shirts, festooned with images of horseshoes, his Double-R-Bar brand, and assorted flora and fauna of the West.

As sensational as Roy's costumes were, those worn by his wife and co-star, Dale Evans, were a match. Dale was declared "Queen of the West" by columnist Erskine Johnson in the late 1940s (the title stuck), and she popularized a now-classic racy cowgirl outfit of a rickracked shirt or tunic top worn with a short-short fringed skirt way above the knee, displaying abundant lengths of lovely gam between her tesselated hem and her ornamental cowboy boots. She and Roy rarely appeared in identical ensembles; instead they often complemented each other by both wearing light-colored, short-crowned hats, deep-yoked shirts with fringe along the sleeves and pockets that swung as sprightly as a hoochie-koochie dancer's, gay kerchiefs, and sensational boots. Dale's boots tended to be short with wide tops, as generally favored by most cowgirls in the 1940s; Roy's were tall with a deep, ornamental-collared scallop in the front ringed with stars, pointing to a spread-eagle inlay wrapping the entire front from top to vamp.

In a *Life* magazine cover story in July 1943 (the cover showed Roy astride Trigger,

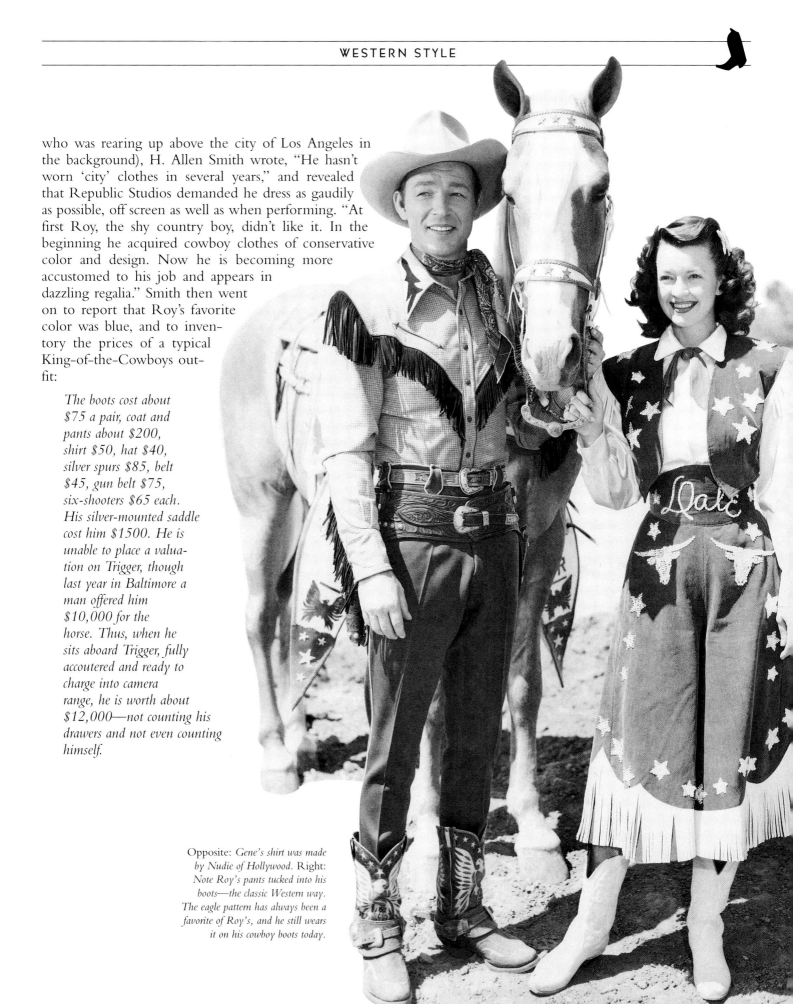

who was rearing up above the city of Los Angeles in the background), H. Allen Smith wrote, "He hasn't worn 'city' clothes in several years," and revealed that Republic Studios demanded he dress as gaudily as possible, off screen as well as when performing. "At first Roy, the shy country boy, didn't like it. In the beginning he acquired cowboy clothes of conservative color and design. Now he is becoming more accustomed to his job and appears in dazzling regalia." Smith then went on to report that Roy's favorite color was blue, and to inventory the prices of a typical King-of-the-Cowboys outfit:

*The boots cost about $75 a pair, coat and pants about $200, shirt $50, hat $40, silver spurs $85, belt $45, gun belt $75, six-shooters $65 each. His silver-mounted saddle cost him $1500. He is unable to place a valuation on Trigger, though last year in Baltimore a man offered him $10,000 for the horse. Thus, when he sits aboard Trigger, fully accoutered and ready to charge into camera range, he is worth about $12,000—not counting his drawers and not even counting himself.*

Opposite: *Gene's shirt was made by Nudie of Hollywood.* Right: *Note Roy's pants tucked into his boots—the classic Western way. The eagle pattern has always been a favorite of Roy's, and he still wears it on his cowboy boots today.*

# Cowboy HATS

You cannot be a cowboy without a cowboy hat. The plain fact is that cowboys didn't really exist before there were singular hats for them to wear; that the so-called "cowboys" who herded cattle wearing miscellaneous soldier's forage caps, Mexican sombreros, Boston bowlers, coonskins, or tweed deerstalkers before the Civil War were thought of by everybody else (and by themselves) as little more than day laborers, like any other workingmen, with none of the prestige and charisma that an audacious uniform tends to engender. But starting in 1865, when John B. Stetson began marketing what he called "The Boss of the Plains"—a huge felt umbrella of a bonnet with a high crown and broad brim—cowboys were well on their way to becoming folk heroes.

All folk heroes need a distinct symbol of their prowess: John Henry had a hammer; Paul Bunyan had an ax; cowboys have their hats. Plain or fancy, fresh off the sizing block or sodden with sweat and trail dust and tattered from years of hard use, a hat reflects a cowboy's state of mind. It is with him always; he wears it indoors at the dinner table and in the dance hall as well as in the sun; he uses it to cover his face when he sleeps in his bedroll at night. In folklore and in real life, it has myriad functions besides shade and head protection: to hold your winnings after a lucky game of poker, to ladle up water for you and your horse, to wave in jubilation or like a semaphore to signal across the prairie, to put on a stick

and hold out from behind a boulder as a decoy to draw an adversary's gunfire.

The most important function of a cowboy hat is to let everyone know what kind of person is underneath it. You can dress a man in a zoot suit or a pair of hot pants and create a fashion curiosity, but put a ten-gallon hat on his head and you have made him a cowboy. One of the worst insults in the West is to declare someone "all hat and no cowboy," the implication being that he doesn't have the guts to live up to the mettle promised by the mighty rig on his head.

The first cowboy hat was manufactured on a lark. John B. Stetson, a milliner from Philadelphia, was roughing it in Colorado with friends in the early 1860s. One night around the campfire he showed them how felt could be made by shaving the hair off beaver and rabbit hides, moistening the fine fur by chewing on it, then boiling it and letting it shrink. He shaped the resulting pad of felt into a high-crowned hat with a broad brim—waterproof and sturdy—which he wore as they went panning for gold in the mountains. According to legend, a passing horseman saw the hat and paid Stetson five dollars for it. Back in Philadelphia, Stetson was so inspired by the sight of the horseman wearing his giant hat that he made a dozen samples and sent them to clothing shops in the West. "The Boss of the Plains," as he called it, debuted just as the cattle business was getting started in Texas. Although some veteran vaqueros continued to wear their sombreros (with a conical crown, saucer brim, and fancy embroidery), Stetson hats soon became the cowboy standard. In an article for *Yippy Yi Yea* magazine, Raymond Schuessler wrote, "Like a peacock needed feathers, John Q. Cowboy needed this headgear."

As familiar a name as Colt, Winchester, and Levi's,

"Stetson" became a synonym for cowboy hat. The Boss of the Plains was followed by the even more capacious Carlsbad (which Hoss used to wear on "Bonanza"), then a whole variety of styles to suit cattlemen, marshals, sodbusters, and outlaws. Texas Rangers took to wearing Stetsons; George Armstrong Custer wore one at the Little Big Horn; Buffalo Bill Cody wore one, as did his Texas rough riders, Annie Oakley, and even, on occasion, Chief Sitting Bull. According to *The Pictorial History of the Wild West,* Wild Bill Hickok and Calamity Jane rode

Girl Crazy, *1943; choreography by Busby Berkeley.*

BIG HAT

into the town of Deadwood (where Wild Bill was shot) wearing "creamy white Stetsons." Will Rogers was a Stetson man, as were William S. Hart and Leo Carillo. Cowboy star Tom Mix liked Stetsons so much he took a trunk full of Tom Mix models (with a high crown and a rakish forward crease) when he went on personal-appearance tours in Europe, where he autographed them and gave them out to dignitaries who came to see his show.

Today cowboy hats are still made pretty much the same way John B. Stetson made the first one, although machines do all the chewing and moistening of the fur. A high-quality hat is made

Cowboy & Buckaroo Hat Creases by Bute

OPEN CROWN · PUNCHER · CENTERFIRE · PEAK · TWO DOT · HOPALONG · RUSSELL · OREANA · RIMROCK · TOM MIX · MONTANA · PACKER · TELESCOPE · CONTRACK · ARENA · HORSESHOE · ROUGHSTOCK · SLOPE · CUTTER · TYCOON · FOREMAN · CANADIAN · CATTLEMAN

BRIMS

STANDARD · RODEO · RANCH · SNAP · AUSSIE

*Bottom left: Roy Rogers developed a unique double-creased crown for his white hat.*

of fur felt, less expensive ones of wool felt. To the ordinary eye, most appear to be brown, black, beige, or gray, but such broad terms are seldom used to describe their color. Cowboy hat makers prefer more evocative designations, such as silver belly, Belgian belly, buckskin, fawn, crystal, pecan, Sudan brown, granite, mist, and smoke. The cost of the hat is determined mostly by how much fur is used, as well as the quality of the fur, and the craftsmanship used to shape it. Hats are graded on an "X" system. In today's market a 2X Beaver will cost a little under $100; a 10X Beaver about $250; a 30X $450. The system takes a leap from 30X to 100X, which might run $1,000. There is no international standard or government agency overseeing the X system, so one company's 5X Beaver hat might actually be better than another's 10X. The real test is the look and feel: better grades are soft, supple, and silky.

Most modern cowboys we have met are exquisite judges of hat quality, and they can spot a cheap one at the skyline. Gary Leffew, world champion bull rider, tells a story about the time some New York high-fashion models came out West to his ranch to shoot an advertisement. They were bedecked in thousand-dollar outfits and priceless Native American jewelry but, Leffew scoffed, "They were wearing thirty-dollar hats." When Leffew suggested to the art director that the cheap hats would ruin the picture—at least for any cowboy who was to look at it—the art director proudly told Leffew he had spent a hundred dollars on his own hat. "It looks it," Leffew said, which

# Hat Etiquette

*Hoot Gibson.*

**A** good cowboy hat will bring many years of pleasure, especially if you follow these simple rules of hat care and etiquette:

1. Never handle your hat by the crown. This breaks the fibers of the fur felt. Always pick up a hat by the brim. When handing another man his hat, hand it to him crown-down with the back facing you; this way, he can simply flip it up on his head without having to turn it around.

2. Never park a hat in a hot car or on a radiator. Heat will make it shrink.

3. Always store a hat upside-down so the roll of the brim won't flatten out. Never put a hat on a bed or bunk: that's bad luck. Cowboys customarily stored their hats on the bunkhouse floor, right beside their bed.

4. Don't try on another man's hat. This is a serious breach of etiquette, almost as bad as getting on his horse.

5. Identify your hat inside your brim. Most good hat shops give you a free insert that says, LIKE HELL IT'S YOURS. THIS HAT BELONGS TO _____.

the art director assumed was a compliment. It was not; to a champ like Leffew, a hundred-dollar hat is scarcely better than a thirty-dollar one. When Leffew told this story, he was wearing a $400 20X-Beaver: his everyday headgear.

Long ago, a hat's crease identified its owner's home. A high crown with three or four front-to-back dents in the side signified the Southwest (but later became known as the Montana poke); a flat top was originally a Northwestern style; a single deep crease—good for water drainage—signified an hombre from a rainy part of the country; a flat, square crown, which helped dissipate heat, was the mark of someone from the desert. Cowboys working the southernmost parts of Texas tended to favor hats as big as sombreros, complete with a *barbiquejo*, or chin strap, now known as a stampede string, to keep the hat from blowing off when riding hard and fast.

Regional differences in hat shapes have disappeared, but there are more than enough styles and creases around to make a hat your own. Many of the vintage cowboy fashions are making a comeback: Tom Mix and Hoppy hats, with tall (seven-and-a-half-inch) crowns and broad (four-inch) brims, are now more popular than they were fifty years ago. We heard these nostalgic ten-gallons scorned by one cowboy as reminding him of dunce caps, but for many others, they bring to mind the romance of old Western movies, when the good guys could be identified literally miles away by the height and whiteness of their lid.

Sometimes the style of a man's hat relates more to his occupation than his place of origin. Rodeo bull riders tend to favor high, wide hats, frequently black—symbols of their audacity; ropers like low crowns for the very practical reason that they don't want to knock their own hat off with their lasso. Cattlemen and ranchers seem to prefer the more conservative styles and buff colors, and in the summer, they switch to cooler, more ventilated straw styles. A whole new slew of hat fanciers has been inspired by what are known in the country music business as "hat acts"—performers such as Hank Williams, Jr. (who owns more than fifty different hats), Garth Brooks, George Strait (who sometimes throws his hat into the audience at the end of his show), Charlie Daniels, and Ricky Van Shelton. There are now hat catalogues that feature styles that duplicate what these performers wear and are named for them—just like sandwiches are named for stars in delis in New York and Los Angeles.

One of our favorite sources for Western headgear, as well as hat-care tips, hat restoration, and general Western haberdashery lore, is the Man's Hat Shop of Albuquerque, New Mexico. On old Route 66 in the center of town, the shop opened for business just after World War II; their catalogue, listing dozens of styles, is hat-fancier's heaven. We quote a few choice descriptions of the hats they offer:

> *Bullrider: When a man climbs astraddle a giant, snorting, quaking hunk of gristle and ire, he'd best be a man of substance; and that's the kind of man it takes to fill out this Resistol 5X Beaver "Bullrider" with its huge 5" brim and 7" crown.*
>
> *Gus: Sometimes a feller just feels too darn ornery to wear an ordinary hat. He needs a topper that makes it clear he's no ordinary cowboy. If you're feeling a tad ornery, let the nostalgic 4X Beaver "Gus" get the word out!*
>
> *Durango: One way to judge a man's character is by his handshake, another is by his hat. The 4X Beaver "Durango," with its solid-looking, subtle roll and broad crease, does more than a firm, honest handshake to mark you as a man to be respected.*
>
> *Dune: Not for the timid, the 4X Beaver Stetson "Dune" hints at a wild heart tamed just enough to stay out of jail. . . . Looks great on women, too.*
>
> *Pecos: Stunning as the country it's named for (almost), the 4X Beaver "Pecos" is a hat you can depend on to protect your fine reputation as well as your hirsute head.*

(For your own Man's Hat Shop Catalogue, call 505-247-9605, or write to them at 511 Central Avenue, Albuquerque, NM 87102.)

Cowboy Joe and Cowboy Jill were manufactured in the early 1950s when the "Roy Rogers Show" was on TV and were patterned after Roy and Dale so kids could enjoy the fantasy of playing with their favorite cowboy couple's fancy clothes. Joe and Jill even had a taste for horses resembling those of Roy and Dale. Joe's Palomino could be Trigger's double, and Jill's mount appears to be buckskin, like Buttermilk.

# Cowboy BOOTS

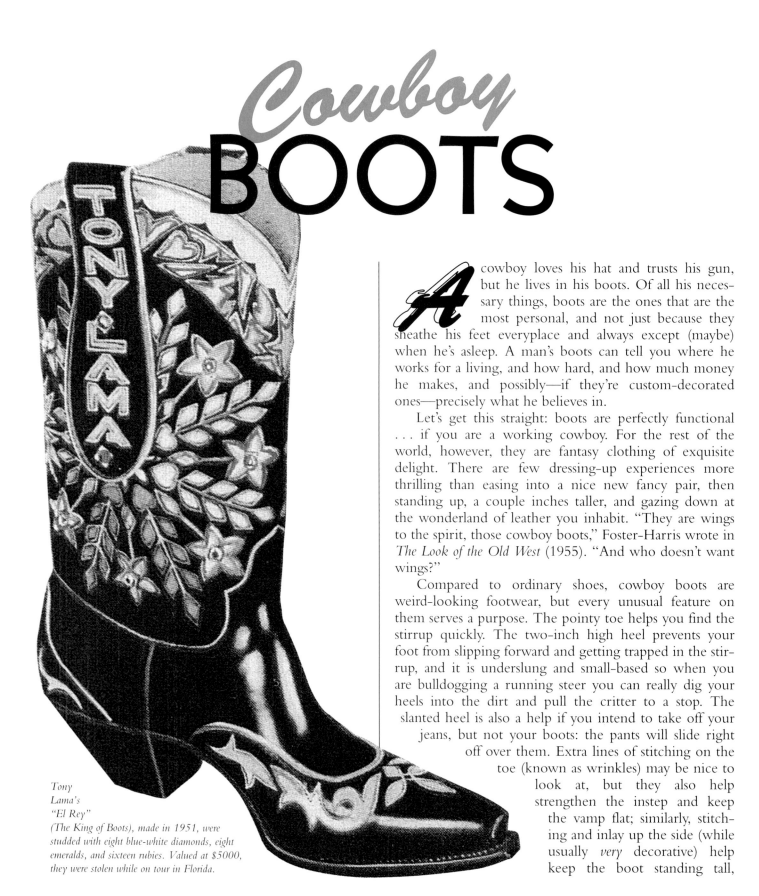

*Tony Lama's "El Rey" (The King of Boots), made in 1951, were studded with eight blue-white diamonds, eight emeralds, and sixteen rubies. Valued at $5000, they were stolen while on tour in Florida.*

A cowboy loves his hat and trusts his gun, but he lives in his boots. Of all his necessary things, boots are the ones that are the most personal, and not just because they sheathe his feet everyplace and always except (maybe) when he's asleep. A man's boots can tell you where he works for a living, and how hard, and how much money he makes, and possibly—if they're custom-decorated ones—precisely what he believes in.

Let's get this straight: boots are perfectly functional . . . if you are a working cowboy. For the rest of the world, however, they are fantasy clothing of exquisite delight. There are few dressing-up experiences more thrilling than easing into a nice new fancy pair, then standing up, a couple inches taller, and gazing down at the wonderland of leather you inhabit. "They are wings to the spirit, those cowboy boots," Foster-Harris wrote in *The Look of the Old West* (1955). "And who doesn't want wings?"

Compared to ordinary shoes, cowboy boots are weird-looking footwear, but every unusual feature on them serves a purpose. The pointy toe helps you find the stirrup quickly. The two-inch high heel prevents your foot from slipping forward and getting trapped in the stirrup, and it is underslung and small-based so when you are bulldogging a running steer you can really dig your heels into the dirt and pull the critter to a stop. The slanted heel is also a help if you intend to take off your jeans, but not your boots: the pants will slide right off over them. Extra lines of stitching on the toe (known as wrinkles) may be nice to look at, but they also help strengthen the instep and keep the vamp flat; similarly, stitching and inlay up the side (while usually *very* decorative) help keep the boot standing tall, even when it's old and worn. If you are a working cowboy you definitely want a tall boot: it protects you from the prick of mesquite thorns, jumping cacti, yucca leaves, and snake bites, as well as the muck in a corral.

The now-classic cowboy boot was developed just as Texans started taking cattle north, right after the Civil War. There is no single known inventor (as there is for the cowboy hat), but the boot, like the Stetson, and like the cowboy who made them his own, was an idea whose time had come. In his definitive book on the subject, *The Cowboy Boot Book,* Tyler Beard wrote that in the late 1860s working cowboys who happened also to be "saddle dandies" created the whole idea of cowboy fashion, including in their repertoire a new-style riding boot with high heels (as extreme as four inches) and pointy toes. Beard writes that such models as "The Drover," "The Stovepipe," and "The Cattlemen" all had tops at least fourteen inches high, some going up beyond the knee; nearly all were black, and until about 1900, when the toe wrinkle was developed, none had any fancy decoration. The first big-name boot makers were C. H. Hyer of Olathe, Kansas (outside of Kansas City,) H. J. Justin of Spanish Fort, Texas (on the Chisholm Trail), and Frederick Leopold of Odessa, Texas.

Vanity is a vice cowboys don't generally admit, but

when it comes to footwear, even stoical wranglers make an exception. Look below the knees of the most taciturn cowpoke you can find, and don't be surprised to find a knock-your-eye-out boot garlanded with trellised rosebuds, flying mallards, or the seal of the great state of Texas. In his book, *The Cowboy* (1922), Philip Ashton Rollins wrote that the cowboy was especially concerned about the size of his feet, disdaining capacious shoes as the foot coverings of people with big, wide paddle paws who walked rather than rode. He had nothing but "contempt for the heavily soled foot coverings of Easterners; [he preferred to] put his feet into decent boots, and not into entire cows." In addition, a cowboy liked his boot with thin soles, Rollins wrote, to give him a

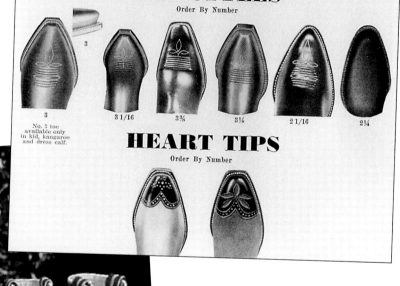

*A trio of collectible pairs for sale at Back at the Ranch in Santa Fe, New Mexico.*

"semiprehensile feel of the stirrup." In fact, cowboys were so obsessed with having little feet that there are apocryphal stories about some who shot off their little toes in order to squeeze into even narrower pairs of boots.

The fancy-boot era began in the 1920s, encouraged by Tom Mix's popularity and the increasing glamour of rodeo. What had once been the unique footgear of a working cowboy, Texas Ranger, or cattle baron became a key fashion accessory for anyone who wanted to advertise his or her allegiance to the West—movie star, down-home musician, or politician. By the 1930s, when hundreds of full-dress Western movies were being made each year, the boot business was thriving. Tyler Beard wrote:

*A myriad of stitched spider webs, decks of playing cards, flowers and vines, prickly pear cacti, longhorns, eagles in flight, a favorite horse or bull, bucking broncs, oil derricks, and even hand-tooled boots resembling saddles became commonplace. Boots in dozens of new leather*

Tony Lama "El Presidente" boots, made of kangaroo, kid, and calf for Harry S Truman.

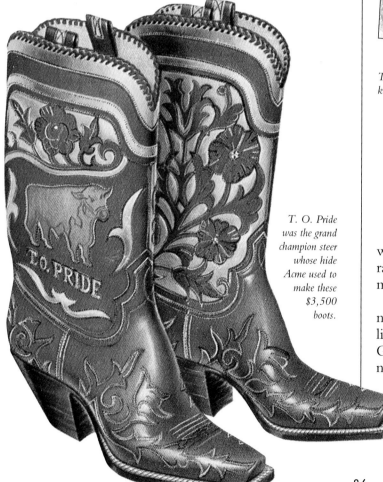

T. O. Pride was the grand champion steer whose hide Acme used to make these $3,500 boots.

*colors and exotic skins, with overlaid and inlaid designs using up to twenty rows of stitching, all pieced together artfully and finished to the boot maker's perfection, appeared on men's, women's and even children's feet all over the country.*

*Life* magazine enumerated the reasons people liked to wear cowboy boots in a 1940 issue that featured dude ranch fashions on its cover: "Comfort, necessity, sentiment, caste, and sheer deviltry."

Cowboy boots retain their Western charisma, but now the majority of people who wear them are more likely to tread across acres of wool carpeting than the Great Plains. After the movie *Urban Cowboy* (1980) detonated a major trend in Western fashion, cowboy boot sales peaked at seventeen million pairs in 1982. Sandra Kauffman, author of *The Cowboy Catalogue* (1980), quoted master boot maker Cosimo Lucchese: "We used to make them to fit a stirrup. Now we make them to fit the gas pedal of a Cadillac." According to *Texas Monthly,* nearly as many cowboy boots are sold in Los Angeles as in Dallas. When Rita Ariyoshi of the *Los Angeles Times* dropped in on an Oklahoma boot maker named Remigio "Pepe" Vega in the summer of 1992, Ms. Ariyoshi found Mr. Vega working on a custom order: 24-inch-tall turquoise-and-cream boots decorated with a replica of a design taken from the ceiling of the Sistine Chapel. They were being made at the cost of seven thousand dollars for a Beverly Hills real estate agent; Mr. Vega was frankly not impressed with the job. "He's seen flashier," Ms. Ariyoshi noted.

Celebrities from Reba McEntire to Axl Rose and

*In 1957 Jim Shoulders was world champion bareback bronc rider.*
*Far right:*
*Four years earlier, Donald G. Linton had Oldsmobile boots custom-made. They are shown in front of his son Ron Linton's vintage DeSoto at P. T. Crow Trading Co. in Albuquerque.*

from Ronald Reagan to Cher are known for their taste in cowboy boots. Elizabeth Taylor got a pair for her most recent wedding; they were white with gold scrollwork and they were spangled with 8.09 carats of white diamonds; their estimated cost was $40,000. Texan Buddy Holly's boots, which are bright green, inlaid with his initials and a bird in flight, sold for $9,075 at a Sotheby's auction in 1990. For many people who aren't stars, buying boots is a unique opportunity to indulge a taste for double-deluxe duds. At one of our favorite boot shops in Albuquerque, P. T. Crow Trading Company, owner Ron Linton has a pair his father, Donald G. Linton, had made for himself back in the 1950s. Mr. Linton, Sr., was regional sales manager for Oldsmobile in Texas, so he ordered boots that are a symphony of different Olds models' names and the marquee's rocket-ship logo, all in dramatic black and white.

If you want a pair of custom-made boots for yourself, get in line: first, to withdraw lots of money from the bank, then to get on the waiting list (sometimes years long) of a top boot maker. And if you are going to all that trouble, you probably want to go visit the boot maker in person (see pages 361–362), so you can have your feet precisely measured and you can look at a pile of cut skins to select exactly which part of which animal looks best where on the boot.

Popular as dazzling new boots are these days (yearly sales have surpassed those of the *Urban Cowboy* era), lots of people prefer old ones—for their classic style, cultural resonance, and fine workmanship, and also because they are already broken in. It is no longer necessary to do as cowboys used to do when they bought new boots—put them on, get them soaking wet, then let them dry and shrink to fit the feet inside, but even the best-made boots require a considerable break-in period before they become totally comfortable.

Many people buy old cowboy boots without bothering to try them on because they have no intention of wearing them. Like a well-seasoned saddle or engraved Colt .45, cowboy boots are functional folk art that evokes the West, and are increasingly used as home decor. It is a stunning sight to behold a well-cared-for pair of vintage snub-nose pee-wees inlaid with Gene Autry's favorite butterfly motif or tall stovepipes stitched with curlicues and swirls, or a whole shelf arrayed with a variety of classic cowboy boots. If it is a really stunning old pair, crafted by one of the legendary shops, such as Lucchese or Olsen-Stelzer, a serious boot aficionado would no more stomp around the dirt in them than you would use an ancient pueblo pot to hold your tuna salad.

# CHAPS

haps, pronounced SHAPS, do serve a purpose: to protect a rider's pants and legs from thorns and brambles, barbed wire, and the occasional nippy steed; they also help prevent flesh burns and bruises in a fall. But beyond their function, they can be wildly decorative, and they are ingeniously tailored to draw the eye to those parts of a cowboy's anatomy where the leather ends and the juicy bits are cameoed. Considering the fact that a cowboy's rear end is sculpted by endless hours of saddle aerobics, it is fair to say that a handsome pair of chaps is a perfect vision of form as well as function.

Chaps is an abbreviation from the Spanish *chaparrejos,* or *chaparreras* meaning leather britches. *Chaparrejos* is derived from *chaparro,* an evergreen oak that grows abundantly in South Texas alongside the thorny mesquite (also the source of the word chaparral). Before there were chaps, vaqueros used *armas* to protect themselves; they were leather aprons attached to the saddle that functioned like a lap robe. *Armas* provided no protection when a man dismounted, so they were reworked into *armitas,* sheets of buckskin attached around the waist that hung to just below the knees, secured there by rawhide thongs. *Armitas* evolved into *chaparrejos,* the full-leather britches that covered the leg.

Like cowboys' hats and saddles, chaps were often tailored to broadcast their wearer's home and occupation. Texans tended to favor "batwing" chaps, with big, curved, flaring leather fronts and back buckles. "Cheyenne leg" chaps (Cheyenne was long considered a fashion center in the West) had no leather in the back from the knee down; the bottom corner inside the leg was rounded off. Indians had their own style of chaps: leather leggings without a seat or front panel, the two halves held together by a buckskin lace known as a whang string. Cowboys in California, Nevada, and Oregon used to go for very short chaps known as chinks (from *chinquedera,* a Mexican word meaning blunt or short) that fell slightly below the knee like the original *armitas* and looked like a pair of fringed culottes. According to Lewis Smith, writing in *Cowboy Magazine* in 1992, "Just a few years ago any Texas cowboy who would dare wear a pair of chinks was leaving himself open to ridicule." But Mr. Smith reported that chinks had grown popular throughout the West, mostly for the ease of movement they allowed when working on the ground with a branding crew.

Chaps reflect the climate. Texans traditionally prefer batwings because they allow air to circulate. Cowboys in the Northern Plains tend to favor "shotgun chaps," going full circle around the legs and tight at the ankles to keep the cold

*Rodeo cowboys in Wyoming.*

89

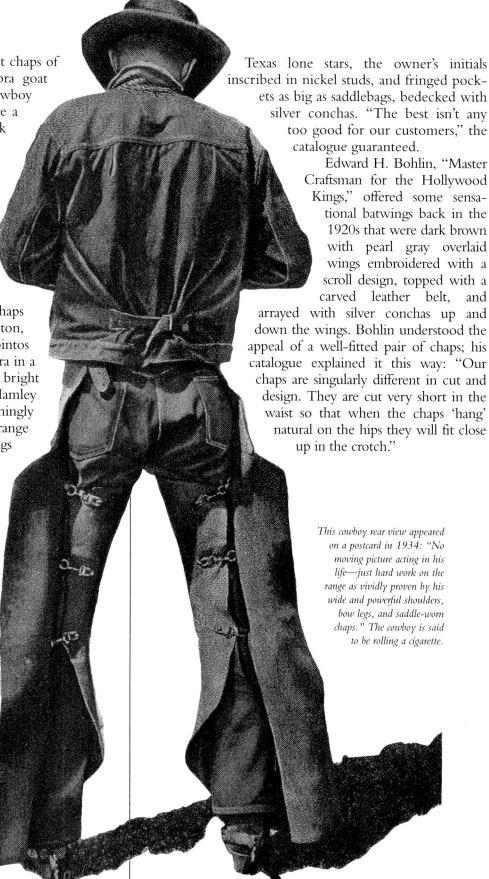

wind out. "Woollies" are the warmest chaps of all, made of luxurious curling angora goat fur, dog hair, or bear hide. For a cowboy riding through a blizzard, woollies are a lifesaver; they also used to be the mark of dudes and riders in Wild West shows who liked them because of their extreme contours—radiating out from the legs in an explosion of fluff that makes the wearer appear to be rising up out of a fur mountain.

Woollies used to come in startling colors. In his book *Cowboy Culture* (1992), collector Michael Friedman shows some astonishing chaps from the Hamley Company of Pendleton, Oregon, made about 1910: they are pintos (multicolored fur) made of fluffy angora in a Halloween motif: black patches on a bright orange background. Another set of Hamley woollies, made in 1912, are of astonishingly long white fur broken up by big orange tassels, and also feature leather batwings inscribed with nickel spot outlines of suits of playing cards, star-and-moon decorations at the hip, and a carved leather belt. "These chaps possess almost every desirable motif element," Friedman observed.

Even utility chaps are decorated to some small degree with fancy stitching, conchas, fringe, beadwork, or hand-tooling. But the most deluxe chaps, made many years ago for rodeo cowboys and cowboy movie stars, are some of the most ornamental articles of clothing known to humankind. The 1923 Visalia Stock Saddle Company catalogue featured a $49.50 pair advertised as "the showiest chaps made": enormous flapping pearlescent leather batwings garlanded with contrasting appliqués of longhorn steer heads and

Texas lone stars, the owner's initials inscribed in nickel studs, and fringed pockets as big as saddlebags, bedecked with silver conchas. "The best isn't any too good for our customers," the catalogue guaranteed.

Edward H. Bohlin, "Master Craftsman for the Hollywood Kings," offered some sensational batwings back in the 1920s that were dark brown with pearl gray overlaid wings embroidered with a scroll design, topped with a carved leather belt, and arrayed with silver conchas up and down the wings. Bohlin understood the appeal of a well-fitted pair of chaps; his catalogue explained it this way: "Our chaps are singularly different in cut and design. They are cut very short in the waist so that when the chaps 'hang' natural on the hips they will fit close up in the crotch."

*This cowboy rear view appeared on a postcard in 1934: "No moving picture acting in his life—just hard work on the range as vividly proven by his wide and powerful shoulders, bow legs, and saddle-worn chaps." The cowboy is said to be rolling a cigarette.*

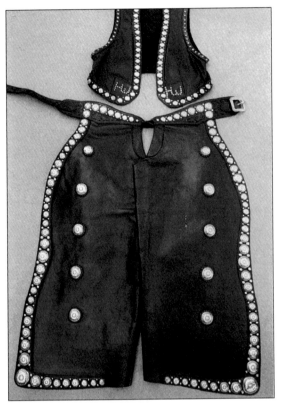

*Chaps, vests, parade gloves, spurs, and collar tips by Edward H. Bohlin, from the collection of George Pitman.*

# BUCKSKIN

Indians were the first Americans to wear buckskin, the yellow-gray leather named because it is traditionally made from the skin of a deer. It was adopted by trappers, pioneers, and scouts for strictly practical reasons—mostly because it was so much stronger than cotton or wool, which could easily get tattered into rags after only a few days on a rough trail. The country's earliest Western heroes, Daniel Boone and Davy Crockett, wore buckskin; so did Buffalo Bill Cody when he was scouting for the 5th U.S. Cavalry in the late 1860s. When Cody began reenacting his exploits on stage and in his Wild West show in the 1880s, he frequently wore a glorious embroidered buckskin jacket, as well as buckskin pants and soft buckskin boots to match.

Since Buffalo Bill, buckskin has remained a popular material for working cowboy garb and for show-business cowboys, although it has gone in and out of fashion among the general public. In the late 1960s buckskin was adopted by many hippies, who relished its Native American connotations, as well as the fact that it required so little care and cleaning.

Strangely, the extra-long fringe seen on buckskin garments worn by such late twentieth-century fashion plates as Cher, George Clinton of the Parliament Funkadelics, and the Judds, actually does harken back to original Indian garments worn many years ago. The native peoples developed clothing with long fringe with function in

Opposite: *Alan Ladd as Shane in wax.* Below: *Guy Madison as Wild Bill Hickok.*

Opposite: *Rodeo cowgirl Vera McGinnis.* Above and right: *Ann Blyth and Fernando Lamas in* Rose Marie.

mind: you could use it to tie provisions to your jacket when you were going on a trip, it served to help garments shed water in the rain, and it could be wielded the way a horse wields its tail, to shoo flies away.

In the movies, however, less flamboyant fringe was preferred for cowboy heroes. John Wayne wore a tight-fitting jacket with modest fringe at the bottom for his first starring role in *The Big Trail* (1930), Gary Cooper wore a three-inch fringed buckskin jacket as Wild Bill Hickok in *The Plainsman* (1936), and serial star Johnny Mack Brown

favored only a single little frieze of fringe down the sleeves of his jacket. Even Roy Rogers and Dale Evans, who were known for yards of fringe on some of their outfits, always liked it a demure length—too short for shooing flies away or for attaching strips of beef jerky to take on the road. On the other hand, Marlon Brando in *One-Eyed Jacks* (1960) and in *The Missouri Breaks* (1976) favors long, wavy, beaded fringe on his clothes. In Hollywood, extended strands of buckskin, like woolly chaps or a too-high hat, brand a cowboy as a popinjay.

# Indian-Inspired Style and FIESTA FASHIONS

The cultural mix that gives the Southwest such vivid character includes a sense of style that owes much to Indians, Spaniards, and Mexicans. In turn, Southwestern style has become one of America's most fashionable looks, sported by women of all races and regions of the country.

As a trading center and magnet for artistic types, the Santa Fe area in particular has always had more than its share of fashionable people. But there is one time of the year in Santa Fe when all stops are pulled and locals dress to kill: fiesta in September. Modern celebration of the fiesta began in 1919, shortly after which a woman named Allie McKenzie noticed that visitors in town for the occasion didn't have the right clothes to wear. Many local citizens who had been to Mexico had brought back "fiesta dresses" and wore them for the occasion—brightly colored cotton, trimmed with rickrack. Miss McKenzie designed her own fiesta dress made of red bandanna material and put it in the window of the Plaza shop where she worked, Gans Crafts. The price was 12 dollars, and before fiesta time she sold as many as she could make.

The gay tiered frocks were soon being made by at least a dozen local women; and each year at fiesta time they staged a fashion show that began to attract scouts from important national department stores. By the mid-1930s, Best & Co. of New York was advertising the New Mexican bandanna dress as "cool, washable . . . the perfect costume for camping, ranching, gardening, or roughing it." In Texas after World War II, similar styles became known as Patio dresses; the fancier ones had flounce tops, for wearing up or off one or both shoulders; the finest of them sported as much as 100 yards of rickrack. In 1950 model and writer Elita Wilson moved from New York to Santa Fe ("I stopped for a night and stayed a lifetime") and began making her own high-fashion version of this party outfit: red flamenco-style fiesta dresses with scalloped black rickrack and ball fringe. She decribed her gloss on the idea as "good taste, glamour, and sophistication."

At the same time fiesta fashions were gaining popularity, Indian styles were also becoming part of the generally known Southwestern look. Nowadays, it is not at all unusual to see women—tourists as well as natives—strolling the streets of Santa Fe dressed in long pleated calico "broomstick" skirts, jewel-toned velvet blouses, and soft buckskin moccasins. Around their waists are silver concha belts, around their wrists are turquoise bracelets. Squash-blossom necklaces or silver pueblo-style crosses hang from their necks. This is a style that is timeless, borrowed from the Navajo Indian women who had been wearing such costumes for more than a century. The cross motif on the jewelry reflected the influence of the early Spanish settlers in the region; the lush velvet blouses and full skirts are thought to have been inspired

by what the wives of the Spanish officers wore around 1860.

Navajo women didn't have delicate fabrics like the military officers' wives; nor did they have irons to keep their clothes smooth. So they used calicos bought at local trading posts and they invented a novel way of pleating a skirt: to get it to look like it had a hundred thin, knifelike pleats, a skirt was soaked, then pulled by hand into pleats and secured by string or pieces of cloth to a wooden pole or broomstick until it dried. When it was finally unbound, the material was closely ribbed and hung elegantly in a manner similar to the multipleated fabrics used by the great designer Fortuny, or by today's Mary McFadden.

Edith Nash was the designer responsible for popularizing this fashion and for giving it the name "broomstick skirt." Mrs. Nash visited Santa Fe shortly after World War I and was struck by the similarity of the indigenous

Left: *Christina Peralta-Ramos.* Below: *Her grandmother, Millicent Rogers, as photographed for* Harper's Bazaar *in 1946.*

*Santa Fe Fiesta fashions.* Bottom left: *Lindee Shaw, wearing a fiesta dress she designed, shows one made in the 1950s by Elita Wilson.*

American Indian clothes to the peasant styles and intricate embroidery she had seen and admired in Europe. She was amazed that these native costumes were unrepresented in the world of New York fashion, so she used them as the inspiration for a collection that included the broomstick skirt, a bandanna-material blouse, and a coat made of faded blue denim and sheepskin. Mrs. Nash's pioneering achievements notwithstanding, some local fashion historians credit Alice Corbin Henderson with being the originator of Santa Fe style when she made a velvet Navajo-style shirt for poet Witter Bynner some time in the 1920s. (Mrs. Henderson's daughter, Alice Henderson Evans, was later a major popularizer of bandanna dresses.)

Designer Agnes James moved to Santa Fe from Dallas in 1937, where she worked with Edith Nash and soon opened her own store, called the Town and Country shop, specializing in lighthearted interpretations of native attire. Mrs. James became the prime interpreter of Santa Fe fashion and continued to embellish the style into the 1950s. One of her signature outfits was a "chile skirt," which featured chile peppers cut from red bandanna fabric and stitched so they appeared to spill out of the pockets of the faded turquoise denim garment. It was worn with a "butterfly blouse" of red bandanna, cut so the short sleeves stood out like wings, and another red bandanna knotted at the corners to form a carry-all purse. One of Mrs. James's other popular styles was called a "saddle pocket skirt." It had a large pocket at the hip made from red gingham; the pocket matched a deep-yoked bandanna cowboy shirt. Located one block from Santa Fe's Plaza, the Town and Country shop also featured clothing with a cowboy look, as well as the flouncy, joyful style of Mexican fiesta wear; the shop became known to fashion-conscious women around the nation as a beacon of Southwestern style. Another landmark, dating back to 1955 and still going strong, is Martha of Taos, a store well respected by both native Taosenos and discriminating tourists for its traditional skirts and blouses. The velvet ensembles at Martha's shop are hand-decorated with old bits of silver, coins, and butterfly conchas all worked lovingly into the design. Martha's dresses are acquisitions for a lifetime. She recently told us that many people who buy them send them back to the shop years later for refurbishing and repleating.

Two of the most important New Mexican designers of the years just after World War II were Kathleen Lienau and Carolina McKee of Albuquerque. Mrs. McKee retailed her work under the trade name Carlotta and specialized in fiesta and playclothes, party wear, and smart casuals, which were described as "suitable for barbecue suppers, patio parties, costume balls, square dancing ranch parties and for wearing after skating and skiing." Kathleen Lienau's work featured a Navajo-type skirt that was not pleated in broomstick fashion but instead had a wide belt and a deep ruffle around the bottom. It was worn with a traditional long-sleeved velvet shirt with a high collar and silver concha buttons. Lienau worked in

THE ORIGINAL
Santa Fe Fiesta Fashions

*Santo Domingo Trading Post.*

earthy muslins and devised her own dyeing process that guaranteed that her clothing would have the same natural hues as true Indian attire. The colors she favored were turquoise blue, adobe tan, forest green, and Aspen gold.

During the 1940s Indian-inspired style leaped onto the pages of fashion magazines and designers' runways. The person who did the most to take it from New Mexico to the rest of the world was Millicent Rogers. Miss Rogers was a woman of immense wealth—ganddaughter of Henry Huttleston Rogers who, along with John D. Rockefeller, had founded Standard Oil, Anaconda Copper, and U.S. Steel. Her friends were the cream of Hollywood society, including Janet Gaynor and Jennifer Jones, and among the men in her life were Clark Gable, Count Serge Obolensky, and Ian Fleming. She was beautiful, described by reporter Tricia Hurst as "tall, with a perfectly proportioned figure . . . and a strikingly exotic alabaster face with wide-set eyes." She modeled for *Harper's Bazaar,* and she was immortalized by Diana Vreeland in a show at the Metropolitan Museum of Art as one of ten American Women of Style.

Millicent Rogers had originally fallen in love with the West in 1947 while on a sight-seeing trip to New Mexico with Janet Gaynor. She was so taken by the land and the Indian culture she glimpsed that she decided to make Taos her home. She regularly took day trips into the outlying pueblos and Indian encampments; these travels were the beginning of a lifelong passion for collecting Native American rugs, jewelry, blankets, and pottery. Like many of the artistic and literary residents of Taos who had moved there from afar (such as Georgia O'Keeffe and the grande dame of the New York City literary salon, Mabel Dodge Luhan), Millicent Rogers was mesmerized by the native culture, and showed her affinity for it by dressing in native garb. She was known for padding in bare feet around the

adobe house she had built, clad in sweeping Indian skirts and velvet blouses, wearing necklaces of turquoise and coral, with silver bracelets on her wrists. Eventually Miss Rogers began to manufacture her own line of Indian-inspired jewelry, and was photographed for *Harper's Bazaar* wearing it, along with armsful of sensational authentic Navajo jewelry from her personal collection.

Millicent Rogers, who had suffered from serious health problems all her life, died in 1953 at the age of fifty. That same year her family established the Millicent Rogers Museum in Taos, dedicated to the appreciation of Native American, Hispanic, and Anglo cultures of the Southwest. Recently the museum sponsored an introduction of the Millicent Rogers jewelry collection—high-quality replicas of the traditional turquoise and silver Indian pieces collected by Miss Rogers during her years in the Southwest.

America's passion for Southwestern style has been spread in large part because so many travelers vacation there, and so many tastemakers have second homes there. In 1956 *Life* magazine singled out the well-heeled town of Scottsdale, Arizona, for a profile titled "Sands of Desert Turn Gold." Once a pioneer boom town, Scottsdale had become home to an Elizabeth Arden "beauty ranch" and a string of luxury hotels. *Life* marveled at dress designers who had set up shops where they charged as much as twelve hundred dollars per outfit, having "provided the country with new fashions based on native costumes and materials." The pictorial spread showed models wearing a bolero jacket trimmed with sequins in a "Navajo design," a "modernized squaw dress cocktail outfit," and a "gaudy handbag made from bands of leather with a metallic finish, available from Lloyd Kiva."

Even New Yorkers fell under the exotic sway of dressing native. In the mid-1950s Milton Grossman, a salesman for the New York-based leather firm Hermann Lowenstein, moved back East after spending a few years in Tucson, Arizona, which inspired him to design a contemporary two-tone "squaw boot." Grossman's upmarket version of the favored footwear of Native Americans was so elegant of line and leather that it was sold at such fine stores as I. Miller and Saks Fifth Avenue, as well as several posh salons on the Upper East Side.

Indian-inspired fashion has made a stunning reappearance since the 1980s, when Santa Fe began yet another steady rise in popularity among tourists, climaxing with Condé Nast's *Traveler* magazine naming it the number-one destination in the world among sophisticated vacationers. Stores all over Santa Fe and other fashionable towns of the West keep seamstresses busy making broomstick skirts and velvet outfits, and after a brief stint of rich-hippie popularity in the 1960s, turquoise jewelry once again has become the hottest-selling commodity in town.

Forty years after its first declaration of Indian-inspired clothes being all the rage, *New Mexico* magazine did a new cover story on its popularity. Instead of photographing visiting socialites in native attire, this time the magazine featured actress and model Jill Momaday, the elegant daughter of Pulitzer-prize winning writer N. Scott Momaday, and a resident of Santa Fe, modeling a traditional Navajo broomstick skirt. Other local beauties modeled fashions that included a chile pepper dress with layers of rickracked ruffles and black material on which were printed tiny red and green peppers. This latest chile

dress was made by the reigning queen of Santa Fe fiesta wear and Indian-inspired fashions, Lindee Shaw, who operates two Fiesta Fashions stores in town, and sells to Saks Fifth Avenue, Henri Bendel, Lord and Taylor, and other expensive department stores around the country. Miss Shaw readily acknowledges that her fashion inspiration comes from the now-classic styles originally popularized in the 1920s.

Many of the venerable stores are still in business, selling the same style clothes they have sold for decades. Martha of Taos continues to craft the same elegant velvet and silver-trim Indian-inspired outfits, and Jeanette's Originals can still be found in Albuquerque, run since 1969 by Sara Gutiérrez. Ms. Gutiérrez recently told a reporter that she regularly ships her Indian-inspired fashions to Paris, and that Nancy Reagan wore one of her fiesta dresses at a White House reception.

*There are two classic poses when wearing a fiesta dress: twirling or seated on the ground, both of which show off its fine pleating, elaborate decoration, and majestic size.*

# *Indian* JEWELRY

*Hasteen Yazie Begay, Navajo silversmith.*

For some sightseers in the West the most exciting view of all is inside a trading post, through the glass of the case where the turquoise and silver jewelry is displayed.

Not all that you see is magnificent. Some "Indian jewelry" is made of blue plastic and imitation silver, cranked out by machines in factories halfway around the globe. The real McCoy—the kind of stuff that gets the juices of connoisseurs and collectors flowing—is exquisitely hand-crafted; some of it is a century old, and some contains stones more brilliant than the sky.

The tribes that produce the best of it are the Navajo, the Zuni, the Hopi, and the Santo Domingans; each group has its own distinct style.

Navajo pieces look blunt and heavy. For many people, they are the benchmark of what all Indian jewelry is supposed to look like; indeed, some early Zuni and Hopi jewelry—before those tribes developed their own unique styles—resembles Navajo work. A Navajo craftsperson works with cast silver that is highlighted with large, bright pieces of turquoise set in a bezel cuff. Traditional Navajo silver work was sand-cast, meaning the design was molded by pouring molten silver into a block of sandstone or volcanic clay, known as tufa. Today's artists often use a more rugged concrete-and-oil mold to create their designs.

Probably the best-known type of Navajo jewelry is the squash blossom necklace, a majestic, ornamental object that was originally developed in the 1880s, featuring a string of stylized silver replicas of pomegranate blossoms and a crescent-shaped pendant, called a naja, hanging from the center. Najas were originally designed as an ornament for horses' foreheads, attached to the fancy silver bridles used by Spanish horsemen. The other Navajo classic is the concha belt, originated around 1870 and made of simple round or oval disks strung on leather. Toward the turn of the century, conchas became more elaborate: scalloped edges, then turquoise stones were added.

Zuni craftsmen are famous for detailed inlays. Turquoise, jet, coral, and a variety of other stones are painstakingly set in silver, creating designs such as the Rainbow Man, knife wing or a geometric pattern. Zunis are also known for using small stones (mostly turquoise or coral) to make cluster patterns on rings, belts, bracelets, or brooches. Another well-known Zuni craft is the "fetish necklace": tiny hand-carved bears, birds, coyotes, and foxes made of turquoise and other stones, strung on multistrand necklaces, creating a magical menagerie.

Hopi jewelry often contains no gemstones. Instead, it uses silver overlay for its effect. The top layer of silver is cut away to form one of the traditional Hopi patterns, such as Pima Siuhu Ki (Man in the Maze), which shows a tiny human figure atop a labyrinth. After the top layer of this "silver sandwich" has been excised to form the design, the underlying piece of silver is etched and oxidized a deep black, creating a dramatic shadowbox

effect. This jewelry came about as a result of a project launched in 1938 by two members of the Museum of Northern Arizona, Dr. Harold Colton and his wife, Mary Russell Colton, who encouraged members of the Hopi tribe to create their own unique style of jewelry that would set them apart from the rest. In 1949, the Hopi Silvercraft Guild was formed, and with the help of the GI Bill, many tribal members who were veterans were trained in commercial jewelry-making skills and silversmithing. Two of the most admired Native American craftsmen of modern times, Charles Loloma and Preston Monongye, are both Hopi.

*A contemporary concho belt by D. Reeves reflects the same fine craftsmanship as the old Zuni manta pins in the foreground.*

I-56 Navajo Girl Proud of Her Jewelry

3B-H1371

Some of the most famous jewelry makers are the people of the Santo Domingo Pueblo, who began pulling away from the Navajo style to define their own early in the century. A classic Santo Domingo piece would be a multiple-strand necklace of hand-drilled turquoise, silver, a shell with a jocla hanging in the front. (A jocla is a double loop of graduated-size turquoise beads—a fashion that began as a handy way to park a pair of beaded earrings when they weren't being worn in the ears.) The delicate beads are known as *heishi;* the best and most fragile ones are miniature masterpieces. Among Santo Domingans, the finer the beads the more desirable the necklace; some experienced artisans make them so fine that it is hard to imagine how they ever got drilled.

In recent times there has been a major revival in pueblo necklaces that feature silver crosses and a "heart of the dragonfly" pendant at the base. Now among the most

sought-after collectibles, some of these pieces date back to 1873 and are testaments to a multicultural heritage. The crosses are derived in part from the Spanish, who explored and settled the region (although long before them, Indians artists had used the cross motif). The large pendant that hangs from the apex of the necklace and looks like a double-barred cross is in fact not a crucifix, but the image of a dragonfly with its double set of wings. The lineage of the dragonfly goes back to prehistory and an ancient tribal legend about a poor little boy who wishes to amuse his sister with a new toy. He fashions a dragonfly of grass and straw and, to his amazement, it flies away. It returns with the Corn Maiden, who bestows a lush harvest and plenty of rain. In return for the favor, the boy paints the dragonfly's image everywhere, reminding mankind of the kindness granted upon them.

Exactly why and how Native Americans started making jewelry is itself a curious story. Indians had worked with bone and shell for ten thousand years, and turquoise has long been considered a sacred "sky" stone—a constant reminder of the forces of nature. Navajo folklore says it will summon rain; Zunis see it as the sacred color of heaven; Apaches traditionally attach a bit of turquoise to a bow or gun stock in the belief that it will help them shoot straight. But it was only in the last quarter of the nineteenth century that tribesmen began to make jewelry out of metal and turquoise together. It began in 1868 when defeated Navajos were released to a reservation in northeastern Arizona. There they adapted farrier skills learned from Mexican blacksmiths to jewelry-making, which became a vital part of their economy because it gave them something to trade.

The earliest jewelry was made of copper, iron, and brass, and on occasion from silver—when buttons or coins could be found and melted down. Jewelry came to represent wealth and prestige to a people stripped by the Indian wars of everything except their dignity. Unlike a hogan or a flock of sheep, it was portable, and a man who wore rows of it on his neck and wrists was somebody to reckon with. For some thirty years the craft of silversmithing increased in popularity among the tribes of the Southwest. About 1880 a Navajo smith named Atsidi Sani first combined turquoise with silver, then taught others of his tribe, who began creating some of the designs now considered classics.

Indian traders played a crucial role in the manufacture of jewelry. They supplied materials and a market for what was created, and in many instances they influenced—or dictated—the design of the work. Trader C. G. Wallace, who has been given credit for essentially originating the jewelry-making industry at Zuni Pueblo starting in 1918, was quoted in *Arizona Highways* some years back as saying, "I never ceased to impress on them that they should stay with tradition." Lorenzo Hubbell, whose trading post in Ganado, Arizona, is now a national historical site, began importing Persian turquoise in 1895 and supplying it to Navajo silversmiths who made jewelry for him to trade.

By 1900 several turquoise mines were open in Arizona, Colorado, and New Mexico. Jewelry-making had become widespread among Native Americans, although the work of individual tribes was not yet distinct. This period is known as the first phase of Indian jewelry, and it came to a close just after the turn of the century.

The second phase was the era of Fred Harvey's influence. Partnered with the Santa Fe Railway, Harvey helped make Indian jewelry a major tourist attraction in the Southwest. Beginning in 1902, the Harvey company set up curio shops to sell native arts and crafts to train passengers. Hopi House, across from El Tovar, the Harvey Hotel at the rim of the Grand Canyon, was designed by Mary Colter (who later designed the Santa Fe railroad's estimable Mimbreño china) to look like an old native dwelling; tourists could watch craftspeople at

*The alluring jewelry case at J. Seitz (see page 349).*

work, then buy some jewelry for themselves. Harvey-commissioned jewelry was soon sold at rest stops all along the Santa Fe rail line, and to train passengers who availed themselves of a Harvey "Indian Detour" trip by motor coach to various pueblos. Suddenly there was a whole new market for Indian jewelry among non-Indians. Compared to the substantial pieces crafted by Navajos and Zunis for their own use in the late 1800s, Harvey House jewelry is lightweight, and although some of it

was modeled on authentic pawn silver, many pieces were simply stamped with motifs chosen for their stereotypical Indian look (arrows, snakes, thunderbirds). Nevertheless, all original Harvey House jewelry is prized by collectors.

By the 1930s, after Nevada mines had been opened up and turquoise became even more abundant, most Indian jewelry was being commissioned by traders and made for tourists—a situation that persists today. The popularity of jewelry among those who aren't Native Americans rises and falls periodically, as do its values. Indian jewelry had a resurgence in the late 1960s and early 1970s when hippies fell in love with all things that were Native American, from tribal living to beadwork to peyote dreams. It was so stylish to look like Cher, Peter Fonda, or other stars who draped themselves in top-of-the-line Indian adornments that some firms simply ground up cheap turquoise, mixed it with epoxy and a plastic base, and made reconstituted stones to sell. Furthermore, some pieces were crafted not by Indians, but by long-haired Anglos who tried their hand at making Indian-style creations. These lesser pieces of jewelry, made by hippies, are jokingly referred to as coming from the "Hippewa tribe."

In the last several years, a significant amount of truly fine contemporary Indian jewelry has been produced. Some of the renowned artists include Joe Caté, Percy Reano, and Jimmy Calabaza of the Santo Domingo tribe, and Charlie Bird, a Laguna/Santo Domingo Indian who makes masterful inlaid pieces, but there are also dozens of other jewelry makers of wide repute whose work has defined a new golden age for aficionados. If you shop at a reputable dealer and are willing to spend some money, you can buy a piece that is not only a good investment, but a pleasure to wear and to look at.

# Along the Turquoise Trail

There are no strict rules about where to find superior Indian jewelry, except to say that getting a great piece cheap is about as easy as stumbling upon an authentic Tiffany lamp at a yard sale. There is a lot of hype about "pawn" jewelry, a term that once signified an old, authentic piece surrendered to a pawnshop by an Indian customer. If the customer didn't reclaim it, it went up for sale . . . and was considered a bonanza by collectors. Nowadays, however, "pawn," "old pawn," and "dead pawn" hardly mean a thing. After all, a new, inferior piece can be (and often is) pawned, too, and it has been at least twenty years since serious collectors raided the pawnshops for treasures.

The most important thing a neophyte browser needs to learn is how to judge the quality of a turquoise stone. There are many grades, from many different mines, and more than a dozen ways to treat them so they look bluer and better than they really are. Some total counterfeits are labeled *turquoise,* referring to their color but not to the stone, which might actually be plastic. One sure way to tell the difference is to heat a sewing needle with a match and press it to the stone: plastic will melt; turquoise won't. (Don't expect many dealers to let you try this!) Beyond measurable quality, some pieces of turquoise have ineffable appeal that, like a diamond's fire or a pearl's luster, give them an edge. In 1915 the first turquoise historian, Joseph Pogue, coined a term: "A good stone must possess an undefinable property called the 'Zat,'" he wrote. "A fine-colored turquoise without the 'Zat' is not worth much."

Above left: *Gallup, New Mexico, famous for pawn-shops with great treasure troves of fine jewelry.*
Above right: *A booth at Trader Jack's Flea Market, a bargain hunter's mecca in Tesuque.*

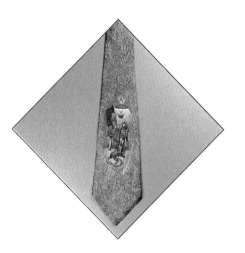

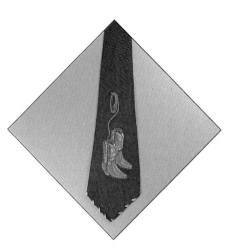

# WESTERN TIES

*from the collection*

*of Ronald Spark*

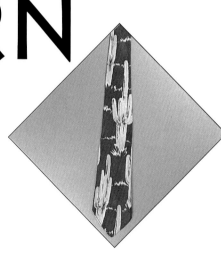

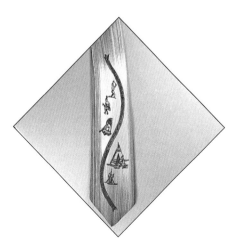

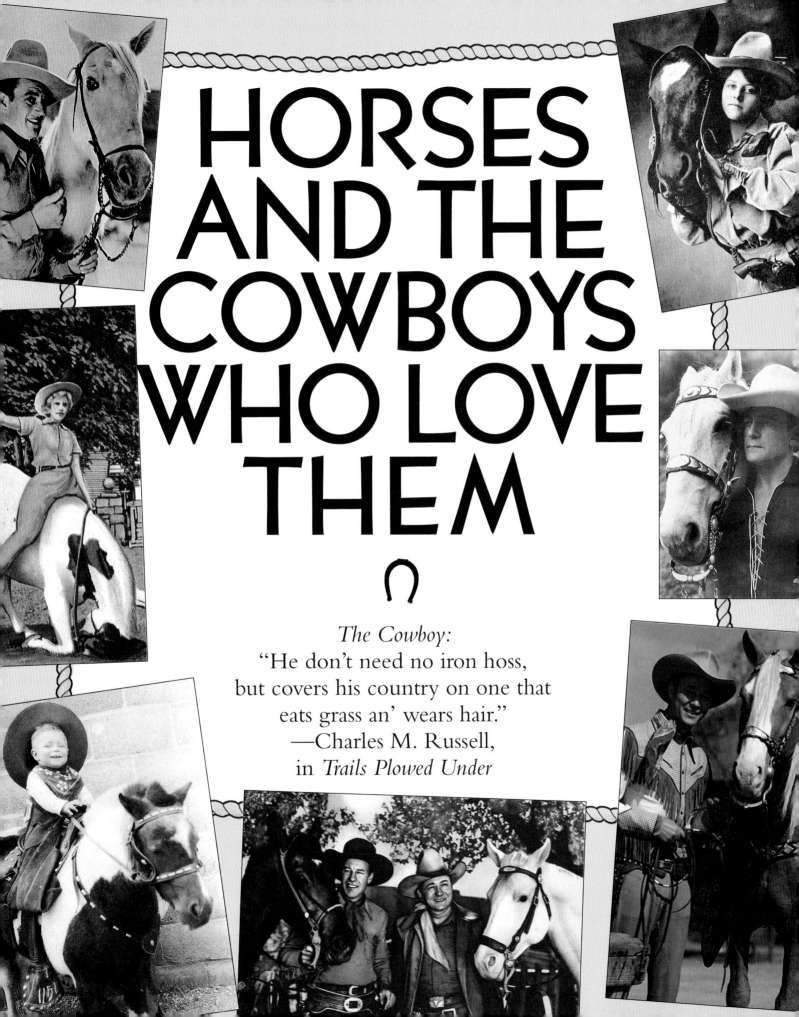

# HORSES AND THE COWBOYS WHO LOVE THEM

☊

*The Cowboy:*
"He don't need no iron hoss,
but covers his country on one that
eats grass an' wears hair."
—Charles M. Russell,
in *Trails Plowed Under*

# *Horses and the* COWBOYS WHO LOVE THEM

owhands don't talk much; they tend not to gush emotions. But there is one subject almost guaranteed to open up their heart: a good saddle horse. Nothing makes a person of the West feel so sentimental as memories of a four-legged critter with a name like Buck, Midnight, Freckles, or Sweet Face, who was an only companion for endless hours on the prairie. A cowboy depends on his horse to make a living, and if he travels long distances to a far-flung line camp or between distant outposts on the frontier, he needs his horse to survive. If a lonesome rider has a secret to tell or feelings to bear while riding through the chaparral, that set of pointy ears that frames his or her view all day long is always ready to listen.

"Thaw out some old-timer of the Cattle Country," Philip Ashton Rollins wrote in *The Cowboy* in 1922,

*and ask him to tell you of . . . horses that he knew. His face will overspread with a reminiscent, loving smile; he*

Opposite: *Iris Meredith listens as cowboy movie star Charles Starrett whispers sweet nothings into the ear of his beloved horse Raider.*

*will say: "But, of all the horses I ever ran across, I knew one once that was all horse. Make no mistake about that. He was a little 'California sorrel' and his name was Mike," and then you will hear a story such as, though truthful, no writer dares to put in print, lest the public brand him as a liar. You will be told of a saucy little devil which suppressed its impudence, and grittily struggled on through snow or desert, to kill itself from effort, but to land its wounded rider in safety; or you will learn of a little brute which came galloping to the house with a blood-soaked saddle hanging from its side, which impatiently nipped the shoulders of the ranchmen that they might hurry more in sending out relief . . .*

A good cowpony is prized for its talents, which include its "cow sense" as a whittler, meaning the ability to separate a cow or calf from the herd by anticipating the cattle's movement and changing direction so quickly that the

designated cow can't go anyplace but where the cowboy wants it. A horse with the talent for whittling (usually a quarter horse) is known as a cutting horse, or peg pony; and cowboy tales of cutting-horse aptitude are legion. Folklorist J. Frank Dobie wrote of one famous strawberry roan who would "watch with his ears. He'd keep both ears pointed at a steer being cut out. If he was behind a cow and a calf, he'd point one ear down towards the calf and the other towards the cow." Another skill that a cowboy's horse needs to learn well is the ability to run behind a cow until the rider throws his lariat, then to veer off and brace himself, squatting back on his haunches, when the cow comes to the end of the rope, then keep the rope just taut enough for the rider to leap off and tie his quarry.

Horses provoke such great emotion because cowboys depend on them so much. Cowboy poet Baxter Black described the charm and value of a ranch horse as "Somewhere between a teddy bear and a good pocket knife," but according to the unwritten Code of the West, even that's an understatement. Steal another man's horse and you'll be hung summarily, ride another man's horse and you'll get whipped, and when you pull into camp, no matter how hungry and exhausted you may be, always hitch your horse, remove his saddle and bridle, and get him his feed before you tend to your own needs.

Frederic Remington, whose paintings and sculpture defined the romance of the frontier well before movies did, chose as his tombstone epitaph the simple words, *HE KNEW THE HORSE*. Remington's idyllic images of men in the saddle, wind against their Stetsons, galloping hard across the prairie, helped create a vision of adventure that was a wondrous antidote to a twentieth century in which civilization had begun to seem like mechanized prison. In Owen Wister's seminal cowboy novel, *The Virginian* (1902), the narrator mounts up and heads West to join the gallant cowboy who has become his idol: "To leave behind all noise and mechanisms, and

Above: *A handsome working cowpony pauses for a drink.* Opposite: *Gene Autry's Champion was equine royalty. Note Champ's bridle.*

From your Pal

Gene Autry
and Champ

# Horse Colors

**American Cream:** according to Edgar R. "Frosty" Potter in his excellent book *Cowboy Slang*, this is a horse that is "pretty close to common cow's cream."

**Appaloosa:** Indian horses from the Nez Percé country, known for their spotted rumps, or spots all over.

**Dun:** anywhere from pale gray to yellowish roan, often with a stripe down their back; sometimes dun is just another name for a buckskin horse.

**Pinto:** a "paint" horse, with spots or splotches of color. Calicos are very brightly colored pintos.

**Palomino:** also known as a California sorrel—"the color of a newly-minted U.S. gold coin," according to the Palomino Horse Association, with a mane and tail that are silver white. Most Palominos are good-sized—1,100 pounds and over 15 hands high.

**Flea-bitten:** gray or roan with small black specks.

**Gruello:** mouse-colored.

set out at ease, slowly, with one pack-horse, into the wilderness, made me feel that the ancient earth was indeed my mother and that I had found her again after being lost among houses, customs, and restraints." Later, in cowboy movies and TV shows that were supposed to be "contemporary," such as the escapades of Gene Autry and Roy Rogers, the gangsters often drive black Packards and shoot tommy guns . . . but they are invariably corralled by Gene or Roy, who rides after them on his horse. More recently, the movie *The Electric Horseman* (1979) was an inspiring morality tale in which Robert Redford frees a drugged and abused stallion from the clutches of evil businessmen, who chase after it, to no avail, in helicopters and cars. Redford's liberation of the horse into the wilderness is a rousing back-to-nature fantasy.

"Something happens to a man when he gets on a horse, in a country where he can ride forever," historian William Brandon observed. Brandon was writing about the spiritual effect that the introduction of horses had on the Plains Indians in the seventeenth century, encouraging them to see their lives with a mythological dimension, and to believe they had a godlike aura as they rode swiftly over the earth. A similar kind of rapture was experienced by many cowboys, particularly fictional ones, who called their horse their home. They became heroic riders of the wide open spaces, the foremost stars of American mythology. The novel *Gene Autry and the Thief River Outlaws* (1944) began with this description of its hero on his trusty horse, Champion:

> *Like all men who lived the greater part of their lives in the saddle, Gene Autry rode as if he were a part of his horse, or the horse a part of him, but there was a deeper unity between these two. Both were more akin to the life in the open than in the settlements. Each recognized certain friendships and duties from time to time but neither man nor beast felt any need to depend on any other creature. They had learned to trust in no help but their own strength, courage, speed, wits, and fighting hearts.*

The original cow ponies of the West were small animals, some no more than six hundred pounds and under fourteen hands high, known for speed and endurance and a talent for traversing rugged trails. They were tough creatures with a wild heritage, the result of what Jo Mora's cowboy memoir *Trail Dust and Saddle Leather* (1946) described as "three centuries of breeding by men who knew horses, and likewise by men who did not, and also of running free on the limitless ranges of those virgin lands." Horses were introduced to North America in 1519, when eleven stallions and five mares were brought to Mexico by Cortes (who used them to terrify and conquer the Aztecs). The conquistadores' horses were a motley bunch: Some were pure Andalusians and Barbs (the latter is a non-Arabian desert horse originally from North Africa), but many more were what Mora described as "an average, general cross-section of the common everyday horse of the mother country."

Like the cattle brought to America by the Spaniards, their equine stock flourished, multiplied, strayed, and ran free. The wild animals were called mustangs, from *mesteño,* meaning of a feral herd. "He craved to wear no man's saddle," Foster-Harris wrote about the mustang in *The Look of the Old West.* "He was quite regularly the doggonedest bucker ever foaled." Known for spirit and stamina, the mustang—also called a broomtail (usually, a range mare) or fuzztail (a range horse)—was often broken to be used as a cow pony, particularly by Plains Indian tribes, although there is a storehouse of sad frontier fables about wild ones who were seized from their herd but were so distressed by captivity that they died of a broken heart.

The stock horses that took cowboys up the cattle trails and rode the range were frequently crosses of the wily little mustang with other bloodlines, introduced for greater size, strength, and temperament: quarter horses, Thoroughbreds, Morgans, and Arabians were all part of the mix that went into creating the American cow pony.

The result has been that American saddle horses are a wondrously variegated bunch, with a taxonomy that can be baffling to a tenderfoot. "This name business is always a tough one to unravel," Jo Mora observed, referring to such terms for horses as bronco—meaning a rough one, usually applied to an unbroken horse; and cayuse—which started as a Northwestern horse term, taken from the Cayuse Indian tribe of Oregon, to describe a paint horse with spectacular markings, but was then generally applied to all native ponies, then to any horse that reminds its viewer of the Old West (in Texas, "to cayuse" used to mean to buck wildly).

In the book *Ranching Traditions,* John R. Erickson, who used to be a full-time cowboy, described what he missed most now that he had retired from life in the saddle. He wrote with affection all about the cowboy life—about branding and berthing cattle, even about the hard work and low pay of the professional ranch hand: But the first thing he talked about, the one part of cowboying he yearned for and missed the most, was his closeness to horses:

> *It's hard for me to drive past a group of horses without going into the ditch, because my gaze lingers on them. I can see at a glance that most of them are idle and need riding, and I think to myself, "Boys, it's too bad we can't get together, because I've got the same problem. We'd both be better with more riding."*

# Trigger and Other
# EQUINE SUPERSTARS

Roy Rogers has known the joy of a good wife, a happy family, and a wonderful career as King of the Cowboys. He also owned a horse named Trigger, the most famous movie animal of all time, and Roy loved Trigger as much as any man can love a horse.

"His sire was a racehorse," Roy told David Rothel, author of *The Singing Cowboys,* "and his dam was a cold-blooded palomino. He took the color, white mane, and tail from his mother and the stamina, speed and conformation from the Thoroughbred side."

His original owner, the Hudkins Stables, named him Golden Cloud, and he had a small role as a youngster in *The Adventures of Robin Hood* (1938), in which Olivia de Havilland rides him sidesaddle through Sherwood Forest. Later that year, when Republic Studios decided to feature Roy Rogers in a series of Westerns, they had several horses brought around for Roy to try. When he mounted Trigger it was love at first whinny.

The magnificent California sorrel (an earlier name for palomino) was featured in Roy Rogers's first starring movie, *Under Western Stars,* in 1938; but before the picture was completed, Roy's first sidekick, Smiley Burnette, suggested the new name—Trigger—because the horse was just that quick. Two movies later, Roy decided he liked the animal so much he bought him, paying twenty-five hundred dollars. Trigger became the co-star of every one of the 87 movies and 101 TV shows that Roy Rogers made.

Trigger was such a natural performer that sometimes he stole the show from Roy, who was known on occasion to curse his mount as "a ham instead of a horse." In a story about the two of them in *Life* magazine in 1943, H. Allen Smith wrote that "the horse has been known to yawn or go into a little dance step at the very moment when the audience is supposed to be giving its undivided attention to Roy. After one such experience at the Earle Theater in Washington, Roy came offstage cussing and in

*Trigger did all his own stunts, except scenes in which he fought another horse. Roy Rogers didn't want his golden Palomino coat blemished by a hoofprint.*

his dressing room announced, 'I'm gonna shoot that so-and-so horse right between the eyes.'"

Trigger had his own fan club with over a million human members. He traveled in an air-conditioned, cork-lined trailer and wore a fifty-thousand-dollar silver saddle studded with a thousand rubies. He put his two front hoofprints in cement outside of Grauman's Chinese Theater and once had a birthday party in the grand ballroom of New York's Hotel Astor. The press relished printing stories that his contract called for at least three close-ups per film. (Trigger frequently did get close-ups and billing equal to Roy's, but he actually worked without a contract.) He was publicized as "The Smartest Horse in the Movies," and his talents included the following feats of skill:

**Walking 150 feet on his hind legs**

**Counting to 25 by stamping his hoof**

**Drinking milk out of a bottle**

**Using a pencil in his teeth to sign the guest register (with an X) when arriving at a hotel**

**Kneeling to pray as Roy sang "Peace in the Valley"**

**Not pooping indoors**

Like Elvis and the Beatles, Trigger was actually put in peril by the intense devotion of those who adored him so much that they yearned to have a part of him. David Rothel reported that so many fans yanked hairs from his luxuriant mane and tail that there were times Trigger actually had to wear a prosthetic tail wig so as to not look bald. In fact, Hollywood horse trainer Glenn Randall, who had taught Trigger most of his sixty tricks, tutored three different look-alike Triggers for personal appearances and live shows; sometimes they were used as doubles in movie long shots. But any film scene that required close-ups was always done by the one and only Trigger, who had a lifelong love affair with the camera.

He retired in 1957 and died at age thirty-three on July 3, 1965. Rogers, who called him "the greatest horse that ever came along," couldn't stand to think of his

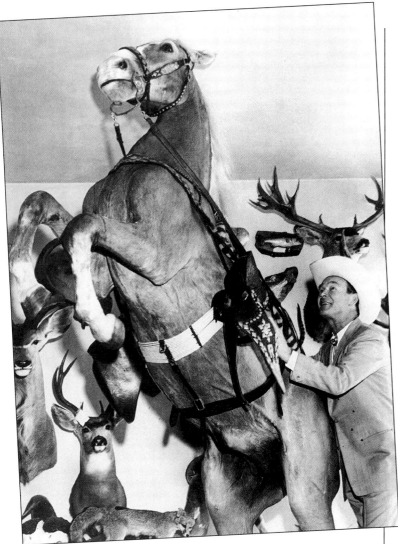

*Trigger is not stuffed. He is mounted, which means that his hide is stretched over an armature.*

which humans play second fiddle to Trigger and Trigger Jr., who star in a melodrama about diamond smuggling (in a trick horseshoe) and murder (by the hard-hitting hoof of an evil stallion); *Under California Skies* (1948), in which Trigger is held for ransom by thugs; and *Trigger, Jr.* (1950), about a killer horse on the loose, with a special taste for palominos!

Gene Autry's Champion—billed as "the World's Wonder Horse"—was second only to Trigger in his fame. Champion shared many of Trigger's beguiling qualities, and he was able to kneel, march, waltz, bow, jump through a flaming hoop, and do the hula, the rhumba, and the Charleston. His hoofprints, like Trigger's, were set in cement outside Grauman's Chinese Theater; and he was reported to travel in a DC-3 with all the seats removed for his comfort. A Tennessee walking horse with a white blazed face and four white socks, Champion was never quite the idolized luminary Trigger was, but he and tiny Little Champ (the comic foil, who used to scamper underneath Champion's belly, much to the old man's chagrin) were key players in

*Below:* Tom Mix on Tony. *Opposite:* William S. Hart rarely smiled *in the movies, but with his pinto Fritz he was clearly a happy man.*

cherished stallion moldering in a grave, so he had him taxidermized, rearing up and wearing a fancy silver saddle in all his glory, the way millions of fans remember him. Now Trigger is the most popular single exhibit at the Roy Rogers and Dale Evans Museum in Victorville, California, where also reside the mounted remains of Bullet the Wonder Dog, Buttermilk (Dale's TV Horse), Trigger Jr. (a good dancer who was often used for personal appearances, but a horse without much film charisma), and dozens of heads of game animals and big fish Roy caught.

Trigger was in a class by himself; no other movie cowboy horse had as many fans as he did, and none got so many good scenes and plum roles. Some of his finest performances were in *The Golden Stallion* (1949), in

Gene Autry's traveling live show and in movies that took place on his Melody Ranch. A souvenir booklet from an Autry show in the late 1940s described their lifestyle: "They live in a deluxe, deodorized stable. Their menus consist of oats with carrots and apples for dessert. Their daily workouts are performed to the din of recorded applause so that when they appear before an audience they will not be frightened by the thunderous cheers

Below: *Buck Jones and Silver.* Right: *Hopalong Cassidy (William Boyd) with Topper.*

which invariably greet their entrances."

Celebrity Western horses are nearly as old as cowboy movies. William S. Hart, the first cowboy movie star, frequently made his mount, Fritz, a key player in the story, and it was Fritz, not a pretty girl, who usually accompanied him when he rode off at the final fade-out. In the prologue he filmed for the rerelease of his great movie *Tumbleweeds* in 1939, Hart, who had been absent from the screen for fourteen years, recalled his dear departed equine pal as he spoke to the audience of looking up toward the Western sky and seeing the old cowboys who had gone to their glory. Loping with the men alongside the ghost herd in the

*The Lone Ranger on Silver.*

clouds was a riderless pinto pony—Fritz, beckoning Bill with a low whinny to join him for the last roundup.

Fritz was known by name to audiences, but it was Tom Mix's Tony who became the first horse superstar.

Tony not only got screen billing along with human actors, in 1922 he starred in his own movie (accompanied by Mix in a supporting role) titled *Just Tony,* in which he leaped over canyons, galloped through fire, swam raging rivers, and in one key scene sauntered over to a table and fetched Mix's six-gun for him. In their book *Box-Office Buckaroos* Robert Heide and John Gilman write that the only thing Tony feared was a dummy horse used by the studio as a stand-in: the fact that it wouldn't whinny back spooked him.

After Tony, it became de rigueur for any star of Western serials to have a horse with a good personality.

Opposite: *Dale Evans and Buttermilk.* Above: *Rex Allen on Koko.* Right: *Whip Wilson on Silver Bullet.*

# HOOFED HEADLINERS

**Tarzan** (Ken Maynard). Tarzan was a real entertainer; in addition to great trick-riding feats with Maynard aboard, he knew how to play dead and dance, and with the arrival of talking pictures, there were even some musical Westerns in which he seemed to swing and sway during musical interludes. He also frequently nudged Maynard into a clinch with a pretty girl.

**Mutt** (Hoot Gibson)

**Silver** (Buck Jones, who also had a horse named White Eagle)

**Silver** (The Lone Ranger) Silver was so named because when Tonto discovered him in Wild Horse Valley he said, "Him look like silver." He was no relation to Buck Jones's Silver.

**Silver Bullet** (Whip Wilson)

**Topper** (Hopalong Cassidy). The first week of production on the first Hoppy film, *Hop-A-Long Cassidy* (1935), William Boyd fell off Topper and broke his leg.

**Silver King** (Fred Thomson). Thomson usually played a good guy, but in *The Sunset Legion* (1928) he played a good guy *and* a bad guy; and in his role as the bad guy's horse, Silver King, who was white, wore a tight-fitting suit of black.

**Midnight** (Tim McCoy)

**Rush** (Lash Larue)

**Diablo** (Cisco Kid)

**Scout** (Jack Hoxie)

**Lightnin'** (Monte Hale)

**Raider** (Charlie Starrett)

**Ko-Ko** (Rex Allen, "The Arizona Cowboy"); Ko-Ko was so named because he reminded Allen of a "wonderful thick cup of chocolate." Star of *Phantom Stallion* (1954), Ko-Ko was billed as "The Miracle Horse of the Movies."

**Rebel** (Johnny Mack Brown). Brown, who came from Alabama, named his horse to honor the South.

**Copper** (Eddie Dean). According to *Movie Western* magazine, "Eddie Dean, PRC's singing cowboy star, sees to every need of his beautiful horse. He knows full well

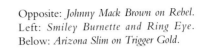
Opposite: *Johnny Mack Brown on Rebel.*
Left: *Smiley Burnette and Ring Eye.*
Below: *Arizona Slim on Trigger Gold.*

*Cordially Yours Tom Keene*

how important his mount is as part of his career as well as to him personally as a trusted companion."

**Ring Eye** (Smiley Burnette). Like Smiley, Ring Eye was a comedian: an old white horse that was sometimes stubborn as a mule, and known for a perfectly drawn circle around his left eye—a mirror image of the Little Rascals' dog, Jiggs.

"Foremost among the up-and-coming gallopers is Blackjack," *Movie Western* announced in 1950. Blackjack belonged to Allan "Rocky" Lane (who played Red Ryder after Bill Elliott), and was said to be a descendant of the Ketchum brothers' herd of horses, known for their spirit back in the 1880s. Blackjack retrieved the newspaper every morning from the mailbox and delivered it to Rocky on the front porch of his ranch. He could count, dance, and answer many questions; and he got equal screen billing with his rider. "His income runs into four figures," *Movie Thrills* reported. Blackjack was known for having more saddles than any other horse except Trigger: "work saddles, flower-stamped everyday saddles, and silver inlaid saddles for dress."

In an article Rocky Lane wrote in 1950 titled "I Doff My Stetson to the American Pioneer and His Horse," he said, "My stallion Blackjack, who is part of me, has no Stetson to doff, but he arches his proud head in tribute to his forebears, those four-legged partners of the early-day cowboys who shared their dangers and their triumphs. As long as cowboys sing 'Old Faithful' in the solitude of the night, or in the glare of a stage spotlight, so long will the horse hold his place in the affections of man."

Above: *Tom Keene on his paint horse.* Opposite: *Allan "Rocky" Lane and Blackjack.*

# The *Well-Dressed* HORSE

Saddlemakers deserve acclaim—they built the leathern thrones from which the cowboy ruled his realm.
—Philip Ashton Rollins, *The Cowboy*

orse livery doesn't change style nearly as much as human fashion, but the quality, ingenuity, and verve that distinguish Western saddles are at least as wondrous as anything that ever paraded down a runway in Paris or Milan. Like most articles of clothing people wear, a cow pony's saddle and tack were originally designed to help deal with some practical issues: in this case, the difficulty of conducting one's business from the back of a very large animal. For example, a bridle makes life easy because it affords a good measure of control of your horse, a saddle with a high padded cantle in back provides all-day comfort, and a horn at the front of the saddle allows you to hitch the end of a rope, thus accomplishing the fundamental task of cowboying, which is to keep a cow where you want it.

Beyond those basic needs, a hundred other problems have been solved by skillful saddle design: tapaderos shield the stirrups and protect a rider's lower legs from cactus thorns and brush; rosaderos, also known as fenders, behind the stirrup leather separate a rider's thighs from a horse's sweat; tie strings, often attached with silver conchas, are used to secure a bedroll, rifle scabbard, and supplies; and the thick, broad skirt, underneath the saddle, helps keep the whole affair in place. To stay put, a saddle also needs a cinch and cinch ring (or a pair of them, if it's a Texas style double-rig, meant for roping hard and fast) and a latigo hitch to hold the rigging; it also needs a corona, or saddle blanket, to protect the horse's back—preferably a soft Angora pad, or a Navajo blanket made with wool that the Indians have dyed red, black, gray, and white.

Real cowboys are obsessed with their saddles more than any modern man thinks about his reclining chair or the upholstery in his automobile. A saddle is, after all, where he spends most of the day, where he rests his head on the prairie at night, and the single most important tool of his trade: "the first, last, and most important piece of equipment of the cowboy," Bruce Grant called it in his *Cowboy Encyclopedia* (1951). "He will sell his horse and almost anything else he owns, but he will keep his saddle. A man without a saddle is no longer a cowboy."

When selecting a saddle, the first thing you need to do is choose a tree (the wood superstructure) that suits you. There are dozens of varieties available, each with a name that evokes its place of origin or someone famous who once rode it: i.e., the Miles City, the Butch Cassidy, the Rocky Mountain Roper, the Association (named for the Rodeo Cowboys Association). One big difference among trees is the fork, which is the leather-covered wooden bridge underneath the saddle horn; they range from a slick fork, shaped like a bell and easy to move around, to a full swell fork, which bulges out above your thighs and tends to hold you in your seat. You'll also want to select the rake and height of your cantle, which will partly depend on whether you plan to ride flatlands or hilly terrain: on the latter, a high cantle helps keep you in your seat. Horns come in all sorts of shapes: the dinner

Opposite: *Don't let this Easter bonnet fool you. Trigger was all stallion until the day he died.*

plate is broad and flat-topped; the duck bill is ovoid and points forward; a slick horn is slim and angles up for quick and easy wrapping with a rope. Stirrups come in different shapes and sizes, too, such as ox-bows and stockman's, and cinches can be mohair or horsehair, with buckles or laces, fastened with latigo straps. Now, do you want tapaderos? And if you do, do you want bulldog taps, monkey-nose taps, eagle-bill taps, or round taps, and do you need them lined with fleece?

Beyond all the strictly practical decisions are many other choices of taste (and pocketbook), such as the degree of fancy leather tooling and silver filigree, and where the tie strings and conchas go. "Once broken in," Michael Friedman wrote in his comprehensive book of Western collectibles, *Cowboy Culture* (1992), "[a saddle] was like an old pair of boots that conformed uniquely to its owner's anatomy." And, we might add, also conformed to its owner's job description, financial status, and state of mind.

The earliest saddles in America were built for fighting. Spanish war saddles carried to the New World by conquistadores were designed with high cantles and high pommels, to provide a secure seat from which a warrior wouldn't likely get knocked off his horse. (The Aztecs, who had no horses, were hardly in a position to fight these armored caballeros, in any case.) In Mexico the war saddle evolved into something more suited for work by cowherds, who were called vaqueros. They required a saddle with a lower cantle (for quick mounting) and a

*A pretty cowgirl, a glittering silver saddle, and a golden Palomino: this cheerful image appeared on a popular 1956 calendar.*

dinner-plate horn up front to which one end of a rope could be easily secured; and they topped their seat with a comfortable leather "mochila" that blanketed the tree. When settlers came to Texas early in the nineteenth century, this is the type of rig that Mexican vaqueros were using there; with the addition of a long leather skirt and a mochila permanently stitched on the tree, it became the classic cowpuncher's saddle.

A sure mark of a rider from the high country was (and still is) called the Cheyenne rig, or Great Plains saddle. Double rigged and with a squared-off skirt as on a Texas saddle, it had a second skirt (also squared), like saddles typical of California. Its most distinctive feature was its cantle, which had a roll of padding at the back, known as a Cheyenne roll. In 1883 Buffalo Bill Cody equipped the riders of his Wild West show with this type of saddle (actually made in Omaha by the legendary Collins brothers).

No one did more to excite the public about the marvels of Western horse wear than Edward H. Bohlin, who was described by *Western Life* magazine in 1967 as the "Michelangelo of Saddlecraft." Bohlin did for saddles what Tom Mix did for cowboys: he took a workaday piece of Americana and elevated it to a maharaja's level of luxe and glamour. In fact, it was Tom Mix who first encouraged Eddie Bohlin to come to Hollywood and make saddles for movie cowboys. They met in 1922 when Bohlin, a young Swedish immigrant who had opened his own leathercraft shop in Cody,

Wyoming, traveled to Los Angeles on a lark to do rope tricks in a horse show. While performing, he wore a fancy calfskin coat he had made for himself. He heard a voice call out to him from the audience: "Hey, kid! What do you want for the coat?" The voice was Tom Mix's; Mix bought the coat and the next day he bought Bohlin's hand-carved traveling bag and walked away in Bohlin's silver-trimmed, alligator-vamp cowboy boots. "I had to walk two blocks barefooted to a street car in order to get back to my hotel," Bohlin recalled in a 1962 article in *The Western Horseman*. But he was seventy-five dollars richer, and he had found a new home for his talents as a leather worker and silversmith.

He set up shop in Hollywood, where he helped make Tom Mix the best-dressed cowboy in movie history and made Mix's horse Tony into the Western film's first fashion-plate equine—draped in precious-metal tack from his flower-concha noseband and breast collar to a saddle with filigreed gold on its skirt and a thick silver rope-roll edge to the cantle. Bohlin supplied ornate saddles, bits, spurs, chaps, gloves, guns, gun belts, and holsters to nearly every fancy cowboy in the movies, including Roy Rogers and Dale Evans, Gene Autry, Hopalong Cassidy, and the Lone Ranger. George Pitman, America's leading authority on Bohlin and his saddles, recently reprinted a 1927 Bohlin catalogue, which was subtitled "Master Craftsman for the Cowboy Kings" and featured one sterling silver–trimmed saddle with filigreed raised steer heads in three shades of gold in the corners, a horn wrapped in a single piece of silver, and stirrup leathers carved with a cowboy on a bucking steer. This particular model sold for $2,750—enough then to buy a small house—and was described thus: "Matchless beauty, incomparable workmanship, and the finest quality materials combine to give this saddle the highest possible rating known to the saddle world. It is the very acme of achievement in precious metal on leather."

Eddie Bohlin retired in 1975 and died five years later, but his shop has gone back into business, and not long ago Bohlin authority George Pitman helped the new owners locate some 220 of Bohlin's antique gold and silver dies, which are now being used again. In fact, saddle-making is one Western craft that is thriving as Americans rekindle their romance with cowboy ways. This was apparent in a breathtaking show put on by the Wyoming Arts Council Gallery

*A classic Main-Winchester-Stone saddle from the 1905 catalogue. "Made exclusively of Cow Boy brand skirting leather."*

UP-TO-DATE SADDLE
FULL FLOWER STAMPED.

G.O. SIMMONS. ENG. SF.

| Full flower stamped, as represented, each | $90 00 |
|---|---|
| Plain, not stamped | " 64 00 |
| Flower border stamped | " 80 00 |
| Checker stamped | " 74 00 |
| With 2 cinchas, add | " 5 00 |
| With tapaderos, add | " 18 00 |

No. 25—Weight, 35 lbs.

in Cheyenne in summer 1992. Titled "The Well-Dressed Horse," the exhibit featured exquisite rose and maple leaf pattern saddles by Chester Hape (he hand-makes about four saddles per year) and Sheridan-style (scroll pattern) saddles by Don King, who's been refining his art since 1946, as well as the fine work of modern braiders (who make reins), weavers (who make coronas), bit makers, and farriers. Also on display was the craft of leather artist Verlane Desgrange, who bases her saddles on historically correct High Plains originals, but makes them to fit modern horses and modern horsewomen—working the leather with tools she has created herself.

Old saddles have become high-priced collectibles. Almost any vintage piece of leather in decent condition is worth something as a token of the West, but the really well-crafted saddles of the big-name saddle makers can cost many thousands of dollars; "having belonged to a famous cowboy can push the price even higher," Michael Friedman noted in *Cowboy Culture*. "If you have the saddle that belonged to Roy Rogers or the Lone Ranger, the price will reflect what the market will bear." Most people who buy such saddles do not put them on a horse and gallop off to Laredo or Laramie. The saddles are bought, like vintage cowboy guns and fine old Native American rugs, as investment-level home decor. George Pitman, describing his spectacular Bohlin originals, wrote, "There is nothing like a gorgeous three-dimensional silver parade outfit to virtually knock your socks off when used for decoration in an exquisite setting with the proper lighting. There is so much more to see than a diamond on one's finger, for example."

# Horse Lingo's Spanish Roots

**M**ost cowboy words for equine things, including saddles, ropes, tack, and the craft of herding cows on horseback, have Spanish origins. This is because it was Mexican vaqueros (from the Spanish *vaca*, meaning cow) who first used horses and ropes to tend cattle in America.

**BRONCO:** a wild horse; from *bronco*: wild

**BUCKAROO:** a cowboy; from *vaquero*: a cow herder

**CHAPARRAL:** a prairie thick with brush, from *chaparro*: evergreen oak

**CHAPS:** from *chaparrejos* (or *chaparreras*): leather overalls

**CINCH:** the strap that fastens a saddle; from *cincha*

**CONCHA:** a decorative silver disc often used on saddles and chaps, from *concha*: shell

**CORRAL:** from *corral*, meaning a fenced yard for animals

**DALLY:** to turn a rope several times around the horn of a saddle after throwing it; from *dar la vuelta*: to give a turn

**HACKAMORE:** a bridle without a bit; from *jáquima*

**LARIAT:** a cowboy's rope; from *la reata*: a vaquero's rope

**LASSO:** from *lazo*: slipknot

**MCCARTY:** a horsehair rope used for reins; from *mecate*

**MUSTANG:** wild horse; from *mesteño*: a gang or herd of mixed ancestry

**PETER MAGAY:** a fiber rope made from the aloe leaf; from *pita maguey*: aloe

**PINTO:** a multicolored pony, also called a **PAINT;** from *pinto*: painted

**QUIRT:** a short horse whip; from *cuarta*

**RANCH:** from *rancho*

**REMUDA:** extra horses; from *remuda de caballos*: a relay of horses

**RODEO:** from *rodeo*: roundup

**SUDADERO:** a saddle skirt's sweatband lining; from *sudadero*: a handkerchief

**TARRABEE:** a paddle used to spin horsehair into ropes; from *taravilla*

**VAMOOSE:** hit the trail; from *vamos*: let's go

# "End of the TRAIL"

**A**dejected Indian brave, slumped in fatigue, his spear hanging low, sits atop a rack-ribbed warhorse whose drooped head is almost on the ground. This is *End of the Trail,* which Karal Ann Marling, author of *Colossus of Roads* (1984), called "the most popular statue of the 20th century." Unlike America's two other most celebrated bigger-than-life sculptures, Mount Rushmore and the Statue of Liberty, *End of the Trail* is not part of an official national park (although it is magnificent to see at the Cowboy Hall of Fame in Oklahoma City); its renown arose less from people looking at it than from people looking at reproductions of it.

No other work of art of any kind, except maybe Leonardo's Mona Lisa or The Last Supper, has had such a long and prosperous life as the inspiration for souvenirs, keepsakes, advertising logos, reproductions of all sizes, and tableaux vivants in which living beings impersonate the sculptor's models. Originally exhibited at the Panama-Pacific Exposition of 1915 in San Francisco, End of the Trail was created by James Earle Fraser to be a triple-life-size monument overlooking the Pacific Ocean—an image that represented the final closing of the American frontier. Fraser, who also designed the Buffalo nickel (see page 252), reportedly had modeled his mournful figure using John Big Tree, a Seneca Indian employed by a Wild West show on Coney Island: Like his famous five-cent piece, the statue combined the heroic grandeur of the West with sentimental longing for the nobler, natural America that civilization had displaced.

The model exhibited at the fair was made of cement, but Fraser had hoped to use it as a prototype for an all-weather beacon of bronze for the ages. "It has been a dream of mine to erect this horse and rider in permanent form on some bold promontory just outside San Francisco," he wrote. "There they would stand forever . . .

driven at last to the very edge of the continent. That would be, in very truth, *The End of the Trail.*"

Fraser's dream was not to be. When the exposition closed, the original statue was sold to the town of Visalia, California. Its actual whereabouts became irrelevant, because by the end of the decade hundreds of thousands of reproductions of it had flooded the art and memento marketplace, and many Americans, unaware of the original sculpture (which Fraser had neglected to copyright), assumed that *End of the Trail* had begun as a classical painting. In a *New York Times* story titled "Most Famous Unknown Sculptor," written in 1951 at the end of Fraser's career, art critic Aline Louchheim wrote that the statue "had been put to illustrative purposes ranging from miniature bronzes for onyx 'doctor's waiting room' ashtrays to a calendar cover bearing the legend:

*Thus ever it is in this world of ours*
*The brightest light will fail*
*Then a tear in the eye and an aching heart*
*When we come to 'The End of the Trail.'"*

In 1932, cowboy actor Tim McCoy, a former government agent for Indian affairs, made a movie called *End of the Trail*, about the white man's mistreatment of Native Americans, fea-

turing a scene in which the statue seems to come alive. Throughout the 1930s, Gene Autry and his "World's Wonder Horse," Champion, frequently appeared at rodeos as a specialty act: Champion bowed to the crowd, laughed at Gene's jokes, kissed pretty girls, untied his tether with his teeth and, as his grand climax, stood upon a pedestal and lowered his head. At the same time, Gene, on Champ's back, lowered his head, too, and the band played "Old Faithful," "So Long, Old Paint," or "As Long As I Have My Horse." It was a heart-wrenching, living version of the sculpture, which Autry himself announced as his and Champion's version of "that famous painting, *The End of the Trail.*"

Gene wasn't the only cowboy with a smart horse to be inspired by the emotional image of the defeated warrior. Many rodeos adopted a similar act and used it as their grand finale. The most famous of the re-enactments was that of rodeo virtuoso Cecil Cornish, who trained his paint horse Smokey to pretend to fall and break his leg, at which point Cornish (who also pretended to be injured in the fall) pulled a gun and aimed it at Smokey's head to put him out of his misery. But before Cornish pulled the trigger, Smokey looked up, pleading to be spared, and hobbled to his feet. The injured rider lifted himself onto Smokey's back, where he slouched in anguish. Smokey limped a few paces, then stopped, unable to proceed, and lowered his head. The stricken horse and its stricken rider stood together, hurt but not crushed, as they struck the classic pose: *End of the Trail.* In his biography of Cornish, *Mr. Rodeo, Himself,* Robert N. Gray wrote, "Seldom would there be a dry eye in the stadium."

When Smokey's *End of the Trail* became old news to rodeo fans, Cornish trained a Brahman bull named Danger to jump over a car and through a flaming hoop, then, in climax, to stand still and lower his head as Mr. Cornish sat on his back, looking forlorn, with his own head cast down toward Danger's hump.

When James Earle Fraser died in October 1953, his obituary in the *New York Times* noted that *End of the Trail* was "being reproduced daily now at every performance of the current rodeo at Madison Square Garden."

*Left: Cecil Cornish performing "End of the Trail" to conclude a rodeo. Following pages: "End of the Trail" is an inescapable Western image. Seneca Chief John Big Tree, who posed for the original sculpture, claimed to also have been the model for the Buffalo nickel and the Pontiac automobile hood ornament.*

END OF THE TRAIL

HARRY MURPHY and "SILVER CLOUD"

GENE AUTRY & CHAMPION
(DOUBLEKY)

# "OLD PAINT"

*I*n 1908 N. Howard (Jack) Thorp published 23 cowboy songs he had gathered in a book called *Songs of the Cowboys,* which he sold for fifty cents a copy. In 1921 he put out an expanded version of 101 songs and poems, including many that he had written based on his own experience as a cowboy, as well as on folk tales he had heard while riding the range. Among the new poems in the 1921 collection was "Old Paint," Thorp's ode to a well-remembered horse.

## OLD PAINT

*Every time I see an old paint horse, I think of you,*
*Old paint horse of mine that used to be,*
*Old pal o' mine that was, the best horse of all, because—*
*That's why, old horse, at last I set you free!*

*I've bought 'em by the thousand, I've owned 'em every-*
*    where—*
*There's one stands out among 'em all alone;*
*Paint-marked everywhere, tail a little short o' hair,*
*Old horse, you never failed to bring me home!*

*'Member when they stole you from Pass City,*
*En locked you up inside the Juarez jail!*
*Said that you had eaten up an entire crop of wheat,*
*En I had to rustle round en get your bail?*

*En I got you cross the river en matched you in a race,*
*En we bet the last red dollar we could scrape?—*
*En how you bit old Rocking Chair, the horse you run*
*    against,*
*En made him turn his head and lose the race?*

*We was both young en foolish in them green days long ago,*
*I don't believe in telling stories out of school!—*
*'Member when we roped the pianner en jerked her out the door?*
*Hush up! Old Paint! you're talkin' like a fool!*

CECIL CORNISH AND HIS WONDER HORSE "SMOKEY" WAUKOMIS, OKLAHOMA

CASE STUDIO '37

*Well, old horse, you're buried, en your troubles, they are done,*
*But I often sit en think of what we did,*
*En recall the many scrapes we had, en used to think it fun,*
*Es we rode along the Rio Grande . . .*
*    Good-bye, old Kid!*

*Pal-O'-Mine*  by *Paul Parry*

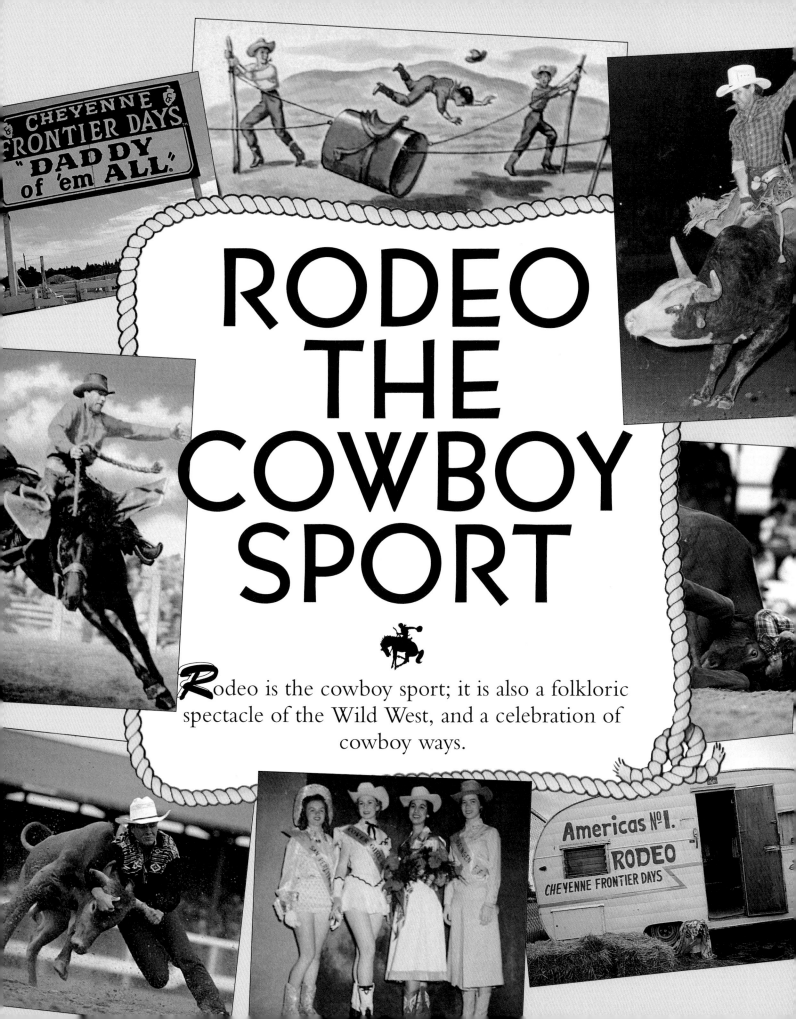

# RODEO THE COWBOY SPORT

**R**odeo is the cowboy sport; it is also a folkloric spectacle of the Wild West, and a celebration of cowboy ways.

# *The Cowboy* SPORT

Rugged cowboys spur their horses in pursuit of fleeing cattle, twirling lariats as they bear down on their quarry. High-riding horse-women burst out of the gate and hurtle full-speed around the arena, racing the clock on a twisting course. Angry bulls go charging after buckaroos and clowns, kicking dirt and bellowing. Outlaw stallions buck with spirit that cannot be broken, dislodging anyone who tries to ride them. These are some of the thrills of rodeo, which is North America's rousing pageant of life on the range. Rodeo is a sport, but for those who perform in it, and for those who love it, it is so much more than scores and standings. Rodeo is a cowboy jubilee.

Most of the big rodeos in the West and High Plains aren't merely rodeos. They are their town's premier cultural event of the year, a celebration of all things Western, and festivities gallop through the streets with the same sense of reckless jubilation that once accompanied the arrival of cowboys after roundup time. In the beginning, about a hundred years ago, they were all named accordingly: the Cattle Men's Carnival of Fort Worth; Frontier Days of Prescott, Arizona; the Festival of Mountain and Plain in Denver; the Black Hills Round-Up of Belle Fourche, South Dakota; the Stampede in Winnipeg; the Cowboys' Convention of Ukiah, Oregon. When they began, all these early rodeos

*Many rodeos, big and small, take place on Independence Day. Opposite: Larry Mahan, known as "Super Saddle," shows some of the things he won at Denver in 1966.*

thrilled participants and spectators alike with the pluck and daredeviltry of men whose home was the wide-open spaces. In doing so, they helped define the American West.

The first rodeos, even before the fabled cattle drives of the 1860s, had an air of festivity. The word *rodeo* (which most people agree ought to be pronounced RO-dee-o, not ro-DAY-o) is from the Spanish word *rodear*—to gather or surround—and one of its original meanings was the driving of cattle to market, which was often part of a town fiesta. When Anglos came to the West and began rounding up and herding cattle, the word lingered to describe not only the range work, but the revelry that followed it when the cowhands finished their cowpunching and had money to spend. Irish novelist Mydne Reid wrote about such an event witnessed in Santa Fe in June 1846, described as "a Donneybrook [sic] fair, indeed. They contest with each other for the best roping and throwing, and there are horse races and whiskey and wines. At night in the clear moonlight there is much dancing on the streets."

At Fourth of July celebrations in communities throughout the Plains, exhibitions of range craft had become common by 1880, when the trail drives and the cowboys who braved them were already beginning to seem like relics of the past. With grazing land in private hands, and with the railroad spanning

Opposite: *Jim Shoulders demonstrates the grit that made him sixteen-times world champion. Forty years ago, when heavy workhorses were still bred for farm work, most bucking stock was considerably bigger than today.*

through the country, cowboys had less work to do, and a professional ranch hand was lucky if he could hire on for branding in the spring and stay through the roundup in the fall. By the end of the nineteenth century, the American West had a significant population of horsemen with unique talents but with little opportunity to exercise them; at the same time, the myth of the West was beginning to mesmerize the nation and the world.

When Buffalo Bill Cody was asked by the citizens of his hometown, North Platte, Nebraska, to stage an Independence Day Jubilee in 1882, he decided to make it an "Old Glory Blowout"—a celebration of recent American history that included an act called Cow-Boys' Fun,

which showed men in chaps, boots, and high hats trying to ride bucking broncos and wild steers, roping, shooting, and racing. Cowboys were becoming entertainment.

In his seminal rodeo history, *Man, Beast, Dust* (1947), Clifford P. Westermeier wrote

> *With pride of heritage and in recognition of the age which had given it birth, the Plains country, in memory of the cattle industry and the unique figure allied with it, the cowboy, annually holds a celebration with gusto in almost every community. Early in this century, from the border towns of southern Texas, northward, and beyond the border into Canada, the cattle industry and the cowboy were being immortalized in rodeo.*

With their spiritual and actual roots in fiestas held by trail hands eager to let off steam, most early rodeos tended to be unruly affairs, not only in the wide-open Western towns that staged them annually each summer, but in Eastern cities when traveling rodeos came to put on a show. In her book *American Rodeo* (1985), Kristine Fredriksson reports that when the 101 Ranch Show came from Ponca City, Oklahoma, to Madison Square Garden in New York in 1905, "They'd all booze it up and they'd ride up and down the streets, whooping and yelling like prairie wolves at a kill. . . . They took in all the leg shows, drank everything in sight, and prized up hell in general whenever the notion struck them." As late as 1940, when the rodeo came to Madison Square Garden, the *New Yorker* magazine considered the dress and behavior of its contestants and complained, "Americana ought to keep its own place and not bob up Eighth Avenue." The writer was especially upset by the sight of men wearing high-heeled shoes—cowboy boots.

Prior to 1950, there probably weren't more than three or four dozen men who could say they made a living rodeoing full time, not only because purses were smaller (indeed they were), but for the main reason that it was difficult to attend enough rodeos to earn a decent wage . . . unless you happened to win nearly every one you entered. But a big change took place as air travel became more accessible and a handful of enterprising cowboys began to realize that they could make more money if instead of spending hours driving hundreds of miles between rodeos, they could get on a plane and fly from place to place. They could even attend two rodeos at once, if their particular event happened to be scheduled on different days in different rodeos.

In 1968 *True* magazine grieved about what it called "a new breed of man" on the rodeo circuit—a man who totes a briefcase instead of a shootin' iron, who hands out business cards, and who doesn't drink or smoke or chew. "Rodeos are another world today," complained the self-described *man's magazine* next to a picture of six-time champion Larry Mahan—well groomed, clean-cut, and sober—climbing into his private jet. "Cowboys carry insurance and go on tour from city to city like professional golfers in spurs. Many of them never worked on a ranch or knew the loneliness of a range line camp."

*True* was exaggerating about how much the sport had changed. Highways are easier to travel now than they were in 1950, and all the big rodeos are scheduled so that it *is* possible to race between them, but even today only the sport's elite can afford to fly. Most cowboys still travel the circuit the old-fashioned way, by driving constantly. Nearly every hock shop west of the Mississippi has a good inventory of rodeo champions' buckles that they pawned to buy the gas to get to Belle Fourche or Vernal or Prairie du Chien to try to win some money. Ropers, who need to carry tack and travel with their favorite quarter horses, have no alternative but to drive, but even bull and bronc riders, whose equipment is little more than chaps and spurs, do most of their traveling between rodeos on the highways, at night, at high speed, with a bag of fast food on the seat beside them and the radio blasting to keep them awake.

"In the rodeo business, you've got to learn to sleep quick," rodeo champion Jim Shoulders philosophized; with equal measures of romance and lament he described the rapture of chasing thousands of miles across the West in a rattletrap sedan, of hoping for the time to get a shower and a cup of coffee before he climbed the chute, of feeling the body heat radiating off the bull as he lowered himself onto the animal's back, praying to God he would last eight seconds, and finally, of winning the world. In rodeo, winning the world means becoming world champion.

Champion, *a sculpture by Edd Hayes outside the Pro Rodeo Hall of Fame in Colorado Springs, shows Casey Tibbs aboard a bronc named Necktie. Inside the bronze are inscribed the words "Ride, cowboy, ride."*

*Barrel racing tests a horse and rider's ability to sprint and turn on a dime.*

Toward the last day of nearly every big annual contest, in whichever saloon has been anointed the rodeo hands' favorite in that town, gypsy cowboys whose cars have broken down somewhere back along the circuit, or who simply trust their luck to keep them going, circle the bar and tables looking to hitch a ride on down the road so they can compete again. Casey Tibbs, one of rodeo's first modern stars, recalled that when he started on the circuit at age fourteen in 1943, he used to lie down on the highway leading out of town to attract motorists' attention in hopes of getting a ride.

Some of the older men travel in a camper with their wives and babies, but most rodeo cowboys, who are in their teens and twenties, buddy up to share expenses and split the driving chores. A lot of them sleep in their cars, unwilling or in some cases unable to lay out the money for motel rooms, and most towns have a "cowboy campgrounds" somewhere near the arena, where contestants can live for the duration of the rodeo. Their cars and pickup trucks circle close, like a wagon train at night; when the day's events are long past, they sleep on bacseats in cluttered nests of laundry, ropes, tack, and menthol-scented liniments, or in sleeping bags on the ground. Sometimes, if there is no fast-food place handy, they roast some meat or heat a can of beans over an open fire, just as their forebears did long ago on the open range.

# *The* EVENTS

Most rodeo cowboys are specialists: They rope (calves or steers), they ride (broncs or bulls), or they wrestle (steers), and they go to a rodeo to compete in the one event they do best.

The pros try to travel to more than a hundred rodeos each year, paying entry fees at each of up to $250. If they place among the top contestants, they win cash—anywhere from $100 at a small-town affair to over $10,000 at Cheyenne, Denver, San Antonio, or one of the other top venues. If they beat everyone else, they get not only the most cash; they also get a big gold buckle to wear. In December, the year's fifteen top money earners in each different event go to the National Finals Rodeo in Las Vegas; after that, the cowboy who has earned the most money in his event during the past year (generally near $100,000) is presented a very big gold buckle that signifies he is champion of the world. (In the early days, several big rodeos, including Pendleton, Cheyenne, and Calgary, each crowned their own "World Champion.") In addition to buckles for bull riding, calf roping, etc., the Professional Rodeo Cowboys Association (PRCA) also awards one extra-fine buckle to the All-Around Cowboy—a man who has won the most money in a single year in two or more events.

Bronc riders and bull riders, whose scores are determined by how well they stay astride a wild animal for an eight-second ride, are the superstars of the game. They have an aura similar to that of a hired gun in a Western movie—the toughest hombre around, a man who lives for kicks but might not be much good on a working ranch.

*Champions in every event win beautiful hand-tooled trophy saddles.*

They are known as roughstock riders because the animals they ride are unbroken, and they are rodeo's superstars because they epitomize cowboy pluck. In fact, bull riding has become so popular these days that there are now some contests around the country with names such as Bullnanza, Bull-o-Rama, Bull Frenzy, Super Bull, and Bullmania, in which all the other events have been completely eliminated for the pure excitement of seeing one determined rider after another try to endure the heat of what some hands like to call "one big snortin' chunk o' chili." Bull riders signify ultimate cowboy charisma because they are free of all the burdens of the cattlehand's trade. Whereas even a bronc rider has to lug around his saddle, and ropers need to take their trained quarter horses with them, bull riders travel light. All they require is their rigging (a rope to wrap around the bull's girth) and their spurs, plus courage and indifference to pain.

## SADDLE BRONC RIDING

The signature performance of rodeo, saddle bronc riding is a feat of skill that comes into the arena straight off the range. In the Old West, wild horses had to be broken so men could ride them. Most big spreads had cowboys who specialized in this arduous task, and there were also traveling outfits who contracted with ranches to come around each summer, after roundup time, and do the breaking. Men who were especially good at it (they did it quickly and authoritatively, and didn't leave behind an animal that hated humans) developed far-flung reputations, and it was only natural for them to want to match their ability against

*"Let 'er buck!"* Above: *Bareback.* Right: *Saddle bronc.*

the most ornery steeds, known as outlaws. On ranches and in early rodeos, bronc riding contests originally had no time limit. A man got on a blindfolded outlaw stallion, the blindfold was removed, and the horse started bucking. The man stayed on until he was thrown off; whoever stayed on the longest was declared the winner.

Nowadays, saddle bronc riding is an eight-second affair, starting when a chute gate opens and horse and rider blast into the arena. If the rider is bucked off in under eight seconds, he gets no score at all. If he makes the eight-second gun, he is evaluated based on four scores, given by two judges, who can award a maximum of twenty-five points each to the horse and to the rider, making a total of 100 points for a perfect ride. The horse is drawn at random, so a cowboy always hopes to get a really rank (meaning high-spirited) one. Its performance is judged on the following criteria, paraphrased from the PRCA rule book:

**1. Front End Moves and Ducks.** Changing direction from side to side as if dodging an obstacle.

**2. How High the Animal's Front Feet Kick.**

**3. Front End Drop.** It should seem as though the animal is sucking backward underneath you with strong effort to throw you over the front of your saddle.

**4. Direction Change or Spin.**

**5. Kicks.** Hard kicks, side kicks, uneven kicks, full extended even kicks, both feet together, high, delayed.

Creates power, drop, rhythm, timing, rocking, and any combination of the above.

**6. Speed and Quickness.**

**7. Timing.** Regularity of speed, kicking effort, and bucking pattern.

**8. Rhythm.** Smooth, even, consistent bucking is preferred over uncoordinated kicks.

**9. Power.** A combination of drop and kick creating stress on the rigging or saddle and jerk on the contestant.

The rule book reminds judges that "If a man makes an outstanding ride on a rank, hard to ride horse, he is entitled to win, not be penalized because he didn't draw one of the cream puffs."

*Jimmy Hazen endures the notorious bucker called Corkscrew. After hanging up his spurs, Hazen became a well-known rodeo announcer.*

"scorn work in any other event except that of bronc riding." Saddle bronc riding is still the classic event, because of its connections to ranch life.

The highest score ever recorded in saddle bronc riding was ninety-five, by Doug Vold on Franklin's Transport, in Meadow Lake, Saskatchewan, in 1979.

## BAREBACK RIDING

The PRCA calls this the most physically demanding contest in rodeo, and the one most likely to result in elbow and lower back injuries. It requires more sheer strength than any other event, because there are no reins and no stirrups. The bareback rider has got to hold on to a bucking, twelve-hundred-pound animal with one hand only; the other has got to stay high in the air. He gets some support and balance

The other half of a cowboy's score is based on how well he does aboard his horse. He is required to synchronize his spurring action with the bucking, placing his feet over the horse's shoulders just before its front feet hit the ground, then quickly drawing them up toward the back of the saddle as the horse lunges up again. He is required to hold on with one hand only and to have his feet touching the horse's shoulder on the first jump out of the chute, then to keep his toes pointed out for the whole ride. He gets credit for the length of his spurring stroke, his timing, and his control, and he is disqualified if he touches the horse, the saddle, or himself with his free hand.

Saddle bronc riders have traditionally been considered the top guns of rodeo. "As a class, they are strongly developed personalities of the rowdy, boisterous type," Clifford P. Westermeier wrote in 1947, adding that they

from his feet and legs, which encircle the horse's rib cage, and which he is required to use to spur the horse vigorously during the entire ride.

The hardest part of bareback riding is to stay on the horse. This is accomplished by holding tight to a rope, called the rigging, that wraps around the horse's chest.

A daredevil bareback rider can choose to ride with a suicide rigging, which means that he wraps the rope around his hand in such a way that it holds him, instead of him holding it. If the horse does manage to buck him off and something's got to give, it will not be the rope rigging; it is usually the bones and ligaments in the cowboy's arm.

Scoring is similar to that in saddle-bronc riding: two judges award twenty-five points each to the horse and twenty-five each to the rider for an eight-second, out-of-the-chutes ride. The highest bareback score on record is ninety-three, by Joe Alexander on Beutler Bros. and Cervi's Marlboro in Cheyenne, Wyoming, in 1974.

## BULL RIDING

Riding a wild bull is not like riding a wild horse. Bulls are fighters; most Brahmans or Brahman crosses, which make up the bulk of rodeo's bovine roughstock, attack things that bother them. They use their horns to gore their quarry, and they swing their heavy heads like cudgels. They weigh up to a ton, but they are nimble; they can spin, twist, reverse, and jump six feet in the air. The mean ones simply do not like people, and they especially do not like people sitting on their backs punching spurs into their hides. To mount one of these creatures and try to stay on top of it for eight seconds as it tries with all its might to heave you off, then gore you, or fling you aside or crush your chest or kick a hole in your skull, is a challenge more dangerous than in any other professional sport.

Bull riding's unique drawing power comes mostly

Top: *Champ Ty Murray sticks on a bull for eight seconds at Cheyenne.*
Bottom: *A cowboy on an airborne saddle bronc in Oklahoma.*

155

from the image of the bulls themselves. Traditionally, they are demonized as red-eyed killers, "wild and vicious human-haters . . . among the meanest, most contemptible, rankest and most easily riled animals on earth," according to 1930s rodeo champ Cecil Cornish in his book *Mr. Rodeo, Himself* (1990). As the *Jaws* movies did for sharks, so the mythology of rodeo has made bulls into an embodiment of evil— a reputation that sells tickets.

As in bareback bronc riding, all a man is allowed to grip (with one hand only) is a rope rigging, which has a big bell attached down below that clangs when the ride begins. If he doesn't last the full eight seconds, he gets no points at all; but if he does go the distance, his maximum score is one hundred, determined by two judges who evaluate both the bull and rider. The bull's score is based on how fast he spins, how mercilessly he kicks, how high he jumps, how suddenly he lunges, how hard he drops, and how cleverly he fades sideways. The rider gets points for aggressiveness (spurring a bull in the neck is worth more than spurring him behind the shoulder), control, and his ability to stay perched high and proud on the middle of the animal's back. In Central Point, Oregon, in 1991, there was a hundred-point bull ride—the only one in history—made by Wade Leslie on Growney's Wolfman.

## CALF ROPING

Roping is timed: whoever does it fastest wins. There is no room for subjective judgment as there is in rough-stock events. Roping is also different from riding a bucking bronc or bull in that it is more about subduing an animal than surviving its fury. Calves, after all, aren't very dangerous or interested in throwing or goring a cowboy.

All a calf wants to do is run away. It is given a head start out of a chute, then a mounted cowboy chases after it, twirling a lariat and carrying a short rope, known as a pigging string, in his teeth. As he throws his lasso around the dogie's neck, his trained horse comes to a quick stop and the cowboy dismounts. He runs along his rope to the calf and flanks it (throws it on the ground), then uses his pigging string to tie three of the calf's legs together. When done, he throws his hands into the air as a signal to the timers to stop the clock; if the calf comes loose in the next six seconds, the cowboy is disqualified. The top calf roping time on record is 5.7 seconds, by Lee Phillips in Assiniboia, Saskatchewan, in 1978.

Opposite: *Veteran Wacey Cathey rides a rank bull.* Above: *Calf roping on the prairie.*

## STEER WRESTLING

Steer wrestlers are a breed apart. Whereas ropers tend to be speedy, agile horsemen, and bull and bronc riders are compact muscle men, most guys who wrestle steers for a living are big, rangy bruisers—the most imposing men in rodeo. The laws of physics demand they be able to pack a wallop. Their job is to drop off a galloping horse onto the back of a running 750-pound animal and wrestle it to the ground in the shortest time possible. They are helped in their effort by a hazer, a horseman who rides along on the opposite side of the steer so it doesn't veer away as the wrestler prepares to jump from his saddle onto the steer.

Dropping off the running horse and latching onto the steer by wrapping both arms around its horns is difficult enough. Then the wrestler has to dig his heels into the ground to stop the forward motion of the steer, and as his boots are plowing up arena dirt, he twists the animal's head as hard as he can, lifting up on the right horn and

"BULL DOGGING"

*A good hazer keeps your steer running straight, but once you drop onto the animal's back, you are on your own.*

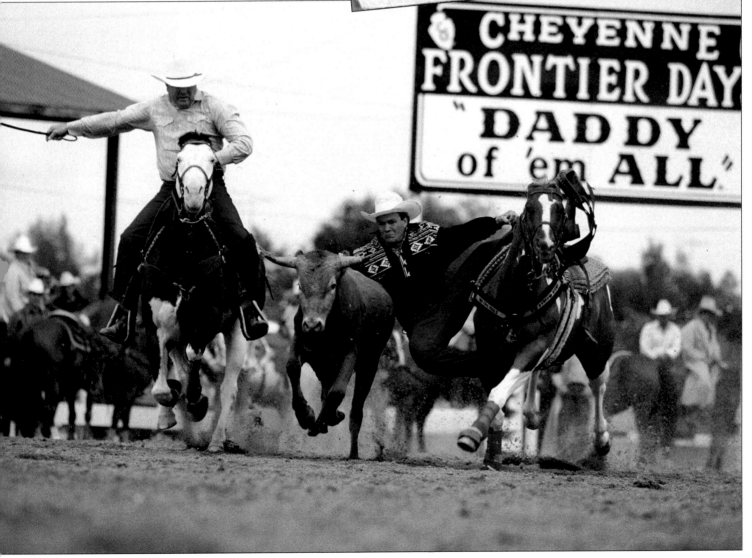

CHEYENNE FRONTIER DAY "DADDY of 'em ALL."

pushing down with his left hand, trying to turn the animal like a corkscrew and wrench it off its feet. As soon as he gets it flat on its side or its back with all four feet and head going in the same direction, the clock stops. Good steer wrestlers need less than 5 seconds to do their job. The record time is 2.2 seconds, set by Oral Harris Zumwalt in Palm Springs, California, in 1939.

In the Autumn 1967 *Oklahoma Today* magazine, Bill Burchardt described how pioneer bulldogger Bill Pickett threw a steer:

*The rider leaped from the saddle. He turned a complete somersault along the length of the steer's back, flying out and down and over the curved horns to fasten his teeth in the side of the steer's mouth. With sheer strength he dragged the running behemoth's head to the tanbark, thrust its horn in the ground, and forward momentum threw the steer hocks over horn in a somersault of its own.*

## TEAM ROPING

A running steer is given a head start out of a chute, then chased by two men with ropes—a header and a heeler. The header must be the first to throw his rope; his job is to lasso the steer around its horns or neck, then dally the rope around his saddle horn and quickly turn the steer away from the heeler, who throws his lariat to catch the steer's hind feet. The clock stops when there is no slack in either rope and both ropers are facing each other with the animal, lassoed front and back and still upright, in between them.

Team roping is the only event in which two contestants work together. The world record is held by Bob Harris and Tee Woolman, who roped a steer in 3.7 seconds in Spanish Fork, Utah, in 1986.

## STEER ROPING

Steer roping demonstrates how cowboys are able to catch and subdue a 750-pound steer that doesn't want to be caught. It can be painful to watch, and of all the rodeo events, it is the one in which animals are most likely to be injured. It is like calf roping, but because a steer is twice as big as a calf, it cannot be picked up by hand and tossed onto its back. What the cowboy does is chase after it on his horse, lasso it around the horns, throw the slack of his rope over the steer's hip, then change directions and ride like crazy, yanking the steer off its feet and, on some occasions, knocking it senseless. When the steer is on its side the cowboy leaps off his horse and ties three of its legs together. The record time for this event is held by Guy Allen: 8.4 seconds, in Garden City, Kansas, in 1987.

## BARREL RACING

Barrel Racing is also known as Girls' Barrel Racing; it is the one event in modern, big-time rodeo reserved for women. Barrel racing is where the money is; top barrel racers earn tens of thousands of dollars in a year, and the world champion takes home six figures.

Scores are based on time. The horse and rider sprint across a starting line and follow a cloverleaf pattern around three barrels, then race back to a finish line. Top scores are under twenty seconds, and sometimes only hundredths of a second separate the top riders; time is added if you knock over a barrel.

# *Championship* BUCKLES

There are loving cups, handsome saddles, and hand-tooled luggage to be won in rodeo, as well as cash, but the prize that means the most is a big gold belt buckle. In rodeo, a buckle is the mark of a champion, and long after the cash is spent and the ribbons and mementos are gathering dust somewhere, that winner's trophy will likely still be gleaming proudly on the belly of the ace who earned it.

Buckles have sentimental value. To pawn one is always a last resort; to wear one you didn't earn is a disgrace, and to wear one you did earn is always good and proper. In an article in *Frontier Times* back in 1971, former rodeo showman Milt Hinkle (he used to bulldog steers by dropping on them from a low-flying crop duster) told the story of Prairie Rose Henderson, who was one of the best-known rodeo contestants in the early years of the sport, and who earned her gold buckle riding saddle broncs. She retired in the 1920s and settled down on a Wyoming ranch. One winter she disappeared in a snowstorm without a trace. Nine years later a woman's remains were found nearby. They were identified as hers by the championship buckle that Prairie Rose always wore.

Every rodeo, from amateur high school tournaments on up to the National Finals, awards a buckle to each competitor who does the best in his or her event. Most

Above: *Cowboy buckles for sale in a pawnshop.* Opposite: *Jim Shoulders wears one of the many he has earned. Shoulders is the winningest cowboy in rodeo history, having earned sixteen World Championship buckles.*

are oval, a few are rectangular, and nearly all are gold-colored metal or silver with gold inlay and sometimes semiprecious stones; even the most modest ones are big—designed to hitch onto a serious, inch-and-a-half-wide belt. A buckle is inscribed with the winner's name and the event for which it was won, and usually with an image of a bucking horse, an angry bull, a steer, or a lariat. Generally speaking, the bigger the buckle the more significant the rodeo that awarded it. There are some championship buckles, from rodeo's gaudier days in the 1950s, that are as big as a prizefighter's belt and virtually impossible to wear. Rodeo groupies are sometimes called buckle bunnies, and it is said they evaluate a potential date by the size of his buckle.

Nearly all winners' buckles are flashy—that's the point of them—but even most of those issued by top rodeos today are of wearable size; proud as a champion might be, it is rarely in his nature to lock his buckle up in a trophy case. When Bob Covin of the *Sunday Oklahoman* interviewed Jim Shoulders a few years after Shoulders retired, Mr. Colvin noticed that when the winningest cowboy in history went about doing chores on his ranch, he wore his 1959 All-Around Cowboy buckle. Shoulders owned sixteen World Champion buckles from which to choose, so the reporter asked him why he wore that one. Shoulders answered, "It holds my britches up."

# Cheyenne Frontier Days Rodeo

NO ONE PERMITTED IN ARENA
DURING SLACK OR PERFORMANCES
UNLESS
DRESSED IN WESTERN...
JEANS BOOTS · COWBOY HATS
AND LONGSLEEVED SHIRTS

DANGER
BULL & HORSE
RUN OUT · ALLEY
KEEP OUT

# *Rodeo* QUEENS

The position of Rodeo Queen is similar to that of other beautiful queens. It lasts only one year, and it is the pinnacle of glamour. To be selected for the job, a woman must be single, young, and pretty. She must be congenial and photogenic. She must be able to answer extemporaneous questions about her personal goals and about issues of the day. In addition, she has to know her way around a horse (horsemanship is a required skill) and how to look sharp in a cowboy hat and boots. Her duty is to be an ambassador of rodeo, which she does by making public appearances during her reign—at fairs, in shopping centers, at schools and senior citizen homes, and before civic groups such as the Moose, the Lions, and the Elks.

Each year, aspirants for the Miss Rodeo America tiara write a brief essay about themselves for the Pageant program book. These self-portraits give a good sense of the kind of character it takes to be a modern Rodeo Queen. Some excerpts from last year's program:

*Rodeo is a traditional part of America, like Mom and apple pie! It is family oriented, respectful of God, and represents a proud part of our American heritage.*

—Sally Money, Miss Rodeo Alabama

*I firmly and sincerely believe that the world's future in all areas depends on the youth of today and tomorrow.*

—Lisa Marie Taylor, Miss Rodeo Arizona

*I've always been fascinated by the American way of life.*

—Theodora J. Smith,
Miss Rodeo New York

*At least once in every person's life, they had a dream of becoming a cowboy. [My goal is] to help others realize their cowboy dreams.*

—Rachelle L. Reavis,
Miss Rodeo Oklahoma

*As Miss Rodeo America I would like to [help] the young people of America set priorities, raise their self-esteem, and attain their goals.*

—Stacey Rae Talbott,
Miss Rodeo Wyoming

*(Miss Talbott became Miss Rodeo America, 1992.)*

Opposite: *These state queens made an appearance at Cheyenne Frontier Days Rodeo in 1992.* Above: *Young Oklahoma rodeo queens gather with a pet pooch, circa 1930.*

# Rodeo's PIONEER WOMEN

In the early days of rodeo, queens were chosen because they rode better and roped better than any of their peers. They were athletes, and they contributed their talent as well as their glamour to the arena. Rodeo began as an anything-goes Wild West show, and women were often featured players—not only as novelty acts. The first female headliner was Prairie Rose Henderson, who was refused entry in the bucking bronc contest at Cheyenne Frontier Days in 1901 until she pointed out to the judges that nothing in

*Three happy cowgirls, including Lucille Roberts (center) and Rene Shelton (right).*

The beautiful Vera McGinnis, a trick rider, toured Europe with a troupe of cowboys and cowgirls in 1924. In London, she gave a command performance for the royal family and rode the royal bridle paths alongside King George V. In 1927, Miss McGinnis shocked the audience at the Fort Worth Fat Stock Show when she performed wearing pants rather than a dress.

the rule book forbade her from trying. Her ride, according to rodeo historian Clifford Westermeier, was magnificent, and "she achieved such notoriety and created such a sensation that many of the rodeos soon included, as a feature event, a cowgirls' bronc riding contest."

Several women's events were on the program at the biggest rodeo staged to that date, in 1916 at Sheepshead Bay Speedway in Brooklyn, a two-week spree at which nearly all the West's renowned rodeo champions were introduced to the East. The stars included Prairie Lilly Allen, who dazzled the crowd with her bronc riding skills; trick riders Tillie Baldwin, Bea Kirnan, and Lottie Vandreau; trick ropers Florence LaDue and Lucille Mulhall; and a fearless woman named Fox Hastings, who not only rode broncs but was also one of the few female steer wrestlers. In her book *The Cowgirls,* Joyce Gibson Roach wrote that Ms. Hastings, who was known for her full-hipped figure, used to call out just before leaving the chute in the steer riding event, "If I can just get my fanny out of the saddle and my feet planted, there's no steer that can last against me."

About the same time Prairie Rose Henderson was making a name for herself, Lucille Mulhall was becoming famous as a cowgirl. An Oklahoma rancher's daughter, Mulhall so impressed Teddy Roosevelt when he saw her performing in a Wild West show in 1900 that that's what he declared her to be—a cowgirl. Until that time, cowgirl was a term unknown

*Cowgirl Montana Bell.*

outside the West, but once Lucille Mulhall was given it, the title became part of rodeo (and after that, of movies, too). Mulhall was five feet tall and weighed ninety pounds, but she was able to ride and rope and bulldog steers as good as almost any man, even encumbered by a long broadcloth skirt and billowing silk shirtwaist blouse. "Cowgirls did not wear pants in the early days," Patrick Dawson noted in his book, *Mr. Rodeo* (1986). "They favored long, split skirts and high-button shoes. Some of them were genteel ladies when they weren't aboard a spinning bronc. Some were wilder than the rest."

One of the best-known female rodeo stars in the early days was Mabel Strickland of Walla Walla, Washington. Fresh out of high school, she won prizes as a trick rider throughout the 'teens, then tried to marry and settle down on a ranch in Idaho. But she and her husband (himself a bronc rider) couldn't resist the lure of the rodeo, so they returned to the sport and hit the circuit in the 1920s. Mabel soon gained nationwide fame not only as a trick rider but also as a bronc rider, a steer rider, and a relay racer. In his *Who's Who of Rodeo* (1982), Willard H. Porter wrote that she was "one of the most beloved cowgirls on the old-time circuit . . . classy and stylish . . . graceful in everything she tried."

MABEL STRICKLAND
QUEEN OF THE
PENDLETON ROUND-UP
— 1927 —

(DOUBLEDAY)

# A Sampling of RODEO GREATS

## GARY LEFFEW

Once known as "the hippie cowboy" because of his long hair, Gary Leffew soared to success as a bull rider in the late 1960s and became champion of the world in 1970. He was different from other rodeo champions. He attributed his victories not so much to grit or gumption or luck, but to the power of positive imaging (programming his mind to think like a winner), which he learned by reading Maxwell Maltz's self-help book *Psycho-Cybernetics*. He also gave credit to garlic cloves and alfalfa tablets, which he ate, and to cod liver oil, which he drank to wash down the garlic and alfalfa. Leffew believed that he could convince himself he was a winner, and by doing so become one; part of the program was to brag and boast before a rodeo like Muhammad Ali before a fight. A lot of his competitors—cowboys who adhered to the taciturn code of the West—thought he was a cocky blowhard, but when Leffew got on a bull, stuck his chest out, gritted his teeth, and called, "Let 'er buck," he made believers out of them all.

Now retired from the arena, Leffew has built upon his reputation as a self-made success and become one of the star veterans of rodeo. He appears in honorary functions at dozens of rodeos every year and has put his talents as a positive thinker to use at the Gary Leffew Bull Riding School, where he tells students, "You've got to get this one thing in your mind: you did not come to the rodeo to wimp out; you came to ride, and you came to win. Remember: you are the stud horse with the fuzzy balls."

*Gary Leffew, Oklahoma City, 1970:*
*Bull riding champion of the world.*

*Superstars Jim Shoulders and Casey Tibbs teach rope know-how to a crippled boy.*

*Casey Tibbs, the greatest rodeo cowboy of all time.*

## CASEY TIBBS

In October 1951, Casey Tibbs appeared on the cover of *Life* magazine and won the saddle bronc riding and bareback riding contests in America's richest rodeo—at Madison Square Garden in New York; then he went on to become All-Around World Champion Cowboy. He was on top of the world, the superstar of a sport that was transforming its image from old-fashioned cattlehand fun into show business.

Casey Tibbs did more than anyone to make rodeo seem big-time. As a rider, he had a style and authority that inspired audiences: Wearing a purple cowboy shirt, with a jaunty bandanna on his neck, he seemed to float above a bucking horse, his chaps flying and spurs flashing like no one had ever seen. Famous for his incandescence on anything that bucked, Tibbs raised hell just as ferociously outside the arena. He relished the high life of a champion, indulged his taste for pretty women and good whiskey, spent money as fast as he earned it, and

delighted in giving chase to state troopers in his purple Cadillac (it matched his shirt).

In 1989, a bigger-than-life-size bronze statue of him aboard the bucking bronc Necktie was dedicated outside the Pro Rodeo Hall of Fame in Colorado Springs, Colorado (see page 376). It is titled "Champion," and sculptor Edd Hayes said that inside the bronze, where no one can see, he inscribed a heart with the words, *Ride, cowboy, ride.* Country singer Charlie Daniels called Tibbs "As Western as the sunset, and cowboy to the core."

## JIM SHOULDERS

Jim Shoulders may have broken more bones than any other rodeo star (one time he broke his leg in five places; *Life* wrote about him under the headline "Mr. Broken Bones"), but his osteo-biography is only partly why he's famous. The really important reason is that he won more World Championship buckles than anybody else: sixteen altogether, including five as All-Around Cowboy, seven for bull riding, and four for bareback bronc riding.

In addition to his talent and his legendary indifference to pain and injury, Shoulders is also significant as one of the first rodeo stars to parlay his arena success into a career as an image—the quintessential rodeo cowboy. Tall and lanky, outfitted in rakish but not gaudy Western wear, and with a slow, Oklahoma drawl and a deadpan wit, Shoulders plays the part of a flinty good old cowboy with ineffable aplomb. He was one of the original Miller Lite Beer All-Stars in TV commercials (with Billy Martin in 1979), and he has been a spokesman for Wrangler since 1948. He chuckled recently when he told us, "I have been associated with Wrangler longer than anybody in the company. I have outlived all the presidents and everybody else there."

After he retired from roughstock riding in 1961, Jim Shoulders became a stock contractor, opened the first bull riding school, and began producing the Mesquite Rodeo, which is now broadcast weekly on cable TV. When he was profiled for *True* magazine in 1960, Shoulders told journalist Paul Friggens, "Don't write anything sentimental—you know, smell of the arena and all that baloney. I don't like to smell an ol' bull any better than you do a typewriter, but it's the only way I know to latch on to $50,000 a year." Friggens summed up Shoulders's significance to rodeo as "what Babe Ruth, Ty Cobb, and Mickey Mantle might conceivably add up to in baseball."

Above: *Jim Shoulders with a suitcase presented by Del's Leather Shop of Riverton, Wyoming, in 1960.* Right: *Ty Murray, reigning all-around cowboy since 1989.*

## TY MURRAY

Ty Murray, modern rodeo's greatest champion, entered six different rodeos over the weekend of July 4th, 1993, and earned money at every one. That weekeend he became the seventh cowboy in history to top the million dollar mark in arena earnings—at the ripe old age of twenty-three. He has won 106 trophy saddles so far and holds the records for single season earnings($258,750 in 1991) and single rodeo earnings ($21,714 at Houston in 1993).

Ty is simply the best there is, and he is a rarity these days: a cowboy who rides bareback, saddle broncs, and bulls with equal skill and success. He has won the PRCA championship buckle every year since 1989, and veteran champ Larry Mahan said he expected Ty to keep the title for at least a half dozen more years. Recently *Prorodeo Sports News* quoted Ty's father Butch as saying, "I can't ever remember Ty not being a cowboy. If he wasn't doing it, he was talking about it." He rode his first calf when he was two years old, won best-dressed cowboy award in a local parade when he was twenty-two months old, and worked all summer when he was twelve years old so he could buy a bucking machine to practice in his backyard. His parents said they took him home from the hospital in a tiny pair of cowboy booties.

# Rodeo Names

odeo has the strangest-named contestants of any pro sport. Cowboys have always seemed to like expressive monikers, from the real West's James Butler "Wild Bill" Hickok, to TV's "Hoss" Cartwright of "Bonanza" and the movies' "Man with No Name." These are a few of the rodeo names we especially like:

**ACE BERRY** (bareback rider)
**BOYD SLICK HANZLIK** (barrel man)
**CHEYENNE PIPKIN** (announcer)
**CODY CUSTER** (bull rider)
**COTTON YANCEY** (announcer)
**COTY BATTLES** (steer wrestler)
**GUMBO LAMB** (saddle bronc rider)
**HOUSTON POWERS** (top cowboy)
**MONK DISHMAN** (bareback rider)
**OTE BERRY** (steer wrestler)
**PINE GILBERT** (top cowboy)
**POW CARTER** (calf roper)
**QUAIL DOBBS** (barrel man)
**RED LEMMEL** (top cowboy)
**ROWDY BARRY** (bull fighter)

**S. Z. ZOOP DOVE** (announcer)
**SKEETER HUMBLE** (saddle bronc rider)
**SPIKE GUARDIPEE** (team roper)
**SPUNK SASSER** (team roper)
**TEE WOOLMAN** (team roper)
**TOOTER WAITES** (calf roper)
**TUTT GARNETT** (steer roper)
**WACEY CATHEY** (bull rider)
**WEASEL HODNETT** (bull rider)

*Tuff Hedeman, bull rider.*

# LANE FROST

The James Dean of rodeo, a young idol cut down in his prime, Lane Frost was a legend even before he died. The Oklahoma bull rider was champion of the world in 1987, at age twenty-four, and the following year he electrified crowds in a season-long duel with a bull named Red Rock, who was as rank as any creature gets, never once having been ridden for a full eight seconds. Frost, who was known for unparalleled riding finesse, as well as for the dashing feather he stuck in the brim of his wide Oklahoma cowboy hat and his boyish good looks, managed to go the distance four out of the seven times. His battle with Red Rock made him as beloved a hero as rodeo has ever had, and a role model for hundreds of up-and-coming bull riders in Little Britches rodeos and high school contests.

The next year, at Cheyenne Frontier Days, Frost drew a notorious wide-horned eliminator named Bad to the Bone. When he predicted an eighty-five-point ride to his buddies in the chutes, they shook their heads in disbelief. Frost managed to complete a successful ride, then let himself get bucked off toward the back, as was his usual dismounting style; but before his score was posted, Bad to the Bone turned around and hooked him with a horn, driving him into the arena dirt and crushing his chest. Frost struggled to his feet and waved for help, then died. His score: eighty-five points.

*Lane Frost with his nemesis, Red Rock.*

*Larry Mahan rode everything that bucked. Usually, though, he didn't use a saddle on a bull.*

# LARRY MAHAN

All-Around Champion Cowboy from 1966 to 1970 and again in 1973, Larry Mahan rode bulls, bareback, and saddle broncs. Known among fellow contestants as "Super Saddle," and described by *Time* magazine as "the cowboy in the gray flannel suit," he did more than any man to make rodeo seem like a modern athletic contest rather than ranch-hand revelry. Rodeo stars before Mahan tended to cultivate their Wild West bravado. They drank heavily, partied all night, and were proud not to have been affected too much by the commercial side of rodeo. Mahan was known for giving out business cards to everyone he met. He piloted his own plane so he could travel more efficiently. He worked out in a gym, and didn't drink or smoke. He kept a journal of written notes about bulls and horses he might draw to ride. He wrote *Fundamentals of Rodeo Riding* and started his own school. He leased his name to a line of Western wear. And—unlike so many rodeo cowboys before him—he retired from the arena a rich, well-invested man.

## CHARMAYNE JAMES-RODMAN

One of the winningest contestants in rodeo history, Charmayne Rodman set a record in 1992 when she won her ninth world championship in a single event. She *owns* the sport of barrel racing, which she began dominating in 1984, while still in high school. Her first season on the road, she mailed in her homework from wherever she was competing, and she won a Dodge truck that she wasn't yet old enough to drive. In 1990 she became the first cowgirl ever to win a million dollars in prize money; in many of her championship years she has earned more than double her nearest competitor. To see her streak around a dirt arena at full tilt, without an inch of slack when she swoops low around a barrel, then charges dead ahead, is to behold a horse and rider in consummate harmony. In fact, Ms. Rodman credits her success to her horse Scamper, a bay gelding whom she has ridden since she began competing. "He's one in a million. He's a miracle," she said. "I doubt there will ever be another horse like him."

*Charmayne James-Rodman with Scamper.*

*Bill Pickett, bulldogger.*

## BILL PICKETT

Bill Pickett invented the sport of steer wrestling. He and four brothers began in the cowboy business as bronco busters in Taylor, Texas, in the 1890s, their handbill advertising "good treatment to all animals . . . catching and taming wild cattle a specialty." Because the cattle they had to catch frequently eluded the lasso by running among mesquite brush, Bill Pickett used a trick he had learned by watching ranchers' bulldogs hold cows immobile: he bit them. Bulldogs were frequently used to flush elusive cattle out of thick brush, then to clamp their jaws down on the big animals' sensitive upper lips. This caused the cow to freeze, allowing cowboys to rope it. Pickett figured out that he could ride alongside a steer, jump onto it, grab its head, then bring it to the ground by latching his teeth onto its lip. Around the turn of the century, Pickett began exhibiting this skill at county fairs in Texas, then throughout the ranching states.

Pickett was the first well-known African-American in rodeo. Although there were plenty of black cowboys (estimated about one in five—mostly freed slaves in Texas), the "Dusky Demon," as he was frequently billed, was permitted to perform at some otherwise all-white rodeos only because what he did was considered an exhibition rather than a true cowboy sport. He became a featured performer with the 101 Ranch Show, and continued to demonstrate his abilities into the 1920s, sometimes wrestling a steer to the ground with both hands tied behind his back. By the time Pickett died in 1932 (a horse kicked him in the head), steer wrestling was on the bill at many rodeos, but few people did it his way. According to Pickett's biographer, Colonel Bailey C. Hanes, "most cowboys were repulsed at taking the snotty upper lip of a steer in their mouths." Furthermore, humane groups protested Pickett's methods, and by the teens, biting was forbidden at most rodeos. Now no one bites a steer, but steer wrestling has endured, and it is still called bulldogging.

# WARREN G. (FRECKLES) BROWN

"Freckles Brown could be elected Governor of Oklahoma tonight," proclaimed steer roper Everett Shaw one evening in December 1967, when Brown received a five-minute standing ovation at the National Finals Rodeo. He had just spent eight hair-raising seconds astride the back of Tornado, a bull that had never before been successfully ridden, but the applause was for more than that historic ride. Freckles Brown had become a legend—indestructible and eternal. He was forty-six years old when he rode Tornado—long past normal retirement age for a bull rider—and he was in his thirtieth year of rodeoing.

In 1962, when Brown was bull riding champion of the world, he had a hard time walking to receive his championship buckle, and he was unable to sit on his championship saddle, because his neck was broken and in a cast from a bull wreck he had suffered at the hands of a

*Freckles Brown waited until the cast was removed from his broken neck to resume bull riding.*

Brahman named Black Smoke at the end of the season. "The amount of try you have," he said, "determines if you really have the desire and courage it takes to be a winning cowboy." He returned to the arena after his neck injury and rode bulls until his retirement in 1974. When Kristine Fredriksson, author of *American Rodeo*, asked him if he worried about getting hurt or dying, he answered, "I'm thinkin' about winnin'. It never crosses my mind that I might get hurt; I don't even think about that."

## THE GREENOUGHS

The Greenoughs are the best-known family in rodeo. The patriarch was Packsaddle Ben Greenough, who ran away from an orphanage in New York, worked for Calamity Jane, and won the first bucking horse contest in Montana in 1898. Four of his eight children became rodeo hands: Marge, Bill, Turk, and Alice. Marge and Alice began in the 1920s with the King Brothers Rodeo, where they learned to ride steers, barebacks, and saddle broncs; they then joined up with "Mr. Rodeo," Leo Cremer, whose traveling show was the most successful rodeo company of its day. They competed from New York to California, in England and Australia; Alice—known as Queen of the Lady Bronc Riders—was riding fighting bulls in Spain when the revolution started. While Alice was a strength rider, and Marge depended more on balance, both of them were equally famous for their high-fashion arena wear, including Alice's giant hat and the bell-bottom riding pants that Marge made using her own portable sewing machine. (Bell-bottoms soon became standard cowgirl attire.)

*The Greenoughs, sometime in the 1930s: Marge, Bill, Turk, Alice.*

Bill Greenough rode saddle bronc, wrestled steers, and roped calves, and Turk was one of the greatest bronc riders of his era, earning championship buckles throughout the 1930s. Turk is also remembered as one of the best stuntmen in Western movies, and for his romance with exotic dancer Sally Rand, whom he married in 1941. Ms. Rand called Turk "my perfect man," and planned to settle down on a ranch on Greenough family land in Red Lodge, Montana, but the marriage ended in 1943—the year Turk won his last saddle bronc riding championship.

Marge's son, Chuck Henson, became one of the all-time great rodeo clowns, selected Clown of the Year by *Hoofs and Horns* (a rodeo magazine) in 1979, and in 1992 Deb Greenough, Bill's grandson, won the bareback riding contest at the PRCA National Finals Rodeo in Las Vegas.

# RALPH (R. R.) DOUBLEDAY

Ralph Doubleday never earned a championship buckle on a horse or bull; he was a rodeo star of a different sort. Doubleday was a photographer who traveled the circuit for well over two decades, starting in 1910 when he took what *Hoofs and Horns* called "the first actual picture ever made of a cowboy in mid-air after leaving a bucking horse." His action shots have never been bettered, and today they provide a magnificent chronicle of rodeo in its Wild-West era. Working with a huge wooden camera that took two strong hands to carry, Doubleday didn't know the modern luxuries of a telephoto lens or autofocus; he didn't even use *rolls* of film, for his camera required five-by-seven-inch glass plates painted with photographic emulsion, which had to be positioned for each single shot. To get a picture, Doubleday planted himself on the dirt floor of the arena, as near to the action as he dared, focusing and framing in an instant, then tripping his shutter at pre-

cisely the moment of peak interest. That night, he went to his rented room, developed the glass plate negatives, and made prints; the next day his assistant—a young girl whom he called his niece—sold the pictures to fans in the grandstand. Many of Doubleday's best rodeo photos were hand-tinted and made into postcards, which played an immeasurable role in broadcasting the allure of the cowboy sport.

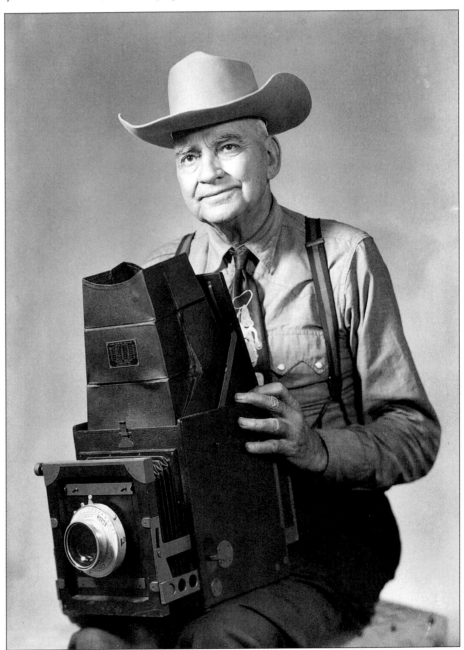

*R. R. Doubleday and the camera he used to capture arena action.*

# *Hall of Fame*
# RODEO ANIMALS

## TORNADO

Bulls are livestock, and unlike horses, they do not often make cowboys feel sentimental. In rodeo, many bulls don't even get steady names—they go by a number, or the label of their contractor or a commercial sponsor, and their names get changed to fit circumstances. Even the rankest ones are forgotten as soon as their bucking career is over. Tornado—a fifteen-hundred-pound red Hereford-Brahman cross with a white face—was a rare exception. Now interred on the grounds of the National

*Freckles Brown endures Tornado in 1967: the greatest bull ride of all time.*

Cowboy Hall of Fame in Oklahoma City, in a plot right alongside those of some of the greatest bucking horses, Tornado was described by his owner, Jim Shoulders, as "the best rodeo bull I ever saw—not the rankest and maybe not the hardest to ride, but the one that put on the best show for the people in the grandstands." He did whatever he had to do to buck men off, he chased clowns around the arena, and he looked mean as hell, although cowboys knew that he was not a killer.

Jim Shoulders discovered Tornado when the young animal was on his way to the slaughterhouse at El Campo, Texas (the bull had flunked a fertility test), and once Shoulders saw him buck, he realized that Tornado was one in a million. He bucked off 220 men before he was finally ridden by Freckles Brown in the National Finals Rodeo in Oklahoma City in 1967—the most famous bull ride ever. When Tornado's bucking career came to an end in 1969, Shoulders put him out to pasture at his ranch in Henryetta, Oklahoma, where he finally died in 1972, at age fifteen, of what veterinarians thought to be hardware disease—a nail or piece of wire, eaten with feed, lodged in one of his stomachs. "He went pretty good," Shoulders said. "Died with his toes up."

# OSCAR

Oscar was a small hump-backed Brahman bull who bucked off 292 of the 300 cowboys who tried to ride him during his career from 1970 to 1978. His violent spin was legendary. Early in his career he was known for his eagerness to maim those he dislodged, but after several seasons of hurling riders off his back, the mature Oscar learned to simply ignore the men he had conquered. Those few who did manage to endure eight seconds of Oscar's ire earned the highest marks (Don Gay got ninety-seven points on him in 1977, and clinched the title of World Champion doing so), and to this day his progeny—many of whom show evidence of his savage bucking style—are bovine aristocrats, and are considered some of the rankest bulls there are.

When Oscar's bucking days were through, his sterling reputation earned him retirement in Colorado Springs, where he spent his sunset years chewing cud and napping in a comfortable pen adjacent to the Professional Rodeo Cowboy Association offices. One time, however, Oscar got loose and vanished. Recalling his arena reputation as a hoofed demon, several of the staff of the PRCA

*Oscar, in retirement.*

mounted horses and went after him, through the streets of Colorado Springs, lariats twirling, ready for a battle royale with one of the scariest bulls that ever came out of a rodeo chute. They found Oscar in someone's backyard, sniffing laundry that had been hung out to dry. The ropes weren't needed. Oscar was happy to see his keepers, and trotted back to the PRCA, where he remained until 1982 when, enfeebled by rheumatism and arthritis, he was put to sleep.

## MIDNIGHT

Midnight was a big black gelding who hated having anybody on his back. Few professional rodeo cowboys could ride him, and in his heyday in the 1920s he was often brought into the arena out of competition, whereupon he was offered up to any person in the grandstand who dared try to survive eight seconds on him. (For a dollar entry fee, you could win a thousand if you stayed aboard, but no one ever did.) In 1930, three years before his last ride (he bucked off the great Turk Greenough at Cheyenne), the Prosser Martin Saddle Shop of Del Rio, Texas, included a poem in its fall catalogue, written by Tim Hinton, a Louisiana cowboy in the U.S. Army stationed in Georgia. Here are some excerpts:

## OL' MIDNIGHT

*Listen, cowboy, I have a story to tell,*
*Of a black Percheron hoss that is tough as hell.*
*He was the mount of a schoolmarm up Canada way,*
*And a well-behaved pony in his early day.*

*The schoolmarm would feed him morning and night,*
*And had 'im so he'd turn to the left or the right.*
*But the lady who rode him to school each day,*
*Turned him loose in the Spring and went away.*
*So the big black horse that I'm talking about,*
*Ate green grass all summer and grew plenty stout.*

*So when the Fall round-up was on in full swing,*
*A cowpoke from Calgary was short one hoss in his string.*
*He told the boss, who was rollin' his pack,*
*That he knew where there roamed a beautiful black.*

*. . .*

*They roped and saddled him, then climbed on the fence,*

*Then some crazy puncher said, "Go get your flank cinch";*
*This was the undoin' of the whole damn bunch.*
*Said Earl to Pete, "I had a hunch,*
*'Cause when I forked that cayuse and he looked around—*
*I had a sneaky feelin' that I was comin' down."*

*Fellers, the way that hoss bucks is simply a fright,*
*So let's name the critter, OL' MIDNIGHT!*
*"Sure," said Smoky, "That's just the thing,*
*And we'll ship the ol' devil to the McCarty-Elliott string."*

*. . .*

*The cowboys have learned to respect this black hoss,*
*'Cause when they get on, they sure get off.*
*But try him they will, and they have lots of fun,*
*Trying to stay up and get the job done.*

*Just a few more words and then I'm through—*
*I'll bet you three to one that he can sack you!*

*. . .*

*They'll see that you are on, and screwed down tight,*
*Open the gate and turn you out right.*

*Then it's Hell, boys; Hell and a terrible fright,*
*But pay off, puncher, 'cause you've left Midnight.*
*Don't get mad and feel all hurt,*
*'Cause you blew both stirrups and hit the dirt.*
*Just pick yourself up with your hat in your hand,*
*And remember Midnight's a horse,*
*And you're a MAN.*

## FIVE MINUTES TO MIDNIGHT

Rounded up in 1924 with a bunch of wild horses on the Sarcee Indian reservation in Alberta, Canada, and saved from the slaughterhouse by a purchasing agent from the Calgary Stampede who bought him on a hunch for five dollars, Five Minutes to Midnight was probably the best bucking bronc in rodeo history. He was named Tumbling Mustard when he started his career in 1926, but he was black like the then-famous bronc Midnight (although he had small white socks on his hind legs and a white blaze on his head), so when Tumbling Mustard started to buck cowboys off as successfully as Midnight, his name was changed. "Little Five" was only about nine hundred pounds, with a fuzz tail and a shaggy coat that always looked unkempt. He bucked off more than two thousand men during an amazing career that lasted until he injured a leg in 1944; even after his retirement, when he was brought back into the arena for ceremonial purposes at a Portland, Oregon, rodeo in 1946, he bucked off the last man to try to ride him. When rodeo officials attempted to put a garland of flowers around his neck to commemorate his magnificent career, Little Five bolted and ran away. He died the following year, and was described in one eulogy as "a tornado of horseflesh, swiveling, spinning, sky-climbing in a blur of fury." His original tombstone on owner Verne Elliott's ranch in Colorado carried these words: "He was the bronc they couldn't break."

inutes of Midnite
Earl Thode the "works"

# "*The Rhythm of* RODEO"

## BY BELVA LOWERY

**B**elva Lowery was born in 1910 on a ranch north of Burwell, Nebraska. When she was eleven years old, Burwell staged its first rodeo as part of the Garfield County Frontier Fair. Mrs. Lowery recalls that her husband, a rancher, and his hired hands (then her three sons) all took part in local amateur rodeos, and each year during the week of the Big Rodeo, the hay crew was dismissed on Wednesday night so that everyone could attend the festivities. Now two of Mrs. Lowery's grandsons are rodeo hands, and when we asked for permission to reprint her poem, she sent us a snapshot of her great-grandson, about five years old, twirling a lariat.

# THE RHYTHM OF RODEO

From the grandstand high 'neath the bright blue sky
    Watch the colorful pageant below.
Hear the rhythmic beat of the galloping feet!
    'Tis the rhythm of the rodeo.

The cowboys' hats, and their spurs and chaps
    And the horses they ride in the show
Plus the colorful crowd, cheering wild and loud
    Are the enchantments of rodeo.

The arena hums with the beat of the drums
    Of high school bands marching by.
And all thrill to Old Glory as the band tells the story
    Of banners unfurled in the sky.

Hear the din and the clatter as the horsebackers scatter
    In the beautiful serpentine ride;
And Indians dressed gaily, doing folk dances daily
    To the beat of drums made of hide.

The rodeo queen, well-mounted and keen,
    Adds glamour to this wild west show.
The officials are cheered, the arena is cleared
    It's on with the rodeo!

The gates open wide. There's bedlam inside
    As the wild scramble comes into view.
There are humor and thrills and quite a few spills.
    There are hometown boys in the crew.

With spurs shoulder high, and a leap to the sky
    A bareback rider comes pronto,
His spurred heels flying, his balance defying
    That zigzagging, sunfishing bronco.

A calf roper's need is talent and speed,
    And a horse well trained and fast
For the calf must be caught, and its kicking fought
    While making a tie that will last.

Look! Out of that chute comes a big husky brute
    A saddle bronc and cowboy together.
He bucks and he bawls, and twisting he falls
    And the unlucky cowboy pulls leather.

A dogging team waits till they open the gates,
    Then the race for the longhorn is on.
When the dogger draws near he leaps for the steer
    And throws him with muscle and brawn.

There's a breathtaking lull when an old Brahma bull
    Goes after the rider he's thrown.
But the spectators scream, when the bull big and mean
    Is foiled by the rodeo clown.

And all of the while, the daredevil style
    Of events on the track catch the eye.
Trained horses pacing, quarterhorse racing
    And trick ropers and riders flash by.

The race of the barrels put on by the girls
    And other events of the show
Are not featured here, but they will appear
    At Nebraska's Big Rodeo.

The Midland Empire Fair and Rodeo, circa 1930.

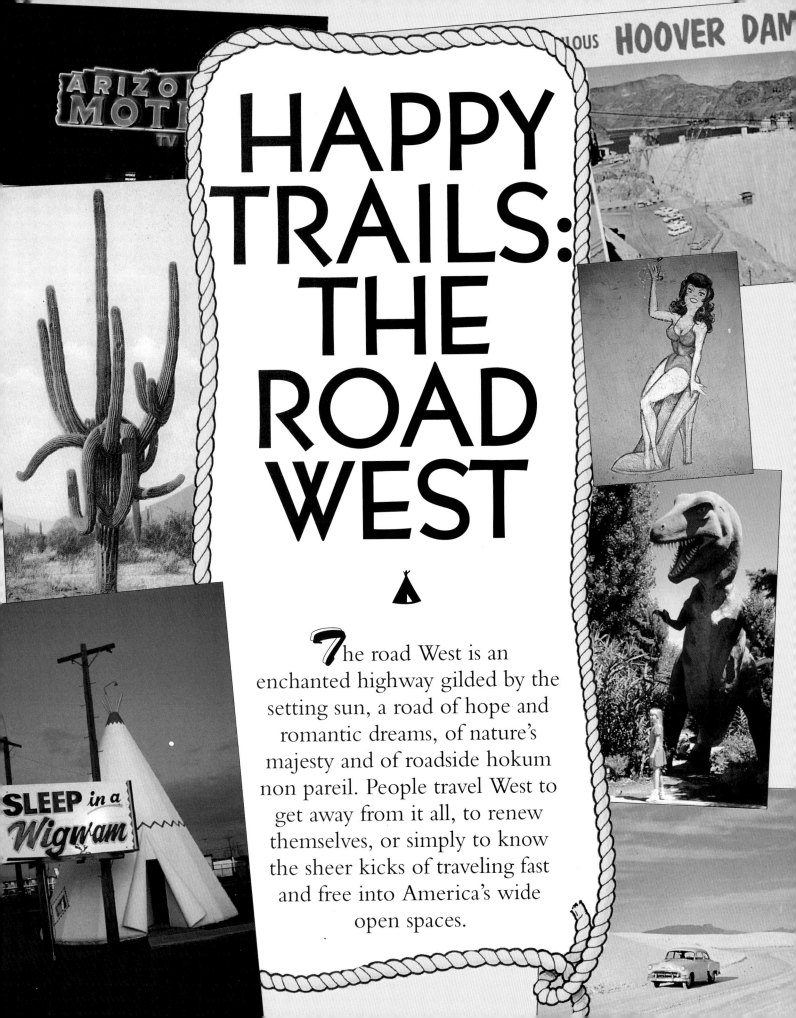

# HAPPY TRAILS: THE ROAD WEST

**7**he road West is an enchanted highway gilded by the setting sun, a road of hope and romantic dreams, of nature's majesty and of roadside hokum non pareil. People travel West to get away from it all, to renew themselves, or simply to know the sheer kicks of traveling fast and free into America's wide open spaces.

# *Happy Trails:* THE ROAD WEST

**7**he West, where the sun sets, holds travelers in its golden thrall. To ride hard along the freedom road under the West's big sky is a kind of elation that travelers have relished from the days of rutted covered wagon trails to those of superhighways lined with Stuckeys. Awesome scenic wonders, awful roadside ballyhoo, and the sheer rapture of *moving on* make the road West a magic place to be. Long before Roy Rogers and Dale Evans sang their theme song, "Happy Trails [to You]," New York newspaperman Horace Greeley exhorted Americans to "Go West, young man" (a summons Greeley expropriated from an Indiana pressman). Even before Greeley, Henry David Thoreau rhapsodized, "Eastward I go only by force; but westward I go free."

Going free is what the road West is all about. It is a road of adventure and of better tomorrows—in literature, movies, and folklore, and sometimes even in reality. The Joad family in John Steinbeck's *The Grapes of Wrath* (1939) flees West along the "Mother Road" to escape the Dust Bowl. When songwriter Bobby Troup got out of the Army in 1945, he vowed to find his future by driving to Los Angeles, a trip that inspired his song, "Get Your Kicks on Route 66." In John Ford's movie *Wagon Master* (1950), the pioneers' historic trek along the Mormon Trail is a rousing story of renewal in America's Promised Land. For Jack Kerouac's desolation angels in *On the Road* (1957), "the darkness of the West" was a spiritual elixir, and the thrill of traveling he extolled—"a fast car, a coast to reach, and a woman at the end of the road"—has had an existential allure for generations of wanderers in postwar America. In *Thelma & Louise* (1991), two women speed West in a blue-green Thunderbird on an intoxicating quest to feel free.

The road takes many forms. It can be the dirt trail of cowboys cantering through the chaparral in the dewy cool of the early morning; it can be the gleaming silver rails of the *Empire Builder,* whisking passengers underneath a cloudless Rocky Mountain sky; it can be the concrete superhighway where truck drivers' noxious diesels drone through the night. The speed and vehicle don't matter; however the trip is made, America's restless nomads have always gone West in search of answers. Their goal might be a fresh start and a brand-new life, or a rollicking family vacation and a station wagon full of souvenirs, or perhaps it's the pure, soulful kicks of traveling fast and free: whether its purposes are grand or goofy, an odyssey into the West is a rite of passage.

In the century before there were cars and highways,

*From a National Van Lines promotional brochure, about 1950: "The covered wagons have disintegrated, like the bones of those who built them, into the dust of the ages, gone but not forgotten."*

the frontier was originally thought to be a perilous wilderness, which homesteaders crossed to find their El Dorado. The trip was not necessarily along a happy trail; the desert in particular was considered repellent and empty. *In Search of the Golden West,* Earl Pomeroy's book about tourism, quotes one early visitor to the Grand Canyon scoffing at its rawness: "It is no place for a gentleman, sir!" And a tourist who passed through Santa Fe in the 1880s complained that the old adobe city was "completely uninteresting and unimaginably ugly. In fact, the people of Santa Fe seem utterly destitute of taste."

Around 1900 the West started to beguile Americans who felt they needed an antidote to the press of civilization. What had once appeared barren, coarse, and primitive began to be perceived as America's unspoiled paradise. "We shall, like the Athenians of old, 'delicately march in pellucid air,'" a Westward-bound train traveler wrote in the 1890s. "We must cross deserts and scale mountains till we reach the Eden of the West." There were no teeming slums in this newly ennobled West; there were no sweatshops or stinking factories. On the contrary, the West became a place to renew one's soul—in the wide-open spaces under skies that were not cloudy all day, in the presence of majestic nature, inspired by colorful native peoples. In the *Atlantic Monthly* in 1903, Mary Austin wrote of the Mojave Desert's "lotus charm . . . deep breaths, deep sleep, and the communion of stars." A traveler to Santa Fe in 1911 described it as "the only picturesque spot in America yet undiscovered by the jaded globetrotter."

Americans grew smitten with the West as a naturalist's utopia, and by the teens and twenties, there were high-

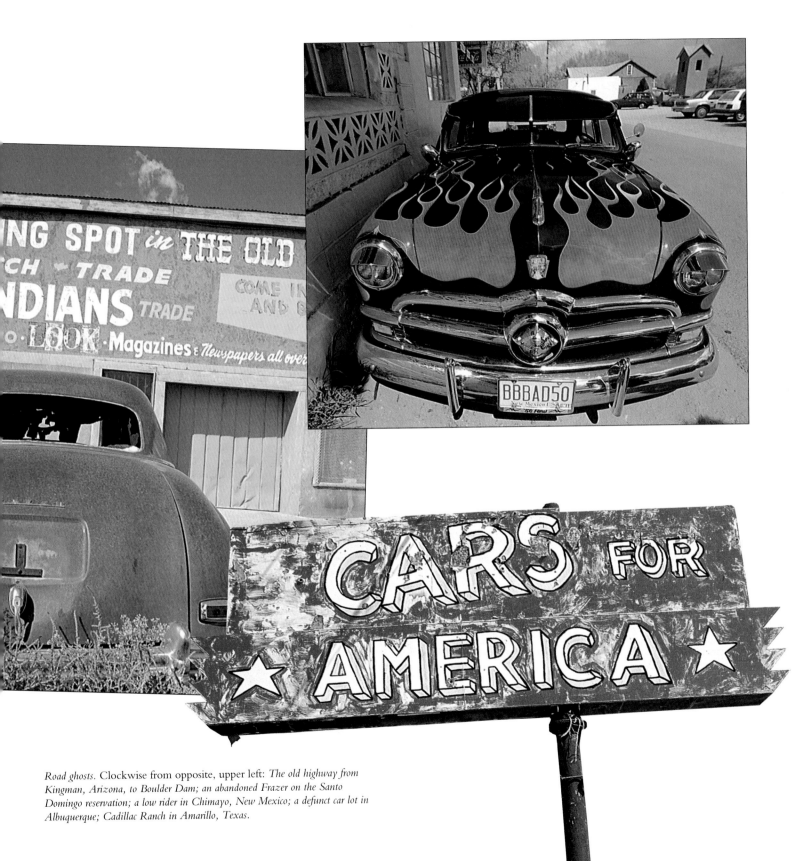

*Road ghosts.* Clockwise from opposite, upper left: *The old highway from Kingman, Arizona, to Boulder Dam; an abandoned Frazer on the Santo Domingo reservation; a low rider in Chimayo, New Mexico; a defunct car lot in Albuquerque; Cadillac Ranch in Amarillo, Texas.*

Left: *Joseph City, Arizona.* Above: *Domingo, New Mexico.*

ways and swift trains to take them there. Luxury hotels throughout the region boasted of their frontier themes: log roofs, animal-skin rugs, cattle skulls on the wall. Glacier National Park Hotel hired Blackfoot Indians to beat a tom-tom serenade for guests in the dining room. The Santa Fe Railroad began issuing its famous Indian-themed calendar, using glamorized paintings of Native Americans to represent the natural dignity and freedom to be found far from the cities of the East. It began its "Indian Detour" service in 1926, and ran trains called the *Chief,* the *Super Chief,* and the *Navajo;* in 1929 it introduced a courier on each of the trains outfitted in Navajo blouse, concha belt, and turquoise necklace who, Earl Pomeroy reports, "had been through 'intensive training under recognized authorities on Southwestern history, archaeology, and Indian lore.'"

Before there were limited-access superhighways, a car trip West was an odyssey into the strange, sometimes scary, and always beguiling subculture of back-road America. It meant traveling along rickety two-lanes that fed you smack through dozens of jerkwater towns along the way, past weathered cattle skulls that decorated gas stations and ancient Model Ts that were abandoned by the roadside where the Okies left them. You passed the pawnshops and the honky-tonks on the wrong side of the tracks, the Woodmen of the World Lodge, the high school and its football field, the town square and its war memorial, the cemetery and the auto salvage yard. You ate chicken-fried steak in a diner on the outskirts of town and slept in the Westward Ho! motel on a Magic Fingers bed under a chenille bedspread, and along the highway, in trading posts and truck stops, you bought an armadillo basket and a rubber tomahawk and a Painted Desert snow globe to remember the fantastic journey.

Millions of families have made the trip; so have vagabonds, pilgrims, and artists of every stripe. The pathfinders have been as different as Brigham Young, Teddy Roosevelt, and *Lolita's* Humbert Humbert, who all sought their own kind of exhilaration and spiritual freedom on the road. The vehicles of liberation have ranged from the horse-drawn Butterfield Stage to the high-horsepower Corvette of TV's "Route 66" and the custom Harley-Davidsons of *Easy Rider.* The trail has changed dramatically over the years, but the theme of the Western road hasn't varied since the days of the pioneers: there is a golden promise just beyond the horizon. "Infinity seemed so close—just down the road," Karal Ann Marling wrote in her book about the roadside marvels of the Plains, *The Colossus of Roads* (1984). "Why, you could almost see the edge of the world, up there ahead, where the highway met the sky!"

One of the popular sentiments on Western souvenir postcards a half-century ago was a poem titled "Out Where the West Begins" by Arthur Chapman. The poem was printed alongside images of winding trails that led through awesome cactus fields, or of cowboys riding free, or of a proud Indian on his horse in a monumental landscape. Here is the last verse of that poem:

*Out where the world is in the making,*
*Where fewer hearts with despair are aching—*
  *That's where the West begins.*
*Where there's more of singing and less of sighing,*
*Where there's more of giving and less of buying,*
*And a man makes friends without half trying,*
  *That's where the West begins.*

Greetings from MONTANA

© CURT TEICH & CO., INC.
P-20
9A-H1Z49

GREETINGS FROM TEXAS

Greetings from PHOENIX
ARIZONA

© CURT TEICH & CO. INC.
9A-H26?
G-19

Greetings From AMARILLO
TEXAS
GATEWAY TO THE GREAT Southwest
HEART OF THE PANHAN...

GREETINGS from ALAMO GORDO
NEW MEXICO

1254

Greetings FROM RUIDOSO
NEW MEXICO

© J. R. WILLIS
G-21

A MESSAGE FROM COOKE CITY

Greetings FROM ARTESIA
NEW...

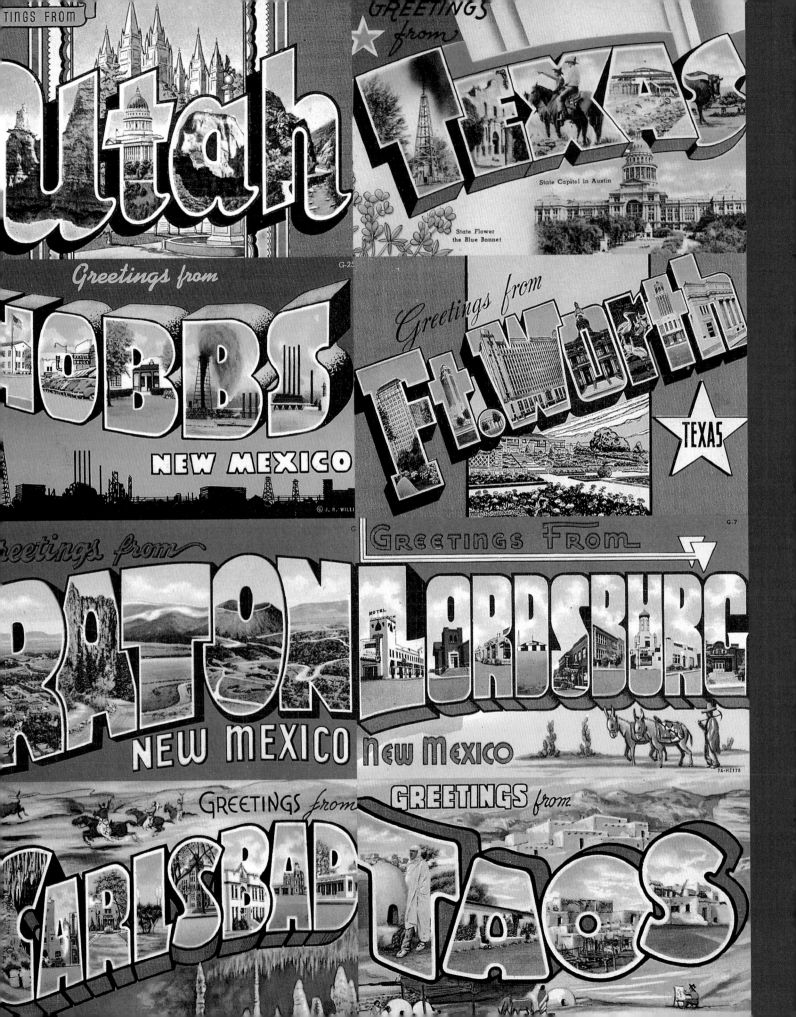

**HIGHWAY U.S. 85**

THRU NEW MEXICO

© CURT TEICH & CO., INC.

Greetings from **DENVER** COLORADO

Greetings from **KEARNEY** NEBRASKA

Greetings From **SANTA FE** NEW MEXICO

GREETINGS from **WEST YELLOWSTONE** MONTANA

WEST ENTRANCE TO YELLOWSTONE PARK

© CURT TEICH & CO., INC.

D-10

Greetings from **DALLAS** TEXAS

MAGNOLIA BLDG.   DALLAS POWER AND LIGHT BLDG.   PRAETORIAN BLDG.   TOWER PETROLEUM BLDG.   REPUBLIC BANK BLDG.   DALLAS GAS

© C. T. & CO.

778

Greetings from **GREAT FALLS**

Greetings from **NORTH PLATTE** NEBRASKA

# Route 66

Route 66 is officially dead. In 1984, the last section of it, running through Williams, Arizona, was superseded by Interstate 40. The new freeway skirted past Williams, which used to call itself the "Gateway to the Grand Canyon" and had made Route 66 its Main Street. In the heyday of Route 66 the town had been crowded with cafés, neon-sign motels, curio shops, gas stations, and tourist information bureaus, but starting in 1956, Route 66—along with so many of the places it passed through—had been rendered obsolete by America's superhighway system. The purpose of the new highways was to separate motorists

*A former gas station, the 66 Diner of Albuquerque was brought back to life in the late 1980s. The menu includes meat loaf and Cherry Coke.*

from towns and thus make their journey safer and more efficient. As mile after mile of Route 66 was bypassed, pieces of the old road went to seed. A few stretches were turned into service routes that paralleled the interstate, while sections that ran through communities were renamed. The last remaining road signs were taken down in 1985. By the time Route 66 was officially decertified, many of its garish roadside enterprises had already started to crumble into ruin.

At the official closing ceremony, however, one loyal devotee of Route 66 told a reporter, "The road is like Elvis Presley. It just won't die." He was right: the freeway once billed as the Main Street of America continues to weave its spell among those who treasure the golden age of roadside culture. On lengths of the venerable turnpike that survive, historical markers now appear, as do new diners and souvenir shops with a Route 66 theme. In 1992, to celebrate the highway's sixty-sixth birthday, each of the eight states it once traversed staged events to celebrate its former glory: old car shows, beauty pageants, and driving tours along its remains.

Now it represents a lost romantic past, but when it was first mapped out in 1926, Route 66 was seen by some people as a soulless bureaucratic mistake. Phil Patton's *Open Road* (1986) noted that in the 1920s, when the U.S. government decided to give roads numbers, the *New York Times* lamented the decision. An editorial proclaimed that assigning numbers rather than names to the

*Route 66 was known as "America's Main Street" because it went straight through so many towns, big and small. It has also been known as the Mother Road, the Glory Road, and the Will Rogers Highway.*

nation's highways stripped them of all their romance: "The traveler may shed tears as he drives the Lincoln Highway or dream dreams as he speeds over the Jefferson Highway," the *Times* sniffed. "But how can he get a 'kick' out of 46 or 55 or 33 or 21!"

There were kicks aplenty to be had on Route 66, the highway that connected the heartland to the West: two thousand rambling miles from Chicago to Los Angeles, veering straight through cities including St. Louis, Amarillo, Santa Fe (bypassed in 1937), and Albuquerque and becoming the Main Street of hundreds of little villages, into cornfields and wheat fields, over mountains, across the Great Divide and down to the desert, alongside scenic wonders, right near the lair where Jesse James and his gang used to hide out (Meramec Caverns, according to hundreds of billboards and painted barns), past Big-Chief highway trading posts and desert viper pits (SEE 'EM ALIVE!), and into small-town speed traps, with promises of clean rest rooms and home-cooked, chicken-'n'-biscuit meals all the way.

The new highway was promoted in 1927 as the main artery for a ninety-day marathon foot race that went from Los Angeles to Chicago, then on to New York (known as the Bunion Derby), but it was not until the 1930s that most of America came to know Route 66—as the Dust Bowl road. Okies and Arkies, displaced from their farms by the winds that swept off the Great Plains, headed West in search of a future. The path they took was Route 66, and it was immortalized in 1939 by John Steinbeck's novel *The Grapes of Wrath* (and the following year in John Ford's celebrated movie version). Steinbeck called Route 66 "the mother road, the road of flight," and he helped infuse its personality with a curious ambiguity that has never gone away: the road of desperation is also the road of hope.

After World War II all kinds of Americans were eager to hit the road. Autos went back into production. Gas rationing was lifted. Families piled in their cars and headed off to see the U.S.A. Thousands of GIs returned home and resolved to find their fortune in the West. One of them was Marine Captain Bobby Troup. Troup was from Pennsylvania but wanted to go to California to pursue his dream of becoming a songwriter, so when he was discharged from the service he and his wife Cynthia got in their green 1941 Buick convertible and set off on a journey that took them from Route 40 in the East to Route 66 and straight into Los Angeles.

Cynthia Troup was a map-reader, and before they even got to Chicago, she suggested that Bobby write a

song about Route 40, but Bobby wasn't much impressed with the road. They picked up Route 66 in Illinois, and when they got to Missouri, Cynthia revised her idea, and came up with a title: "Get Your Kicks on Route 66." Bobby measured the distance from Chicago to L.A. on the map, discovering it was more than two thousand miles. From Missouri to California the Troups saw the sights, and Bobby worked on the song. Six days after arriving in Los Angeles, he played it for Nat King Cole, who loved it. Cole recorded it—with a slow, bluesy beat—and it was a hit. "And why not?" Susan Croce Kelly asked in her book *Route 66* (1988). "A big portion of the public was making the same trip that the Troups had made, down the same narrow, crowded highway, with the same hopes of a better future Out West." "Get Your Kicks on Route 66" has since been recorded by artists from the Andrews Sisters to the Rolling Stones as well as by Natalie Cole (Nat's daughter), and it has become the foremost anthem of America's romantic attitude toward highway travel.

The rapture of the highway in this country is a love affair that burns especially hot in the wide-open spaces of the West. Powered by the great V-8 engines of Detroit in its lordly days, America's particular attraction to Route 66 was in some ways a cheap and vulgar love affair—as tacky as a flashing neon tepee advertising Injun Curios in Tucumcari, but it was also a love that could feel as pure and sublime as a purple sunset straight ahead on the Staked Plains of the Texas panhandle. The magic of the Mother Road was formulated out of those strangely complementary extremes: the tumult of garish roadside kitsch and the reckless joy of speeding into nature's virginal splendors.

The impolite razzle-dazzle of roadside commerce can seem nostalgic when we look back at it in photos and linen-finish postcards, but to many concerned citizens in postwar America, Route 66 had become an awful eyesore. In fact, Cynthia Troup remembered her trip with Bobby in 1945 as a journey through a very unsightly landscape. She was appalled by the Will Rogers Memorial in Oklahoma that displayed (and still displays) the clothes he was wearing when his plane crashed and he died; nor was she thrilled to see Jesse James's alleged hideout. "To me it was just a long road with cheap motels and restaurants," she recalled. "What I really can't believe is that he doesn't have Albuquerque in the song."

In 1960, when superhighways were being built from Chicago to Los Angeles, auguring the end of Route 66, the magic of the doomed road was recalled by an hour-

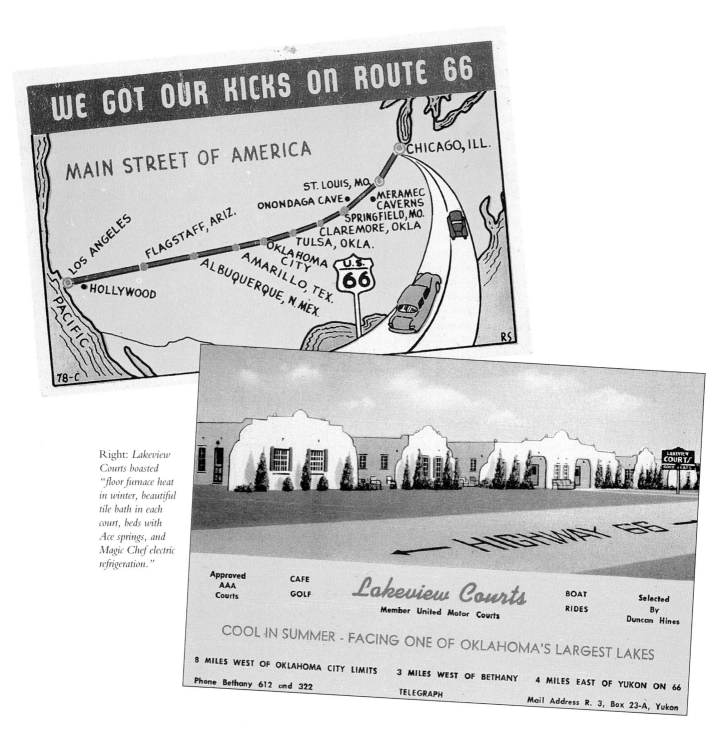

Right: *Lakeview Courts boasted "floor furnace heat in winter, beautiful tile bath in each court, beds with Ace springs, and Magic Chef electric refrigeration."*

long television series that lasted until the fall of 1964. "Route 66" never broke into the top twenty–rated shows, but it earned a cult following for its weekly dramas about two footloose guys (Martin Milner and George Maharis, the latter replaced by Glenn Corbett in 1963–64) who roamed the country in a Corvette convertible finding plenty of adventure and always looking sharp (despite the fact that their car's trunk scarcely had room for a couple of toothbrushes and change of underwear). In fact, Route 66 itself rarely figured in the stories, most of which took place elsewhere, but writer Sterling Silliphant said that he chose the title for its symbolic power: "Route 66 [is] an expression of going somewhere . . . It's the backbone of America."

# *Natural* WONDERS

In the West, nature has a character all its own: it is spectacular and it is odd. The Western landscape is known for its vastness, and for picturesque curiosities: a seemingly precarious Balanced Rock as big as a two-car garage, a million-year-old forest of petrified wood . . . and another forest of giant saguaro cacti instead of trees; a painted desert as colorful as a kaleidoscope . . . and a desert of nothing but blanched white sands (inhabited by mice and lizards that are also white). The very names of its sights suggest its grandeur: the Grand Canyon, the Royal Gorge, Big Bend, Monument Valley, Zion National Park, the Garden of the Gods. For many people, the main purpose of traveling West is to see these strange and remarkable places—to stand in wonder and take pictures or buy

*Camel Rock, north of Santa Fe, New Mexico.*

Everyone is Friendly Here

Greetings from *The Scenic West*

Opposite: *Canyon De Chelly*. Above: *Aerial view of the Grand Canyon.*

postcard views, then look at the images and think profound thoughts about the world we live in. "Everywhere you look, there's something to see," rhapsodized *The Golden Guide to The Southwest* in 1955 as an introduction to its roster of the marvels travelers would find.

Western vistas inspire awe, and most tourists think of them as beautiful. But it wasn't always so: toward the end of the last century, people traveled to see the sights of the frontier not because they were so majestic, but because they seemed so grotesque. Earl Pomeroy's classic travel history, *In Search of the Golden West,* describes Victorian sightseers going West to see its "dreadful reminders of the turmoil of the creation"—a primeval geological panorama unblessed by Europe's noble history or by the cultivating hand of white men. Wealthy tourists prided themselves on their refinement, to which the Wild West was a dramatic contrast. Put another way, they tended to think of nature in the West as an example of bad taste: unruly, savage, and gross. It was a notion that was never

completely overcome: in 1945 photographer Ansel Adams complained that too many sightseers looked at a rock formation or a desert as if it was "merely a gargantuan curio"; in 1960 art critic Harold Rosenberg described the Rocky Mountains as a perfect example of American kitsch . . . because they were so obvious, blatant, and excessive.

Vulgar as it may have seemed to Victorian travelers, the spectacle was fascinating to them nonetheless because it was so peculiar—a kind of nature's freak show. The Garden of the Gods, a group of unusual rock formations near Colorado Springs, was proudly advertised by the Denver and Rio Grande Railroad in the 1880s as a "curious freak of nature." Earl Pomeroy quotes visitors to the Garden of the Gods as looking at the rocks and being thrilled to be able to see in their strange shapes "a stag's head, curious birds and crawling serpents, an eagle with pinions spread, a seal making love to a nun, and an elephant attacking a lion." A 1905 tourist brochure called

# America's Version

**B**efore Americans learned to love the West for its own sake, it was a common tourist strategy to appreciate it as a kind of poor man's Old World. It was long the policy of guides in the Garden of the Gods to encourage sightseers to imagine that the jagged stones resembled Grecian temples, English castles, and the Great Wall of China; guides on early Santa Fe passenger trains that passed inhabited pueblos in the Southwest advised their passengers to consider how much the Native American villages were like ancient Babylon and Nineveh. As late as the 1930s, the Greyhound Bus Company issued a poster boasting that it was possible for travelers to "See All the World . . . Right Here in America!" The poster showed some of the West's natural wonders along with a list indicating which important sights around the world they were every bit as good as. The roster included:

| AMERICA'S VERSION | THE WORLD STANDARD |
|---|---|
| Nevada Desert | Arabian Desert |
| Montana Plains | Russian Steppes |
| Grand Canyon | Petra, Arabia |
| Death Valley | The Dead Sea |
| ("both are hundreds of feet below sea level") | |
| Petrified Forest | Egypt (near Cairo) |
| Casa Grande, Ariz. | Inca Temples, Peru |
| ("ruins of prehistoric races") | |
| Rocky Mountains | Swiss Alps |
| Taos Pueblo | Liberian Villages |
| West Texas | Argentine Pampas |
| San Antonio | Monterrey, Mexico |
| ("large, picturesque Mexican section") | |

**DEATH VALLEY NATIONAL MONUMENT**

PROTECT NATURAL FEATURES
WILDLIFE SANCTUARY
FIREARMS PROHIBITED
PRESERVE DO NOT DESTROY

TOWNE'S PASS ENTRANCE

*Postcard views of the wonders of the West. This page, top to bottom: "Leap for Life, Grand Canyon, Ariz. This spectacular leap was performed by a Park Ranger at a point known as Douglas Fairbanks Rock about five minutes walk east of El Tovar"; Taos Pueblo, showing "Indian Boys singing to their sweethearts"; the Petrified Forest; Hopis surveying the Grand Canyon. Opposite page: Dante's View, near the Furnace Creek Inn— "Beyond, the long, bony fingers of the Panamint Range reach out into the valley."*

the garden's most famous formation, the Balanced Rock, "the most photographed object in the United States."

Like clouds, the West's geology has always inspired people to see things in it, and to name it accordingly. A picture postcard of Camel Rock, north of Santa Fe, issued sometime in the 1940s, enticed tourists with this description: "Nature, the great sculptor, has fashioned rocks into many fantastic shapes and forms resembling human beings and animals, but nowhere has she done anything more realistic than this Camel Rock just alongside Highway No. 285 about 13 miles north of Santa Fe, New Mexico. Here, for centuries, this lifelike portrayal of a camel lying down looks forever toward the north over a waste of unwatered soil, scrub pine, and cedar."

It wasn't necessary to see specific animals and anthropoids in Western rocks to find them fascinating. Because the West is so *visually* dramatic, it has long been popular to infuse its sights with a kind of geological melodrama, as did this stirring account of the Petrified Forest, published in the 1930s by the Fred Harvey company to encourage train travel: "From remotest epochs earth has striven against the seas in her struggle to free her face to the air. She is most deeply scarred by the conflict in the Petrified Forest, where her triumph is complete, but her wounds are bare, and with them many a secret she thought to lock forever in her bosom."

There isn't a sight in the West that has inspired more rhapsodizing than the Grand Canyon, which was a major tourist attraction by 1900, when rail service brought sightseers right to its edge. Four years later, Fred Harvey built Hotel El Tovar, a luxury resort made of boulders and rough-hewn pine logs, at the rim of the canyon, from which disembarking Santa Fe train passengers could venture down on muleback rides. "The Grand Canyon is not the eighth wonder of the world, but the first," proclaimed a souvenir pamphlet published in the 1930s. "This sublime gorge is 217 miles in length, a terrific trough 6000 to 7000 feet deep, and ten to twenty miles wide, peopled with hundreds of gorgeously colored pyramids and minarets carved from its painted depths. It has been likened to a 'Giant Paint Pot.' The blues and the grays and the mauves and the reds are second in glory only to the Canyon's size. The colors change with each changing hour."

*Monument Valley, on the Utah-Arizona border.*

# CACTI

When Walt Disney dramatized the flora and fauna of the southwest in his 1953 Academy Award-winning documentary, *The Living Desert,* cacti were featured as shrewd survivalists—known as "the juicy ones," or succulents, for their amazing ability to store water. The movie showed them protecting their juicy selves by brandishing their spines, which scared off hungry critters that wanted to eat them, but it also showed how many different kinds of wildlife lived inside them, which made the biggest cacti—in Disney's words—"desert skyscrapers."

The succulents of the Southwest desert, which extends through most of southern Arizona and New Mexico, west Texas, and the southeastern tip of California, are such strange plants, and so unlike commonplace shrubs or trees, that frontier lore is filled with stories that give them personalities as complex and as willful as any mammal's. Reg Manning, in his "who's who of strange plants of the southwest American desert" entitled *What Kinda Cactus Izzat?* (1941), described the cactus as a "non-belligerent surrounded by powerful aggressors," a plant that "knows how to maintain its independence. It never goes looking for trouble—but it can dish out plenty of misery to anybody who tries to push it around."

Above: *Varieties of cacti near Carlsbad Cavern.* Opposite: *Ray Manley photographed a happy family outside of Tucson about thirty years ago.*

The trouble a cactus can dish out comes mostly from its spines, which are vestigial leaves, impervious to desiccation in the sun. The spines discourage animals from trying to get at a cactus's flesh, where it stores water; they also serve the giant saguaro cactus as baffles, shielding the stem from winds that might evaporate its moisture. Sitting on a barrel cactus and getting a buttock full of spines is always a source of great fun (for onlookers) in cartoons and Western movies, but not all cacti have the same kinds of spines: some have long needles, some have barbs, some have spines that are more like thistles. For the person in whom they are embedded, however, cactus spines are seldom a laugh, especially barrel-cactus spines, which are flat, thick, and hooked at the tip.

It's worth pointing out that yuccas, which have sharp-pointed leaves and flourish in the desert, are *not* cacti, although they are frequently mistaken for them. In fact, they are members of the lily family, and include the giant Joshua tree and the century plant, from which tequila is made. The best-known varieties of Western cactus include:

## PRICKLY PEARS

They have jointed, flat pads and live about twenty years; they are easily potted, and aren't unique to the Southwest. Their blossoms are mostly yellow, and their fruit, known as a tuna, is sweet when ripe.

## CHOLLA

They are cylindrical and jointed, and include among their number the notorious "jumping cactus," which is so loosely connected that pieces of it can easily break off and attach themselves to a passing pant leg or sock. Staghorns, which grow as high as twelve feet, are also chollas; their hole-riddled trunks and branches were the basis of "Cacticraft," a now-lost souvenir art that turned the dead plants' skeletons into floor lamps, picture frames, and other knickknacks of interest to tourists in the 1940s and 1950s.

## BARRELS

They resemble stout barrels, and their tissue contains water that many desert wanderers—in movies, anyway—

Opposite: *Ricky Nelson came to Arizona to film* Rio Bravo *(1959). The above picture was captioned "Sweet doll with that dangerous look."*

have tapped to survive. (Sap from most cacti can be poisonous.) Cactus candy is made from barrel cactus pulp, although all the sweetness is added in the processing; the pulp itself has little flavor.

## ORGAN PIPE

As high as twenty feet, organ pipes are a night-blooming cactus that grow a new branch on any arm that is injured or stunted by a cold snap on a winter night. This causes them to become broad and thick, with dozens of arms crowded together and branching out as wide as the plants are tall. They bloom in May and June, and their fruit, which is covered with needles that are easy to remove, is among the sweetest of all cactus fruits. An amazing field of organ pipes is visible at the Organ Pipe Cactus National Monument in southern Arizona, where they share space with saguaro, jumping cholla, barrel cacti, ocotillo, and mesquite bushes.

# SAGUARO:
## LORD OF THE DESERT

The saguaro cactus (pronounced sah-WAH-ro), towering over the Sonoran sands as high as fifty feet, with its candelabra arms reaching skyward, is the king of cacti. It is tough and enduring, but it is also endangered. There is even a black market in saguaro (for lawn decoration) because they are protected in their natural habitat and they cannot be grown commercially. It takes one a hundred years to reach maturity; the giant saguaro have been living twice that long.

Really old saguaros begin to resemble elephants, at least around the joints where, when full with water, their skin seems to sag and wrinkle under their immense weight. The upraised arms of a tall saguaro can give it a strangely human bearing that make it appear as regal as a soldier standing at attention, or as awkward as a bad jitterbugger. Reg Manning wrote that "Driving through a saguaro forest for the first time makes you a little self-conscious. You get the odd feeling of walking into a crowded room, where everybody stops what he was doing and watches in embarrassed silence till you have passed through."

Saguaros may resemble humans, but they are smarter and better equipped when it comes to surviving in the desert. They use their vertical pleated stems like an accordion, expanding and contracting them as they need to store moisture. During a desert rain, a saguaro soaks up water from its far-flung roots, and as the water is piped upward, the ridges swell and pull apart, giving the stem a bloated look. After months of dry weather, the ridges contract as the moisture dissipates, and a dry

*Herb Wood stands next to the cacticraft clock he made. Below: A cacticraft lamp.*

# Some Saguaro Facts

It takes fifteen years for a saguaro to grow from a seedling to one foot tall; it doesn't sprout arms until it is seventy-five years old.

A saguaro can produce as many as forty million seeds in its lifetime. Of these, only one will likely grow to maturity, spread by desert fruit bats.

It can suck up two thousand pounds of water in a single rainy day. It is 98 percent water, and can weigh as much as fifteen tons.

Its roots can extend sixty-five feet in all directions, and they can absorb enough moisture during one rainy season to keep the plant alive and blooming through four years of drought.

During a rainy period, when a saguaro is busy absorbing moisture, it can bleed to death from a single knife wound. In an ordinary dry spell, the cactus insulates itself from gouges by secreting a plaster-like material that forms a hard, wooden scar. These hard

*Along old Route 66 in Arizona.*

hollows, carved by birds, are known as "saguaro boots," and when a cactus dies, the boots remain on the desert floor long after the flesh has decomposed.

An old, dying saguaro can be a stunning sight: as the succulent tissue dries and falls away from the arms and stem, the skeleton of woody ribs remains upright, waving in the wind like the arms of drowning men until the cactus topples at its base and falls to the earth.

saguaro will appear as emaciated as a human after a Pritikin diet.

In the spring, a saguaro flowers at night, at the tips of its branches. The small white blossoms (the state flower of Arizona) are shaped like little horns and are visible at sunrise, but they close in the heat of the day. Later, in the summer, an edible red fruit appears where the flowers grew; the fruit is sweet and tasty, but hard to reach, and usually gobbled up by birds as soon as it is ripe.

In the summer, woodpeckers manage to get past the saguaro spines and drill holes in its flesh, where they live until the following year, when they like to find a new place to nest. These abandoned holes, which quickly develop a firm, corklike surface (to keep moisture from leaching out) are then occupied by elf owls and purple martins, or lizards and mice. It is not unusual for literally hundreds of desert animals to make their homes inside a single giant saguaro cactus.

The Saguaro National Monument, established in 1933 on both sides of Tucson, is the ideal place to experience saguaros in their natural grandeur—a cactus forest for miles.

*Plaster cacti for sale near the Saguaro National Monument in Arizona.*

# Roadside Wonders
# OF THE WEST

**M**any people like to travel West to see God's handiwork in such sights as Carlsbad Caverns and the waterfalls of Yosemite. Some prefer to relish what the hand of man has wrought, and they go West to cruise along highways shimmering with fabulous neon signs, to eat at funky beaneries built to resemble giant coffeepots, and to buy a ten-gallon hat as big as the one Hoss wore in "Bonanza." Roadside connoisseurs go West to follow the trail of signs that guide them to Wyoming's two Little Americas, the biggest gas stations on earth, where they can buy a bumper sticker announcing they were there; they pose for snapshots standing underneath a sixty-ton concrete buffalo, in Jamestown, South Dakota, or in the doorway of the only house in North America made entirely of salt, in Grand Saline, Texas.

Roadside ballyhoo is as much a part of the character of the West as canyons filled with odd-shaped rocks and deserts ablaze with color under spectacular sunsets. No region of the country is as much in love with its own iconography as the West;

*The Tack Room: a Tucson landmark.*

and the roads that run through it are a constant reminder of that love: motels sprout giant totem poles and neon signs shaped like covered wagons and feature coffee shops with Indian tacos and cowboy burgers on the menu and rooms with chenille longhorn steers and maps of Texas on the bedspread. "Howdy!" says the sign on one side of the souvenir trading post; "Whoa! You Missed Us!" says another sign farther up the highway.

The Navajos called their part of the world "the land of time enough and room enough"; perhaps it is that same combination that makes something magical happen along the Western roadside. Things that normally would be too minor or ridiculous to command attention back home are suddenly captivating and evocative. Set amid the majesty of nature, the concerns of modern man—from his endless need for a cold drink to the eternal quest for discount moccasins—can make a journey through the West a poignant odyssey. Writing about the road trip Humbert Humbert takes across America with his beloved *Lolita*, Vladimir Nabokov exclaimed, "Nothing is more exhilarating than philistine vulgarity" and he marveled at the roadside's endless selection of "Sunset Motels, U-Beam Cottages, Hillcrest Courts, Pine View Courts, Mountain View Courts, Skyline Courts, Park Plaza Courts, Green Acres, Mac's Courts."

Once an exotic destination reserved for the idle rich (or just the idle), the West began to attract more ordinary tourists in the 1920s and 1930s, thanks to the construction of highways and the greater availability of cars. After World War II, when so many Americans were eager and able to hit the highway, roadside entrepreneurs began to vie with one another to catch travelers' eyes. In most cases, the strategy was a simple one: promise an experience that is uniquely Western. Build a hotel that looks like a hacienda, erect a sign in the shape of a saguaro cac-

Left: *"America's newest and most luxurious desert hotel, five minutes from the heart of Las Vegas."* Above: *A jackalope.*

tus, a tribal chief, or a cowboy on horseback. Trading posts positioned statuary on their roofs that showed longhorn steers, jackrabbits, and roadrunners; on their walls were painted giant primitive illustrations of the hand-loomed rugs sold within. What tourist in search of a Western adventure could drive past a roadside café that had a mechanical buckaroo outside, waving his hat at cars? What hungry family could ignore a sign that showed cowboy-style ham and eggs painted in colors brighter than nature?

When two-lane roads started being bypassed by superhighways in the 1950s, many of the old trading posts, motels, and frijole palaces fell on hard times as business dried up and blew away like tumbleweeds in a dust storm. Amazingly, though, some of the great sights survived. Establishments simply hung on: the Santo Domingo Trading Post in Domingo, New Mexico—once a main stop on the rail line, now a forlorn piece of real estate far from the highway between Albuquerque and Santa Fe—continues to attract customers who relish merchandise and signs that seem not to have changed since Greer Garson shopped there in the 1940s. Some other road-side attractions are long defunct, but their signs remain: a sexy cowgirl lounging in an oversize high-heel shoe lifts her champagne glass in a toast on the outside wall of the boarded-up City Lights saloon in Truth or Consequences; a femme fatale models a cowboy hat outside an old dry-goods shop in Holbrook; an empty lot still promises "Cars for America" on the road west of Albu-querque. The signs are faded, falling down, but curiously compelling in the rarefied Western air—ghosts of a vanished era.

Left: *"If you haven't stopped at the Jack Rabbit [on Route 66], you haven't been in the Southwest."* Below: *Dixon, New Mexico.*

*Lariat* MOTEL VACANCY

*Wyoming* MOTEL

EL PUEBLO LODGE

$16 95 WK NICE
21 95 FRE & C

THE WESTWARD HO

*The* *Capri* MOTOR HOTEL WELCOME to the Best MOTEL in the West

WESTERN HILLS MOTEL RESTAURANT

VACANCY 1 DOUBLE BED $20

*Paradise* MOTOR HOTEL KITCHENETTES DAY·WEEK·MONTH DOUBLE $16

ARIZONA MOTEL TV POOL RV MONTHLY SPACE

TOURIST HOME

VACANCY

COLOR T.V.

HEATED POOL

Western Holiday MOTEL

Desert Sands

MOTOR HOTEL

bow & arrow LODGE

VACANCY

RAINBOW MOTEL

NO VACANCY

WESTERN

Western MOTEL AIR CONDITIONED

PHONE

SINGLE 15.88

PUEBLO COURT

GHOST RANCH LODGE & RESTAURANT

FLYING M RANCH

MOTEL

STANDARD VACANCY

FREE CABLE TV

| 1 GUEST | 2 GUESTS | 3 GUESTS | 4 GUESTS |
| $3. | $4. | $5. | $6. |

FAMILY UNITS

THERMOSTAT HEAT

# Twenty-five Unnatural WONDERS OF THE WESTERN ROADSIDE

## BIG PILE OF BONES (NORTH OF DIXON, N. MEX.)

If you are in the market for a set of longhorns to mount on your car or in your den, or if you need some cattle skulls to decorate your porch or patio, or if you've just got a hankering to surround yourself with jawbones, rib cages, and vertebrae—all picked clean and gleaming white—this is the boneyard for you. On the road to Taos out of Española, the Big Pile has acres of bones of every size and shape for sale at reasonable prices. And if you happen to have a skull you hanker to get rid of, or to swap for a better one, come on down. At Big Pile of Bones, they've never met a part of a skeleton they didn't like.

## CADILLAC RANCH (AMARILLO, TEX.)

Alongside Interstate 40, formerly Route 66, five miles west of Amarillo, ten Cadillacs were half-buried in the ground, nose down, in 1974. They range from a 1948 fastback coupe with mere bumps for tailfins to a Coupe De Ville from 1959, the year fins reached their maximum height and pointiness. When a group of creative people known as Ant Farm first put them in the ground (in a neat row parallel to the road and at the precise angle of the sides of the Great Pyramid of Cheops), one of the artists called the arrangement "a white trash dream"; the rich man who commissioned them, Stanley Marsh 3 [sic], said they represented "the great escape . . . sexual free-

some other things. One of the several buildings that compose this huge trading complex is covered entirely in cattle skulls; another, when we passed through in 1992, was named *Dances with Wolves,* for the Kevin Costner movie. What's most amazing about it all is the exterior: the roofs and the russet bluffs behind the buildings are occupied by lifesize plaster effigies of buffalo, horses, mules, antelope, grizzly bear, and a ghostly Indian driving a buckboard, while all the facades and signs are painted shades of red and yellow so extreme that they literally imprint themselves on your retinas and will tint everything you see for miles down the road.

dom, the freedom to make choices, and the ability to just go." Over the years, the cars' rumps, which were in good shape when their noses were interred, have been used by passersby as an opportunity to express themselves: in the first few years with simple hearts and maxims scratched by knife into the paint, then with big-bore bullets (looming up in the flat landscape, the fins make a great set of targets), and in the last several years with spray-paint graffiti.

## CHIEF YELLOW HORSE TRADING POST (LUPTON, ARIZ.)

Nestled against a red-rock butte near the New Mexico border along Route 40, Chief Yellow Horse Trading Post has everything . . . and everything MUST GO!: 50 percent off ten thousand pairs of moccasins, 67 percent off Indian jewelry, 75 percent off Navajo sand paintings and kachina dolls, and—if you play your cards right—90 percent off

## CHISHOLM TRAIL MURAL (YUKON, OKLA.)

A handsome painted mural showing cowboys and cows passing through Oklahoma (which was then Indian territory) on their way from Texas into Kansas in the late 1860s. Its sponsors, including One-Hour Moto Photo and Big Ed's Hamburgers, are listed below the picture, which you can't help seeing if you keep your eyes right as you travel west on old Route 66 during daylight. We got to town late in the afternoon, and thanks to Tom Snyder's *Route 66 Traveler's Guide,* knew enough to stick around until dark, when the lights go on at the huge Yukon Flour Mill across the road: a fantastic show. One other reason for visiting Yukon: it's Garth Brooks' hometown, and there is a sign on the outskirts saying so—an excellent photo opportunity.

# CORN PALACE (MITCHELL, S. DAK.)

September is the best time to come see the Corn Palace, when the exterior wall space on this Byzantine edifice is freshly covered with multicolored corn cobs, oats, barley, sorghum grain, and assorted grasses—all precisely arranged to form immense murals. The pictures, which are gloriously framed in abstract designs also made from local produce, illustrate a different subject each year, but the consistent theme is the good life in South Dakota: pheasant-hunting, vacation fun, and the like. Above the pictures rise fiberglass minarets painted with images of buffalo. The front of the palace features corn portraits of performers who are headlining at that year's Corn Festival, on stage in the 3,500-seat auditorium inside. Marching bands have been a big part of the festivities since John Philip Sousa conducted here, but the star who performed at the Corn Palace most (five times) is the Dakotas' favorite son, Lawrence Welk.

THE WORLD'S ONLY CORN PALACE, MITCHELL, S. D.

## DINOSAUR GARDENS (VERNAL, UTAH)

There are dinosaurs by the side of the road from coast to coast in America—some of them are so big that you can climb a staircase and visit religious shrines inside their bodies—and there are dinosaur parks with dozens of fanciful specimens, some we have seen with Day-Glo tennis balls for eyes. But the sad fact is that most of this country's population of roadside dinosaurs are falling-apart wrecks. That's why it is such a pleasure to see the dinos of Vernal, Utah. Sculptor Elbert Porter spent fourteen years creating these fourteen fiberglass and polyester resin beauties, which are arrayed in a park adjacent to the Utah Field

House Natural History Museum: the handsomest and best-maintained dinosaur garden in the land. They are anatomically correct and lifesize (some as long as eighty feet), and they have faces that blaze with emotion; the landscape they inhabit simulates Jurassic foliage; and they are illuminated at night in the summer, when you can take an evening stroll past their waterfall and through their swamp.

## EL VADO MOTEL (ALBUQUERQUE, N. MEX.)

The quintessential Route 66 motel, with the prettiest sign in Albuquerque (the city with the best roadside signs in the West): an Indian chief with a headdress in rainbow neon colors. El Vado is a white adobe motor court built in 1937 in what some of its old postcards call "Spanish pueblo style," which means a series of low-lying white units with exposed vigas outside and rough-hewn beam ceilings in the rooms. It used to advertise steam heat and tile baths; today it boasts cable TV and free local phone calls. It is spanking clean and picturesque enough to attract many customers who are traveling connoisseurs of the bygone American roadside, and who prefer its quaint charm to the no-surprises ambience of a chain motel.

## FARMER JOHN MURAL (TUCSON, ARIZ.)

Leslie Grimes painted three murals for the Farmer John Meats Company in the West, and although the one he did in Vernon, California, is probably the widest known—because it was featured in the background of a scene in Antonioni's film *Zabriskie Point* (1970)—the one on Grant Street in Tucson is the one we like most. It is a wraparound panorama of Western life that includes saguaro cacti, purple mountains, fleecy clouds overhead in an enormous sky, grazing cows, and angry bulls—one charging and upending a cowhand. Leslie Grimes died in 1968 when he fell off a scaffold, but Tucsonian Marie Spark has assured us that the mural is regularly touched-up and repainted by Arno Johnson, who maintains its verisimilitude.

## GARDEN OF EDEN (LUCAS, KANS.)

The Garden of Eden is located on a pleasant, tree-lined residential street, but it isn't nearly as peaceful as you'd expect Eden to be. In fact, it is a parcel of fuming chaos in the form of concrete and limestone statues that depict such bloody tales as Cain slaying Abel, the crucifixion of the working class, and warfare between the U.S. cavalry and Native Americans. In the midst of the gruesome statuary is a walk-through mausoleum containing S. P. Dinsmoor, the man who created this environment (to educate mankind) between 1905 and 1933. Dinsmoor was 64 when he began the project, which would put him on the far side of 150 years old today . . . and, to be frank, he looks it. As his Last Will and Testament requested, he is enshrined in a coffin with a glass window so visitors can look in and see what a moldering man looks like.

## GHOST TOWN (COLORADO SPRINGS, COLO.)

Ghost Town is more than just some dusty old mining camp. For one thing, it's all indoors. And whereas the enchantment of a real ghost town is its sparseness, the fun of this one is marveling at how much stuff it has managed to pack into its twelve different buildings. "Turn back your watch 100 years," warns a billboard outside, but the fact is that time goes haywire in this place, which is filled with furniture, tools, curios, mementos, and displays from many different decades past. There are an Old West sheriff's office and old-time saloon, buckboards and early automobiles, a nickelodeon and a completely outfitted Victorian home, Franklin D. Roosevelt's bulletproof limousine, and a pair of ice skates once worn by Mrs. Roosevelt.

## GIANT JACKALOPE (DOUGLAS, WYO.)

Most jackalopes are only heads, mounted on wood plaques for the rec room. This giant jackalope is full-bodied, and inhabits the out-of-doors: on Center Street in Douglas, Wyoming, the town where the legendary horned rabbit of the West was invented some sixty years ago (see page 268). It is well over six feet tall and made of fiberglass: an irresistible place to have your picture taken. A sign outside of Douglas, which long ago declared itself the Jackalope Capital of the World, warns motorists to *Watch Out for Jackalopes* despite the fact that Jackalope Hunting Licenses (available in many town souvenir stores) describe it as "perhaps the rarest animal in North America."

## HAROLD WARP'S PIONEER VILLAGE (MINDEN, NEBR.)

The Midwest and West have an abundance of pioneer museums, but Harold Warp's place stands out because of the breadth of his devotion as a collector. Warp, the son of immigrant pioneers, spent his life acquiring things that showed, in his words, "man's progress since 1830." This meant virtually *everything:* tools, cars, motorcycles, locomotives, dishware, entire buildings (a firehouse, a Pony Express station, a sod hut), thousands of fishing lures, one entire building filled with home appliances, a collection of trivets, a collection of hat pins, a collection of musical instruments, twenty-two airplanes, one hundred tractors. The inventory continued to grow even after Warp opened the Village in 1953, and some of the more modern displays include the development of the snowmobile, outboard motors, TV technology, and atomic power. At last count there were twenty-six buildings spread over twenty acres containing more than fifty thousand things.

## MAY'S EXOTIC WORLD OF GIANT TROPICAL INSECTS (COLORADO SPRINGS, COLO.)

There are grander things to see in Colorado, but we couldn't help falling in love with this museum/campground/ souvenir shop with its colossal goggle-eyed plaster bug—big as a horse and named Hercules—above Route 115 south of Colorado Springs. Hercules's limbs have been chewed away by wildlife, or possibly stolen by vandals, so he hovers above the earth on unseen prosthetic legs, but all the real insects in the museum are shipshape and under glass. Mr. May collected them around the world; and what impressed us even more than the weird beetles was the vintage inventory of souvenir merchandise for sale in the room just outside the gallery—keepsake pens and pencils,

ViewMaster discs, and excellent postcards of glamour girls in bathing suits surrounding Hercules when Hercules was whole. May's is at the end of a long, wooded road: a trip back in time to a lost style of roadside charm.

## OLD RIP'S FINAL RESTING PLACE (EASTLAND, TEX.)

Old Rip was a pet horned toad who belonged to the son of Eastland Justice of the Peace Ernest Wood, and who was put into the cornerstone of the town courthouse, alongside a Bible, when the building was dedicated in 1897. (Mr. Wood's motive for entombing his son's live toad is unclear.) Thirty-one years later, when the courthouse was demolished to make way for a new one, Old Rip hopped out—dusty and confused, but eager to find some ants to eat. The froggy phoenix toured the nation, even visited the White House. When he died for good the following year, his tiny body was embalmed and placed in a silk-lined coffin made especially for him by the Abilene Casket Company. The coffin is now visible behind a glass window at the front of the new Eastland Courthouse, where a granite monument marks the death-defying lizard's final resting place.

# OLD TUCSON (TUCSON, ARIZ.)

Old Tucson consists of 140 buildings originally constructed in 1939 as a set for the movie *Arizona,* which took place in 1865 and featured some one thousand modern Tucsonians in roles as extras, playing their ancestors. Many classic Westerns were subsequently made here, including Anthony Mann's *Winchester '73* (1950) starring Jimmy Stewart and Howard Hawks's *Rio Bravo* (1959), starring John Wayne, Dean Martin, and Ricky Nelson. Today's visitors are treated to daily mock gun battles in the street featuring a burro-powered wagon to haul away the actors playing dead bodies. Also featured are stagecoach rides for the whole family, live music, a petting zoo, an old-time saloon, a Wizard of the West Illusion show (Lillie Langtry's garter is made to disappear), and—the drawing card that has proven to be one of the most alluring of all the Western-themed spectacles on the road—tours of the sets and soundstage where exciting cowboy movies and TV shows are still sometimes made.

# PONDEROSA RANCH (INCLINE VILLAGE, NEV.)

When "Bonanza" first went on the air in 1959, the Ponderosa Ranch where it was supposed to take place did not exist except as soundstages in Hollywood. Outdoor scenes were filmed at the north shore of Lake Tahoe in Nevada; at the beginning of each episode, the titles appeared over a burning map that showed exactly where Ben Cartright and his three boys (Adam, Little Joe, and Hoss) lived. In the 1960s the program grew so successful that viewers started making pilgrimages to Lake Tahoe to see the ranch. An entrepreneur named Bill Anderson built it for them—faithful to the one on TV—and opened his gates in 1967, when "Bonanza" was number one in the ratings. Over the years, his attraction expanded from a mere ranch house into a Western theme park that now includes the Church of the Ponderosa (where you can really get married), horseback trails, haywagon breakfast rides (including Ben's recipe for scrambled eggs and houseboy Hop-Sing's sausage), and a lunch specialty named for Ben's fattest son: the Hossburger.

## ROY ROGERS– DALE EVANS MUSEUM (VICTORVILLE, CALIF.)

If only for the fact that Trigger is here, along with Dale's horse Buttermilk and Bullet the Wonder Dog, taxidermized in all their former glory, this museum is a landmark for all who love the West of the silver screen. Exhibits include some of Roy's spectacular saddles, rifles, shirts, boots, a custom Pontiac (with six-guns for door handles), a clear bowling ball with Trigger's image in the center, as well as thousands of assorted mementos from the distinguished singing, acting, parenting, and charity careers of the ultimate cowboy couple. Tapes of many of the movies Roy and Dale made are for sale in the gift shop.

## SALT PALACE (GRAND SALINE, TEX.)

"We are the only salt house in North America," said the woman in charge of the Salt Palace, and when we asked her about salt houses on other continents she admitted that she had heard of none. So this may be the only salt house on earth! In fact, by the time you read these words, it might not exist at all, but don't worry: If it does get torn down, it will only be to make way for a bigger, better salt house next door, which was in the planning stages early in 1993. The problem, you see, is that a house made of salt needs to be sealed well or else it crumbles when it gets moist, and the Salt Palace has been falling apart for years. The new one, we were assured, is going to be sealed to a fare-thee-well, and only two of its walls will be made of salt, anyway. Inside this amazing building, built to honor the deposits that put Grand Saline on the map, there are salt pellets and salt blocks for cattle, pictures of the first salt mine, and a really old movie about the history of salt extraction in this part of Texas. A souvenir salt shaker is also available for purchase, but you will find absolutely no pepper shaker to go with it.

## SANTO DOMINGO TRADING POST (DOMINGO, N. MEX.)

Here's the place to stock up on rubber tom-toms, child-size feathered war bonnets, and deerskin moccasins in styles that haven't changed since Lucy and Desi traveled West with the Mertzes. It is far off the main road halfway between Albuquerque and Santa Fe; you will know you have arrived when you spot the rusted hull of a Frazer automobile in front of a faded sign announcing, "THIS IS

IT: MOST INTERESTING SPOT IN THE OLD WEST. AS FEATURED IN LIFE, NEW MEXICO, LOOK MAGAZINES AND NEWSPAPERS ALL OVER U.S."

The cavernous, wood-floored interior is a wonderland of kitsch and collectibles, including a trio of magnificent old rugs from Navajo Chee Dodge, the first tribal chairman. The rugs cost $45,000, but for those on a budget there are bolo ties for men at $3.95 each ("Popular, Neat, Comfortable"), spears with bendable points at reasonable prices, and beaded belts "for the small fry" that look straight out of Hoppy's era. Many things for sale are marked by signs that appear not to have changed in decades. "Give your tootsies a real break," a placard above the moccasins advises customers, "Greer Garson says: MMMMmmmm, butter-soft and yummy! and Sooo comfortable."

"Trader Fred" Thompson, a former insurance man from Rochester, New York, has operated the Trading Post, which is on Santo Domingo land and subject to tribal law, since 1951. He is now in his eighties and going strong, and asks most guests to sign in at the register at the front of the store. It is the size of four big-city phone directories, and contains the names of people from every country on earth.

in the 1870s. So they designed a picture of a beautiful woman fifteen feet high and eight feet wide, and put her in an evening gown made entirely of money. The low-cut dress is wide and full, from just above her nipple line to the floor. It is made from 3,261 silver dollars, some of them minted in Carson City, and it is cinched at the waist with a belt of twenty-eight twenty-dollar gold pieces.

## TOMBSTONE (TOMBSTONE, ARIZ.)

Tombstone, site of the Gunfight at the O.K. Corral, bills itself as "The Town Too Tough to Die." Once the toughest silver mining camp in the West, it is now one of the most fun-filled tourist attractions, offering not only the O.K. Corral with the Earps and the Clantons posed mid-battle, but also an adjacent electronic diorama, called the Historama, narrated by Vincent Price, which entices customers with the promise they will hear the "dread Apache war cry pierce the air!" Also on the bill of fare: Boot Hill, the graveyard where unlucky gunslingers were buried (and where there is now a big gift shop); periodic gun battles (with blanks) in the street; and Grandma Fudpucker's collectible shop, specializing in Emmett Kelly, Jr., clown figurines and Tiffany-like lamps.

## SILVER QUEEN OF NEVADA (VIRGINIA CITY, NEV., IN THE SILVER QUEEN CASINO)

Lee and Ruby Carel, proprietors of the Silver Queen, wanted to honor the Comstock Lode, which yielded more than a billion dollars' worth of silver and made Virginia City one of the most prosperous places in America

## TOM MIX MONUMENT (FLORENCE, ARIZ.)

Near this spot on Highway 89, the great cowboy movie actor Tom Mix died in a fatal one-car crash on October 12, 1940. He went out of the world as he had lived: fast and rolling in money. Speeding west out of Florence through the Sonoran desert one night, he suddenly saw a washed-out bridge ahead. He hit the brakes, his car flipped over, and his neck was broken when his head got conked by the suitcase loaded with gold pieces that he always used to keep in the backseat. To mark that unhappy event, there now stands a poignant monument by the side of the road: a cenotaph topped with a silhouette of a riderless horse. On the plaque memorializing his life is a handsome portrait of Mix along with Tony, the horse he loved.

## TORNADO'S GRAVE (OKLAHOMA CITY, OKLA.)

Tornado was the greatest bull in rodeo history (see page 181). Just outside the Cowboy Hall of Fame, he is interred along an ambling path that takes visitors past some magnificent bronzes of cowboys as well as monuments to a select few of their best-remembered animals: Baldy ("A Great Cow Pony"), Steamboat (a horse, "Symbol of the Spirit of Wyoming"), Hell's Angels ("Great Bucking Horse"), and Midnight (a horse: "Please, God, Rest His Soul"). Tornado is the only bovine creature honored here; his marker eulogizes such talents as "bucking, jumping, and spinning . . . clown- and barrel-fighting" but notes that "He was not a killer bull. He bucked just hard enough to toss his rider. The better the cowboy rode, the harder Tornado bent to his task."

# TUCSON RODEO PARADE MUSEUM (TUCSON, ARIZ.)

Every year as part of Tucson's gala Fiesta de Los Vaqueros in late February, the city stages the longest nonmotorized parade in America: 350 Conestoga wagons, stagecoaches, buggies, buckboards, and fringe-top surreys, along with detachments of high-stepping horses and riders in full regalia. In the weeks before the event, the Parade Museum opens up to the public; and it is really fun to see. Don't expect million-dollar silver saddles, though; this homespun exhibit, in what was once Tucson's first airplane hangar, features an assortment of prairie schooners and buggies, lots of old saddles and tack, a bunch of colorful Old West storefronts with costumed dummies inside, pictures of the Parade Committee posing in their matching outfits over the last several decades, and some really hospitable gents from the Parade Committee who are more than happy to show you around. Our personal favorite exhibit is in the left-hand corner as you enter: the Cisco Kid's aqua-blue horse trailer, for hauling around his favorite horse, Diablo.

# WIGWAM VILLAGE (HOLBROOK, ARIZ.)

What adventuresome lad or lass hasn't dreamed of sleeping Indian-style in a wickiup under the stars way out West? Here's your chance: a whole village of wigwams (actually, tepees: a wigwam is arched or oval, without a point) available at reasonable rates, with color TV and ample parking. What a fantastic roadside vision they are, especially in the evening when the white concrete cones glow like ghosts of old Route 66 against the Arizona sky.

Each tepee is a single unit with a quartet of lifelike lodge poles sticking up from the spire like a kewpie doll topknot. There are concrete flaps around each door (which is made of wood); inside, in lieu of a fire pit on the floor, there are individual heating controls, and a nice new air conditioner in every unit. Opened by Chester E. Lewis in 1950, this highway landmark followed a design originally patented in Kentucky in 1936; five years ago it was completely renovated. The office now contains a Wigwam museum, gift shop, and petrified wood display near the registration desk.

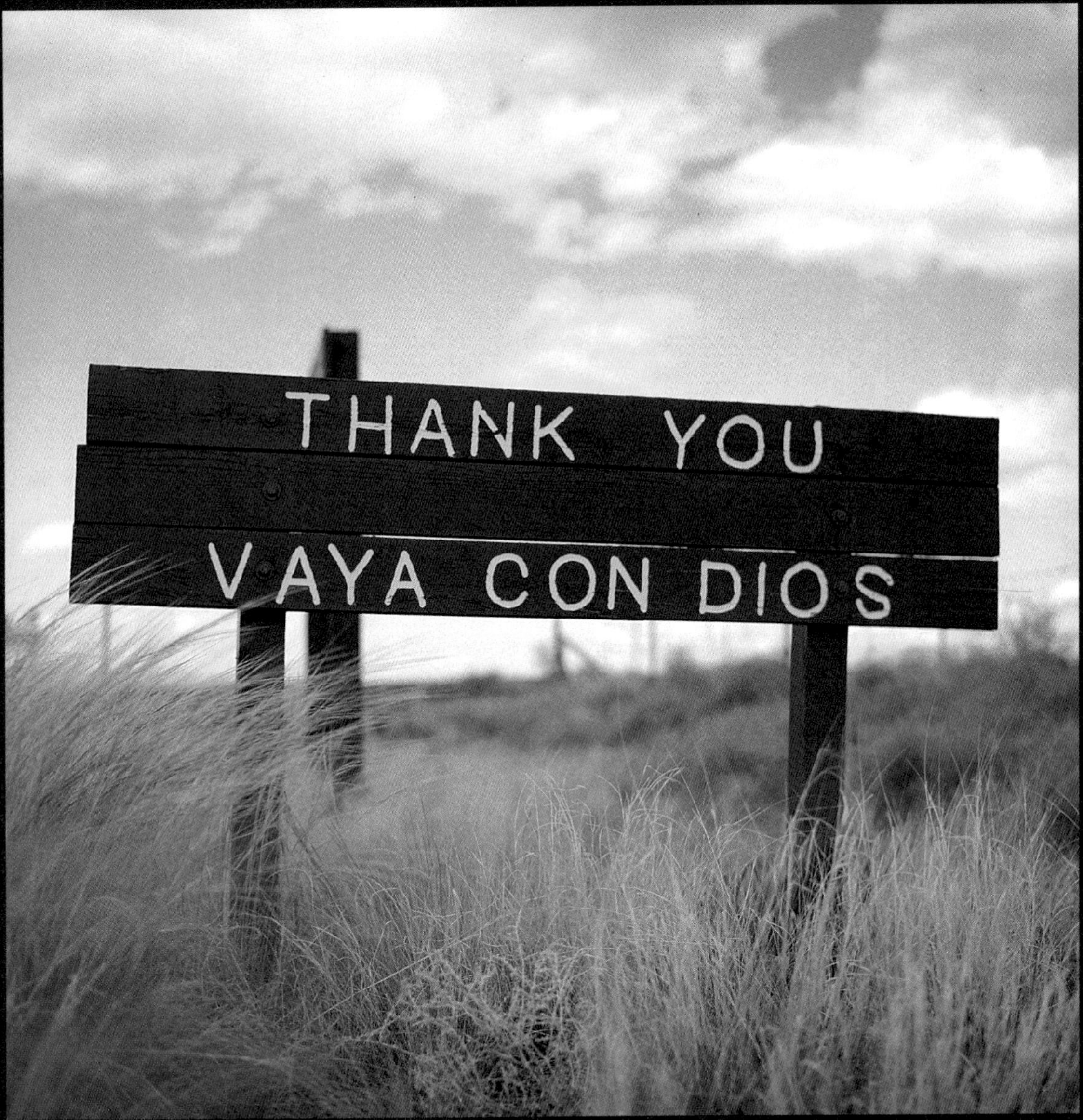
THANK YOU
VAYA CON DIOS

# CRITTERS

The population of the West includes a cast of animals that are as much a part of American mythology as cowboys and Indians: lonesome longhorn cows, majestic woolly buffalo, coyotes howling at the moon, stubborn jackasses, and roadrunners scooting among the sagebrush. Wildlife has always been part of what makes the West so alluringly wild.

Texas Diamond Back Rattle Snake

RAGS

# CRITTERS

7he creatures of the West are magnificent, ugly, scary, scaly, and in some cases, deadly. Many of them have become symbols of the exotic nature of the desert and the High Plains. Humans have always had a strange relationship with the unusual fauna they encounter in the region. Some have been admired and some have been ennobled; the useful ones have been domesticated; the hide and flesh of some have been hunted without mercy; those that have been declared dangerous enemies have been targets of extermination campaigns. What is especially interesting about the critters of the West is how they provoke so much emotion. Their ability to fascinate us humans has elevated many species to legendary status.

No one was more influential than Texas writer J. Frank Dobie in helping people appreciate the critters of the West. Starting with his first book, *On the Open Range* (1931), Dobie wrote with fathomless curiosity and respect about longhorns, coyotes, mustangs, roadrunners, lizards, and snakes (and also about a lot of interesting humans). Every species he explored was given its proper place not only in nature, but in folklore. In his last book, *Rattlesnakes* (1965), he recalled something that had happened to him in 1942. He wrote that he had grown up believing that a decent man always does two things: he shuts every gate he opens, and he kills every rattlesnake he gets a chance at. But he changed his mind (about snakes, not about shutting gates) after an encounter with a rattlesnake in the brush country of southern Texas:

*He was a big one, and when he rattled and I got a whiff of his odor—apt to be strong in the dog days of August—the blood rushed up into the back of my head just as many a rattlesnake had sent it rushing. But I didn't even try to find a stick to kill him. I stood still and watched him glide off into an old badger hole under some cedars. While the hair was getting stiff on the back of my head I had two thoughts that caused my inaction. In the first place, despite my instinctive revulsion, that rusty old rattler suddenly appeared to me as something natural, native, and honest belonging to the land that I belonged to—a fellow creature that I would not want to*

*see exterminated. In the second place, it came to me how honest he is with his poison, not even the gleam of a manufactured smile on his face.*

Even rattlesnakes, Dobie believed, have their own kind of nobility.

One of the most interesting things about the wild animals of the Western range is how naturally we attribute to them human traits and characteristics: the august buffalo, the cunning coyote, the comical roadrunner, the reckless mustang, the outlaw longhorn cow. Walt Disney's documentary movie *The Living Desert* (1953) gave every natural thing in the Southwest, including plants, a vivid personality, but it was

*Mounted coyote, Cheyenne, Wyoming.*

movies of the mid-1950s, the American desert was frequently the origin of malicious mutants (also because it was the desert where some A-bombs had been tested): the giant ants of *Them!* (1954), the mountainous spider of *Tarantula* (1955), and the volcano-bred *Black Scorpion* (1957, set in Mexico). And there was the terrifying *Giant Gila Monster* (1959), which had a special taste for teens in hot-rod cars. Creepy-crawly desert fiends were reprised in *Bug* (1975), about fire-breathing cockroaches that invade a Western town, and *Tremors* (1989), about giant slimy desert worms that suck people under the sand.

The distinctive critters of the West have qualities that make them seem acutely different from animals typical of other parts of the country: the prairie dog, who isn't a dog at all, but barks like one; the coyote, who sings arias; the gila monster, who is the only poisonous lizard on earth; the horned toad, who isn't really a toad, and whose unusual talents include squirting blood from his eyes to deter aggressors. They are fascinating because they have adapted to the harshest environment, and some of them can seem like throwbacks to prehistory. What follows is a roundup of lore, legends, and some amazing facts about the most astonishing of these species.

*The back of this postcard says, "Texas: America's last frontier and land of the modern pioneer!"*

the critters, each referred to as *he* or *she* rather than *it,* that were the stars of the show, and that seemed to possess as much human emotion as any of the 'toons in *101 Dalmatians* or *Lady and the Tramp.*

A lumbering tortoise in *The Living Desert* engages in a jealous feud with another male of his species. He loses his girlfriend to the foe and creeps away, a beaten terrapin; even though he is a loser in the romance department, viewers are assured that he feels "glad to be alive." Nasty desert peccaries are depicted as a rampaging pack of piggy juvenile delinquents who gang up on a faint-hearted bobcat and chase it to the top of a cactus. Then there is Mrs. Rat, matriarch of a family of kangaroo rats, who saves her happy little litter by vanquishing an evil snake who wants to eat them. In a victory celebration, we learn "what a jolly rumpus the little rats made, dancing and jumping and bouncing about." Walt Disney must have had a soft spot for the desert rodents, considering that a certain mouse had been his original cash cow.

Because the desert is such an otherworldly and unfriendly kind of place, many of its animals can seem not only peculiar, but downright malevolent. During the short-lived cycle of giant-insect horror

# Longhorn CATTLE

The West became a legend because of Longhorn cattle. Without them, there would have been no roundups, no trail drives, no rustlers, no hired guns, and no range wars. There would have been no wicked cattle towns in Kansas, no Boot Hill cemeteries, and no moonlight riders singing sagebrush lullabies to keep the restless dogies quiet in the night. Without cows to move, there would have been no cowboys. (In the West the word *cow* can refer to both sexes of the bovine species—bulls as well as cows.) The romance of the West was founded, to a large degree, on the story of what happened when millions of head of longhorn cows were driven from their home on the range in Texas to the railheads of Missouri and Kansas.

Longhorns were uniquely suited to make that harsh journey. As J. Frank Dobie put it in his 1941 biography of the breed, *The Longhorns,* "They could walk the roughest ground, cross the widest deserts, climb the highest mountains, swim the widest rivers, fight off the fiercest bands of wolves, endure hunger, cold, thirst, and punishment as few beasts of the earth have ever shown themselves capable of enduring." As a breed, they had spent three hundred years before the great cattle drives of the 1860s perfecting their survival skills. They were descendants of the first cattle to arrive in the New World—horned Spanish Andalusians brought by Christopher Columbus. The conquistadores and missionaries who followed brought bulls and cows into Mexico, and many of these cattle wandered free, north into Texas territory. In this sparsely populated land, the strays multiplied and adapted to the natural hardships they faced. The fittest survived, developing resistance to parasites and predators, learning to use their formidable horns to fend off wolves and grizzly bears, and to bushwhack thorny shrubbery that grew above edible scrub grass. They evolved into lean, sturdy, independent critters—tall and heavy-boned, seemingly impervious to the elements. By the middle of the nineteenth century, there were four million of them browsing wild on the open range: Texas longhorns.

The fantastic curving horns that gave this breed its name could grow as wide as ten feet or more from tip to tip, although most spans were under six. Once the horns reached their maximum dimension, their owner began to develop wrinkled skin at the base, becoming what was known as a mossy-horn cow. By its maximum age of fifteen, or sometimes as much as twenty, an old, half-ton mossy-horn might have a glove of skin extending halfway out its hornspan. They were lanky beasts, rangy and agile compared to the thick, lumbering beef cattle of today. The breed was also known for its amazingly diverse coloration—most were shades of red, yellow, and brown, but there were also mousy gray *grullas,* brindles (with orange and tan stripes), whites, blacks, and paints, as well as linebacks, which had a stripe straight down their spine. In his *Look of the Old West,* Foster-Harris wrote of them, "Regardless of their color, they could run like deer, swim like sea lions, and fight like catamounts."

Longhorns were fiercely protective of their young; at night in the spring after calving season, the cows of a herd were known to gather around their newborns, horns facing outward to deter aggressors. "Tough, wary, wiry, self-reliant, liberty-loving," is how S. Omar Barker described them in a paean he wrote for *New Mexico* magazine in 1942, which he concluded with his remembrance of a longhorn named Old Wildy he knew as a boy, back before the turn of the century:

*This cow was a beautiful golden yellow lineback who had never seen the inside of a corral since the day of her branding. When the rest of the cattle "swooked" in from all directions for salt, Old Wildy always kept her distance, close to the timber's edge, ready to vanish into its somber, protecting depths at the first move of a horseman toward her. She wintered on the range, sometimes alone except for that season's calf. Wild as a deer, and apparently as fast on her feet, the yellow lineback kept her liberty for years. We simply weren't cowhands enough to bring her in. And neither, it turned out, were the two shore-nuff cowboys who tried to help us. When Old Wildy finally came home she rode in skinned and quartered, on a couple of packsaddles. I remember looking at her golden yellow hide, white bellied, white stripe down the back, as it hung out on the fence, and almost wanting to cry. For although just a button at the time, I somehow sensed that the love of freedom, even in a yellow lineback cow, was a longhorn heritage too admirable, too God-given, to be rightly destroyed for the mere sake of meat.*

The longhorn cow was a symbol of the Wild West not only because of its independent nature, but because of the respect it earned by surviving the trail drives that began in the 1860s. When the first herd of them traversed the Chisholm Trail into Abilene in 1867, townsfolk erected a bandstand and invited the Texas cowboys to drive their herd straight through town. It was a glorious moment for the drovers, for the townspeople (to whom the arrival of the cattle meant prosperity), and for the longhorns themselves. Music played, flags waved,

politicians orated, and thousands of the Texas-born animals, gaunt from the rigors of the trip and as wild as any free-ranging outlaw bull, loped through the streets of Abilene toward the stockyards.

Cattle drives were the foundation for most cowboy lore, and for a world of cow lore, too. Perhaps the greatest hero among the cows that made the journey was Old Blue. He was a male, a mulberry longhorn steer that led the herds of trailblazing cattleman Charlie Goodnight, from Palo Duro in the panhandle of Texas into Dodge City, eight years in a row. "His hooves were hard and bright as polished steel," J. Frank Dobie wrote, describing Old Blue as a sober character who came to think of himself as a seasoned wrangler more than mere livestock. "The older he grew, the more philosophical he became," Dobie noted, recounting tales of his knack for making those who followed him do what he wanted them to do, just by a proper bellow, glance, switch of his tail, or flutter of his dewlaps. By the end of his career, Old Blue was reputed to be able to prevent a stampede just by bawling at the agitated young cows in his thrall. He never

*"My breed is now extinct."*

OLD TIME
TEXAS LONG HORN STEER
HORNS MEASURING 11 FT. 2 IN.

flinched when a jackrabbit jumped in his path, and if nervous cows did start stampeding, he simply stepped aside and mooed authoritatively at the running reprobates. Old Blue was longhorn royalty: he slept with the horses, and was given apples, corn, and chunks of bread by the chuck wagon cook. He finally died at the age of twenty; today his horns are in a museum at West Texas State Teachers College in Canyon.

Old Blue joined the ghost herd in the sky in 1890, by which time the reign of the Texas longhorn was over. Grazing land had expanded northward into Colorado and Wyoming, and railroad tracks had been laid to meet it in the North as well as in the South; all the open country on which longhorns thrived was being sliced by barbed wire into farms and ranches. Cross-country treks became impractical as well as pointless, and the longhorn's hardiness and survival skills, which had suited it so well for the brutal cattle drives, had lost their appeal. By the time the frontier had been transformed into private land, longhorns—symbol of the free range—seemed obsolete. As feed-lot cattle, they took far too long to mature (they didn't reach peak weight until they were ten years old), and they were lean instead of plump. Even their horns could be a liability once they were penned for slaughter; they caused too many cuts in hides that might otherwise have become perfectly good leather. Crossbred with Durhams, Devons, Polled Anguses,

and Brahmans, the longhorn gradually vanished in favor of stock that was docile, uniform in size and shape, and tender-fleshed. By the turn of the century, the lanky, leggy longhorn was despised by fat-beef men, who considered it to be lowly scrub cattle.

In 1927, when the U.S. Congress decided to honor Western history by establishing a national herd of longhorns, Forest Service rangers could find exactly three bulls, twenty cows, and four calves in all the nation that had the pure characteristics of the breed. These surviving specimens were taken to the Wichita Mountains Wildlife Refuge at Cache, Oklahoma, and most of the other cows and steers that looked principally longhorn were used by impresarios as novelty exhibits at stock shows and rodeos.

The pure Texas longhorns recovered by the government, along with a few sturdy specimens still in private herds, eventually became the foundation of what are today known among the handful of longhorn ranchers as the Seven Families—seven different genetic pools used to strengthen and perpetuate the breed (not only for history's sake, but also for their lean and therefore nutritionally fashionable beef). The current population of longhorns is about 150,000—the same number of cattle that were driven north into Kansas on their way to slaughter in a single month in the summer of 1871.

Opposite: *Bobby, The World's Most Educated Steer, rider unknown.* Above: *Longhorns at the Pro Rodeo Hall of Fame, Colorado Springs, Colorado, 1992.*

# BUFFALO

7he biggest of all native North American creatures, and once so prolific that it blanketed the grasslands of the Great Plains in herds that stretched for miles, the buffalo is a symbol of the natural grandeur that was lost when the West was won. No other hoofed creature was so impressive to behold, especially in its tremendous herds, which inspired observers to eulogize America's boundless horizon and the Great Plains' splendor, and to describe the earth as "one big robe . . . black, as if in motion." Its near extinction in the late nineteenth century was declared by the writer N. Scott Momaday to be "perhaps the greatest offense committed against this land."

Although related to the common cow (and scientifically a bison rather than a true buffalo), the American buffalo impressed many of those who saw it in its glory as a symbol of just how different the West was from anyplace else. With its cumbersome hump-shouldered body, heavy horned head with bearded face, and shaggy neolithic pelt, here was an animal that seemed to belong to the era of woolly mammoths, or to a strange Arctic tundra. Its strength was awesome, and many yarns were spun about its charging other animals with its head lowered, tossing wolves and even grizzly bears high into the air. It was also considered a monstrously filthy beast because it relished dunking itself in mud holes (which are still known in much of the Plains as buffalo wallows) until the mud became a thick coat impermeable by bugs. When bugs did make them itch, buffalo frequently

S-1

Native Arizona Buffalo

*1950: Tovrea's Meat Processing Company supported this buffalo in a Phoenix zoo as a keepsake of the past.*

*William F. Cody earned his famous moniker as a buffalo hunter. He brought a small herd to Europe with his Wild West show.*

scratched themselves by rubbing up against a tree, stripping it of all its bark or simply uprooting it.

During a thirty-year period after 1869, when the golden spike was driven at Promontory Point, Utah, uniting the Central Pacific and Union Pacific railroads, the continent's buffalo population was reduced from some sixty million to under a thousand. First they were hunted for hides and for meat, which were shipped via the new rail lines across the country, then to Europe; they were so plentiful that some hunters took only the tongue, which was supposed to be the best part. Their enormous numbers made them easy to kill, and occasionally, they weren't smart enough to run away when they were being shot at. Instead, a group of bulls gathered in a circle, with their horns facing outward—a defensive posture that was formidable against such natural

enemies as wolf packs and mountain lions, but only gave human beings an opportunity to reload their rifles and kill them all. As the animals were eradicated in the southern Plains, hunters moved north. In 1882, two hundred thousand hides were shipped back east.

Throughout the 1870s buffalo were destroyed for sport; in one famous contest, a Dodge City hunter named Thomas Nixon managed to drop 120 of them in forty minutes by alternating between rifles so that he could draw a bead while an accomplice reloaded the second gun. When Grand Duke Alexis of Russia came to America looking for a Western adventure in 1871, Buffalo Bill took him out to a herd, where the overwrought nobleman emptied his six-shooter at an animal twenty feet away . . . but missed. Cody handed him his own mighty .50 caliber Springfield rifle; Alexis rode to within

Chief Iron Tail
The Indian on the Nickel, Oklahoma

*Chief Iron Tail, who claimed to be the model for the Indian on the nickel, took his name from the way buffalo hold their tail when fleeing danger.*

ten feet of a grazing bull and fired. The animal toppled, and Cody later wrote that, "corks began to fly from the champagne bottles." For non-royals, there were excursion trains into the prairie that promised to stop close enough to the herds so that passengers could point their guns out the window and destroy animals without ever having to set foot in the grass. When such a train or a hunting party quit its killing grounds, there were often so many carcasses left behind that even wolves had too much to eat, and acres of slain buffalo rotted in the sun.

But the slaughter wasn't carried out only for amusement. Buffalo had been a vital part of Plains Indian life for centuries—as food, for hides, and as a spiritual totem that the Indians believed had been created by a Supreme Being to sustain them. The U.S. government encouraged and approved of the decimation of the buffalo as a way to deprive recalcitrant Native Americans of a primary food source, forcing them onto reservations, where they were switched to beef. U.S. General Philip Sheridan, notorious as an Indian fighter, described the extermination of buffalo as "the only way to bring lasting peace and allow civilization to advance."

When the U.S. Treasury issued the buffalo nickel (designed by James Earle Fraser) on February 21, 1913, both sides of the famous five-cent piece featured images that stood for a frontier that was long gone. Sioux Chief

Iron Tail, who claimed (along with at least two other Native Americans) to have been the inspiration for the coin's Indian head (which was accompanied by the word *LIBERTY*), was making his living posing for picture postcards and playing a savage in the Miller Bros. 101 Ranch Show. The majestic buffalo on the other side of the coin had been modeled after Black Diamond, a specimen born in New York's Central Park Zoo. In fact, by that point there were more buffalo in zoos than in the wild. Those few that remained free, supposedly protected in a small government herd in Yellowstone National Park, were mostly taken by poachers, but in 1941, three surviving bulls and fifteen cows were transported to public lands in southern Utah, where they were allowed to propagate. These, along with a few private herds, including those established by cattle-drive pioneer Charles Goodnight of Texas and Pend d'Oreille Indian Samuel Walking Coyote of Montana, became the saviors of the species. Goodnight and Walking Coyote kept them safe and bred them, and in fact, there are some eighty thousand buffalo in the West today—enough to supply low-fat meat for novelty steaks and burgers on restaurant menus. Because their natural predators are all nearly extinct, the remaining buffalo thrive and multiply—so much so that the herds of free ones are periodically thinned in organized kills by buffalo hunters.

# ASSES

Stubborn, comical, and eccentric, the ass and its kin are some of the most colorful creatures in folklore. Distinguished from their sleeker equine relatives by a blocky, big-eared head and an upright mane, asses have generally been considered graceless beasts of burden, with none of the charisma of a swift stallion, a potent bull, a winsome cow, or even a faithful dog. They are known mostly for their recalcitrance, which helped make them the butt of countless cowboy jokes and tall tales; there was never an outlaw with a reputation for insubordination as bad as theirs. Another thing that has won them disrespect is their harsh, tuneless braying, for which they got such derisive nicknames as "desert nightingale" and "Rocky Mountain canary." It is surely no compliment to be called a jackass, but as much as oxen, cows, and horses, asses were indispensable to the conquest of the West.

In cowboy movies every grizzled prospector and desert hermit keeps a homely ass as his companion; usually it is a little burro with a big name such as Antiphone or Beelzebub or Margarita, which might wear a straw hat (with holes cut out for its high conical ears), and be known to chew tobacco and laugh like a buck-toothed hyena when a tenderfoot gets thrown from a horse or steps in a cowpie. These improbable critters are renowned for their extraordinary, and in many cases supernatural, talents: their ability to forecast the weather by the way they bray, their uncanny steadiness when transporting loads of dynamite over mountain passes, their acuity in spotting rattlesnakes and gila monsters in the path ahead and refusing to press on. One amazing tale, recounted by Levette J. Davidson in *The Brand Book* (1950), concerns a sleepy prospector riding through the Rockies on his sleepy burro. Both man and animal doze off, but the burro, being a steadfast creature, keeps trudging along in its sleep until it trudges right off a high cliff. The prospec-

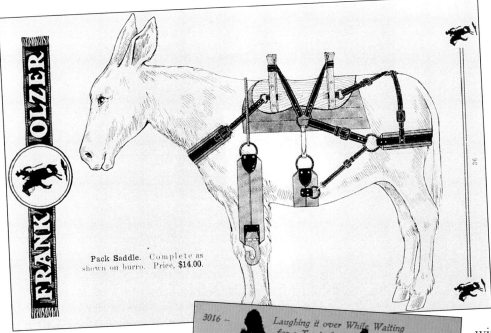

Pack Saddle. Complete as shown on burro. Price, $14.00.

3016 — *Laughing it over While Waiting for a Tenderfoot.*

speed supplies out to mining towns and Army posts. The most acclaimed of these teams were the twenty mules used to haul borax from mines in Death Valley to Mojave, California, in the 1880s.

The best-known burro of the West was named Prunes, who worked in the mines around Fairplay and Alma, Colorado, for over thirty years starting late in the last century. His owner, Rupe Sherwood, allowed him to retire, after which Prunes wandered around the community of Alma from kitchen door to kitchen door each morning seeking handouts of pancakes, his favorite food. According to Frank Brookshier in his book *The Burro* (1974), Prunes lasted until the winter of 1930 when, in his dotage, he got trapped in a shed in a snowstorm. When he was found, he was still alive, but failing; all his teeth had fallen out, and he was no longer able to even gum a pancake. He was put to sleep, and some time later a monument was erected to mark his life. It reads: "*Prunes, a Burro—1867–1930. Fairplay, Alma, All Mines in This District.*" After the animal's death, Rupe Sherwood composed a poem called "Me and Prunes" to remember his companion. The first verse goes like this:

*So poor old Prunes has cashed in.*
*Too bad, still in a way*
*I'm glad the old boy's eased off*
*and calling it a day.*
*I'm going to miss him scand'lous!*
*The world won't seem the same—*
*Not having him a-standin' here*
*hee-hawing in the game.*

Sherwood died a year after Prunes. Before his passing, he requested that his ashes be buried alongside those of his beloved burro.

tor wakes as they are falling, then wakes his burro and calls, "Whoa!" The trusty burro obeys and pulls to a dead stop just a few feet above the canyon floor, whereupon they compose themselves and continue on their way.

Despite their irascible nature, as pack animals asses have no peers. They can negotiate precipitous trails where horses simply cannot fit or maintain sure footing. They are faster and more nimble than oxen, and they have a reputation for going farther on less food than any other beast of burden. For pack trains, mules were the most prized animals because of their ruggedness and dispatch, and a string of eight or ten of them was the epitome of deluxe frontier transportation, often used to

Top: *The catalogue of the Arizona Saddlery Company, around 1910.* Opposite: *"Ghost Riders in the Sky," a hit song about the legendary twenty-mule wagon trains, was sung by Stan Jones, a former Death Valley ranger.*

# An Ass by Any Other Name

**J**ust to set things straight, *donkey* is simply another name for a domesticated *ass* (*Equus asinus*), of which there are several different sizes, from miniature to mammoth; they come in various shades of gray, brown, and beige, and, rarely, with spots (under one thousand spotted asses are currently registered with the American Council of Spotted Asses). The males are *jackasses,* the females are *jennys,* or *jennets;* there are also *burros,* which is merely a Mexican-flavored term for the same animal, although it is usually applied to smaller, fuzzier donkeys and never to mammoth asses. *Mules* are half-asses, the hybrid of a female horse and a male ass; male mules are known as *stallion mules* or *horse mules;* females are called *molly mules. Hinnies* are the reverse of mules: the offspring of a stallion and a jennet. Mules and hinnies, although sexually normal, are sterile.

Death Valley
"Ghost Riders in the Sky."

# COYOTES

**7**he coyote is a small desert dog that typically inhabits gift shops of the American Southwest. It sits on its haunches and wears a bandanna on its neck, and it turns its snout up toward the moon, pursing its lips to howl. You'll see it sculpted of cottonwood, imprinted onto T-shirts and tote bags, and made from wax into a candle with a wick spouting out of its mouth.

It's only right that artists and craftspeople create so many coyotes, considering it was the coyote that created mankind, at least according to Native American folklore. Some stories say that Old Man Coyote created the whole world and all the animals in it; there are yarns describing a primordial conference to which he invited all the other beasts, soliciting their ideas as to what human beings ought to be like. Each egotistically urged that its own species should be the model, but Coyote wanted something better than any of them—a creature that combined some qualities of each, including a doe's eyes, a bear's feet, and especially the Coyote's own wiles. A big fight ensued, and all the animals started to fabricate their own designs, but being the craftiest of the bunch, Coyote got his way: he waited until the others slept, then destroyed their half-formed creations and breathed life into his own, begetting mankind as we know it. Other fables credit him with creating the moon and the stars and the winter snows, always through trickery and mischief, and there are legends in which he uses his cunning in trades

"I'm Wild About The Desert"

Desert Blues

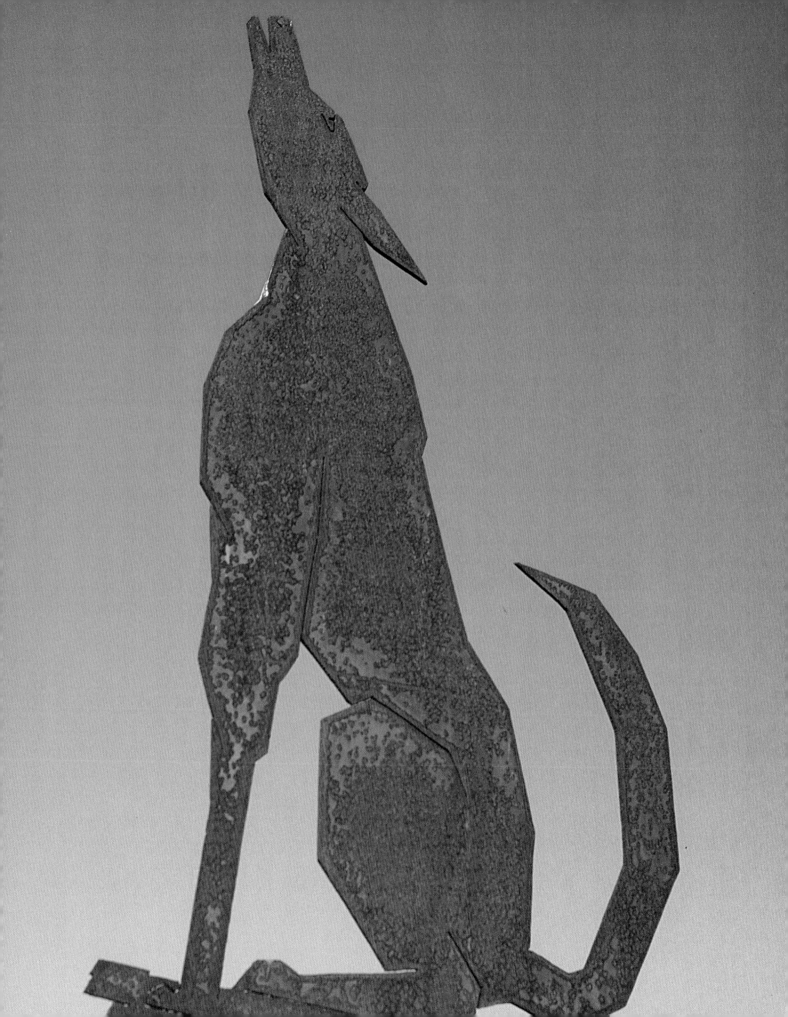

with mortal people, usually swindling them out of their best horses, jewelry, and fancy clothes.

In nature, as in folklore, the coyote is a notoriously shrewd being. If he weren't, he likely wouldn't have survived a century of settlers' efforts to eradicate him as a predator of livestock. Coyotes are known for their uncanny ability to avoid entrapment and stay out of sight—survivalistic qualities that are frequently condemned by their frustrated hunters as cowardice. They like meat and will eat carrion as well as fattened sheep, and are skillful at catching mice, frogs, rabbits, and even grasshoppers; when there is no meat to be had, they can get along on seeds, beans, berries, weeds, and grass. Farmers have long told tales of their devilish talent for always choosing the plumpest chickens in the coop or the ripest melons in the field, and trail-drive folklore is replete with stories of cowpokes awakening to find their horses wandering away because coyotes snuck up in the night and ate their leather tethers.

What coyotes do best is sing, especially at night when the moon is out. They customarily begin with an overture of short, piercing yips that leads into a long, ghostly wail. One coyote can sound like many, and a few can seem to fill the desert with song. In his book *Wonders of the West,* Oren Arnold described the coyote's howl as "the true call of the room-enough," and Texas folklorist J. Frank Dobie described it as "seeming to express remembrance of something lost before time began." It is not uncommon for families of them to howl in harmony around their den, letting other faraway groups know where they are, and at the same time providing cowhands with an eerie sagebrush serenade.

With the notable exception of Wile E. Coyote, the hapless (and ultimately harmless) nemesis of the Road-runner in Warner Brothers cartoons, coyotes have long been thought of by most Americans as capable, stealthy predators with an aptitude for evil—a reputation encouraged by ranchers, who feared for their stock and have lobbied to eradicate them. "Bushwhacker upon the flanks of the buffalo ranges; the pariah of his own race, and despised of mankind," wrote Ernest Ingersoll in *Coyote Wisdom* (1938). "He is the Ishmaelite of the desert."

Starting in the 1980s, however, the coyote has enjoyed a pop culture image makeover and has gone from criminal to cute, and from moonlight murderer to playful prankster. The rehabilitation is partly due to a new appreciation of Native American mythology and cowboy lore, and also to the increasing glamour of Santa Fe, New Mexico, as a tourist destination. Older kinds of Southwest souvenirs, such as bleached cattle skulls, armadillo baskets, and lucky rattlesnake charms all have a certain uncouth quality out of sync with Santa Fe's burgeoning image as a place where refined people come to shop. On the other hand, the carved wooden coyote, wearing a scarf and looking as amiable as a pet pooch as he raises up on his front tippy toes to croon toward the sky, has proven to be an enchanting emblem of a tourist-friendly town, with just the right measures of natural animal attraction and folkloric heritage. No one can say exactly how it suddenly got so popular among home decorators and in gift shops, but by 1987 it had become a commonplace sign of Southwest chic, and in 1989 it was featured prominently in a comical poster by artist Jerome E. Milord, who drew a woman wearing heaps of silver and turquoise lying flat on her back in the middle of an extravagantly appointed adobe home. The caption reads "Another Victim of Santa Fe Style." The coyote got so overexposed that by the end of the 1980s, some locals, exasperated by the influx of sightseers it had come to represent, began to put bumper stickers on their cars that showed the howling coyote in a circle with a slash-bar through it—the international nix sign.

# ROAD-RUNNERS

7he galloping ground cuckoo known as the roadrunner does not say "meep meep!" like the cartoon character when it races along the road ahead of horses, wagons, stray golf balls, or autos. Its cry is more a sibilant "croot croot!" interspersed with a harsh cackle and the clicking of its bill. Furthermore, wily coyotes are rarely interested in chasing after this long-legged, big-footed bird; the roadrunner's real predators are eagles, hawks, bobcats, and domestic cats, as well as human hunters who have found the high-crested speed demon an irresistible target, and who have justified shooting it because it is believed to eat young quail (it rarely does).

The one trait of the Mel Blanc-voiced Roadrunner of cartoon fame that *is* true to life, and to desert folklore, is its knack for outwitting enemies. Usually, however, it is roadrunner prey rather than its predators who get hoodwinked. Although most of the roadrunner's diet is such relatively easy-to-nab fare as lizards, bugs, toads, scorpions, and rabbits, it is also known for its ability to attack and kill a rattlesnake, which it does by engaging in a flurry of feints, dodges, kicks, and turns, forcing the rattler to strike, at which point it eludes the fangs and leaps on the back of the reptile's head, then pecks it to death. Sonora Desert tales also credit roadrunners with the talent for sneaking up on a resting rattler and stealthily surrounding it with a corral of cactus pads. The bird then makes a racket, causing the snake to wake and strike out, impaling itself on the thorns.

Known as *paisano* in Mexico and *chaparral cock* in Texas, the roadrunner inhabits lowlands from the southern Pacific coast into west Texas, and it is the state bird of New Mexico. It *does* have the capacity to fly, with ease and gliding grace for short distances, but it much prefers scampering along in its hunt for bugs and such, and it generally does so in a recurring pattern that has endeared the busy-seeming critter to human observers. Many country folks have come to know a roadrunner by its regular, daily rounds as it zooms past the back porch at 10:15 A.M. sharp, screeching to a stop by fanning its long tail upward, surveying the scene, then streaking off again to return every day for another look-see at dusk. In her marvelous "Naturegraph," *Roadrunner* (1984), Virginia Douglas tells the tale of a pair of them that used to visit a ranch outside of Santa Fe at the exact time the rancher fed his chickens (roadrunners like cracked corn, too), then roosted with the chickens at night; another pair delighted in visiting a mine near Hachita each day just so they could get chased by the miner's dog who, of course, never caught them.

Roadrunners are inquisitive fowls, and Southwest homesteaders have often told of being carefully scrutinized by one as they built their homes and worked their land. In some cases, the birds have made friends with people, as well as with people's pets, but they are usually too wary to get within touching distance. According to Virginia Douglas, there was one exceptionally friendly one in the western Arizona desert at Quartzsite that decided to take up residence in a town telephone booth, where customers used to stroke its head feathers as they made their calls. One local citizen took the bird home and gave it the run of his cabin, which it enjoyed immensely . . . although it returned every night, like clockwork, to roost in its favorite phone booth.

The actual top speed of a roadrunner is a bit under twenty miles per hour on a straightaway, but it seems faster because of the way it changes direction on a dime, zigzagging among cacti and thickets of mesquite in its quest for tasty lizards or, apparently, for the sheer pleasure of racing.

In 1962 *Picturesque New Mexico* magazine printed this poem, titled "Road Runner," by Inga Kent, age eight, of Las Cruces:

Runner, Runner, bird of the state,
How fast you run, it's very great.

All you do is scurry 'long.
You never stop to sing a song.

How gaily prance with head so high,
You never lift your feet to fly.

But still I like you, oh so great.
Runner, Runner, bird of state.

CONCHA'S ROADRUNNER SERVICE

*Because of their speed, roadrunners are an especially popular motif for automobile service stations, as well as for restaurants that deliver food.*

# ARMADILLOS

The fame of the armor-plated armadillo has little to do with qualities the living animal possesses—although admirers laud its tenacity and adaptability and the toughness of its flexible bony shell. Among tourists and collectors of Western kitsch, armadillos are renowned mostly because they become such nice souvenir baskets when they are dead. For many years, an armadillo basket was as popular a keepsake from a trip to Texas as were alligator ashtrays from Florida and cypress-knee lamps from the Louisiana swamps.

According to *The Amazing Armadillo* (1984), a truly amazing book by Larry L. Smith and Robin W. Doughty containing *everything* there is to know about the subject, armadillo baskets were invented—actually discovered—and first marketed by Charles Apelt of the Apelt Armadillo Farm and Basket Company outside of Comfort, in the Texas Hill Country. Mr. Apelt stumbled upon what would be his life's work one day in the late 1890s while plowing the fields of his farm. Farmers have always disliked armadillos because they root up plants and dig burrows that can cause livestock to stumble and twist a leg, so Apelt heaved a few rocks at the varmint and killed it. He skinned it, then hung up the skin on a shed door to dry. Later, he returned to find that the sun had caused the armadillo carapace to curl up, with the tail reaching toward the head, resembling a basket. At that moment, Charles Apelt beheld his destiny; within a few years, he was selling armadillo baskets from a souvenir shop he opened on his farm, as well as wholesaling them to stores all around the state, especially

around military bases, where soldiers bought them as mementos of their stay in Texas.

Apelt sold plain armadillo baskets (in natural shades of beige), deluxe baskets with colored silk lining and festoonery, painted baskets, and also table lamps with armadillo shell shades, and even chandeliers made from matched groups of armadillo shells, as well as such other frontier-themed knickknacks as rattlesnake skins and "Aztec" pottery, plus starfish lamps and baskets made of coconut shells. His customers eventually included curio shops all over the world, and by the time he died in 1944, he (and many competitors) had helped make armadillo baskets as prominent a symbol of Texas as the Alamo.

There were no armadillos in the United States when the battle of the Alamo had been fought; they started arriving about the time Texas joined the Union. Attracted by north-of-the-border insects (which they wanted to eat), as well as by the fact that settlers were busy killing off their

A Group of Armadillos

© CURT TEICH & CO., INC.

*An armadillo family in the wild.*

*Armadillo baskets for sale.*

natural enemies (wolves, bobcats, coyotes, and cougars), the hump-backed mammals began swimming across the Rio Grande and darting past dusty border posts; a few were even carried into the country by human beings, as novelty pets or as stuffing for tacos. By 1900, the armadillo was common throughout South Texas. (We mean the familiar nine-banded armadillo, a creature just over two feet long and weighing about fifteen pounds; other varieties range from the pink-fairy armadillo of Argentina, which is the size of a guinea pig, to the giant armadillo of Bolivia, which can weigh up to 130 pounds.) By 1950 armadillos were nearly everywhere in Texas, and well on their way toward Louisiana, Oklahoma, and Arkansas. Now they range through most of the Southeast, but in the United States armadillos remain, by reputation and by character, as Texan as a mockingbird or a longhorn cow.

Although they are eaten regularly in Central and South America, armadillos never made a big hit as food in the United States, mostly because they look like troglodytic rats. Their meat is considered poor people's fare, closer to rodents like muskrats and squirrels than to respectable human victuals, and 'dillos became known, pejoratively, as Hoover hogs during the Depression. Even many self-sufficient rural hunters don't like to eat them because they live in burrows underground and, in folklore, are known as "grave diggers" because they supposedly feast on newly buried corpses. Nonetheless, Hondo Crouch, the epi-

curean mayor of Luckenbach, Texas, entered a recipe for armadillo chili in the Terlingua World's Chili Cook-Off in 1969 (it didn't win); Crouch was also known for devising the armadillo weight-loss plan: "Eat nothing but armadillo for a month, but you have to catch all the armadillos you eat—really takes the weight off!"

In addition to scouring the countryside for wild armadillos, Charles Apelt had also raised some in captivity, a few for sale as pets or to zoos, but most for medical-research facilities. Because armadillos have a natural body temperature of ninety-three degrees, similar to human body extremities such as the nose and ears, they make an ideal host for *Mycobacterium leprae,* the bacilli that cause leprosy; they can also be used to prepare lepromin, which is used in diagnosing leprosy patients. When Mr. Apelt's family finally closed the Armadillo Company in 1971, there was a sudden dearth of armadillos in leprosy research facilities, but the gauntlet was quickly picked up by Sam Lewis, a San Angelo entrepreneur who had contrived the sport of armadillo racing at carnivals in the mid-1960s, and whose reputation was also based on the fact that he had invented the jalapeño-flavored lollipop.

The armadillo developed countercultural cachet via cartoons and caricatures by the Austin artist Jim Franklin, who has been called "the Michelangelo of armadillo art," and who, starting in the late 1960s, produced all sorts of armadilliana, including posters that showed hipster armadillos smoking marijuana and a giant armadillo trying to copulate with the state's capitol dome. Larry Smith and Robin Doughty report that by the mid-1970s the armadillo had become a fundamental icon of "Texas chic," and a symbol of "laid-back, unconventional living."

In 1979 and again in 1981, armadillo supporters lobbied the Texas legislature to make the anteater-shaped animal the state mammal, but both times opposition from anti-armadillo forces squashed the effort. "We ought to just kill 'em all," argued Representative Bennie Bock of New Braunfels, where gardeners consider them nothing but a nuisance. Although it has never attained state-mammal status, it was named Official State Mascot in 1981 by executive decree that lauded it as having "the attributes that distinguish a true Texan." These attributes included respect for the land, adaptability, and love of freedom, as well as "skin as tough as a cowboy's boot."

# *Horned* TOADS

The horned toad is no ordinary frog. In fact, it isn't a frog at all. It is a lizard about four inches long with pointy scales along its side and a crown of sharp spines on its head which, combined with its broad, frowning mouth, make it look like a bulbous little sourpuss in a suit of armor. The Texas horned lizard is the most common variety, and it has long been kept by kids as a pet (although few owners provide it a proper diet of large, living ants), but its rarer relative, the regal horned lizard of the Sonora Desert, is the one whose amazing repertoire of survival skills has mesmerized humans for centuries:

*It can use the jutting spines along the back of its neck to plow down into sand and bury itself with only its eyes and nose visible above the ground surface.*

*It can seem to hibernate, and it will spend the early part of most days in the desert lying flat and still on a rock, absorbing the sun's heat.*

*It can squirt blood out of its eyeballs (by raising its blood pressure to a stratospheric level). It can shoot from one eyeball or two; the stream can travel up to four feet, and it makes a sound similar to that of just-poured seltzer water.*

*It can blow itself up with air so that it resembles a football, thus becoming impossible for a snake to swallow.*

*It can deflate its lungs and become stiff as a wood plank, making you think it is dead.*

*The concept for this strange old postcard probably came from the horned toad's ability to puff itself up, also from its reputation as a desert ruffian with a tough attitude.*

A TEXAS HORNED TOAD SMOKING A CIGARETTE—T18

# *Deadly* CREATURES

hich bloodthirsty animal is most likely to kill you in the desert? The hissing sidewinder, with its rattles clicking like castanets of death? The hideous gila monster, which is said to spit clouds of poison gas, and whose tough, boney skin is believed to be impervious to slugs from a Winchester .30-.30? The stinging scorpion? The hairy tarantula? The slavering coyote? The loathsome-looking buzzard? The answer is: none of the above. The frightful desert fiend with the highest probability of inflicting a fatal injury on a person is the plump yellow honeybee. Even the bee isn't much interested in murdering anybody, but statistically it is the beast most likely to sting you, and (again, statistically) the one most likely to induce a life-threatening allergic reaction in a human. All the other animals—those fabled creepy-crawly assassins of countless dime novels, low-budget Westerns, and mutant-creature horror movies—will do just about anything to avoid human contact, and even if they do happen to sting or bite, the main thing you ought to worry about isn't their venom, but the panic you will feel because of all the ridiculous fables about how deadly desert critters are. It is far more probable that you will be killed because of your own hysterical, reckless driving rushing to a doctor than by anything an animal has done.

In the rogue's gallery of notorious desert critters, these four are usually thought of as the most malevolent:

*The scorpion: sudden death lurks in a shoe or sugar bowl.*

# RATTLESNAKE

Beady-eyed, fork-tongued serpents that travel mostly by night, rattlers eat rodents and do their best to stay away from human beings. Nevertheless, they are the most infamous of all the enemies offered up by the desert. They announce their presence by a hiss and a rattling tail as they coil like a spring and appear ready to strike. In the movies, when you come across a rattler behaving this way, you are supposed to either shoot it instantly or freeze, still as stone, because snakes are known to lunge toward anything that moves. In fact, a snake will sometimes strike out toward a sudden movement, but it is not likely to attack if you simply back away and leave it alone: the rattle is its way of saying, "go away." If you do move away and it does decide it really wants to sink its fangs into you anyway, its maximum land speed is two to three miles per hour, and because it has only one lung, it has almost no long-distance stamina.

When a rattlenake does strike, it injects its venom (through its fangs) in order to immobilize prey and to begin to break down its tissue (thus beginning digestion) for eating in one, tender, trouble-free piece. A rattler is smart enough to know that a human is just too big to consume in one piece, which is the only way it eats. Unable to chew with its unfused jaws, it can open them shockingly wide—wide enough to engulf a good-size rabbit and ingest it by slowly slithering forward, transforming the poisoned animal into a huge lump of food that moves down toward its stomach. (Such a meal is so big and nutritious that a mature rattler needs to eat only about ten times each year; after injecting its venom, a snake needs three full weeks to build up a new supply.)

## RATTLER FACTS

1. For an hour after it dies, a rattler's reflexes are still intact; so a dead one can still strike and bite.

2. Contrary to myth, the number of rattles do not indicate how old a snake is.

3. A rattlesnake often bites without first rattling.

4. The rattle is actually more like a buzz, which can range from twenty cycles per second (in the cold) to eighty-five cps. (in temperatures above 100°F.).

5. Only one half of one percent of all people bitten by a snake actually die as a result.

*Milking Rattlesnake, Ross Allen's Reptile Institute, Silver Springs, Fla.*

PHOTO BY SAM ANDRE "PIC MAGAZINE"

Tarantula *(1955) featured Clint Eastwood as a pilot who tries to kill the giant spider by dropping a bomb on it.*

There are several different kinds of rattlesnakes in the United States, not including the legendary monstrous one in the Arbuckle Mountains of Oklahoma—it's rumored to be twenty feet long, broad as a big dog, and with scales and studs along his back that are so bright they can blind a victim in the sun. Among real rattlesnakes in the Southwestern deserts, the diamondback is usually considered the most frightening; the sidewinder, also known as the little horned rattler, is the most peculiar, known for a loopy slither through the sand that makes it look as if it is hurling itself along.

## TARANTULA

Tarantulas are the big and hairy spiders that starred in the movie *Arachnophobia* (1991). Natt N. Dodge, in the booklet *Poisonous Dwellers of the Desert* (1976), recounts

tall tales of them leaping at hapless human victims from as far away as ten feet, sinking their gruesome fangs into a neck, and inflicting a painful bite that causes a slow, excruciating death. In fact, the timid tarantula has terrible vision, and pounces on its favorite prey—a grasshopper—from no more than six inches away, which is about as far as it can see. It does have fangs, and if it uses them on a human, the bite will hurt. It injects no poison, however, and the rare lingering effect is usually due to a secondary bacterial infection. Therefore, the proper treatment of tarantula bite is the application of iodine.

## SCORPION

If you are stung by a scorpion, you will likely feel numb where the stinger pierced your flesh, but unless you are a baby or an extremely allergic person or the stinger gets you in the neck, along the backbone, or on your genitalia, numbness is all you've got to worry about.

A scorpion is a scary-looking little armored bug, with pincers in the front (to hold its prey) and a long, curving tail tipped with a bulb full of poison and a stinger. It injects its poison with a quick flick, paralyzing quarry (usually a centipede or soft-shelled beetle), then tearing at its flesh with a set of hard mandibles. It is especially worrisome because it can pop up almost anywhere—not only under rocks in the desert, but in sleeping bags and in woodpiles and even in dresser drawers and kitchen cabinets. If you are in scorpion country (southern Arizona), you should consider shaking out your shoes every morning and looking under your sheets and blankets when you go to bed at night.

# GILA MONSTER

One of the best dumb horror movie premises was *The Giant Gila Monster* (1959), which featured teenagers in hot-rod cars trying to escape from a forty-foot-tall lizard. What the lizard did was kill them and eat them, and that was quite awful indeed, but frightening as it was, we believe that the producers missed a good bet in not making the scariest thing about the gila monster a feature of the film: the way it smells. These big stinkers have such a reputation for their bad breath that some folk tales describe them as having no anus at all; they are believed to be walking septic tanks who turn waste into venom and eliminate it out of their mouths by injecting it whenever they bite their prey. When they are not inoculating victims with putrefied stool, the very air they exhale is a steady torrent of gaseous fumes. In their book *Gila Monster* (1991), David E. Brown and Neil B. Carmony quote an article from the *Arizona Citizen* on May 15, 1890, that told of a woodcutter in the Huachuca Mountains who failed to rise from his sleeping bag in the morning. His companions discovered he was dead, and spotted a gila monster slithering away. And yet there wasn't a wound or bite mark on him. "We must suppose," the newspaper concluded, "that his death was caused by the mere exhalation of the lizard."

Gila monsters do have anuses, and their anuses have scent glands that broadcast an aroma, but it's not nearly as strong as a skunk's; their breath is not notably worse than that of other lizards, although it does have a clammy quality. In fact, they themselves have an extremely delicate sense of smell (via receptors in their mouth), which helps them locate their favorite foods, which include bird eggs, smaller reptiles, and newborn rodents. Their reputation as loads of festering feces is probably derived from the fact that the gila monster, like many reptiles, eats only intermittently, and can live off what it stores in its tail through a winter or a long drought. In the early spring, when gila monsters come out of their underground burrows (to which they will likely return for the whole span of their fifteen-to-twenty-year life), their tails drag behind them like limp little ropes; after they spend a few weeks chowing down on bird eggs, nestlings, and newborn rabbits, the tails swell up as wide as their bodies.

At about twenty inches long, with a gorgeous black-and-coral stripe pattern in its beaded skin, the gila monster is the biggest lizard native to the United States; along with its Mexican variant, the *Heloderma horridum* (meaning terrible, studded-skinned thing), it is unique among lizards in its capacity for injecting poisonous venom when it bites. Despite this fact, and despite its name, it poses almost no danger to humans, except for humans who actually put their hand inside its mouth. It waddles slowly with a wide-legged gait that is anything but ominous; although it is agile when it needs to be, and capable of snapping and hissing in its defense, it tends not to attack like a lunging snake. When it decides to bite something, it does so with deliberation; venom is secreted from glands in the lower jaw, slowly, as it clamps down hard and chews the poison into the flesh of its victim.

*Gila monsters are impervious to cactus thorns.*

# JACKALOPES

**7**he jackalope is the most easily sighted varmint in the American West, if you know where to look: in souvenir stores. Most jackalopes are furry and a foot or two tall; many are only heads, mounted on wood plaques; there are some six-footers, covered with fur, that can be found under tents on the midways of state fairs and big rodeos, where they are outfitted with saddles so customers can climb aboard and have their picture taken.

It is plain to see how the ridiculous creature got its name: body and ears like a jackrabbit, horns like an antelope. It was invented in Douglas, Wyoming, in 1934 when a couple of taxidermist cut-ups named Ralph and Doug Herrick decided to plant the antlers of a small dead deer on the head of a big dead jackrabbit. They sold their trophy (it was a head only, mounted on wood) to a local saloon, where it was hung above the bar and no doubt caused many a bleary customer to wonder what in tarnation he was drinking.

N-33                          *Cowboy Riding a Jack Rabbit*

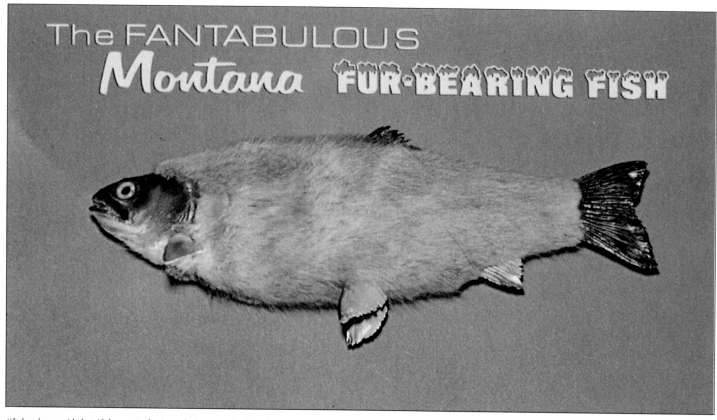

*"It has been said that if the exotic fur is made into a neck piece the wearer enjoys immunity from numerous ailments."*

Since then the aberrant animal the Herricks designed has been reproduced thousands of times and has become the reigning star of tall-tale critters.

Well before jackalope creation day, outrageous animals, as well as improbable fruits and vegetables, were a popular postcard motif in the time-honored tradition of frontier braggadocio. The theme of most of them was unbelievable hugeness. Twenty-foot ears of corn, man-size melons, and potatoes as big as a railroad car were dramatic images that showed the folks back East just how incredibly fertile the wide-open spaces were; some cards touted the rivers' bounty by featuring trout and pike that dwarfed fishermen's boats; hunters back home were bedazzled by plump prairie chickens that lorded over bison. Abundance wasn't the only point of these Barnumesque enticements to the wonders of the West; sheer strangeness was also a big part of their appeal. Some cards featured buxom cattle with pretty girls' faces, scorpions the size of a house, buzzards that sat on fence posts discussing the fate of thirsty desert wanderers, or cowboys mounted on giant rabbits rather than on horses.

The Herrick brothers' 3-D jackalope readily made the leap from trophy to star of tall-tale postcards, of which there have been hundreds of variations in the last sixty years. It also established a small industry of similar mutant souvenir trophies, ranging from a rattlesnake with tiny antlers to a trout with a muskrat's pelt instead of scales. Fur-bearing trout abound in folktales collected in the late 1930s, which include at least two stories that explain their origin: a spill of hair tonic into a Colorado stream, or a school of especially frisky trout that got loose in a silver fox farm. No oddity, however, has had the charisma of the original horned hare of Wyoming.

*Opposite: Jackalopes in bars and roadside stores frequently wear sunglasses.*

# SKULLS

*T*he cattle skull is an unusual kind of memento mori—too common to retain the kind of disturbing deathly aura attached to a desiccated human head, and yet still a reminder that death at nature's hand feels a little closer out West than in gentler parts of the country. Traditionally, in the desert—but especially in movies about cowboys and pioneers in the desert—skulls are a portent of nature's brutal efficiency: denuded by scavengers of all their meat and moisture, they warn those who dare pass by of what will happen to any person or any creature that falters. Like buzzards circling over a thirsty wanderer, bleached bones along the trail are a sign that the grim reaper is close at hand.

Curiously, they are some of the most popular decorative objects in the West. With antlers attached, they serve as coat racks and hat trees, as shields above doorways and as household bibelots. Antlers alone, whether shed (as by deer) or sawed off the skull of an animal to which they were attached for life, have sometimes been used as the ornamental superstructure for a table, chair, or hassock, which is then upholstered with hide from the animal whose equipment they presumably once were.

The best-known use of the skull as a pictorial charm is in the art of the painter Georgia O'Keeffe, who started bringing bones back East after her summers in New Mexico in the 1930s. She used them as a repeated motif in some canvases and painted single skulls in such grand works as *Cow's Skull—Red, White and Blue* (1931) and *Ram's Head with Hollyhock* (1935). She even painted landscapes with assorted animal pelvises and vertebrae in the foreground. But it was mostly her renderings of bleached-white brain pans that helped make bones into an emblem of austere Southwest desert beauty.

Mary Emmerling, the design master who shows people how to lead lovely country-style lives, explained in her book *American Country West* (1985) that "sun-bleached skulls from the countryside mingle easily with potted cactus plants on the porch," and (speaking of antlers) advised readers that "It is not uncommon to see animal afterlife curling around a tree, embellishing the side of a barn, or serving as an unexpected arbor or archway." Although Ms. Emmerling's sensibility is far too refined to make note of it, it should also be said that antlers from Texas longhorn steers have long been a favorite automobile ornament in the Southwest, most especially on large Cadillacs equipped with musical horns that moo and bellow instead of merely beep, driven by show-offs with money to burn. (The

Left: *Tex Terry equipped his Cadillac with steer horns.* Above: *A building on the road from Tucson to Nogales.* Opposite: *Skulls for sale in Lupton, Arizona.*

roadster in which movie cowboy star Tom Mix had his fatal accident was equipped with a six-foot longhorn span mounted on the radiator.)

The great cattle drives of the 1860s and 1870s originally gave cattle skulls their aura of frontier enchantment. So many animals died along the way from Texas up to Kansas and Missouri that trails were marked by their bones. Then, after grazing ranges had been established farther north, the punishing winter of 1886–87—the coldest anyone in the West had ever known—strewed the High Plains with bones of animals that froze to death. In *The Longhorns*, J. Frank Dobie quoted one line rider describing cattle as "gathered around ranch houses, bellowing and bawling and crowding up to the windows and looking in, in appeal for help." By the spring thaw, their carcasses were piled high along barbed-wire fences and were damming rivers and blocking roads. Some 90 percent of the cows in Colorado and Wyoming had perished in the cold, and "for years bones bleached on windswept foothills against the high Rockies . . . lay scattered from one side of the land of buffalo grass to the other."

The dead animals' skulls were picked up by frontier survivalists, grizzled hermits, eccentric Indian traders, and settlers who couldn't afford anything store-bought in the way of home decor. Nailed onto cabin walls, inside and out, they became bold signs of pioneer pluck and toughness, of homesteaders who had weathered the worst nature could throw at them. Originally there weren't a lot of civilized middle-class citizens who would consider something so gruesome as a proper object to hang on a parlor wall, or even on a polite front porch. But as the frontier came to an end and as its romance was kindled, bleached bones became a way to honor the ruggedness of the land and the bravery of the settlers who overcame its hardships.

So the cattle skull was transformed from an omen of imminent death into a proud token of Western heritage, and, more recently, into a vital element of high fashion, Santa Fe style. Nowadays, most skulls sold in gift shops and at roadside stands are retrieved from boiling pots at slaughterhouses, although interior designers prize older ones that look like they came from cattle who died on the range and whose remains have weathered the ages.

Top: *Detail of a cowboy boot custom-made in El Paso.* Above: *Outside the Chimayo Trading Post in Española, New Mexico.* Opposite: *At the Hubbell Trading Post in Ganado, Arizona.*

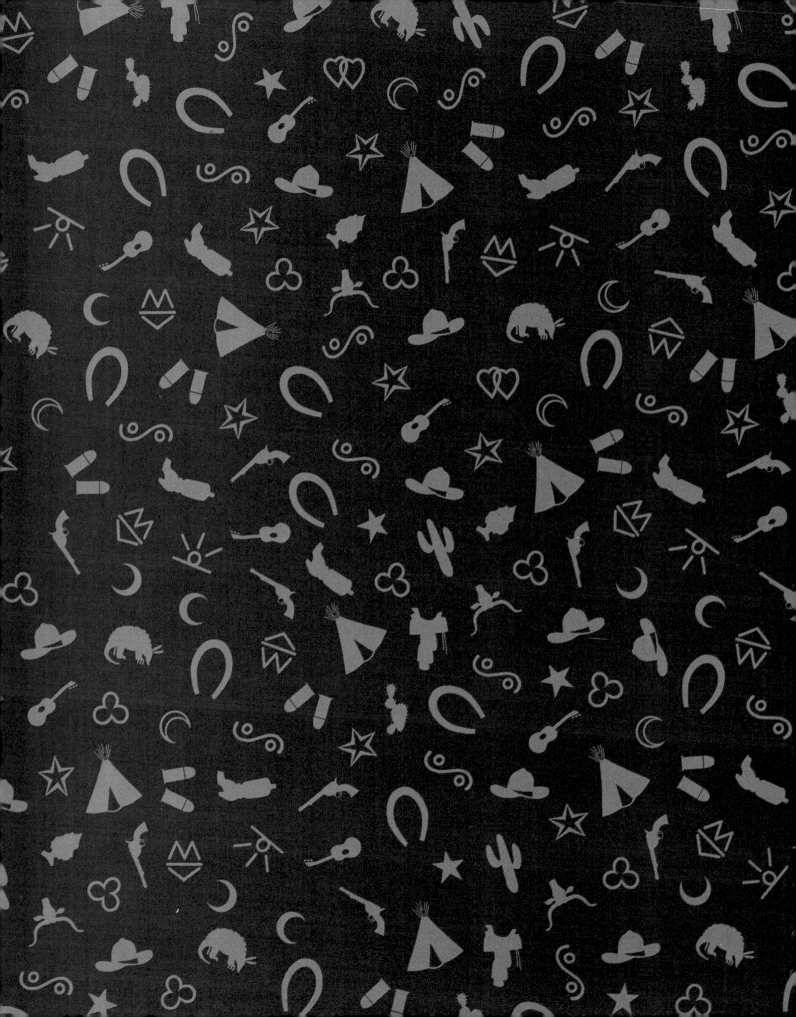

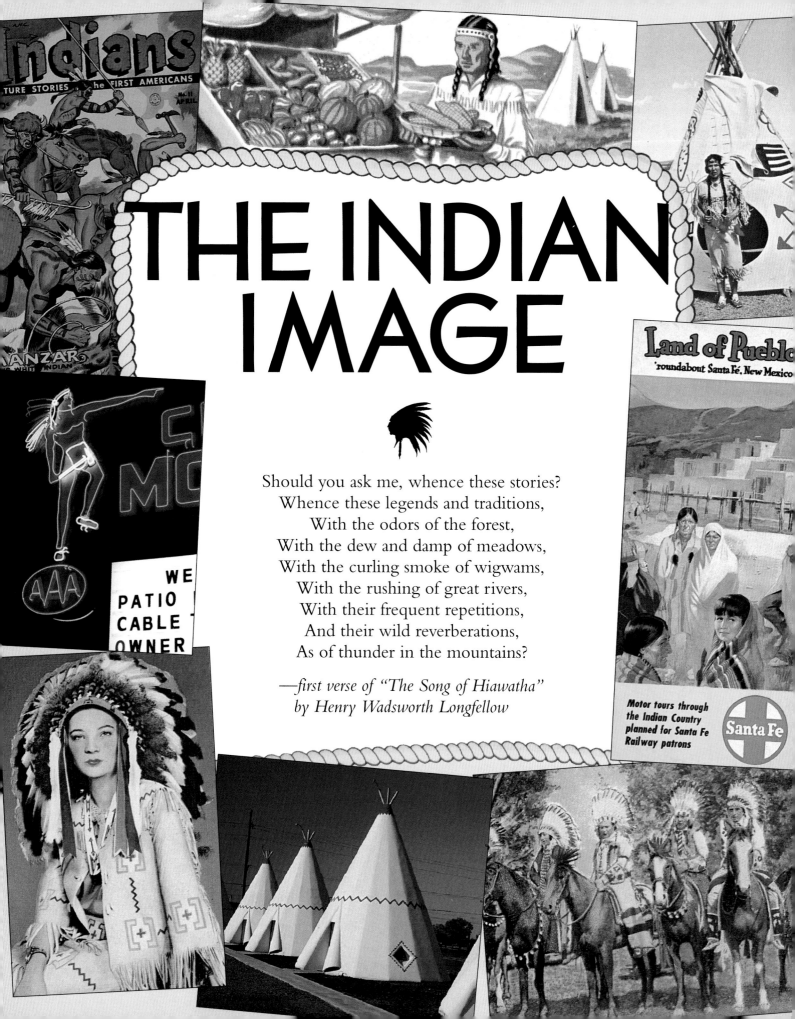

# THE INDIAN IMAGE

Should you ask me, whence these stories?
Whence these legends and traditions,
With the odors of the forest,
With the dew and damp of meadows,
With the curling smoke of wigwams,
With the rushing of great rivers,
With their frequent repetitions,
And their wild reverberations,
As of thunder in the mountains?

—*first verse of "The Song of Hiawatha"
by Henry Wadsworth Longfellow*

# The Indian IMAGE

In 1907, the American Indian became the best-known Western advertising image prior to the Marlboro cowboy. It was that year that the Santa Fe Railroad issued the first of its annual calendars, featuring paintings of Native Americans engaged in tribal activities or simply looking august and exotic. Hundreds of thousands of these calendars, meant to be enchanting invitations to come visit the Southwest, were sent free throughout the land each year for more than three quarters of a century. The railroad had tickets to sell, and the Indians on the calendars (as well as in advertising) proved to be a powerful lure. "The Santa Fe Indian," T. C. McLuhan wrote in her enlightening book about the impact of the railroad on Southwest Indian life, *Dream Tracks* (1985), "possessed an aura of glamour. An intangibility. An ineffable essence. . . . Simplicity. Freedom. Nobility." Even before that first calendar, the Indian image had become a symbol of the West, and it has remained a symbol ever since—so powerful that it has obscured the reality of Indian life.

The true story of America's native peoples, and of what happened to them as the West was won—and as

Above: *"The Sunrise Call."* Opposite: *Joan Taylor in* Rose Marie *(the 1954 version), known best for its musical production number, "Indian Love Call."*

their lands were lost—has been called this nation's great unfinished business. It is a story that is grand and colorful, gilded with lofty ideals, stained by wave upon wave of unspeakable tragedy, and almost always tinged by fear and fascination—and misunderstanding—on the part of white people. "Why do you call us Indians?" a tribesman asked Pilgrim missionary John Eliot in 1646. As Robert F. Berkhofer, Jr., points out in *The White Man's Indian* (1978), there were some two thousand different cultures in North America when white people arrived; each saw itself as separate and distinct. But the newcomers lumped them all together and misnamed them, simply because Columbus thought he had landed somewhere near India.

(The proper name for indigenous Americans is still very much an issue. Some tribal spokespeople prefer "Native American," which is technically correct. For the most part, though, Native Americans we have encountered in our travels still frequently use the term "Indian," at least when talking to outsiders. Among themselves they aren't likely to use either "Indian" or "Native American"; instead, "Navajo," "Choctaw," "Cherokee," etc., are the words that really tell a listener who they are. Some

Cameron, Arizona.

teams traditionally adopt names such as "Indians," "Braves," and "Chiefs" for their connotation of never-say-die ferocity; in the last few years, the Atlanta Braves fans' rallying gesture—the tomahawk chop—has become a sore point among many Native Americans and their sympathizers, who see it as a disrespectful cliché. (Actually, a freehand chop was originally devised in the early 1980s at Florida State to cheer on the university's Seminoles; it became a Braves' trademark in 1991 only after a foam-bedding salesman named Paul Braddy began marketing foam tomahawks.)

For Indians, it hasn't necessarily been a wonderful thing that their image—however exalted, ferocious, or magical—has veiled their existence as human beings. One original obstacle to perceiving the native people of this continent as equal beings was that the United States was founded on a firm belief in natural law, at a time when nature and all things close to it were thought to hold the key to truth and virtue. "Nature itself had become holy," wrote William H. Goetzmann and William N. Goetzmann in their book *The West of the Imagination* (1986). "Primitive people [were equated with] nature and nature's laws, thus making them, in their grand simplicity, the people closest to God." So while the natives of America represented a problem to be reckoned with—they had to be evicted from their homelands for westward settlement to proceed—they also took on a role in white people's eyes as nature's truest surrogates. The complexities and refinement of their ancient cultures notwithstanding, Indians became the U.S.A.'s own race of "noble savages." They were considered primitive, and therefore linked to the earth and wise in the ways of cosmic law.

James Fenimore Cooper's Leatherstocking Tales, *Last of the Mohicans* in particular, helped crystallize this sentimental image in print—of a heroic race doomed by the onslaught of civilization. George Catlin, originally of Philadelphia, realized it on canvas in lyric paintings that depicted the

tribes are even battling these labels. A faction of Navajos want to shed the word *Navajo,* which was derived from the Spanish term *Apaches de Navajó* [*Navajó* was the Spanish name for what is now northern New Mexico and Arizona], and return to what they used to call themselves—*Diné,* meaning simply "people." The former Papagos—also a Spanish name, meaning bean people—who live in the Sonoran desert south of Phoenix, Arizona, have already officially reclaimed the more traditional name of Tohono O'odham, meaning desert people.)

One reason for tribal interest in reclaiming original names is that the rest of America has always felt free to appropriate the names, as well as the likeness, of indigenous peoples for products of all kinds—from Red Man chewing tobacco to Crazy Horse beer, Navajo Van Lines to Chevrolet Apache trucks and Jeep Cherokee station wagons. High school, college, and professional sports

Indians of the West (and of the East) as a glorious breed of people, enveloped in nature's dignity; in his words: "their long arms in orisons of praise to the Great Spirit in the sun, for the freedom and happiness of their existence." Writing about the red man he painted, he described him as a being "in the innocent simplicity of nature, in the full enjoyment of the luxuries which God has bestowed upon him . . . happier than kings and princes can be, with his pipe and little ones about him." He described his subjects as "Lords of the forest" and "Nature's proudest, noblest men," and the West they inhabited as "the great and almost boundless garden spot of the earth."

To Catlin, the Indian was a vanishing idol, a baleful victim of the march of civilization. He wrote, "From the towering cliffs of the Rocky Mountains, the luckless savage will turn back his swollen eyes on the illimitable hunting grounds from which he has fled; and there contemplate, like Caius Marius on the ruins of Carthage, their splendid desolation."

Catlin was so disturbed by the awful effects of settlement on Indians and their land that as early as 1842 he wishfully imagined the West being transformed into a kind of huge nature preserve, where Indians, like an endangered species, would be protected. It would become "a *magnificent park,* where the world could see for ages to come the native Indian in his classic attire, galloping his wild horse, with sinewy bow, and shield and lance, amid the fleeting herds of elk and buffaloes . . . A *nation's Park,* containing man and beast, in all the wild and freshness of their nature's beauty."

The enduring influence of Henry Wadsworth Longfellow's epic poem "Song of Hiawatha," published in 1855, was due in great measure to its setting in the past, on the verge of the coming of the white man. Its Indians (who lived in the East) were not a roadblock standing in the way of manifest destiny, but a simple, happy people living in harmony with the earth . . . and gladly welcoming the black-robed missionary who comes

"Song of Hiawatha"
Pipestone, Minn.

# The Chiefs

**BETWEEN CHICAGO AND THE WEST AND SOUTHWEST**

**Santa Fe**

Headed by the *Super Chief* and *The Chief*, the Santa Fe great fleet of trains between Chicago and California offers a choice of fine accommodations to satisfy every taste and fit every pocketbook. And between Chicago and Texas, it's the *Texas Chief*.

For smooth-riding comfort...friendly hospitality... delicious Fred Harvey meals...fascinating scenery...travel Santa Fe—*the Chief Way!*

R. T. Anderson, General Passenger Traffic Manager, Santa Fe System Lines, Chicago 4, Illinois

to convert them to Christianity at the end. Written in drumbeat meter like a legend chanted around a campfire, the poem's idyllic descriptions of the ways of the Ojibways and Dakotas cast a nostalgic spell so powerful that even as a very real policy of bloody extirpation was being waged by the United States against intransigent natives, thousands of schoolchildren learned to give recitations of the poem—to honor America's first people. Young white students dressed in dyed feather headdresses and mock buckskin, and delivered their verse complete with an elaborate system of hand signals to indicate a wigwam, a rising moon, and baby Hiawatha being rocked in his linden cradle "safely bound with reindeer sinews." The most oft-repeated part of the heroic tale was from the section titled "Hiawatha's Childhood":

*By the shores of Gitche Gumee,*
*By the shining Big-Sea-Water,*
*Stood the wigwam of Nokomis,*
*Daughter of the Moon, Nokomis.*
*Dark behind it rose the forest,*
*Rose the black and gloomy pine trees,*
*Rose the firs with cones upon them;*
*Bright before it beat the water,*
*Beat the clear and sunny water,*
*Beat the shining Big-Sea-Water.*

By the time Buffalo Bill Cody began to mythologize the frontier in his Wild West shows in 1883, it was impossible to envision the West remaining wild any longer. The frontier was on the verge of being "closed." The West had been won, Indian resistance had been broken, and with rare exception, the surviving Indians had surrendered. "Some of my best friends were Indians," Buffalo Bill once boasted, speaking in the past tense; and out of friendship—as well as showmanship—he made them part of his spectacle. Along with longhorn cows, buffalo, coyotes, and cowboys,

PICTURE PUZZLE BUBBLE GUM

*Opposite: Indian majesty, selling train tickets. Above: Indian savagery, selling bubble gum.*

Indians became featured players in the exhilarating pageant of the frontier that originally defined the pop-culture West.

Most of the Indians employed in the Wild West show were Dakota Sioux, and thanks in part to their role in Buffalo Bill's pageant, they became *the* symbolic Indians of North America. It was the Sioux who camped in circles of white tepees (their word was *tipi*), who painted their ponies for war, who smoked peace pipes, and who wore spectacular eagle-feather headdresses, fringed buckskin shirts, and beaded moccasins. To many people unaware of the diversity of Native American cultures, they formed the basis for the singular image of the American Indian.

And of course under the direction of Buffalo Bill, who knew that audiences would not spend money freely to see peaceable natives sitting together in equanimity, they did their best to yelp and cavort and behave like wild Indians were supposed to do. They chased after a covered wagon train, ululating and wielding their tomahawks, and in a grand melodramatic finale, they massed as an army of feathered savages and re-created "Custer's Last Charge" (the word *stand* was then considered too defeatist), including battle with the U.S. Cavalry on horseback, hand-to-hand knife and fistfights, and a chilling climactic moment when a Sioux brave reached down to take the scalp of General George Armstrong Custer. Imagine the awe and horror audiences felt when, immediately after this blood-curdling mayhem, Hunkpapa Sioux chief Sitting Bull—the very man who had directed the massacre of Custer's troops less than ten years earlier—rode out before them, in full-feather regalia. Many in the audience took the opportunity to jeer Sitting Bull as Custer's murderer.

After one season with the Wild West show, in 1885, Sitting Bull (a U.S. government captive since 1881) was allowed to go to the Standing Rock Sioux reservation in Dakota; Buffalo Bill Cody—with whom he had become fast friends—gave him a gray horse from the show to keep. It was a trick horse that had been trained to sit and wave its hooves in the air at the report of a gun. In 1890, at the height of the Ghost Dance frenzy (a belief that spread through many Western reservations that wild—but peaceful—dancing would soon bring forth an Indian Messiah who would renew the buffalo herds, restore Indians to their land, and make white men vanish), Major General Nelson Miles ordered the rearrest of Sitting Bull for fomenting the allegedly subversive cult. (It was a trumped-up charge; in fact, Sitting Bull was skeptical of Ghost Dancing.) When police arrived, more than a hundred Ghost Dancers rallied to protect the venerable chief; in the confusion, shots were fired. At the sound of the guns, Sitting Bull's horse began to perform its theatrical dance—sitting on

*This brochure promised walks "along the paths of the Indians, worn inches deep in solid rock by moccasined feet."*

its haunches and waving a hoof in the air as it had learned to do in the Wild West show: an unsettling coda to the image white men had created for the vanquished chief. The Sioux leader, whom police later accused of resisting arrest, took a bullet and fell dead. But his horse continued to perform in the midst of the melee—stunning onlookers who thought the horse itself had been seized with the Ghost Dance spirit.

Even before the Ghost Dance cult animated the Plains reservation dwellers and became a catalyst for the final awful massacre at Wounded Knee in the Badlands in 1890, the Indian wars had come to a symbolic close in the Southwest when Apache leader Geronimo surrendered for the last time in 1886 in Skeleton Canyon on the Arizona-New Mexico border. Geronimo, who was already notorious as the "Tiger of the Southwest" for his ability to wage guerrilla war and to elude capture, became the most famous Apache in America. After serving time at hard labor in Florida, Geronimo was allowed to appear in Pawnee Bill's Wild West show, where he was billed as "the worst Indian that ever lived." Outfitted in flamboyant eagle-feather headdress, he rode before the crowds in a Locomobile touring car, gunning down a live buffalo from the passenger seat—a performance advertised as "The Last Buffalo Hunt." Never mind that, as a Chiricahua Apache of the Southwest mountains, it is likely Geronimo had never shot a buffalo and had never worn headfeathers. He had become the supreme image of an Indian on the warpath, and that image, in the popular mind, necessarily included a warbonnet as well as a wake of dead buffalo.

Indians soon became one of the prime tourist attractions in the Southwest. Subdued on reservations and no longer an obstacle to settlement, they still carried a whiff of danger, which provided the traveler with the kind of wild game-park thrill George Catlin had once imagined. Beyond their curiosity value as an only recently defeated enemy, Indians were also intriguing because of their crafts skills. The opening of Hotel El Tovar at the rim of the Grand Canyon in 1904 provided visitors not only with a close-up view of nature, but with a view of America's natural people—Indians—making jewelry at Hopi House, a crafts studio built by the Fred Harvey Company just across the way from the hotel. In Albuquerque, Harvey's Alvarado Hotel opened an entire room devoted to the display (and sale) of native pottery, baskets, jewelry, and rugs.

In 1926, encouraged by the success of El Tovar and tour buses that took tourists around the rim of the Grand Canyon, the Santa Fe Railway, in conjunction with the Fred Harvey Company, introduced "Indian Detours." Now someone traveling coast-to-coast by rail could pay extra and stop in Winslow, Albuquerque, or Santa Fe for a guided excursion into Indian country. Groups of Detourists stepped off the train and boarded elongated Packard Harveycars with eleven upholstered swivel seats and broad Pullman-style windows for two- or three-day trips. Each car was driven by a cowboy-mechanic in a ten-gallon hat and riding boots, and each was hosted by a specially trained "courier," who was a college-educated white woman in an Indian velvet shirt and silver concha belt. According to company literature, the couriers all

Tourist attractions. The Fred Harvey postcard at upper right says: "Comely Indian maidens and aged squaws meet the train and sell their wares."

had supplemented their education with "special training on archaeological and ethnological history." Their job was to make the trip an experience that brought travelers so close to Indians they could touch them:

> *Greeting guests upon arrival by train, it is thereafter their privilege to fill the pleasant dual role of hostesses as well as guides. Couriers' friendships with representative Indians in many pueblos assure their guests of intimate glimpses of Indian life not otherwise obtainable.*

Just as movies consummated the transformation of cowboy from hired man to folk hero, they further flattened the Indian image into a familiar stereotype. Hollywood's Indians were based primarily on the whooping Sioux of the Wild West shows, and while silver-screen red men have ranged from tragic innocents to bloodthirsty demons, certain aspects of their role in movies have been consistent: Indians are always symbolic of something, and they are usually clichés, outfitted in what Ralph and Natasha Friar, in their book *The Only Good Indian* (1972), described as the "instant Indian kit" of buckskin and warbonnet, with tomahawk and bow and arrow. They all live in tepees, pound drums, ride beautiful pinto ponies, and communicate in an elementary language of grunts and hand signs. They are simple people—simple and happy or simple and wicked, depending on what the plot requires.

In the 1950s Hollywood's image of Indians began to change. Starting with Delmer Daves's *Broken Arrow* (1950), about a white man in love with an Apache girl (played by Debra Paget, not an Apache), it became more common to see Indians depicted as innocent victims rather than scalp-hunting fiends. A number of red men had always been featured trusty sidekicks, such as the Lone Ranger's Tonto or Little Beaver (played by juvenile Robert

Blake), the junior companion of Wild Bill Eliott as Red Ryder, and of course, there were plenty of comic characters, such as Chief Thunderthud and Princess Summerfall Winterspring on television's "Howdy Doody." But after *Broken Arrow,* such movies as Robert Aldrich's *Apache* (1954) and Douglas Sirk's *Taza, Son of Cochise* (1955) actually purported to deal with the Indian question as a troubling issue in need of solutions; both movies set forth a policy of peaceful coexistence.

Indians were the subject of a great cultural vogue starting in the late 1960s, thanks mostly to hippies, who liked to see themselves as tribal sorts of people. Headbands, moccasins, body paint, and turquoise jewelry were all adopted by flower children as symbols of their closeness to North America's original tribes. Wearing beads became "a symbolic rejection of a corrupt society and a return to the communal values of American Indians," announced Columbia University student rebel Ted Kaptchuk in a 1968 *Eye* magazine fashion story. In *Flashing on the Sixties* (1987), which includes an account of the New Buffalo hippie commune in New Mexico, Lisa Law wrote, "The Indians of the Taos Pueblo helped the New Buffaloers by being friends and teachers, and the young Indians in turn gained self respect when they saw other men with long hair."

In 1971 the Raiders (formerly Paul Revere and the Raiders) hit the top of the *Billboard* chart with "Indian Reservation (The Lament of the Cherokee Reservation Indian)," about the sad fate of Native Americans forced to live on reservations. Originally written by John D. Loudermilk in 1963 and recorded by Don Fardon in England, it became a monster hit in the United States—the biggest-selling single in Columbia Records' history to that date. Two years later Cher went native in Bob Mackie beads and buckskin for her "Sonny and Cher Comedy Hour" on television, and had a number one hit with "Half-Breed," a socially conscious song with an Indian theme.

As national shame over the Vietnam war escalated, the cause of Indians became a favorite one among many concerned people in the entertainment business, who saw parallels between the U.S. government policies toward the indigenous people of the American West and those of Southeast Asia. Starting in 1970 for about a half-dozen years, Hollywood produced dozens of diligently pro-Indian, anti-Army pictures. Setting the tone for many, *Soldier Blue* (1970), billed as "the most brutal and liberating, the most honest American film ever made," dramatized the Army's 1864 Sand Creek slaughter of Indians. According to director Ralph Nelson, it was meant to parallel the My Lai incident in Vietnam, and it is, even today, shocking in its depiction of senseless bloodshed (mostly by whites against Indians). It featured a plaintive title song written and performed by Cree activist and folk singer Buffy Sainte-Marie; however—as usual—the Indians in the movie were mostly anonymous, and all the major roles were played by whites (including Candice Bergen and Peter Strauss). Another 1970 picture, *A Man Called Horse,* was scrupulous in its attempt at realism, including dialogue spoken in Lakota Sioux; nevertheless, *The BFI Companion to the Western* quotes the Native American newspaper *Akwesasne Notes* about it: "Same old savage stereotype. White actors playing cigar store Indians." Reportedly the Sioux who allowed the film to be made on their reservation became "the laughing stock of Indian America."

Chief Dan George, an actor from the Tse-lal-watt tribe of British Columbia, provided audiences with another perspective on Native Americans in the 1970s: he was smart and he had a sense of humor. First as Old Lodge Skins in the savage history lesson *Little Big Man* (1970, from the novel by Thomas Berger), and then as Lone Watie, Clint Eastwood's traveling companion in the resonant epic *The Outlaw Josey Wales* (1976), he provided both films with unexpected tenderness. George's addition of intellectual whimsy to the Indian image has been echoed in many films since, perhaps most effectively in *Thunderheart* (1992), about an earnest FBI agent (Val Kilmer) who comes to terms with his mystical Indian heritage while solving a murder. Spiritual as its plot may be, *Thunderheart* is notable for the pranks and fun enjoyed by its Indian supporting cast—Graham Greene as a witty tribal cop and Chief Ted Thin Elk as a shrewd old Sioux medicine man who's addicted to television shows and

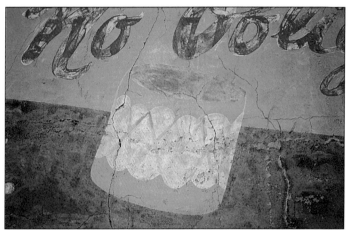

*A painting on the wall of the Santo Domingo Trading Post between Albuquerque and Santa Fe: "Most interesting spot in the old West."*

who always seems to be hoodwinking Kilmer.

The traditional image of Indians has broadened tremendously thanks to many popular books with Indian characters and themes, from the bestselling historical novel *Sacajawea* to the embarrassingly successful book of bogus Native American maxims, *The Education of Little Tree.* Novels and nonfiction by Tony Hillerman, Louise Erdrich, and Michael Dorris, the latter two of Native American descent, have created compelling alternatives to old stereotypes, but probably the most influential recent pop-culture portrayal of Indians was a movie—*Dances with Wolves* (1990). After a decade in which Indians hadn't been seen much on screen, director-star Kevin Costner revived the ultra-noble image in an Academy Award-winning movie that *U.S. News & World Report* declared the catalyst for a new era of "Native American chic." Costner's romantic parable extolled the Lakota Sioux as a loving, peaceful, loyal, emotionally expressive, ecologically responsible, and joyous culture who find themselves besieged by U.S. soldiers who are nothing but evil predators. As Union officer Dunbar, Costner is so smitten with the Sioux that he changes sides and joins them, even falls in love with one (who happens to be a white woman raised by them, thus allowing the plot to dodge the issue of intermarriage); when they name him Dances with Wolves, he declares that he knows for the first time who he really is. Audiences loved the three-hour fable, which, along with Clint Eastwood's *Unforgiven* (1992), is credited with resurrecting the Western genre.

We recently stumbled across a Western scene that said a lot about the enduring power of the stereotyped Indian image in contemporary life. In Window Rock, Arizona, headquarters of the Navajo nation, there is an immense red-rock arch shaped like a portal that rises up above the sandstone buildings that house tribal offices and the federal Bureau of Indian Affairs. It is an awesome natural sight, but when we came to town in the spring of 1992, it was not possible to get near it because a television commercial was being filmed in front of it. Surrounded by

*This Kevin Costner–inspired shop at the Chief Yellow Horse Trading Post in Lupton, Arizona, sells many Indian souvenirs at up to 80 percent off their retail price!*

lights, reflectors, a camera, a microphone boom, and about a dozen crew members in T-shirts and jeans, a Navajo stood with the rock formation rising up behind him. He was a very handsome old man wearing a velvet blouse and draped in a spectacular suite of Navajo silver and turquoise necklaces. The camera crew had recruited him for the occasion, hiring him for his noble appearance. When he was cued, he looked into the camera and spoke in a voice that quivered with portent, delivering his single line over and over again, perhaps three dozen times, until he said it exactly the way the director wanted. "In nature, all things are balanced," the red man repeated, each time holding up a perfumed loofah sponge you can buy at your favorite department store.

We asked one of the crew members about the commercial being filmed. He explained that the concept behind it was to emphasize the sponge's closeness to the earth. An Indian was chosen to deliver the message, he said, because "They're more in touch with nature than anybody else."

# Strange Names
# AND SIGN LANGUAGE

ndians in old Hollywood movies are generally too busy chanting and dancing or looking silent and wise to talk much; when they do speak English, they tend to employ many more nouns than verbs, and they use pronouns incorrectly: "Him great buffalo hunter. Buffalo gone Happy Hunting Grounds." This ridiculous image of Indian communication derives from the very real fact that many of the languages of Native Americans (there are more than two hundred separate ones) combine whole ideas into an evocative single word, so that verbs become redundant, and in some of the languages, pronouns simply do not

exist. English has approximately ten times as many words as any Native American tongue; and so it used to be that, while many Indians did learn English words, they never accustomed themselves to the foreign language's strung-out sentences.

Another reason that much is lost in translation is that Indians favor poetic expressions of feelings rather than blunt ones, painting word-pictures that make clear and perfect sense in their own language, but sound childish in English. "Him speak with wise tongue" is a case in point, as is "Rifle strong medicine." Bruce Grant's *Concise Encyclopedia of the American Indian* (1958) gives these typical examples: "My heart is warm" instead of "I am glad"; "He has a big heart," meaning "He is brave"; and "hearing with the eye," which was an Indian way to describe written European languages. In the introduction to *Indian Sign Language* (1929), William Tomkins said that an old Sioux friend once said to him, "May the Great Mystery make sunrise in your heart."

Indian names are also typical of the way their languages are structured to create images rather than labels. Tribespeople never select a random word without intrinsic meaning to call a person; rather, names are chosen to reflect a unique personality trait or an accomplishment. Traditionally, the Cheyenne did not name a boy until he had engaged in battle; his name told how he fought. The names Native Americans bear are often entire expressive phrases when they get translated into English. Some of the historical classics include Snow on Her (one of Sitting Bull's

*Opposite: Indian Love Call. Right: "The American Indian had a literature and a language long before the white men came to this land."*

## INDIAN SYMBOLS

BEAVER IN HOUSE

RAIN PRAYER

LOUD TALK

SPIRITS ABOVE

WARRIORS IN CANOE

BEAR DEAD

MEDICINE TEPEE

EAT

WILKES

COPYRIGHT BY
E. C. KROPP CO.
MILWAUKEE

X30

CHEROKEE INDIANS'
CEREMONIAL DANCE

K-14 GREETINGS FROM THE GREAT SMOKY MOUNTAINS NATIONAL PARK

## Aya gatlunska utanu uwahoop-p.

## Uwahoop-p-p!! Yoh!!

Egwa, *Great*
Dutsusda, *Smoky*
Gatusi, *Mountains*
Aya, *I*
gatlunska, *make*

utanu, *heap much*
uwahoop-p, *whoopee*
Yoh, *an expression of*
*great astonishment*

*The Cherokees of North Carolina originally called their home "The Land of 1000 Smokes"—now the Smoky Mountains.*

wives), One Who Yawns (Geronimo's original name, before Mexicans started calling him Geronimo after St. Jerome), Dull Knife, Pony That Walks, Sleeps in Saddle, and Man with Worn-Out Moccasins. Names were often subject to mistranslation when going from a native language into English. A Dakota Sioux whose tribal name was Young Man Whose Very Horses Are Feared became known to U.S. soldiers as Young Man Afraid of His Horses. The Hunkpapa Sioux leader with the imperious name Bull in Possession became known to the world as Sitting Bull because the pictograph of his name looked like a buffalo that was relaxing. Crazy Horse was actually His Horse Is Crazy.

It was long believed that Indian languages had no grammar whatsoever, that they were simply spoken hieroglyphics, without meaningful syntax. This is not true, but the complexity of their logic makes them impenetrable to outsiders. When we travel in northern Arizona, we often try to tune our radio to a Navajo sta-

tion, and we like to eavesdrop on Navajo conversations in local cafés. The sounds we hear are so wonderfully strange that it is easy to understand how the fabled Navajo "code talkers," working for the U.S. military in World War II, were able to communicate verbal messages in a code that proved to be unbreakable by this country's enemies: their native tongue!

Still, the image of the taciturn Indian, able to muster "How!" and "Ugh!" but little more in the way of speech, is a cliché that has been slow to die in popular culture. One of the reasons is that Indians also developed an eloquent sign language. Rather than speak long strings of English words, which can seem pedestrian, they frequently intersperse a few words with demonstrative signs. Similar to the ancient pictographs of the cliff-dwelling Anasazi, as well as to pictorial writing that was common well into the nineteenth century, sign language creates an image of the topic by use of the hands and arms (but never by the face, which should always remain composed).

It is a very logical way of communicating. To signify a time, you point to the place in the sky where the sun would be, and to signify a length of time, you show how far the sun would travel. For *horse,* you hold up your hand with your index and little fingers raised, like pointy equine ears; for *tepee,* you hold your index fingers at a sixty-degree angle, crossed at the first joint. To pose a question you raise your right hand to shoulder height, with fingers and thumb extended and turn it back and forth two or three times, as if shaking something loose. Sign language even has a basic additive syntax. For example, if you want to ask if a grizzly bear is nearby, you sign *question,* then hold cupped hands to your ears (indicating really big ears), then claw downward with both hands, like a bear's paws. To say *we,* you combine the signs for *me* and *all.* To say *today,* you combine *day* and *now.* To ask *Have you had supper?* you combine *question, you, eat,* and *sunset.*

Sign language was developed in the early eighteenth century, when Indians began coming to the Plains because they had been displaced by white settlement and because the horse—introduced by the conquistadores to North America—gave them a mobility they hadn't previously known. Horses also changed the way they hunted buffalo, and it was in buffalo country, when different tribes found themselves stalking the same herds, that they needed a way to communicate. Instead of learning one another's complex languages, they signed and gestured, and by the mid-1800s Indian sign language was so well evolved that people from different tribes could have detailed conversations without saying a word. In 1885 it was estimated there were over 110,000 fluent sign-talking Indians in America.

In *Indian Sign Language* William Tomkins wrote that "there is a sentiment connected with the Indian Sign Language that attaches to no other. . . . It has a beauty and imagery possessed by few, if any, other languages."

Tomkins was eager to point out that Indian Sign Language was very different from ordinary deaf-mute signing, which was based on European languages rather than on the languages of Native Americans. The word *think,* for example, is indicated in the language of the deaf by placing extended fingers against one's forehead, pointing to the brain. When Indians want to express the idea *think,* he noted, they place their right hand against their left breast, then draw it forward, as if pulling something from their heart. Tomkins concluded his enthusiastic remarks with a tip for those who wanted to talk with their hands like Indians: "The beauty of Sign talk depends upon the manner of making the gestures. Movements should not be angular or jerky, but should rather be rounded and sweeping in their rendition. It is inspiring, and a thing of beauty, to witness a sign conversation between two capable Indian sign talkers."

*The man in this picture is making the sign for "yes."*

PLAINS

Indians Speaking Sign Language

# The Chief MOTIF

Chief Snow Cloud

(John Rogers)
Author & Publisher of:
"A CHIPPEWA SPEAKS"

In popular culture, you can spot Indian royalty by the munificence of their feathered headdresses. Chiefs and princesses have big ones: huge circles of golden eagle feathers around their head, streaming back, sometimes to the ground, like a coronation tiara and train. In truth, the shape and size of a headdress does not necessarily signify that its wearer is a chief. It *does* tell you which tribe he belongs to, and it also might indicate what he has accomplished. Many tribes wear no feathers on their heads, and this is also true of their chiefs. The Blackfoot and Omaha prefer fur hats; the Iroquois like buckskin turbans.

Among the Dakota Sioux, whose war bonnets are the most spectacular of all, eagle feathers serve as military decorations; and each has a particular meaning. A red-tipped feather was earned for killing an enemy; a split feather shows that the wearer of the headdress was wounded in battle; notches tell how many times a warrior has counted coup—touched a live enemy or an enemy's tepee with his "coup stick" (a long, bent shaft decorated with otter fur; coup could also be counted by stealing an enemy's horse). Therefore, in tribes that do wear feathered headdresses, it is likely a chief will have a big one. But he doesn't get it because he is chief; on the contrary, it is more likely he became a chief because of accomplishments indicated by his headdress.

*Chief Snow Cloud spent part of each year in Hollywood, where he provided the movie colony with novelty birch bark canoes and other Chippewa crafts.*

RED TOMAHAWK

TINGLEYS
STORE

REDSKIN

BIG CHIEF
DRILLING COMPANY

# TEPEES

ollywood stereotypes notwithstanding, all Native Americans do not live in tepees, and they never have. Some lived in earth lodges, some in thatched wickiups, stone-and-adobe dwellings in caves or on the sides of cliffs, pole-and-adobe huts on mesas, log-and-earth hogans, or dome-shaped wigwams made of poles and bark. But of all the places in which Indians have traditionally kept house, the conical dwellings made of hides wrapped around a frame of smooth, barkless poles are the ones that became part of their pop-culture image, as much as tomahawks and feathered headdresses. Originally popularized as an Indian symbol when Sioux performers in Wild West shows built picturesque tepee towns around the fairgrounds, the tepee has now become a fundamental icon of the Western roadside—used as a sign of hospitality by motels, trading posts, and restaurants.

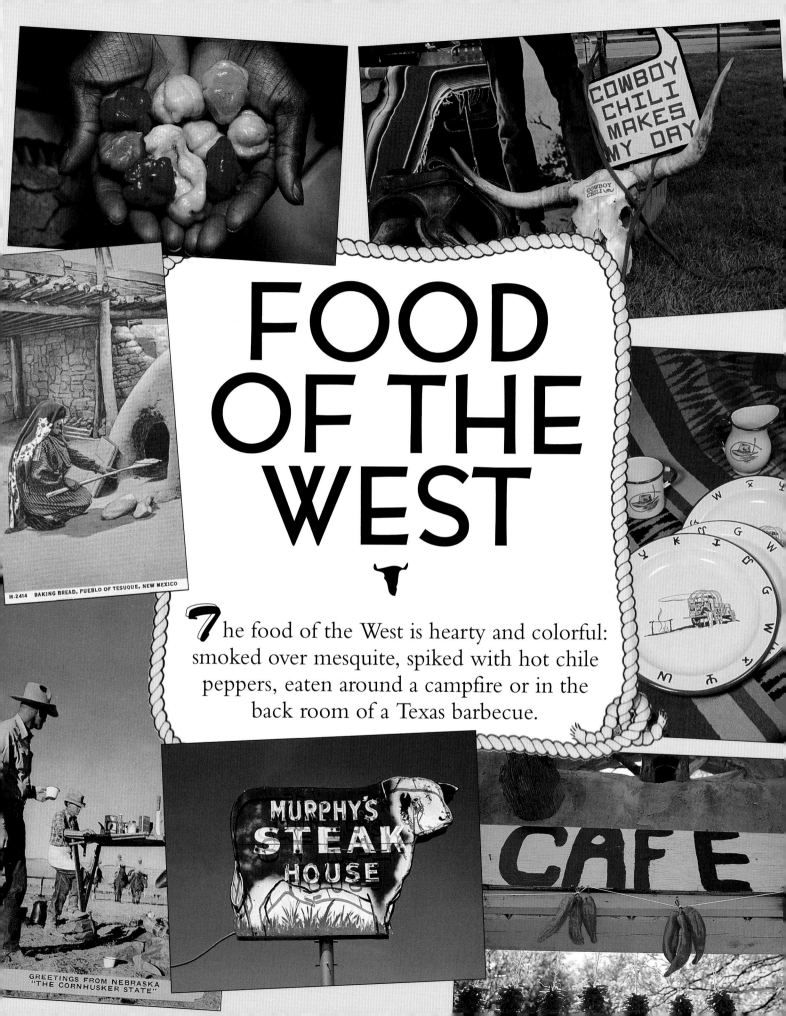

# FOOD OF THE WEST

*7*he food of the West is hearty and colorful: smoked over mesquite, spiked with hot chile peppers, eaten around a campfire or in the back room of a Texas barbecue.

H-2414   BAKING BREAD, PUEBLO OF TESUQUE, NEW MEXICO

GREETINGS FROM NEBRASKA
"THE CORNHUSKER STATE"

COWBOY CHILI MAKES MY DAY

COWBOY CHILI

MURPHY'S STEAK HOUSE

CAFE

# Come and GET IT!

The grub of the West is brash—from jerked beef to bull's balls by the slice, and from Frito pie (in a slit-open Fritos bag) to piñon-crusted striped bass with red chile aïoli (in a swanky restaurant in Santa Fe). Western food is almost always served without formality and in huge amounts. It is made to stick to your ribs; and even when it doesn't always taste great—as is sometimes the case in greasy-spoon cafés and weather-beaten truck stops—it can still be mighty entertaining. Western vittles, and the places where they're served, brim with character.

Duncan Hines, who was America's pioneer traveling gourmet before he became a cake mix, once wrote, "The best meal I ever ate was an order of ham and eggs in a frontier café where the click of the roulette wheel in the back mingled with the clatter of dishes at the front counter. That was in Cheyenne, Wyoming, about 1899." Mr. Hines had eaten many more aristocratic meals in his career, but the ham and eggs he recalled so fondly from his early days saved his life after he had gotten lost in a snowstorm and finally wandered on foot into Cheyenne where he found Harry Hynds's café (and also subsequently met the woman who became his wife). The point of his story was that the pleasure of a memorable meal usually involves a whole lot more than the food itself; it's the circumstances that make it extraordinary. That is why the food of the West is so especially fabled: it bristles with connections to adventure and romance that give it an extra measure of pleasure and meaning, and flavor, too. It can suggest all the high spirits of frontier mythology—of pioneer mettle and cowboy self-reliance.

Originally, the cooking of the West suffered the worst reputation of any regional cuisine in America. The West was wild, and so were the rations pilgrims faced when they went there. Despite the lingering flavor of the Hacienda cookery brought from Mexico by Spanish settlers, and regardless of how

*Cowboys tend to like coffee with a kick; in some cafés, "cowboy-style" coffee means a brew that tastes as if it has been on the range all day.*

advanced pueblo ecology had been before the conquistadores arrived (Hopis and Zunis are believed to have practiced crop rotation and to have developed sophisticated techniques to preserve the harvest by in-ground freezing, sun-drying, and smoking), most Americans who lit off for the frontier to make their fortune or start life anew considered themselves hardscrabble survivalists in a savage land. "Our daily 'bill of fare,'" pioneer Annie D. Tallent recalled of her life in the Black Hills, "consisted of the following articles, to wit: For breakfast, hot biscuit, fried bacon, and black coffee; for dinner, cold biscuit, cold baked beans, and black coffee; for supper, black coffee, hot biscuit, and baked beans warmed over. Occasionally, in lieu of hot biscuits, and for the sake of variety, we would have what is termed in camp parlance, flapjacks."

*Judy Garland as a Harvey Girl.*

Whether traveling by train or car, westward wanderers felt nearly as bad off as the famished pioneers of pre-Civil War days. When Emily Post wrote *By Motor to the Golden Gate* in 1916, she delighted in the many physical hardships she faced along the road but she was not nearly so sanguine when it came to describing some of the meals she encountered: "anemic chilled potatoes, beans full of strings, everything slapped on plates any which way, and everything tasting as though it had come out of the same dishwater." Even train travel, in the first several decades after the completion of the transcontinental railroad in 1869, was a notorious gastronomic obstacle course. The historian Lesley Poling-Kempes described the grub available to passengers (who were allowed exactly twenty minutes to disembark, scurry into a trackside beanery, and wolf it down) as an "insult to a traveler's stomach." She wrote, "Meat was greasy and usually fried, beans were canned, bacon rancid, and coffee was fresh once a week. Pie, if found, was of the dried-fruit-and-crust variety, biscuits were known as 'sinkers,' and eggs were shipped 'fresh' from back East, preserved in lime. A 'chicken stew' of prairie dogs was not uncommon."

The one person who did the most to transform the reputation of Western food from vulgar muck to robust nourishment was Fred Harvey. London-born Harvey had arrived in the United States in 1850 at age fifteen; after knocking around New York, then New Orleans, as a busboy, he opened his own café in St. Louis in 1857, but it did not survive the Civil War. Harvey worked as a freight agent for the railroads, and at the same time began operating a couple of eat-stops along the Kansas Pacific line. Then, just as most trackside food was earning its scurvy reputation as inedible slop in the 1870s, Harvey went to the fledgling Atchison, Topeka, and Santa Fe and convinced them that they could offer something very special to their westbound passengers: good meals. All the train line had to do was provide him café space in their depots and ship his provisions free. They also provided him the use of their telegraph lines to inform each Harvey House up ahead just how many customers were on the train, and how many of them planned to eat in the à la carte lunchroom or more expensive (seventy-five cents per meal) dining room (where a man was required to wear a jacket). Harvey, in turn, would make good, honest, even sometimes elegant, food one of the great lures of Western travel. When the train pulled into the station, the food was ready, the coffee was freshly brewed, and customers were allotted a hospitable thirty minutes to enjoy their meal before the conductor signaled its end by calling "All aboard!"

Starting in 1883, when he fired the all-male work force at the Harvey House in Raton, New Mexico (for getting in a barroom brawl and arriving at work the next day all bruised up), Harvey staffed his restaurants with Harvey Girls, lured from the East by the promise of decent pay, clean uniforms, the romance of the West, and unimpeachable respectability. Advertising for girls who were "of good character, attractive, and intelligent," Harvey made absolutely certain that no one would mistake

them for prostitutes or gold diggers. They were required to live in a dormitory, to go to sleep every night at an assigned bedtime, and to conduct themselves, on and off the job, according to strict rules of deportment and grooming that forbade nail polish, jewelry, makeup, and gum chewing. Harvey House chaperones had to approve any gentleman who wished to see a girl socially. A hundred thousand women, ages eighteen to thirty, took up the challenge between 1883 and the 1950s, and the pert, decent image of the Harvey Girl entered popular folklore (especially via the 1946 Judy Garland musical, *The Harvey Girls*). Duncan Hines sang their praises as "those famed waitresses of song and story" and commended their contribution to the salubrious atmosphere at Harvey Houses throughout the West: "They were always neat and clean;

*Cookie is breaking eggs in his iron skillet while cowboys enjoy coffee and a smoke.*

their uniforms starched and spotless, their hair smoothly combed."

Like his girls, Fred Harvey's food became universally recognized as a paragon of virtue. Every city along the Santa Fe rail route had a Harvey House, and as would later be true of Howard Johnson's in the early days of interstate highways, travelers knew that Harvey Houses could be counted on for a filling as well as scrupulously hygienic meal. Menus were planned across the country so that passengers on any one train encountered different meals every stop along the way. Railroad refrigerator cars allowed Harvey to serve planked Lake Superior whitefish in Ashfork (Arizona) and Bluepoint oysters on the half-shell in Topeka (Kansas). Cold fruits and vegetables were carried East from California; he supplied milk and butter to the West from his own dairies; a Fred Harvey pie (made from fresh, not dried, fruit) was always sliced into four, not six or eight, pieces; and in some Harvey Houses, even water for French-roasted coffee was freighted in to eliminate the sulphur taste of native wells.

The debut of the Santa Fe *Chief* and *Super Chief* in the 1930s helped make a train trip West into a truly deluxe experience. *Super Chief* dining cars featured not only USDA prime beefsteak and butter-basted brook trout, but also pheasant *à la Perigueux* and jumbo frog legs *au beurre noir*. Harvey himself was long gone by this time (he died in 1901), but his name has continued for decades (via his progeny) as a beacon of good food. "It's almost worth taking a trip just to eat a Fred Harvey meal!" boasted a 1947 Santa Fe advertisement that showed a cowboy and his son gazing with awe and admiration at a passing *Super Chief,* the lad calling out, "Gee, that's eatin'!"

Opposite: *Colorado Springs, Colorado.* Above: *A Texas souvenir plate shows the Lone Star State's six flags: those of Spain, France, Mexico, the Confederate States of America, the U.S.A., and the Texas Republic. The most powerful culinary allegiances are to Mexico and the Confederacy.*

The appetizing image of the West was improving in many ways by the 1930s, and not only because of Fred Harvey's good name. The vast national anxiety of the Great Depression encouraged a lot of people to refocus their attention on bedrock regional values, to discover local heritage and character (as expressed so vividly by the WPA Writer's Project). The frontier, which could so easily be seen as unspoiled and immune to the worries of the modern world, was a rich lode of just such inspiration. It became the symbolic American place; its history was close enough to still feel vivid, but past enough to bear a nice sentimental haze as a kind of golden age and consecrated region where freedom and individuality blossomed . . . nourished by the wholesome, open-air cookery of homesteaders and chuck wagon cooks. In addition to the poetically remembered square meals eaten by pioneers, the West featured colorful ethnic shadings, too, from the earlier Spanish settlers and the Pueblo natives, both of which were still there for all to see . . . and to savor.

So as America learned to appreciate its regional identity, the West grew in stature from a brutal wilderness with sparse, vulgar, even tainted chow to a picturesque Eden abounding with fresh fish and exotic game, friendly cowboy feasts around the campfire, earthy Indian recipes for native corn and squash, and colorful, spicy Mexican fiestas. When Crosby Gaige wrote the *New York World's Fair Cookbook (The American Kitchen)* in 1939, Gaige began with a salute to Native Americans for their gift of corn, then went on to glorify what was called the "lavish luxury inspired by abundance" that typified eating in the Southwest: "Spanish ideas and Indian simplicity and native products [including] beans, maize, spices (notably peppers) and red chocolate . . . wild turkey, meats, game, fish, fruits and vegetables."

In the decade after World War II, the food of the

region was further popularized as an agreeably rugged and admirably unaffected cookery. With the exception of the fare that could be found in the cosmopolitan cities of the Pacific Coast, Western meals were thought of—for better and for worse—as unsophisticated, forthright, and filling, the modern heir to a tradition born of ranch kitchens and campfires. Describing dinner at the T-Dart Dude Ranch outside of Phoenix in her 1960 book *How America Eats,* Clementine Paddleford wrote that the "cooking was ranch-style, and that's what the city folks liked . . . served outdoors. Maybe bacon and eggs with hot dropped biscuits made on a griddle. Sometimes there were pinto beans for the main dish or a stew and often the meal was a huge bowl of thick vegetable soup."

The social status of Southwestern cooking fell very low in the 1960s, when many Americans grew enamored of European food. Inspired at the beginning of the decade by the Continental cuisine of the Kennedy White House, gourmets suddenly found themselves with Lyndon Johnson as president—a barbecue-eating, beer-can-chucking (and increasingly unpopular) Texan who, as a lark, installed a fountain that spouted Fresca just outside the Oval Office. It was a time when some dissatisfied citizens began to feel embarrassed by this country's exasperating lack of cultural sophistication, and from this perspective, the rough-hewn grub identified with the Southwest was anathema. Case in point: in their *Salute to American Cooking,* published in 1968, Stephen and Ethel Longstreet offered typical recipes from every region of the country, but when it came to the frontier, they appear to have flagged in their enthusiasm for what Americans really ate, and included among their *representative* Southwest dishes such painfully artful concoctions as "Texas Beef Stroganoff," "Death Valley Scotty's Sweetbreads" with Marsala wine and grated Parmesan cheese, and "Spitted Pheasant Yosemite" rubbed with olive oil and basted with sherry.

However, it wasn't long after LBJ left the White House that all kinds of downhome, regional Americana got popular in the 1970s ( Jimmy Carter, CB radios, *Smokey and the Bandit*), and one of the great discoveries—or rediscoveries—for many culinary adventurers was the cooking of the West: barbecue, Tex-Mex, New-Mex, chili, and chimichangas. Such foods are informal and fun, and that was their charm at a time in history when more and more Americans wanted to disdain culinary pomp.

Fajitas, for example, invented in Texas, became an immensely popular dish in sleeves-up restaurants not only because they taste good, but because they are impossible to eat with any decorum. Nachos, once available only in Mexican restaurants, have become possibly the nation's favorite hot snack food, at home and in taverns: easy to make, easy to eat while having drinks and watching a football game on television.

In the 1980s, a strange thing happened to Western cookery. It was a time when a new generation of chefs sought to embellish and reinvent American cuisine by using local ingredients but Cordon Bleu techniques, and when foodies fairly worshiped anything different and exotic. This phenomenon was known as New American Cooking. It happened to a degree in every region of the country, but no chefs were as inspired as those of the Southwest, whose tortilla soup, goat cheese enchiladas, and mesquite-grilled *anything* became the country's foremost signatures of culinary connoisseurship. Chile peppers, blue cornmeal, paddles of cacti, unusual game animals, and even *huitlacoche* (a New Mexican corn fungus with a mushroom flavor) were all part of the New West's image, and helped reinstate Santa Fe's reputation as a gourmet mecca, an image it maintains today.

Such fanciful fare is popular in fine restaurants around the country that serve their own version of high-fashion Western food, but they are far removed from the unadorned Western chow that beguiled so many travelers in earlier years. That time-honored taste of the region is still available, and you can savor it when you plow into a Navajo taco at the Tuba City Truck Stop in Arizona, sample Daddy Bruce's sublime barbecue in Denver, chaw on a flap of jerky from Jiggs' Smoke House along old Route 66 in Oklahoma, gobble hot carnitas from Roque's Carnitas Wagon on the Plaza in Santa Fe, compare and contrast the green chile cheeseburgers at the Tesuque Market in New Mexico to the Caesarburgers at the Split T in Oklahoma City, and ingest a length of hot gut sausages in the back room of the Southside Market in Elgin, Texas. As the women of the Junior League of Odessa (Texas) noted in the introduction to their *Wild Wild West Cookbook* (1991) (which contains nary a single recipe that uses sun-dried tomatoes or a demi-glace, but a dynamite one for Odessa Firemen's Chicken-Fried Steak), "There is nothing like puttin' on a pair of boots, meetin' friends and eatin' some good food."

# BARBECUE

arbecue is like religion: first, because it can make you swoon in jubilation; and second, because it has so many different sects. There are true believers who are convinced that *their* kind of barbecue is the *only* good and true one, and that people who use an unorthodox type of wood for their fire, or make sauce a little differently, are heretics.

The barbecue of the West is as different from the pig pickin's of the South and the urban smokeshacks of the Midwest as the Archbishop of Canterbury is from the Reverend Jesse Jackson.

So, please be forewarned, all ye who think of barbecue as pork butt with sweet red sauce, or baby back ribs or shreds of swine in vinegar, or sandwiches with sweet slaw and hot meat in buns: what we're going to honor here is something else, and to those who love it, it's the only kind, and it's the best. "Texas has more great barbecue places than anywhere else," wrote Alan Richman when he traveled around the country for *People* magazine looking for the country's ten best barbecue establishments, noting that the last wish of Arthur Bryant, the far-famed pit man of Kansas City, was to be buried where he first savored majestic barbecue . . . in Texas.

Nearly everything edible gets barbecued out West, including rattlesnakes, Gulf shrimp, pizza (topping only), and goat's heads, but it is beef, beef brisket in particular, that defines barbecue at its best in cowboy country. Most times when pork is on the menu, it is a second-class citizen; chicken, mutton, and fish and their ilk are basically novelty items more than genuine contenders for serious appetites. As for sauce, which is so vital in other regions' formulas for stellar barbecue, it hardly bears discussion in certain parts of Texas; many of the best barbecue parlors offer no sauce at all to accompany their meat, the philosophy being that barbecue means one and only one thing: beef infused with smoke, unsullied by catsup-like condiments.

(Parenthetically, on the subject of what, precisely, the word *barbecue* means:

It is a verb that suggests cooking by means of smoke and an open fire.

It is a noun with several related but not identical meanings: barbecue is the meat served in a barbecue [a restaurant] that barbecues it using a barbecue [a pit with a grate for meat and a place for a fire].

*Curtains in the window, a working neon sign: a quite swank barbecue restaurant.*

It is also a synonym for the kind of picnic at which barbecue is served.

Similarly, the word *pit* means both the specific apparatus used to cook the meat and the establishment where the cooked meat is sold; i.e.: "All great pits have a pit in the back room." We have chosen the spelling *barbecue* merely for the sake of consistency, but we have nothing against barbeque, barbie cue, bar bee que, bar-b-q, or just plain BBQ. And as for the origin of the word, our favorite among the many speculations is that it comes from the French *barbe à queue*, meaning beard to tail.)

The place to relish the essential Western-style barbecue is the back room of a small-town meat market in the heart of Texas, where customers dine sitting on a bench at a picnic table, and where the air might be perfumed by the delicious rank aroma of an adjoining one-room sausage factory as well as by hickory, oak, and mesquite smoke leaking from the brick and metal pit. Eateries like this can still be found throughout the extraordinarily appetizing region known as the Hill Country, harkening back to the earliest days of commercial barbecue, about a century ago.

Outdoor, open-pit cooking has been a Southern community ritual since colonial times, and Texans, whose gastronomy owes much to Dixie, have long enjoyed it as well, at political rallies and Fourth of July picnics and, most conspicuously, at the famous XIT Ranch around Dalhart, where it is a tradition every autumn to pit-cook several tons of beef over cords of mesquite wood in trenches dug with bulldozers (sides of cow are heaped in the trenches using dump trucks). But around the turn of the century, butchers in central Texas added a new twist to the idea of barbecue when they figured out that instead of throwing away unsold cuts of meat, they could prolong their salability if they cooked them using an indoor "pit" made of fire bricks. They then set up a table or a counter somewhere near the pit, where customers could come eat this smoked meat, accompanied by sliced white bread for mopping up its juices, and beer or Coke or Dr Pepper to wash it down. So the barbecue parlor was born, presided over by a pitmaster, who is to Texas cookery what the cinnamon bun baker is in Iowa or the maître d' is in New York: a revered culinary god, with the power to make your meal a blessed occasion.

The meat of choice is brisket, which starts tough, but has enough fat nestled in the muscle so it bastes itself as it steeps on

*Pittsburg, Texas, 1977.*

the grate enveloped in smoke, becoming more supple than any other cut of beef, so tender it actually falls apart when you pick up a slice of it. The primary secret of producing such sublime meat—and the essential skill of all great pitmasters—is to keep the fire low enough so that the brisket is cooked not by flame (which would cause its juices to boil away) but by the warmth of a constant haze of smoke, which insinuates itself into the fibers, turning them limp and voluptuously tender, striated with glistening veins of fat, and encased in a blackened crust.

PICTURE PUZZLE BUBBLE GUM

All pits, whether jerry-rigged from old oil drums or architected out of iron and brick, are designed with a firebox at one end and a smokestack at the other, with a grate in between where the meat is set to bathe in smoke that wafts from the burning wood toward the flue. If the fire is low and slow, and the temperature of the pit is sustained at an ideal 175 degrees, it takes a good twelve hours, or sometimes as much as twice that, for the meat to attain maximum succulence. It is a delicate job to keep the fire at just the right level and ensure a constant flow of smoke, to rearrange the dozen or so briskets so each imbibes the smoke on the hot spots of the grate, and each has opportunity to breathe. To adulterate this process by mopping the meat with sweet sauce of any kind is heresy to the traditionalist pit men of the Hill Country,

although many east of Dallas (in the sphere of Dixie influence), as well as most pit men outside of Texas, do apply a marinade or sauce to flavor the meat as it cooks.

No barbecue restaurant is formal; the great pits of central Texas are informal *in extremis.* Most don't have any sort of menu, since everybody comes for the same thing: brisket, by the pound, or by the half pound if you are on a diet, and maybe a sausage link or two on the side. Of course there are no waiters. Present yourself at the back counter and tell the pit man how much you want. He forks a brisket off its grate inside the pit, cleaves a heap of slices, about a quarter-inch thick apiece, and slaps them onto butcher paper. The paper is your plate and serving tray in one; use it to carry food to a table, to catch dripping juices and hunks of falling brisket as you eat, then to wrap up your end-of-meal debris for tossing in the trash can. It is *de rigueur* for a pit man to offer some sort of bread with the meat. The customary choices are spongy white bread (good for sopping up all the natural gravy that spills out) or saltines, generally doled out by the half-stack. Some pits also provide onions and jalapeño peppers for chewing, a bottle or two of hot sauce on the tables, and maybe even some seasoned beef juice to use as gravy. Beverages are generally purchased from a soda machine against the wall.

# Great Western
# BARBECUES

Of the Magnificent Seven eateries listed here, the Kruez Market offers the classic Texas butcher shop experience. The others, in Texas and beyond, vary in their classicism, but none are less than sublime in their taste and atmosphere.

**Louie Mueller's**
**206 West Second Street**
**Taylor, TX**
**(512) 352-6206**

You wouldn't rightly call Mueller's a restaurant, not even a café. It is an eat-place, fashioned out of a room that was a school gymnasium many decades ago, now dimly lit by a cloudy skylight in the stamped tin ceiling. There are no balanced meals, no *plats du jour.* Eat beef by the pound, hot links, and maybe potato salad on the side, served on butcher paper and a molded plastic cafeteria tray.

**Kruez Market**
**208 South Commerce Street**
**Lockhart, TX**
**(512) 398-2361**

Kruez (say "Krites") has been smoking meat since the beginning of the century, and they don't even have plates, but they do twist up the ends of the butcher paper so the meat's juices don't spill when you carry it from the pit to a table.

**Southside Market**
**1212 Highway 290**
**Elgin, TX**
**(512) 285-3407**

Although the brisket (and even the mutton) is exemplary, it's sausages, known hereabouts as hot guts, that have made the Southside Market a beacon for more than one hundred years.

**Sonny Bryan's Smokehouse**
**2202 Inwood Road**
**Dallas, TX**
**(214) 357-7120**

Mellow brisket is heaped into gigantic sandwiches, well sauced and sold with good side dishes such as french fries and pork and beans, as well as tumblers of iced tea.

**Jake's Rib**
**100 Ponderosa**
**Chickasha, OK**
**(405) 222-2825**

Jake's is known for its mammoth portions of pork ribs, pork chunks, sliced brisket, fiery sausage links, and thick, smoke-flavored pink bologna steaks.

**Jiggs' Smoke House**
**exit 62 off I-40**
**Clinton, OK**
**(405) 323-5641**

Jiggs' is an outpost of a smokehouse specialty that has become something of a rarity in modern times: genuine beef jerky. It takes two big hands to bend one, and a healthy set of teeth to rip off a chaw. Chew, chew, chew: the salty cured flavor inundates the mouth with more intensity than a plug of Skoal.

**Daddy Bruce's**
**1629 East 34th Avenue**
**Denver, CO**
**(303) 295-9115**

Daddy Bruce Randolph came to Denver from Arkansas, via Texas and Arizona, so his barbecue is fundamentally Southern-style, meaning sauced with a sweet, peppery, garlicky red stuff, but with an unmistakable frontier panache.

# Chili,
# TEXAS-STYLE

*T*exas chili is a bowlful of attitude. It is ornery, rude, and starts fights and feuds. It inspires homesickness, chauvinism, braggadocio, tears (of agony as well as longing), dozens of tumultuous cook-offs each year, and more philosophizing than Marcel Proust's madeleines. Will Rogers called it a "bowl of blessedness"; Kit Carson's final wish, as he lay dying, was for one last taste of it; and President Lyndon

*At the Texas Centennial Exposition in Dallas, the Walker's Austex Chile Company booth featured Mexican-costumed attendants serving chile con carne and hot tamales.*

Johnson said, "There is simply nothing better." Food writer John Thorne determined that chili's unique appeal was its masculinity, and quoted a professor of contemporary mythology who called it "Disgusting stuff . . . the pure embodiment of rampant male chauvinism." Many people think of it as lowly fare, right down there with pulpy meat loaf and deep-fried corn dogs, but those who love it exalt it more than a grand cru vintage wine, and worry over its preparation more than they would over a truffle soufflé.

*Mexican chili stands in old San Antonio. "As day dawns," this vintage image was captioned, "the queer hotel keepers put out their fires, fold their tables, and silently steal away until another night."*

To be precise, the inamorata in question here is chili con carne, which is, simply, meat in pepper sauce, or, more precisely, coarsely ground or chunked beef, with an ample measure of fat or suet, simmered for a long time with chile peppers or chile powder, cumin, garlic, and a dash of oregano. In the last hundred years, people have customized this basic formula with thousands of other ingredients, including booze, beer, eyes of bulls, shaved chocolate, snake meat, red ants, and one tap of the ash from a good Havana cigar, and of course beans, tomatoes, and onions. In Texas, where it was invented and first served, and where it has been declared the Official State Dish (in 1977), most chili eaters—however else they customize the recipe for their own personal bowl of red—disdain beans and macaroni above all, and pretty much hate tomatoes and onions, too. "You may as well learn," advised Jane Trahey in her marvelous *A Taste of Texas* cookbook in 1949, "that the tomato and bean messes

served from Forty-Second Street, New York to Stockton Street, San Francisco, have absolutely no relation to real chili."

A true Texas bowl of red is a stunning vision, reminiscent of a Technicolor sunset created in a Hollywood studio: opaque currents of molten mahogany, lustrous orange, and cordovan are flecked with grains of spice and swirled with rivulets of limpid grease. The texture is faintly grainy from the pulp of roasted chile peppers, thick enough to cling to the heaps of dark, spice-saturated meat chunks that fill the bowl. If it's good chili, its aroma hovers close, and you can almost see it floating up like a pokey cloud above the crimson brew. If you are a serious chili eater, you will first partake of that smell, closing in to above the bowl to inhale—not too close or too deeply, lest the peppers' heat burn your eyes—thereby putting your central nervous system on bowl-of-red alert. After the aroma, but before the taste begins to pleasure your tongue, there is heat. Instantly, when the first spoonful hits your mouth, the fire of the pepper jolts your body, perhaps causing goose bumps or a quick shiver. Then there is warmth—not thermal warmth, but a glow akin to passion—and as the warmth spreads to every nerve ending in your body, the flavor of the chili comes on strong. It is earthy but rarefied, bracing and dizzying at the same time, a comfort and a thrill. The authority of bull meat ballasted with grease and armed with the punch of the peppers make chili con carne a truly sublime eating experience: literally breathtaking, sweat-provoking, and joyful.

Chili began as a poor person's meal in San Antonio long before the Civil War—a clever way for Mexican families to stretch a low-down cut of beef by hacking it into lots of little pieces and stewing it with peppers. As curry spices did for bad meat in India, the peppers gave a new zest and taste appeal to verge-of-rotten food, and the first documented description of this dish (in 1828) describes it as containing "nearly as many peppers as there are pieces of meat." Sometime around 1880, chili stands were set up in San Antonio's Military Plaza. The plaza was a respectable market during the day, but at night it became an anything-goes zone, where people went to drink, smoke marijuana, trade in stolen goods, and bargain for whatever pleasures they desired. The chili stands were nothing but open-air charcoal and mesquite fires set up among the confusion, with adjacent trestle tables and communal benches where chowhounds could sit and eat. Their repertoire was billed as "Mexican food," but was in fact axiomatic Tex-Mex: tamales, enchiladas, chili verde, frijoles, *atole* (cinnamon-flavored hot chocolate), and of course, chili con carne. The grub was dished out by women who became known as chili queens—colorful characters in native costumes, with roses pinned to their frilly peasant blouses, and popular for their flirty ways with customers. Nearly all descriptions of the San Antonio chili queens made much of their virtue (*they* were not for sale), but chili con carne's enduring status as a vaguely wicked dish was established by its association with the disreputable after-dark scene of El Mercado.

By the time the chili queens and their wares were banished for health-code reasons in 1937 (then reinstated in 1939, then banned again, for good, in 1943), chili was famous . . . or perhaps the better word is notorious. The chili stands of San Antonio had become an inspiration for chili parlors all across Texas and the West: short-order joints with none of the amenities of a nice restaurant—just a cauldron full of chili, some crackers and beer to go

with it, and a shady atmosphere (with waiters and waitresses who may or may not have been chili queens, and may or may not have been virtuous). Discharged military mess sergeants, out-of-work trail cooks, and diner chefs whose businesses went bust during the Great Depression all had the proper butch attitude to become chili parlor proprietors, and by World War II, chili had become the archetypal low-class café meal, served in open-all-night hash houses on the wrong side of town. At best, you might expect to find a semirespectable bowl of red at a drugstore counter or in a truck stop, but most nice restaurants simply did not serve it, and nice people (who weren't supposed to have breath that smelled of garlic and spice) didn't eat it. And because chili con carne can be made with the cheapest grade of meat and is so easy to prepare in large amounts, it also became— in Frank X. Tolbert's words—"a standard entree in most jails in the Southwest." Tolbert, author of *A Bowl of Red*, reported that many ex-cons, discharged from the Texas state prison system, found that chili on the outside just wasn't up to snuff, and so wrote to the warden begging for the recipe of the jailhouse chili they remembered so fondly.

Chili con carne's status as an outlaw dish gave it a taboo charisma that, starting in the 1950s, has made it the last word in reverse chic for any hearty eater who wants to prove he or she is not a culinary sissy. Probably the celebrity who did the most to give chili a glamorous (but in no way aristocratic) cachet was Elizabeth Taylor, who made gossip-column news in 1962 by sending telegrams to Dave Chasen, of Chasen's restaurant in Beverly Hills, pleading that he air-freight his chili, ten quarts at a time, to her movie location in Rome, where she and Richard Burton were busy filming *Cleopatra* and carousing. Chasen's chili con carne, like the restaurant's other famous dish, a "hobo steak," has never actually been listed on the menu, but both are well known among the ritzy clientele, who presumably indulge in such conspicuously vulgar foods as a relief from their ordinary diet of quail eggs and lobster thermidor.

To the dismay of Texas chiliheads, Chasen's chili contains beans. To help spread the True Word about beanless chili con carne, the Chili Appreciation Society International, originally founded in Dallas in 1951 with the slogan "The aroma of a good chili should generate rapture akin to a lover's kiss," opened a chapter in Los Angeles in 1964. A few years later they began sponsoring chili cook-offs, and the rowdy cook-offs have since grown into major media events, with corporate sponsorship ranging from Pepsi to Pepto-Bismol.

# Three Famous Bowls of Red

## FUNDAMENTAL CHILI

(adapted from Frank X. Tolbert's recipe)

*3 pounds lean beef*
*2 bottles of beer*
*⅛ pound kidney suet or 1/4 cup vegetable oil*
*4 jalapeño chile peppers, or less for mild chili,*
*    stems removed*
*2 tablespoons crushed cumin seeds*
*1 tablespoon salt*
*1 tablespoon cayenne*
*1 teaspoon oregano*
*1–3 cloves chopped garlic, to taste*
*Optional: masa harina*
*Optional: 2 cups tomato sauce*

Marinate beef 6 to 8 hours in beer. Reserve beer and cut beef into small, bite-size chunks or grind it very coarsely.

Heat kidney suet (or oil) in a pan and sear the beef in the suet until it is gray.

Puree peppers, seeds and all, in a blender with just enough water to make a catsup-thick paste. Combine pepper puree with beer marinade and beef in a large pot. Bring to boil, then lower heat and simmer 30 minutes. Remove pot from heat.

Stir in cumin, salt, cayenne, oregano, and garlic. Return to heat, bring to boil, then lower heat, cover pot, and simmer about 1 hour, stirring occasionally. Masa harina may be added to thicken the chili (without it, this recipe makes a fairly soupy chili . . . which is the authentic way), also tomato sauce can be used to give the broth some body, if desired. Continue cooking, at a very slow simmer, until meat is tender.

Remove chili from heat and refrigerate at least 8 hours. (After this 8 hours, it will be easy to skim off grease from the top, if desired.) Reheat. Serve with beans and crackers on the side.

**6 servings.**

## LYNDON JOHNSON'S PEDERNALES RIVER CHILI

(from a recipe by Zephyr Wright;
*Air Force One* never flew anywhere without a
supply of this chili on board)

*4 pounds coarsely ground beef*
*1 cup finely chopped onion*
*2 cloves finely chopped garlic*
*1 teaspoon oregano*
*1 teaspoon crushed cumin seeds*
*2 tablespoons chili powder*
*2 (16-ounce) cans tomatoes*
*2 cups hot water*
*Salt to taste*

Brown meat until gray in a heavy stew pot. (If meat is not fatty enough, you may have to use a few tablespoons of oil.) Add onions and garlic and cook until onions are translucent. Add all remaining ingredients. Bring to boil, lower heat, and cover. Simmer 1 hour. Skim off grease before serving.

**Serves 8.**

## ALLAN SHIVERS' CHILI

(Mr. Shivers was once governor of Texas.) "Put a pot of chili on the stove to simmer. Let it simmer. Meanwhile, broil a sirloin steak. Continue to simmer the chili and eat the steak. Ignore the chili."

"It's a wonder he was ever elected," Frank X. Tolbert observed in regard to Shivers's attitude toward chili.

# The Cult of
# THE POD

In New Mexico, a lot of people love chile, but hate chili. The difference is that chile, which New Mexicans generally spell with an "e," refers to the pod, and to a meatless bowl of pureed pod usually served alongside other meals. Chili, with an "i," is a spelling that local fanatics save for Texas-style chili con carne (with meat), which they abhor.

The chile pepper is one of New Mexico's two state vegetables (along with the pinto bean), although technically it isn't a vegetable at all. It is a berry, like the tomato, and the most popular variety is about six to nine inches long. It is verdant green, but turns a scintillating red when it ripens. In the autumn, at harvest time, the peppers are woven into *ristras*—gorgeous scarlet wreaths that hang outside on adobe walls so the pods can dry in the sun (then be plucked and used in cooking). All along the roads lead-

*Harvest time in the foothills of the Sangre de Cristo Mountains.*

ing through pepper-growing country, wisps of loamy smoke curl up above green fields into a turquoise sky as farmers roast chiles in big mesh drums over wood or propane fires. The roasting pods smell luscious and tasty, and as the drum's mesh rubs the singed, blackened skin from the peppers their flesh turns supple and they glisten celadon green. Many of the stands sell pepper sandwiches: nothing but delicious, limp roasted peppers piled up between slices of sturdy bread.

To celebrate the chile harvest, the town of Hatch has a Chile Festival each year around Labor Day. There is a cooking contest, blue ribbons are awarded to the farmer who brings the loveliest pods; and a Red Chile Queen and a Green Chile Queen are crowned. The citizens march through the streets of town in a parade that includes floats that look like enormous pods, bowls of chile, and frying pans full of peppers.

New Mexico chile peppers tend to be hot but not dangerously so, and they are fleshy enough to be ideal for stuffing, roasting and peeling, and chopping into salsas. Their flavor, in the words of Santa Fe chef Mark Miller, "is unlike that of any other chile in North America: sweet and earthy, with a clarity that seems to reflect the skies and landscapes of New Mexico." In his *Great Chile Book* (1991), Miller enumerated these wonderful qualities of the pod:

•Chiles are good for you. They are low in calories, low in sodium, and cholesterol-free.
•Historically, chiles have featured prominently in homeopathic and herbal remedies.
•The healthiest quality of chiles is that they open the soul to new experiences!
•Chiles have succeeded in bringing the world together and have proven themselves roving ambassadors.

Below: *Juanita Martinez brews a batch of chile in Socorro, New Mexico (1979).*
Right: *Hatch, New Mexico, 1991. The seated women dressed like red and green chiles are riding a parade float sponsored by a local dentist, which is why their stools look like teeth.*

# *International Connoisseurs of*
# GREEN AND RED CHILE

**T**he International Connoisseurs of Green and Red Chile was founded in 1972 in Mesilla, an old frontier town in the southern Rio Grande Valley where most of New Mexico's chiles are produced. The ICGRC, now eight thousand members strong and headquartered in Las Cruces, publishes *Chile Connoisseurs News,* a quarterly gazette with lists of upcoming hot food festivals and cook-offs, hints for home chile gardeners, roasting and peeling tips, and recipes. Membership requirements in the ICGRC aren't too stringent (send them ten dollars and unless you are a convicted Texan, you'll likely be accepted), although if you join while you are visiting Las Cruces, you might be required to stand at attention before a civic official, with a brace of native New Mexican chiles raised in one hand, and make the following pledge:

*On land and on sea, in this nation and abroad, and even into outer space, I hereby pledge my allegiance and loyal support to chile in all forms and preparations for reasons gastronomical, for reasons cultural, for reasons historical and reasons economical. Furthermore I take this pledge with chile in hand and in full view of those who appreciate the finer things in life.*

Aspiring chileheads interested in joining are invited to write to: International Connoisseurs of Green and Red Chile 311 North Downtown Mall Las Cruces, NM 88001.

*All year, chile ristras decorate homes, gardens, and shops throughout New Mexico, but they are brightest in the weeks after the fall harvest.*

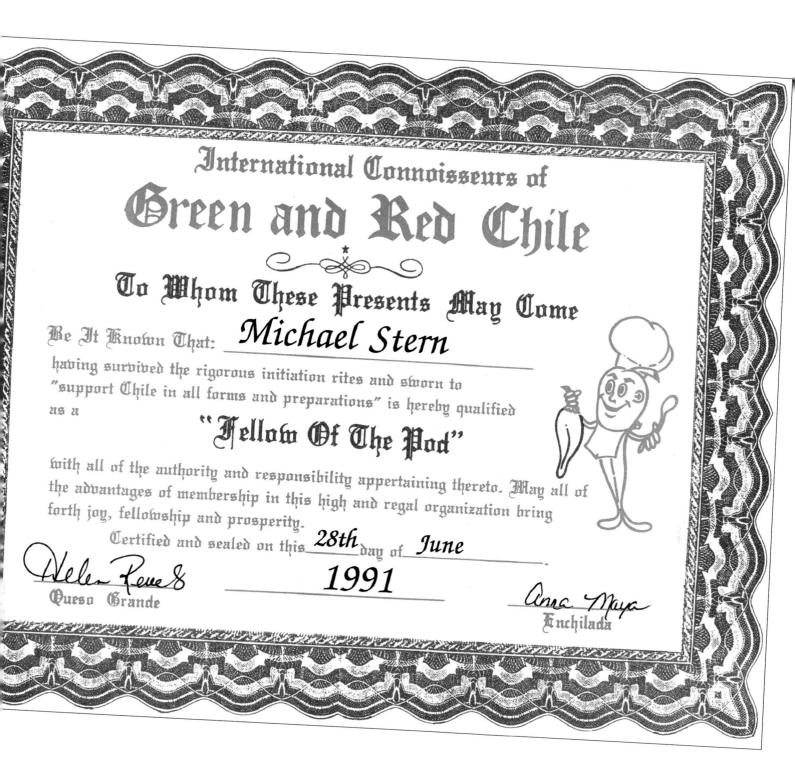

International Connoisseurs of

# Green and Red Chile

★

## To Whom These Presents May Come

Be It Known That: **Michael Stern**

having survived the rigorous initiation rites and sworn to "support Chile in all forms and preparations" is hereby qualified as a

## "Fellow Of The Pod"

with all of the authority and responsibility appertaining thereto. May all of the advantages of membership in this high and regal organization bring forth joy, fellowship and prosperity.

Certified and sealed on this ___28th___ day of ___June___

___1991___

*Helen Reyes*
Queso Grande

*Anna Maya*
Enchilada

# Hot, Hotter, Hottest CHILES

**M**ore than their keen flavor and the gorgeous colors they come in, the thing that makes chile peppers special is their heat. It is heat that can cause distress or ecstasy, or both, simultaneously, and it is heat that makes them addictive. No one knows for sure why people enjoy eating something that hurts so much; some psychologists see it as daredeviltry, like bungee-jumping or Brahma Bull riding. Eating super-hot peppers can be an expression of gustatory machismo every bit as impressive as slugging down shots of mescal with the worm at the bottom of the bottle.

Scientists speculate that the peppers' real appeal is more complex—their heat stimulates the body to produce endorphins, which create a sense of well-being like that known by long-distance runners who break through the wall of pain into a sense of overwhelming pleasure. The hotter the peppers you eat, the more endorphins you produce: agony stimulates ecstasy. After you have experienced that unique chile pepper glow, the sight or even the thought of hot pods can trigger a Pavlovian response that can be stronger than the lust for any other food, except possibly chocolate.

Paul Bosland, America's foremost chile breeder, once clued us in to a pepper farmer's favorite practical joke, based on the botanical fact that the heat of peppers is all in a substance called capsaicin, which is concentrated inside the pods in their placenta, the fleshy part to which the seeds are attached. The joke goes like this: carefully slice a piece from the wall of a really hot pepper and eat it, suffering little distress, then give the butt of the joke a piece of the wall with lots of the placenta attached. Now, watch the person combust in agony! (Note: If you try this at home, have ice cream or other dairy products, or potatoes or bread, ready as a salve: they're the best ways to dilute the effect.)

Peppers' heat is commonly calculated in Scoville Units, a measure originally developed in 1912 when pharmacologist Wilbur Scoville needed a way to test peppers used as the active ingredient in Heet, a muscle salve he helped invent. Jalapeño peppers, which most people consider pretty hot, rate about 5,000 Scoville Units. The hottest of all peppers, the Habanero, has been measured at 300,000 S.U.; a teaspoon of minced Habaneros is enough to transform a gallon of innocuous salsa into a four-alarm tongue trauma. Smaller chiles tend to be hotter, and one of the most insidious qualities of these pretty little pods is that long after they are added to a recipe, their capsaicin continues to leach out, amplifying the heat of the dish as it sits there. So a carne adovada you make to be quite hot at four in the afternoon might be unbearably incendiary when you reheat it for dinner at eight.

Peppers' heat also makes them healing agents. Capsaicin's power to provoke the digestive tract is what makes it the active ingredient in any number of salves and liniments, creating a warmth that relieves maladies ranging from hemorrhoids and shingles to postmastectomy pain and cluster headaches. Peppers are a source of treatment for allergic rhinitis and provide the secret thrill in some chewing gums used by ex-smokers to replace the kick of nicotine, and they are a time-honored folk remedy (in Mexico) for stomach aches. In addition, chile boosters are fond of pointing out that they are loaded with vitamins C and A and beta-carotene, and have been credited with speeding up people's metabolism, thus aiding weight-reduction plans.

*Opposite: Religious Experience hot sauce, made in Colorado, comes in four strengths—Mild, Original, Hot, and the Wrath.*

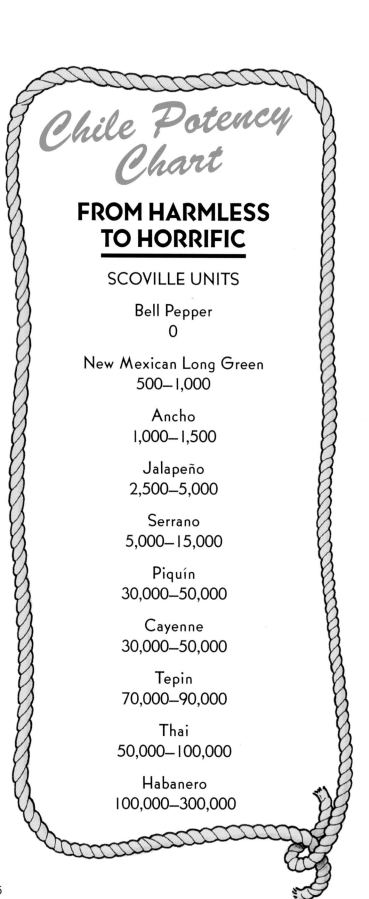

## Chile Potency Chart

# FROM HARMLESS TO HORRIFIC

### SCOVILLE UNITS

Bell Pepper
0

New Mexican Long Green
500–1,000

Ancho
1,000–1,500

Jalapeño
2,500–5,000

Serrano
5,000–15,000

Piquín
30,000–50,000

Cayenne
30,000–50,000

Tepin
70,000–90,000

Thai
50,000–100,000

Habanero
100,000–300,000

# Cooking
# RED AND GREEN CHILES

owls of red chile and bowls of green chile are staples in the New Mexican kitchen. They can be used in any number of recipes, such as enchiladas or burritos, or to flavor almost any kind of meat. They are also served as a companion dip-and-dunk (for warm flour tortillas) with breakfast, lunch, and dinner.

## RED CHILE

*¼ cup finely chopped sweet onion*
*2 cloves garlic, finely chopped*
*2 tablespoons olive oil*
*1 teaspoon ground cumin*
*2 tablespoons flour*
*½ cup powdered red chile*
*2–2½ cups water*
*Salt to taste*

Sauté onion and garlic in oil over medium heat. When onion is translucent, stir in cumin and flour. Continue cooking, stirring constantly to blend flour into oil, until mixture barely begins to brown, 2 to 3 minutes. Remove from heat.

Combine chile with 2 cups water, mixing well. Using a whisk and mixing constantly, slowly pour this chile mix into the pan with the flour and oil. Return pan to medium heat, continue whisking, and cook about 5 minutes, or until mixture begins to simmer. Lower heat if necessary to keep it from boiling rapidly. Continue stirring as mixture thickens, adding a bit of water if necessary

to keep it from getting pasty. When sauce is smooth, and about as thick as a heavy cream soup, remove from heat.

**Makes 2 cups.**

*(Will keep about a week, well covered, in the refrigerator. Some people like to puree it before using to smooth out any lumps and eliminate the grainy texture.) Use this sauce as a dip for tortillas alongside (or on top of) fried eggs. Or add cooked hominy or beef or pork to make it into a stew. It is also the fundamental flavor in enchiladas and burritos.*

## GREEN CHILE

*¼ cup finely chopped sweet onion*
*1 clove garlic, finely chopped*
*2 tablespoons olive oil*
*2 tablespoons flour*
*½ teaspoon ground cumin*
*1½ cups chicken broth*
*1½ cups roasted and peeled green New Mexico chiles, chopped (Roast chiles on an open fire or under a broiler, until skin blisters. Peel off the skin and remove seeds, wearing gloves to protect your hands.)*
*¼ teaspoon oregano*
*1–2 tablespoons chopped jalapeño peppers, to taste (this will depend on how hot the green chiles you use are)*
*Salt to taste*

Sauté onion and garlic in oil over medium heat. When onion is translucent, stir in flour and cumin. Use a whisk

*Like corn (another New World crop that dates back to prehistory), chile peppers are appreciated as decoration as well as food.*

and stir constantly to blend the flour with the oil. When the mixture begins to brown, remove it from the heat. Slowly stir in the broth, whisking constantly to prevent lumps. Add green chiles and oregano. Return to heat. Bring to very low simmer, stirring frequently. Cover and cook about 10 minutes. Taste and add jalapeño peppers and salt, if necessary (if using canned chicken broth, it won't likely be).

**Makes 2 cups.**

*(Will keep about a week, well covered, in the refrigerator; but you will need to heat it up before using and—if graininess and a few lumps bother you—puree it as well.) Use this sauce as a dip for tortillas alongside (or on top of) fried eggs, or as the basic flavoring of enchiladas. Or add tomatoes, pureed tomatillos, cooked hominy, ground cooked beef, or chunks of cooked pork to make it into a stew.*

# Where to Eat
# HOT CHILE IN NEW MEXICO

## Angelina's
## Española, NM
## (505) 753-8543

There are ordinary tables in the middle of Angelina's dining room, but the choice seats are around the perimeter, in small, semiprivate eating areas, each of which is outfitted like a different Old West place: a teepee, a hacienda, a jail, a bank. It's fun, funky decor, but what's really great is the food: zesty huevos rancheros, bowls of hot-hot red and green chile, carne adovada, and puffy sopaipillas on the side.

## Chope's
## Route 28
## La Mesa, NM
## (505) 233-3420

A café and tavern in the Rio Grande Valley in the heart of chile-growing country, this whitewashed building surrounded by chile fields is crowded at lunch with local planters. Not to be missed: red or green enchiladas, chile rellenos, meaty tamales, and bowls of red or green chile, plain or *con queso*.

## Coyote Café
## 132 West Water
## Santa Fe, NM
## (505) 983-1615

The source of "Nouvelle New Mexican" food, from red chile onion rings to tenderloin of pork with apple and red chile chutney. Chef Mark Miller says the inspiration for his imaginative cuisine is ancient pueblo food, as might have been enjoyed by twelfth-century cliff-dwelling Indians. Be that as it may, late twentieth-century Americans have gobbled up his inventions, putting this restaurant at the cutting edge of food fashion.

## Dave's Not Here
## 1115 Hickox
## Santa Fe, NM
## (505) 983-7060

Far from the bustle of the Plaza, Dave's Not Here (named for the former proprietor) is an insiders' favorite, renowned for its superb chiles rellenos and gigantic hamburgers. Be sure to leave room for a piece of gooey chocolate layer cake made by local masseuse Tracy Conrad.

### Dora's
**401 East Hall St. (Highway 85)**
**Hatch, NM**
**(505) 267-9294**

Hatch bills itself as the Chile Capital of the World, and there is no better place to sample honest, hometown versions of all the fire-eater's classics: bowl of red, bowl of green, huevos rancheros, chile rellenos, also exemplary menudo (a tripe and hominy stew renowned for its ability to cure hangovers).

### M&J Restaurant
**403 Second SW**
**Albuquerque, NM**
**(505) 242-4890**

### Nellie's
**1226 West Hadley**
**Las Cruces, NM**
**(505) 524-9982**

A joint. Fluorescent lights. Cinder-block walls. Humming Dr Pepper cooler. And oh, such succulent chile rellenos: big meaty pods battered and fried and served piping hot with grand refritos on the side.

### The Pink Adobe
**406 Old Santa Fe Trail**
**Santa Fe, NM**
**(505) 983-7712**

Santa Fe's own "21 Club" since it opened in the 1940s, The Pink Adobe is favored by long-time citizens as well as visiting celebrities. It even boasts its own "power table"—#10, in the back of the Dragon Room bar, where owner and founder Rosalea Murphy holds court every night. The food is classic Santa Fe (as opposed to nouvelle), including swell chicken enchiladas and apple pie with rum sauce, as well as Steak Dunnigan smothered with mushrooms and chopped chiles—a dish that is a true taste of this city's culinary history.

### Roque's Carnitas Wagon
### on the Plaza
**Santa Fe, NM**

A food wagon parked around lunchtime at the corner of Palace and Washington streets, Roque's menu is limited to one wonderful thing: carnitas. That's strips of sirloin sizzled on a grill and heaped into a warm tortilla with a fiery jalapeño salsa. Find a bench, or eat standing up leaning over a garbage can: this is a sloppy, drippy, and unforgettable feast.

Also known as the M&J Sanitary Tortilla Factory, M&J is one of the most memorable cheap-eats experiences in Albuquerque. The dining room is an airy hall with spacious vinyl booths and rough-textured walls covered with love letters to the restaurant written by satisfied customers. The carne adovada just may be the best in the West, especially when loaded into a burrito; also recommended: enchiladas (blue or yellow corn).

## Santacafé
**231 Washington Avenue**
**Santa Fe, NM**
**(505) 984-1788**

An impressive mingling of Southwestern ingredients with oriental style and gourmet amenities. It's very, very fashionable; but it is also very, very delicious, especially the chile-spiked brioche at the beginning of the meal, the peppery dumplings and spring rolls with dipping sauces, and one autumn all-vegetable meal we recall as being the very image (and flavor) of a utopian harvest, including all sorts of beans and legumes and the sweetest corn we ever ate.

## Tecolote Café
**1203 Cerrillos Road**
**Santa Fe, NM**
**(505) 988-1362**

Breakfast: atole piñon hotcakes, made with blue cornmeal and studded with roasted piñon nuts; French toast made from cinnamon-raisin or orange poppy seed bread; corned beef hash atop a hot tortilla, smothered with red or green chile; the "sheepherder's breakfast," which is spuds and jalapeño peppers cooked on a grill until crusty brown, then topped with two kinds of chile and melted Cheddar cheese. Need we say more?

## Woolworth's
**58 East San Francisco**
**Santa Fe, NM**
**(505) 982-1062**

*Specialité de la maison*: Frito pie, served across the lunch counter in a slit-open Fritos bag, with a plastic fork planted in its heart and a sheaf of paper napkins to hold it so you can eat while you walk around town. Don't laugh. This really is a tasty treat: the chile topping on the chips is just hot enough to give your tongue a buzz, and just the right level of juiciness so some Fritos down below stay crisp, while others near the top turn to strips of limp, salty cornmeal.

*Roque's carnitas.*

# The Bean PALACE

*Roy Rogers prefers lemon pie to beans. We once overheard his wife, Dale Evans, tell him, "Honey, you don't eat enough to keep a bird alive."*

**B**eans are the soul food of the American West. Jim Shoulders, world-champion rodeo star, remembered that when he came to New York City from Oklahoma to the rodeo at Madison Square Garden in the 1940s, he traveled with beans in his suitcase. He brought a pan, too, and every night before the show he and his traveling partners cooked cowboy beans on a hot plate at the Belvedere Hotel. "There wasn't a restaurant in New York that served decent pinto beans back then," Shoulders said; and he simply didn't feel right about rodeoing on a stomach full of New York City food. All top hands consider beans an essential part of a healthy diet— preferably the mottled tan ones called pinto beans (meaning *painted*), cooked long and slow with chunks of salt pork for flavor until they are still whole and plump, yet soft enough to scarcely resist the pressure of the gentlest bite.

Because dry ones were easy to carry on the trail and to cook over a campfire, beans were always a range staple— simple, filling, nutritious, and a cowboy favorite well into the

*Gary Cooper, playing a rodeo star, shows Merle Oberon how tasty a bowl of beans can be in* The Cowboy and the Lady *(1938)*.

canned-foods era. Although beans are pretty basic, refritos, which are made from leftovers the next day, can be a deluxe kind of treat. Refritos are the specialty of ranch kitchens, border town cafés, and haciendas throughout the Southwest. Although refritos means *refried,* they are in fact fried only once; but the frying can infuse the humble nuggets with a luxury they never knew when whole.

Here are recipes for basic pinto beans, then refritos.

The plain beans make an ideal companion for a bowl of red or a bowl of green, with big, soft flour tortillas for dipping and mopping—a classic meal. The refritos go well with just about any frontier food, from huevos rancheros in the morning to full-dress Tex-Mex combo plates. They're also an excellent ingredient for a plate of *nachos grande*—on top of chips, with melted cheese and hot peppers, tomato chunks, and maybe cooked and seasoned beef.

## FRIJOLES

2 cups dried pinto beans
Water
⅔ cup chopped onion
3 cloves garlic, chopped
4–6 ounces salt pork, cut into ½-inch cubes
1 teaspoon whole cumin seeds
Optional, to taste: 1–2 tablespoons powdered red chile
Freshly ground black pepper to taste
Salt to taste

Wash beans, removing grit and pebbles. Soak in water overnight.

Drain the beans well, pick over them again to remove any impurities.

Use about 5 cups of water, or enough to cover the beans by about 1½ inches in a large saucepan. Bring to boil. Simmer 20 minutes. Add all remaining ingredients (except chile, salt, and pepper). Cover pan and gently simmer the beans about 3 to 4 hours, stirring once or twice per hour, removing any foam that comes to the surface, and adding water, if necessary, to keep the beans moist. If spicy beans are desired, add the powdered chile about 2½ hours into the cooking process. When the beans are tender, and the cooking liquid is thickened to the consistency of milk, they are done.

Serve beans, with their pot liquor, seasoned to taste with salt and pepper. (One favorite trick of frijoles cooks is to take about a half a cup of the beans and a few tablespoons of the cooking liquid and puree them. Then add this thickener back to the beans to make a more substantial liquid.)

**8 servings (or 4 servings, with enough leftover for 4 servings of refritos the next day).**

## REFRITOS

3–4 tablespoons lard (bacon fat will do)
3–4 cups cooked pinto beans, with their cooking liquid
Optional:
    ½ cup chopped onion
    1 cup grated Monterey Jack cheese
    6–8 ounces zesty sausage, cooked and crumbled
    Roasted and peeled green chiles, to taste
    Chopped jalapeño peppers, to taste

Heat lard in large, heavy frying pan over medium-high heat. Sauté onion until limp if onion-flavored refritos are desired. Add beans with their liquid, about a half a cup at a time, to pan (careful: they will splatter and sizzle when they hit the hot fat). Use a potato masher or the back of a heavy spoon to mash the beans—either thoroughly if you like them smooth or leaving some lumps and half-mashed beans for texture's sake. Once all the beans are added and mashed (they will absorb their cooking liquid as you mash them), continue to cook 15 to 20 minutes, until the edges of the mess of beans begin to turn crisp.

Serve hot, topping individual hot servings with grated cheese, sausage, or chiles, if desired.

**4 servings.**

# FRIJOLE BEANSES

by N. Howard Thorp, 1919

I've cooked you in the strongest gypsum water;
I've boiled you up in water made of snow;
I've eaten you above the arctic Circle,
I've chewed on you in southern Mexico.
In the camp-fire, on the stove, or in the oven,
Or buried in the ashes overnight,
You've saved my life on more than one occasion—
Oh, frijole bean, you're simply out of sight.

Of course you know, as far as one's digestion
Is concerned, you'd ever break it plumb in two
Without a single moment's hesitation—
Least that's the reputation given you.

Well here's to your health, you little brown frijole,
Your health I'll pledge and by you always stand;
You're eaten by the rich and lowly,
You're an outlawed product of our Western land.

Oh, little bean about you's such a savor,
Such a muchness, such a taste that you have got;
A particularly satisfying flavor
When we've added sow and chile to the pot.
Then good-bye, my little pard, I hate to leave you,
You've been with me on many a long hike;
So I'll eat the last of you that's in the skillet,
Then saddle up old buck and hit the pike.

# Chicken-Fried STEAK

Not everyone is enamored of this cheap cut of cow that is breaded and deep-fried in a skillet like chicken (hence, the name). Here is how Edna Ferber wrote about a chicken-fried steak dinner in her novel *Giant,* in 1952:

*Enormous fried slabs, flat, grey, served with a thick flour gravy. Mashed potatoes. Canned peas. Pickles. Huge soft rolls. Jelly. Canned peaches. Chocolate cake.*

Ferber's description was supposed to make readers commiserate with poor Leslie Benedict, the novel's sensitive, Virginia-bred bride (played by Liz Taylor in the movie) who finds herself confronted not only by her Texas in-laws, but by their idea of a good meal. The gray slabs of meat, accompanied by bottles of catsup and other common condiments, turn her stomach; they are an example of (in Ferber's words) "American food cooked and served at its worst, without taste or imagination."

Chicken-fried steak always seems to inspire extreme reactions. Hordes of serious Southwestern eaters—sophisticates as well as Bubbas—adore chicken-fried steak precisely because of its inalienable lowbrow character. It is all but illegal to serve one on fine china or with good silver or accompanied by any wine, even from a bottle with a screw-top. It's even rather strange to eat one in a dining room at home: the kitchen table, preferably covered with oilcloth, while a Frigidaire hums in the background, feels more appropriate, the proper attire being a strap T-shirt. Of course, it is entirely at home in a café with fluorescent lights and gum-chewing, pencil-tapping waitresses with beehive hairdos and pointy harlequin eyeglasses. We are talking here about a hunk of feed completely uncontaminated by nutritional sanctimony or food fashion, a classic symbol of downhome cooking. It is found on virtually every café menu in the West, even into Arkansas and the South, and for those who appreciate its pleasure, it is truly one of this land's greatest comfort foods, right up there with meat loaf and Jell-O and

Jewish chicken soup as a dish you don't merely like; you *long for it,* especially when you crave cooking like Mama used to make.

Like so many good things to eat, it began as a way to dress up an unappealing piece of food. Chuck wagon chefs sometimes fried meat in grease to ease the monotony of range grub; moms began to make it during the Great Depression, when times were lean and meat was scarce and tough. Texas had enough cooks of middle European heritage that Wiener schnitzel and its aristocratic ilk were at least vaguely familiar, so that chicken-fried steak could be considered a kind of cut-rate version, made from stringy beef instead of veal. The process begins by giving a slab of inexpensive beef (round steak or worse) a severe beating with a mallet or an old Coke bottle until it has given up all its fight and become tender. Then you take the battered meat, dredge it in eggs and flour, and skillet fry it until it is crisp and dark golden brown. The pan drippings, all funky with little chunks of sizzled crust, make an ideal base for gravy. Add a mound of mashed potatoes and a hill of black-eyed peas on the side, and maybe some biscuits and a tall glass of iced tea. The result is a culinary ultimatum that no zealous eater can resist.

In all its country glory, made the way it ought to be, chicken-fried steak delivers satisfaction that few other foods can offer. It can even verge on being elegant, or as elegant as you would ever want Mom's home cooking to be. Its tan crust, brittle but luxuriously sumptuous, gets melded to the meat so that every mouthful is a perfect mix of crunch and chew. If the beef is properly tenderized, you can cut it nicely with firm pressure of a fork's edge, then push that forkful through the gravy that surrounds it. The taste is only gently beefy, the heft of the meat leavened by the crisp crust and milky softness of the gravy.

That gravy, by the way, is a point of controversy among chicken-fried steak aficionados. Do you ladle it

atop the steak, or do you put the steak on top of the gravy? Steak-on-top-of-gravy people say they like to *see* the broad golden crust, uncovered, before they dig in; and they like to keep it absolutely crisp. The gravy-blanket school of chicken-fried steak aficionados prefer the cascading gravy look—a great river of pepper-speckled sauce spilling over the entire plate, including the steak and potatoes, handy for biscuit-dipping wherever you choose to dip.

# ODESSA FIREMEN'S CHICKEN-FRIED STEAK

(loosely based on *The Wild Wild West*,
by the Junior League of Odessa)

*6 round steaks, about 4 ¥ 4 inches each, tenderized by
  butcher*
*1 egg, beaten, combined with 1 (12-ounce) can evapo-
  rated milk*
*1 cup flour, mixed with 1 teaspoon pepper*
*2–3 cups lard or vegetable oil*
*1 cup milk*
*Salt and pepper to taste*

Put the steaks between pieces of wax paper and use the edge of a sturdy coffee mug to beat the steaks hard, a full 3 minutes per steak.

Soak the beaten steaks in the egg and evaporated milk mixture for 10 minutes.

Remove steaks from the egg and evaporated milk mixture, then dredge each thoroughly in the flour and pepper mixture. Return them briefly to the egg and milk mixture, then to the flour once again.

Heat oil in heavy skillet until very hot but not smoking (360 to 375 degrees). Use enough oil to have about ⅔ inch in skillet.

Slide the steaks into the hot oil and cook them 8 to 10 minutes, or until they are dark golden brown on the bottom. Turn, and cook the other side about 6 more minutes, or until well browned.

Remove steaks from oil with slotted spoon and drain on paper towels.

To make gravy, pour off all but 2 tablespoons of the oil in the skillet. Return the skillet to the heat, and sprinkle 2 tablespoons of the remaining flour over the hot oil, stirring constantly for a full minute, scraping up browned bits of crust from the bottom of the skillet.

Stir in milk, a little at a time. Continue cooking and stirring until the gravy is thick. Add salt and pepper to taste. (Gravy should be quite peppery.)

Serve with mashed potatoes and/or biscuits, black-eyed peas, or collard greens.

**4–6 servings.**

*While on location shooting* Jubal *(1956) at Jackson Hole, Wyoming, Glenn Ford cooked himself a steak at the campfire. (*Jubal *was a Western-themed version of* Othello, *featuring Ernest Borgnine as a rancher who becomes insanely jealous when he thinks Ford is making time with his wife, played by Valerie French.)*

# *Tuba City* TACOS

There is an old truck stationed in a lot alongside the road that leads to the reservation town of Tuba City, Arizona. On the flatbed back of the truck a sign directs passers-by to the restaurant "Where the Stars Come to Eat." The sign points to a cinder-block building with the words "Let's Eat" on its outside wall. This is the Tuba City Truck Stop Café, a restaurant sometimes visited by celebrities who come to this area to make a movie in the picturesque countryside.

Usually the customers are strictly local. Native Americans sit at tables sipping coffee, reading the *Navajo Times,* and conversing table-to-table in their ancient, indecipherable tongue. Most of them arrive in up-to-date pickups, and many wear Levi's and polo shirts, but a surprising number are dressed traditionally. Women wear wine-red velvet blouses and are adorned with turquoise-nugget necklaces. Concho belts and heavy silver bracelets

circle waists and wrists. Men wear their hair long, wrapped in the traditional Navajo bun, which hugs the nape of the neck and is secured by a fabric wrap.

Although the menu at the Tuba City Truck Stop Café features such venerable native specialties as mutton and hominy stew, as well as all-American hamburgers, the best thing to eat is the Navajo taco, a new-West invention that got popular about twenty years ago and is now a café staple throughout the region. Like a Tex-Mex taco, it is a melting-pot creation, but in this case the traditional ingredients (seasoned ground beef, shredded yellow cheese, tomatoes, iceberg lettuce shreds) are served atop a pedestal of Indian fry bread. The bread makes the difference. Fried quickly in hot oil, it puffs up into a faintly crisp, chewy pillow, tough enough to stay intact, but with just the right absorbency to help mop juices from the chili-flavored beef on top.

Navajo tacos are easy to make at home. Fry bread itself is good to eat even without the elaborate taco toppings, like a giant sopaipilla: simply drizzle honey on the warm circle and you've got a tasty breakfast, or a fine companion for a mutton stew.

## INDIAN FRY BREAD

*2 cups all-purpose flour*
*2 teaspoons baking powder*
*1 teaspoon salt*
*3 tablespoons solid vegetable shortening or lard*
*⅔ cup warm water (approximate)*
*Oil for frying (about 1 cup, depending on size of pan)*

Mix together the flour, baking powder, and salt. Cut in 2 tablespoons of the shortening until the mixture is mealy. Slowly stir in enough water to form a ragged dough.

Melt and cool the remaining tablespoon of shortening.

Turn the dough onto a floured board and knead 2 minutes, or until smooth. Roll the dough into six equal-size balls. Brush each with the melted and cooled shortening. Cover them with a towel and let them rest 15 minutes.

Heat fat in deep skillet to 375 degrees. When the oil is hot, take a circle of dough and flatten it with the heel of your hand or a rolling pin into a 6-inch circle. To keep it from puffing like a giant sopaipilla, use a sharp knife to

cut four or five 1-inch-long slits through the dough. (Or if you do want your fried dough to be a balloon-like pastry, don't cut it.)

Ease the circle of dough into the hot fat. Cook it 30 seconds until brown, then turn it and cook the other side until golden brown. Drain on paper towels. Flatten and cook the other circles and serve immediately.

*Navajo tacos are best when served on HOT fry bread, so the best technique is to prepare these toppings first, then make the bread:*

## TUBA CITY TACOS

*1 clove garlic, minced*
*1 tablespoon vegetable oil*
*1 pound ground beef*
*1 tablespoon chile powder*
*1 teaspoon salt*
*½ teaspoon ground cumin*
*2 cups cooked kidney beans, warmed*
*2 cups shredded mild yellow Cheddar cheese*
*1 cup shredded iceberg lettuce*
*1 chopped tomato*
*1 cup prepared salsa, hot or mild to taste*

Sauté the garlic in the oil in a medium-hot skillet. Add beef and seasonings and cook until the beef is brown. Drain off fat.

To assemble the taco on a plate, top a disc of warm bread first with beef, then beans, cheese, lettuce, tomato, and salsa. Serve immediately with extra salsa on the side.

**6 Navajo tacos (serves 4–6).**

# *Sock* COFFEE

offee has always been a cowboy staple, and a lot of Westerners like theirs cowboy-style, which as more than one diner waitress has explained to us, means that it "tastes like it's been on the range all day."

Ranch hands and cowboys on big trail drives were lucky because they likely had a cook who could brew coffee for them. But line riders and wanderers had to fend for themselves, and real coffee was a rare luxury at the far reaches of the frontier. So the clever ones learned to brew a substitute by using rye, wheat, or toasted acorns.

Cowboys who had to travel light might not be able to take along a coffeepot, which is how this unusual recipe came to be. It is adapted from a marvelous book called *Texas on the Half Shell* (1982) by Phil Brittin and Joseph Daniel. They attribute it to a gent named Smokey, and advise the reader that it "ain't no joke!"

## SOCK COFFEE

*1 clean sock*
*coffee*
*water*

Into a clean white sock, spoon as many heaping tablespoons of ground coffee as you want cups to drink, then add one more tablespoon "for the sock." The coffee should be ground medium fine. Tie the sock well and immerse it in a pot containing enough water to match the amount of coffee. Cook until coffee is desired strength "or until the color of the sock matches the one you used yesterday morning."

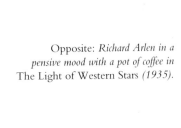

Opposite: *Richard Arlen in a pensive mood with a pot of coffee in* The Light of Western Stars *(1935).*

# "The OYSTER"

The sign upon the café wall said OYSTERS: fifty cents.
*"How quaint,"* the blue-eyed sweetheart said, with some bewildermence,
*"I didn't know they served such fare out here upon the plain?"*
"Oh, sure," her cowboy date replied, "We're really quite urbane."

*"I would guess they're Chesapeake or Blue Point, don't you think?"*
"No ma'am, they're mostly Hereford cross . . . and usually they're pink.
But I've been cold, so cold myself, what you say could be true
And if a man looked close enough, their points could sure be blue!"

She said, *"I gather them myself out on the bay alone.
I pluck them from the murky depths and smash them with a stone!"*
The cowboy winced imagining a calf with her beneath.
"Me, I use a pocket knife and yank 'em with my teeth."

Above: *Poet, large-animal veterinarian, and team roper Baxter Black with his cow pony and dog.*

*"Oh, my,"* she said, *"You animal! How crude and unrefined!
Your masculine assertiveness sends shivers up my spine!
But I prefer a butcher knife too dull to really cut.
I wedge it in on either side and crack it like a nut!*

*I pry them out. If they resist, sometimes I use the pliers
Or even Grandpa's pruning shears if that's what it requires!"*
The hair stood on the cowboy's neck. His stomach did a whirl.
He'd never heard such grisly talk, especially from a girl!

*"I like them fresh,"* the sweetheart said and laid her menu down
Then ordered oysters for them both when the waiter came around.
The cowboy smiled gamely, though her words stuck in his craw
But he finally fainted dead away when she said, *"I'll have mine raw!"*
—by Baxter Black

# SHOPPING GUIDE

## WAY OUT WEST SOURCES

A list of personal favorites: places we like to shop, catalogues we pore over, and periodicals we depend on. Some stores carry all kinds of Western-themed merchandise; rather than list them in every category, most such places are included here under their best specialty.

# NATIVE AMERICAN JEWELRY

### Arrowsmith's
402 Old Santa Fe Trail
Santa Fe, NM 87501
(505) 989-7663

Arrowsmith's is known for its array of cowboy collectibles (see below), but the jewelry case contains some dazzling pre-1950s treasures. There was a Zuni bracelet for sale here not too long ago that was one of the most beautiful we have ever seen.

### Buffalo Dancer II
Taos Pueblo
Taos, NM 87571
(505) 758-8718

A small native-run store with a nice assortment of reasonably priced jewelry.

### Cameron Trading Post
Cameron, AZ 86020
(602) 679-2231

An immense, antique trading post with everything from cold drinks and snack foods for travelers to cases full of jewelry ranging from common to magnificent. There used to be a guest hogan on the premises, for the use of Indians who traveled here in the summer to trade.

### Case Trading Post
Wheelwright Museum of the American Indian
704 Camino Lejo
Santa Fe, NM 87501
(505) 982-4636

The Case Trading Post, designed to resemble an old trading post from a century ago, is located in the basement of a magnificent museum that was founded in 1937 by Mary Cabot Wheelwright to preserve Navajo culture. There are rugs, knickknacks, and a significant inventory of hard-to-find books, but we are especially fond of the display case in the back of the trading post that features some very nice old pawn jewelry.

### Chimayo Trading Post
Española, NM 87532
(505) 753-9414

Moved to its present location in 1930, this historic trading post descends from one that opened more than a century ago. Today it still has the spirit of a vintage frontier emporium, stocking a wide range of goods from sublime Native American artifacts to ridiculous postcards. The two gents who run the place really do trade; we once swapped a seldom-worn necklace for a beautiful bracelet and some other things.

### The Common Ground
19 Greenwich Avenue
New York, NY 10014
(212) 989-4178

Although The Common Ground also has a fine selection of old pottery, moccasins, and other Indianalia, what we like best about this store is its selection of old jewelry. It always amazes us that in New York City, thousands of miles from the turquoise mines of the Southwest, it is possible to find such a well-chosen collection at reasonable prices.

### Cowboy Hall of Fame Gift Shop
1700 Northeast 63rd Street
Oklahoma City, OK 73111
(405) 478-2250

Something for everyone, from cowgirl T-shirts to "Young Guns" souvenirs and Western-themed lamps and bric-a-brac for home decor, as well as a big selection of unusual books. A great place to browse because the buyers are discriminating; they stock a broad array of high-quality new Native-American jewelry that is definitely worth close inspection.

### Dewey Galleries, Ltd.
74 East San Francisco
Santa Fe, NM 87501
(505) 982-8632

The *crème de la crème* for the serious collector. The Dewey Gallery has some of the most beautiful things in town. It is not the place to bargain hunt, but you can be assured of the highest level merchandise. The Dewey Gallery is also on the cutting edge of Western collectible trends, so if you see it here you can be assured it is worth investing in.

### East West Trading Co.
727 Canyon Road
Santa Fe, NM 87501
(505) 986-3489

Despite its high-ticket location, East West feels like a colorful old trading post somewhere in the boondocks. It is an enormously fun place to shop because you never know what you'll find, from collectible kitsch to Old West antiques. Bo and Jim, the gentlemen in charge, are always ready to bargain. There is a surprisingly big assortment of old pawn jewelry, and some nice reproductions as well.

### Foutz's Indian Room
Farmington, NM 87401
(505) 325-9413

For generations the Foutz family has been known and respected as traders throughout the Four Corners area. Located in downtown Farmington, this shop is well worth a visit for its extensive selection of old and new jewelry. Many customers are traditionally dressed Navajo women and men, who come here to trade or sell their things.

### Guns for Hire
Santa Fe Village
27 Don Gaspar
Santa Fe, NM 87501
(505) 989-7273

Why is a store called Guns for Hire listed under jewelry? Because R. "Bear" Campbell is a master at repairing silver Indian jewelry—at reasonable prices, while you wait. His partner, Steve "Shorty" Kniesel (he's the one in the bowler hat), is a master leather worker. The two of them are available for Old-West gunfights and trick-shooting demonstrations.

### Hanging Tree Gallery
416 Romero NW (Old Town)
Albuquerque, NM 87104
(505) 842-1420

We have found some really unusual items here, such as a 130-year-old Navajo pendant complete with the history of who owned it and wore it. Owner Quentin Edgerton loves such rare pieces, and he is great fun to talk to.

### Hi-Ho Silver
c/o Marcia Spark
P.O. Box 43414
Tucson, AZ 85733
(602) 323-8714

Marcia Spark has a keen eye for finding unusual and rare items. Her specialties include Indian pawn jewelry, folk art (antique and contemporary), and cowboy kitsch. She is a private dealer, so showings are by appointment only. If you do visit Marcia, be sure to see her husband Ronald's collection of vintage neckties, particularly those with a Western motif. They, alas, are not for sale.

### Hopi Arts and Crafts Co-op Guild
Second Mesa, AZ 86043
(602) 734-2463

The place to find the very distinctive silver Hopi jewelry, as well as pottery, kachina dolls, textiles, and baskets. Some of the silver pieces on display represent the highest quality to be found.

### Elaine Horwitch Galleries
129 W. Palace
Santa Fe, NM 87501
(505) 988-8997

Elaine Horwitch is renowned as one of the top galleries in town for successful painters and sculptors, but we have snuck it into our jewelry listing because one wall of the large space is loaded with some of the most wonderful Indian jewelry in town. It has all been selected by the legendary Dickie Pfaelzer who, at seventy-eight, is the grande doyenne of Santa Fe style and the best-dressed woman in town. If you want to look half as sharp as Dickie does, these jewelry cases might be a good place to start.

*Jane Stern (left) and Dickie Pfaelzer.*

## The Jewel Box
601 North Central
Phoenix, AZ 85004
(602) 252-5777

A pawnshop in an unglamorous part of town, The Jewel Box is the best place in the state to find fabulous old jewelry at fair prices. It has been around since 1945, and is run by Morrey and Honey Reznik, whose finer pieces have been featured in *Arizona Highways*. Several cabinets are stocked with museum-level pieces from the C. G. Wallace collection, which are not for sale.

## Skip Maisel's
510 Central SW
Albuquerque, NM 87102
(505) 242-6526

Our favorite bargain-hunting stop in Albuquerque. Not only does this old-fashioned store have one of the great vintage Southwestern facades, but everything inside is rock-bottom reasonable. Note the stunning modern rugs in the window; as for jewelry, you can complete a Christmas list here in one stop, from low-priced bric-a-brac to some truly majestic older pieces.

## Morning Star Traders
2020 East Speedway
Tucson, AZ 85719
(602) 881-2112

Here are Indian goods (and some cowboy things, too) selected with a real connoisseur's eye. On our last visit to this two-story shop, we fell in love with an elaborate silver parade saddle that featured the heads of Indian chiefs stamped all over; we admired antique silver flatwear cast in the Indian style, some with turquoise embedded in the handles, and found many very high-quality examples of old pawn jewelry, as well as excellent new things, too. Also: pottery, baskets, and rugs. Nothing here is cheap, but everything is of the finest quality.

## Morning Talk Indian Shop
Taos Pueblo, Box 2328
Taos, NM 87571
(505) 758-1429

Nothing old or very precious here in this pueblo shop, but they do have a very good selection of new jewelry at fair reservation prices.

## Packard's on the Plaza
61 Old Santa Fe Trail
Santa Fe, NM 87501
(505) 983-9241

"In town" prices are the rule, but Packard's—a store with a venerable lineage in Santa Fe—is still the place to find some of the best and most beautiful work done by contemporary Native American craftspeople.

## Rainbow Man
107 East Palace Road
Santa Fe, NM 87501
(505) 982-8706

Feast your eyes on one of the finest arrays of older jewelry (as well as incredible vintage cowboy collectibles, Edward S. Curtis photographs, art, and trade blankets—see below) for sale anywhere in the Southwest. Despite the store's high-rent location on the Plaza, prices are fair; the salespeople are knowledgeable and eager to explain what you are looking at. Rainbow Man is one of the supreme Santa Fe shopping experiences.

## Tony Reyna's
Taos Pueblo Lodge 1
Taos, NM
(505) 758-3855
and
Kachina Lodge 2
Taos, NM
(505) 758-2142

Both of Tony Reyna's shops have an enormous assortment of fine old pieces and nice new ones. We like the shop off the pueblo better because it seems to have a wider range of goods.

## Richardson Trading Company and Cash Pawn
222 West 66 Avenue
Gallup, NM 87301
(505) 722-4762

A genuine piece of history at the southern edge of the Navajo Reservation. Navajos, Zunis, and other pueblo people have been coming to trade in Gallup since before the turn of the century, and in 1913 in order to encourage the U.S. government to build a road between Arizona and California (eventually known as Route 66), trader C. N. Cotton organized a motorcade along the wagon trail from Gallup to Albuquerque. Gallup has since been a main trading stop for native people and whites alike. Richardson's opened for business nearly a century ago, and it remains today what it has always been: a place Indians come to buy, trade, pawn, and store their valuables, as "live pawn." The cases are crammed with jewelry, some old and some new, and you will find amazing items here that you won't see anywhere else, like a bolo tie and turquoise-encrusted belt buckle so huge they could only fit a giant. The old pawn is especially nice, and the staff is especially shrewd about what they are selling.

## Millicent Rogers Museum

P.O. Box A (4 miles north of Taos on Highway 3)
Taos, NM 87571
(505) 758-2462

The late Millicent Rogers was a pioneering collector of Native American jewelry, some of which is on display in this elegant museum. The gift shop has a very fine selection of pieces for sale; of special interest is the line of reproduction jewelry from the museum collection.

## Saity Jewelry

725 Fifth Avenue (Trump Tower, Level 5)
New York, NY 10022
(212) 308-6570
and
48 East 57th Street
New York, NY 10022
(212) 223-8125

David Saity's stores are the Tiffany of Native-American jewelry. They are both located in the heart of the poshest shopping area of Manhattan, and their merchandise is the cream of the crop. Mr. Saity started collecting jewelry many years ago, first as a hobby before it became his business, and much of what he has for sale simply isn't made anymore. Among the knock-your-socks-off items on display are a squash blossom necklace fully embedded with turquoise on one side; flip it over and you see that it is equally embedded with coral on the other. There is also an amazing belt that shows detailed scenes of Indian life on each of its elaborately carved silver conchas.

## Santo Domingo Indian Trading Post

2049 South Plaza NW
Albuquerque, NM 87104
(505) 766-9855

Run by the Santo Domingo Tribe and located in Old Town, this is a great place to get the fabulous multistrand bead necklaces that the Santo Domingans are known for,

and at very fair reservation prices. They also repair jewelry as well as "wrap" old necklaces—a craft they know as "pueblo wrapping."

## J. Seitz & Company

9 East Shore Road (Route 45)
New Preston, CT 06777
(203) 868-0119

The best place in Connecticut for anything Southwestern. You can rely on owner Joanna Seitz's impeccable taste to bring the best of the West back to her friendly shop. There is no old pawn jewelry here, but everything she sells is stunning and authentic looking. Also for sale: Western clothing and boots, furniture, gifts, and select antiques.

## Shalako Traders of Old Santa Fe

115 East San Francisco
Santa Fe, NM 87501
(505) 988-4374
and
137 East Palace
Santa Fe, NM 87501
(505) 986-8347

Both Shalako Traders are crammed full of treasures, and despite the cluttered appearance, goods are well marked in a way that separates the vintage jewelry from the new stuff. We found some amazing bargains in both stores, as well as very friendly service.

## Sherwood's Spirit of America

325 North Beverly Drive
Beverly Hills, CA 90210
(310) 274-6700

Yes, this place is in the heart of Beverly Hills, on the most exclusive acre of real estate in America, but don't be surprised to discover that many prices are in fact no higher than in trading posts of the Southwest; some are actually less. Proprietor Moke Kokin is one of the nation's top authorities on Western collectibles; buying or browsing here is an exhilarating experience.

## Tobe Turpen's Indian Trading Co.

1710 South Second Street
Gallup, NM 87301
(505) 722-3806

One of the oldest and most respected trading posts in Gallup. Many serious collections began with purchases here, and although today's selection contains more new than old jewelry, it is still well worth a stop for the possibility of unearthing a treasure.

### Turquoise Lady of Old Town
2012 Plaza Drive NW
Albuquerque, NM 87104
(505) 842-5064

Tucked away off the Old Town Plaza, the Turquoise Lady's collection has been featured in books on Native-American jewelry, and the contemporary work on display shows a selective eye.

### Wright's Collection
Park Square
6600 Indian School Road, NE
Albuquerque, NM 87110
(505) 883-6122

Wright's has been selling good-quality Native-American jewelry since 1907. The selection today includes very fine examples of contemporary Indian artistans, as well as some beautiful older pieces.

# COWBOY COLLECTIBLES AND FURNITURE

### American West Gallery
520 4th Street
Ketchum, ID 83340
(208) 726-1333

Alan Edison's serious gallery has vintage cowboy and Indian artifacts from a hundred years ago, as well as collectibles from the 1930s, 1940s, and 1950s. Also vintage art and posters, Pendleton blankets, and some fantastic antique Western furniture.

### Anteks
5814 West Lovers Lane
Dallas, TX 75224
(214) 528-5567

A Texas-sized shop with *everything* you can imagine for furnishing a home, Western-style, including antique and reproduction tables, chairs, beds, pillows, lamps, and accessories, plus some fun theme T-shirts.

### Arrowsmith's
402 Old Santa Fe Trail
Santa Fe, NM 87501
(505) 989-7663

Chaps, saddles, gunbelts, and all the best things that made cowboys celebrated for their fashions. Count on seeing at least one stunning parade saddle on display.

### Back at the Ranch
235 Don Gaspar
Santa Fe, NM 87501
(505) 989-8110

Owner Wendy Lane has a wonderfully funky fashion sense, and a good sense of humor as well. We loved her wall-mounted Naugahyde horse head, as well as the goofy Western-style ashtrays and knickknacks, but the best things are wearable, including fine vintage and custom-made boots, hats, and a wide array of snappy modern Western duds, too.

**Big Horn Gallery**
1167 Sheridan Avenue
Cody, WY 82414
(307) 527-7587
and
On the Square
Jackson Hole, WY 83001
(307) 733-1434

Cody is the center of the cowboy-furniture revival, known as the look of the New West. The Big Horn gallery displays the best work by local artists and artisans.

**Big Sky**
114 West Houston St.
New York, NY 10012
(212) 674-6821

Merv Bendewald, a Montanan who has brought carloads of genuine cowboy gear to Manhattan at Whiskey Dust (see "Western Clothing," below) recently opened a second shop featuring the best of Western furnishings. Big Sky, located on a street named Houston (which is pronounced "How-ston" hereabouts), is a bonanza of Wild Western furniture (antiques and reproductions), fabrics, and accessories. If you are uncertain about what to do with all this delicious stuff, Big Sky advertises "Consulting Trail Boss Available." We assume "trail boss," in this context, is a synonym for interior designer.

**Blondie's American Collectibles
and Pony Expresso Bar**
Main Street
Florence, AZ 85232
(602) 868-0966

A small nostalgia shop crammed with all kinds of memorabilia, not limited to Western things, including a dandy three-piece "Come-and-Get-It" chef's apron and plenty of Elvis and Marilyn souvenirs. We were impressed with the selection of handsome vintage boots and some deluxe hand-painted ties with cactus and cowboy motifs.

**Cactus Country**
57 Whitfield Street
Guilford, CT 06437
(203) 458-9593

Sue Lapham's happy Western store in the heart of Yankee country has everything from Western-themed tableware to books on the West, Native American jewelry, and cedar-scented soaps that smell like a night on the prairie.

**Cadillac Jack**
6911 Melrose Avenue
Los Angeles, CA
(213) 931-8864

Don and Penny Colclough have set up a cowboy collectible store that draws the Hollywood crowd in search of vintage cowboy culture. Daryl Hannah, Judd Hirsch, Penny Marshall, and Jon Lovitz are some of the celebs who have been spotted here shopping for their cowboy fix. Specialties include furniture, posters, and lamps from the 1940s and 1950s.

**Canyon Road**
111 Cherry Street
New Canaan, CT 06840
(203) 972-6661
and
250 Greenwich Avenue
Greenwich, CT 06830
(203) 629-8595

Canyon Road has a good selection of everything Southwestern, from chile pepper posters to cowboy-cut shirts and beautiful silver and turquoise-studded belts. Last time we visited, they also had a good supply of Religious Experience hot sauce! For anyone in the Northeast who can't hop a plane to Santa Fe, this is a good place to stock up.

**Cowgirl Hall of Fame**
519 Hudson St.
New York, NY 10014
(212) 633-1133

This place is famous in Gotham as a choice place to eat such distinctly non-urban vittles as cracker-fried catfish, chuck wagon chili, and chicken-fried steak with cream gravy. But there's more. In addition to being a restaurant and a swell place to meet and/or have a party (in the paneled Living Room Lounge or Portrait Library), the Cowgirl Hall of Fame—which actually helps support its namesake in Hereford, Texas, and is decorated to the nines with eye-popping memorabilia and photos of champion cowgirls—also has a general store. The shop is diminutive, lodged between the dining room and the bar, but it is hugely fun! There are great T-shirts, salt-and-pepper shakers, cattle skull Christmas tree lights, frontier foodstuffs, and lots of other things that will supply you with a spicy taste of Texas in Manhattan.

**Crybaby Ranch**
1422 Larimer
Denver, CO 80202
(303) 670-0773

A huge and wonderful collection of everything vintage and cowboy, specializing in stuff from the 1930s through the 1950s. If you are interested in collecting the West, don't leave Denver without visiting this store.

**Dakota**
317 East Colorado Avenue
Telluride, CO 81435
(303) 728-4204

Cowboy furniture, decor, accessories.

**Deep Texas**
2173 Portsmouth
Houston, TX 77098
(713) 526-2464

A dreamy store full of cowboy icons including refinished antique ranch furniture as well as modern Western-style home decor, vintage movie posters, and a passel of gifts and Texas foodstuffs.

**East West Trading Co.**
727 Canyon Road
Santa Fe, NM 87501
(505) 986-3489

If you can pull your eyes away from the jewelry cases long enough to notice, East West has a fine selection of frontier collectibles ranging from first- and second-generation Colt .45s in fancy gunbelts to cowboy kitsch such as bronzed "Trigger" clocks and lamps that look like cacti.

**Fighting Bear Antiques**
35 East Simpson
Jackson, WY 83001
(307) 733-2669

Proprietors Sandy and Terry Winchell know all there is to know about antique Western furniture, and they have more genuine Molesworth than anyone. This two-room shop is for serious collectors of dude ranch furniture, spurs, bits, branding irons, fireplace screens, chaps, and vintage art and photos; there is little in the way of cheap cowboy kitsch.

**Friedman Gallery**
5 Post Road West
Westport, CT 06880
(203) 226-5533

Michael Friedman, one of the most knowledgable and respected collectors of Western memorabilia, and author of the book *Cowboy Culture,* runs this extraordinarily selective gallery. There isn't a huge amount of merchandise, but what there is, is all magnificent. A fine place to find anything from deluxe vintage chaps to a never-used set of rodeo-motif glasswear. We purchased a fine old china statue of Roy Rogers and Trigger that we love!

**Furniture Etc.**
17 Main
Kalispell, MT 59901
(406) 756-8555

Genuine antique Molesworth funiture as well as modern, locally made lodgepole and willow chairs and tables.

**Homestead**
223 East Main
Fredericksburg, TX 78624
(512) 997-5551

Cowboy furniture for the bedroom, including lodgepole bed frames, custom linens, curtains, and curtain rods.

**Horse Feathers**
P.O. Box 698
Rancho de Taos, NM 87557
(505) 758-7457

This plentiful selection of merchandise shows a good sense of humor as well as a love affair with Hoppy and Roy and Trigger and all the heroes that made us baby boomers want to grow up to be cowboys.

**Legends**
411 Guadalupe
Santa Fe, NM 87501
(505) 982-0230

A very personal kind of trading post, with a wide-ranging assortment of cowboy and Indian collectibles and what the proprietor calls "Southwestern unusuals." Last time we visited, we bought a beautiful steer-head bolo tie and admired Clayton Moore's (the Lone Ranger) personal gunbelt.

## Manitou Gallery

1715 Carey Avenue
Cheyenne, WY 82001
(307) 635-0019

The Manitou Gallery is known around the world by serious collectors looking for vintage saddles, beautiful bronzes and paintings, and the rarest cowboy and Indian collectibles. While visiting Cheyenne for the Frontier Days rodeo, we picked up the single best-looking hand-braided horsehair stampede string for a cowboy hat we ever saw.

## Martin-Harris Gallery

60 East Broadway, Suites 3–5
Jackson, WY 83001
(800) 366-7841 or (307) 733-0350

Antiques, collectibles, memorabilia, including vintage saddles and other leatherware and a selection of modern "new West" furniture.

## Mongerson-Wunderlich

701 North Wells
Chicago, IL 60610
(312) 943-0833

The best place in Chicago to shop for cowboy collectibles, clothing, and home decor—new and used, pricey and affordable. A supremely tempting place to look around.

## Old West Antiques

1215 Sheridan Avenue
Cody, WY 82414
(307) 587-9014

Cody can feel like the cowboy capital of the West, and one of the main reasons is this place, with its fantastic selection of genuine cowboy collectibles, including many rare antique saddles, chaps, spurs, guns, and gunbelts. For those who can't get to Cody, it is possible to shop by mail from the Old West catalogue.

## One Eyed Jack's

1645 Market Street
San Francisco, CA 94103
(415) 621-4390

Looking for a nice cow skull to hang on the wall? Well-worn cowboy boots like they don't make anymore? A Hopalong Cassidy "Shoot with Hoppy" box camera? These folks just might have it in their inventory of collectibles, furniture, accessories, and vintage cowboy clothes.

## Rainbow Man

107 East Palace Road
Santa Fe, NM 87501
(505) 982-8706

The middle room of this resplendent shop is devoted mostly to Western collectibles. Wow, what treasures! The stock changes as the rarities are bought and sold, but you can count on a plethora of cowboy lamps and toys, spectacular Santa Fe rail line memorabilia (posters, china, menus), and old Western movie posters. Last time we visited, the walls were covered with huge, original Buffalo Bill Wild West show posters from the turn of the century . . . about three thou apiece.

## Rancho

322 McKenzie Street
Santa Fe, NM 87501
(505) 986-1688

Owners Barbara and Chuck Cooper explain that Rancho is about "The Tradition & Romance of the American West," and anyone with a taste for cowboy collectibles will feel they have gone to heaven as soon as they pass through the doorway here and find themselves surrounded with what just may be the most exquisite collection of Westernalia for sale anywhere . . . from a mint vintage "Comic Book Corral" to a five-foot-tall, $10,000 drum from a turn-of-the-century cowboy marching band, and a couple of rooms full of hard-to-find but affordable real Western clothing. You can't miss Chuck and Barbara, either. She is drop-

dead gorgeous and looks great in her thigh-high Western skirt, and Chuck, from his cowboy boots to the tip of his ten-gallon hat, looks ready for a trail drive.

### T. P. Saddle Blanket
304 Main Street
Great Barrington, MA 01230
(413) 528-6500
and
Routes 11 & 30
Manchester Center, VT 05255
(802) 362-9888

Wonderful Western department stores in the heart of New England. Best known for the clothes they make and sell (see below), Saddle Blanket is also the place to find "Montana Ranch" furniture, made from cedar poles: beautiful things, and as right-looking in a ski cabin in the Green Mountains as in a Great Plains ranch.

### Saga
806 Federal Road
Brookfield, CT 06804
(203) 740-9509

A potpourri of home accessories, decor, jewelry, and art—cowboy and Indian themed, modern and vintage—make this a fun place to browse and buy. You'll find blankets, pots, turquoise, foodstuffs, a few books, and all sorts of bibelots with a Southwestern accent.

### Santa Fe
3571 Sacramento Street
San Francisco, CA 94118
(415) 346-0180

The best of the West in the Bay area. High-end antiques and collectibles including cowboy and Indian trophies, old pawn jewelry, and vintage furniture. Also some fine art.

### Santa Fe Dave's Outlaw Furniture
1310 Cerrillos Road
Santa Fe, NM 87501
(505) 983-4237

Owner Dave Hall likes to boast that his store is *not* on the Plaza and sells *no* cute coyotes. In other words, this aims to be a place for people who actually live in Santa Fe rather than for tourists passing through. They will fix old and broken vintage furniture, and sell all kinds of locally made cowboy-themed goods, which are categorized in some advertisements as "Cheap stuff, same old stuff, stuff, and good stuff." A one-of-a-kind shopping experience.

### Shaboom's
5811 North Seventh St.
Phoenix, AZ 85014
(602) 222-5432

We swoon when we walk in the door of this cluttered place, which is a treasure trove of movie-buckaroo collectibles, all sorts of Western ephemera, gorgeous old boots and dude ranch attire, plus lovely Cacticraft lamps and furniture from the 1930s through the 1950s. Last time we visited, there were four "Comic Book Corrals" for sale.

### T and A Antiques
155 West Pearl Aveunue
Jackson, WY 83001
(307) 733-9717

A terrific slumgullion of collectibles from the Golden Age of Cowboy Funk. Lamps, old clothing, jewelry, Roy and Hoppy memorabilia, and stunning furniture make this a soup-to-nuts place to hunt for treasures.

### T-M Cowboy Classics
364 Main Street
Longmont, CO 80501
(303) 776-3394

"The best cowboy kitsch (memorabilia) shop in Denver," according to *Westward* newspaper, T-M is a treasure trove of frontier-themed home decor from the 1950s, including lamps, ashtrays, bedspreads, dishwear, bookends, and bronze buckaroo clocks. In addition to the inventory of curios, owner Tom Bice manufactures his own pine-and-leather furniture in what he calls "the macho, Western look."

### True West
P.O. Box 148
Comanche, TX 76442
(915) 356-2140

True West is run by Tyler and Teresa Beard, who deal in Western Americana of all kinds, including reproduction Westward Ho dishware and props for movies. They supplied the furniture for Euro Disney's Cheyenne Town and Tyler Beard wrote the book on boots—literally (*The Cowboy Boot Book*). If you are serious about collecting the West, give them a call. A brochure is available.

# WESTERN-DECO FURNITURE MANUFACTURERS

*Many manufacturers do not sell directly to consumers; but if you call them, they can tell you who does. Several have catalogues available.*

**Jimmy Covert**
907 Canyon Avenue
Cody, WY 82414
(307) 527-6761

Cody, Wyoming, is the center of a boom in cowboy furniture; Jimmy Covert, who apprenticed with Ken Siggins (see Triangle Z, below), is one of its top practitioners. He does reproductions of cowboy deco pieces from the 1930s, as well as original work using lodgepoles, driftwood, and leather upholstery created by his wife, Lynda Covert.

**Cowboy Furniture**
1516 Pacheco Street
Santa Fe, NM 87501
(505) 983-8001

L. D. Burke makes all kinds of custom cowboy furniture, including kid-sized Wild West tables, chairs, and bureaus, but he is best known for his fantastic decorated mirrors, which are framed with silver buckles and dots, rowels from spurs, and cowboy maxims. His first mirror said "America, Love Her or Saddle Up."

**Elkhorn Designs**
P.O. Box 7663
Jackson Hole, WY 83001
(307) 654-7890

Amazing furniture made from amazing antlers, including huge, pointy lighting fixtures, fireplace sets, candle holders, and tables and chairs.

**Lure of the Dim Trails**
Cowboy Chic Pine Furniture
22647 Ventura Boulevard #358
Woodland Hills, CA 91364
(818) 702-0538

Molesworth-inspired furniture, including chairs with bowlegged gunfighter silhouettes on the back, illuminated bucking-horse lamps, and also fabrics with a Western motif. Jerry England also sells cowboy antiques and memorabilia.

**Ron McGee's Wild West Furniture and Supply**
P.O. Box 3010
Apache Junction, AZ 85220
(602) 983-1788

Ron McGee told Elizabeth Clair Flood, "I make the kind of furniture a cowboy can put his feet on and spit on." Not only is it tough barnwood, frequently with a "chipped paint" look, it's imaginative, using Wild West motifs such as barbed-wire drawer-pulls on a bureau and horse-bit hooks on a hat rack.

**New West**
Patrick Ranch
2119 Southfork
Cody, WY 82414
(307) 587-2839

Cited as top designers by *Metropolitan Home* magazine in 1992, Mike and Virginia Patrick were described by Elizabeth Clair Flood in her lavish book *Cowboy High Style* as creators of "unabashed visions of Western fantasy." These include chairs with cowboy and cowgirl silhouettes for backs or moose antlers for arms, and a rodeo chandelier with ropers, cows, and arena clowns around the circumference.

**Old Hickory**
403 South Noble Street
Shelbyville, IN 46176
(800) 232-2275

Since 1899 Old Hickory has specialized in furniture made from hickory saplings, including the furniture for the Old Faithful Inn at America's first national park. They make rockers, bar stools, tables, headboards, and some fabulously rustic coat trees and deck furniture; upholstery includes leather straps, hickory slats, woven cane, and fabric. For a rugged Western look, you won't find a finer outfitter. Old

Hickory furniture is not cheap, but it is made to last several lifetimes, and it looks it. An early Old Hickory sales brochure included this pitch:

> *Old-fashioned comfort*
> *Old-fashioned days,*
> *Old-fashioned workmanship,*
> *Old-fashioned ways,*
> *Old fashioned material,*
> *Old-fashioned care,*
> *All these combined*
> *In the Old Hickory chair.*

## Rustic Furniture
10 Cloninger Lane
Bozeman, MT 59715
(406) 587-3373

Western lodgepole furniture combined with curvaceous Adirondack willow give Diane Cole's chairs and tables an especially lyrical appearance.

## Sweet Water Ranch
P.O. Drawer 398
Cody, WY 82414
(307) 527-4044 or [store, in Denver] (303) 293-3171

Faithful reproductions of Wyoming furniture maker Thomas C. Molesworth, whose sleek leather furniture, accented with bulging burl wood and Chimayo weavings, was the epitome of cowboy designer style in the 1930s and 1940s.

## Triangle Z Ranch Furniture
P.O. Box 995
Cody, WY 82414
(307) 587-3901

Ken Siggins will repair your antique Thomas Molesworth furniture, or make glorious lodgepole pieces to order (if you can wait—he's very much in demand). According to Elizabeth Clair Flood, Mr. Siggins had built tables and chairs for Tom Brokaw's second home in Montana, and forty lodgepole and rawhide chairs for the Proud Cut Saloon in Cody.

## Western Heritage Designs
P.O. Box 208, Highway 6
Meridian, TX 76665
(817) 435-2173

Milo and Teddy Marks use matched sets of Texas longhorns as legs for their tables and chairs (a fashion popular in the 1880s in Texas, according to *Cowboy High Style*); they also hand-carve cowboy-themed benches and tables that they say are "so sturdy you can do the Texas Two-Step on it."

## Willow Run Woodworking
2330 Amsterdam Road
Belgrade, MT 59714
(406) 388-6848

Some of the finest new, but vintage-looking, furniture made today comes out of Rob Mazza's studio. He is known especially for his cowboy lamps with rawhide shades, and for Molesworth-like chairs and couches featuring lipstick-red leather upholstery.

# NATIVE AMERICAN RUGS AND BLANKETS

**Becker Gallery**
102 Center Street
Jackson, WY 83001
(307) 733-1331

The Becker Gallery has a fine collection of old Navajo weavings in addition to a carefully selected supply of pueblo pottery, blankets, and Plains Indian beadwork.

**Case Trading Post**
Wheelwright Museum of the American Indian
704 Camino Lejo
Santa Fe, NM 87501
(505) 982-4636

In a subterranean location below the Wheelwright Museum, the thoughtfully conceived Case Trading Post looks straight out of history. Rugs and blankets are slung over one another in a casually authentic manner, and they have some beauties. This is an especially good place to shop because the staff really know their stuff—it is a museum, after all!

**Cow Canyon Trading Post**
P.O. Box 88
Bluff, UT 84512
(801) 672-2208

A quaint outpost in the middle of nothing but gorgeous scenery; the selection of rugs here (mostly new) is outstanding, and the prices are reasonable.

**Dewey Galleries**
74 East San Francisco
Santa Fe, NM 87501
(505) 982-8632

As is true of everything the Dewey Galleries sell, the weavings are museum-quality and priced accordingly. The staff knows their merchandise, so if you are looking to seriously invest, this is a good place to consider.

**Hubbell Trading Post**
P.O. Box 388
Ganado, AZ 86505
(602) 755-3254

One of the historic sites for a shopping pilgrimage to the West, the Hubbell Trading Post made its reputation on buying and selling Navajo rugs. Today there is still a very large assortment to choose from, old and new, large and small, and mostly quite expensive.

**The Kaibab Shops**
2841-43 North Campbell
Tucson, AZ 85719
(602) 795-6905

A cluster of small boutiques with everything from Southwestern clothes and cowboy kitsch jewelry (a tie clasp with little dangling silver chaps), and some knock-your-socks-off Zuni bracelets that would be at home in the finest collection. Best of all are the Navajo rugs: high quality, fair prices, and a broad selection.

**Nambe Trading Post**
Route 11, Box 83-B
Nambe, NM 87501
(505) 455-2513

The town at Nambe has two great sights in it: a beautiful mission-style church and a trading post that specializes in Navajo rugs. Owner Ruth Romero (who wears the most stunning silver squash blossom necklace we have ever seen) has been trading rugs for some time now, and the selection here is very, very good.

**The Rainbow Man**
107 East Palace Avenue
Santa Fe, NM 87501
(505) 982-8706

Owner Bob Kapoun, author of *The Language of the Robe,* is a respected expert on the subject of Indian trade blankets, and in the back room of his store you will find more grand ones than you will see in any other one place at one time. Even if you aren't a blanket-hound, it is worth a trip to the back room to see Misty, a somewhat shy senior citizen canine who has made a fine home for herself in the cavelike space under a big table, where she lies on her personal rug and surveys all who shop here.

**Sherwood's Spirit of America**
325 North Beverly Drive
Beverly Hills, CA 90210
(310) 274-6700

You will find only top-of-the line collectibles at Sherwood's, and the well-trained staff, who sell to Hollywood's high rollers, know the merchandise well enough to help you make a knowledgeable choice.

**Teec Nos Pos Trading Post**
P.O. Box 940
Teec Nos Pos, AZ 86514
(602) 656-3224

Teec Nos Pos means Cottonwoods in a Circle. The original Teec Nos Pos Trading Post was built in 1905, and its name was given to a distinctive local weaving style often based around a lightning-bolt pattern. Rebuilt after a fire in 1959 and now owned by Russell Foutz of the Foutz trading post dynasty in the Four Corners area, Teec Nos Pos is still a fine place to shop.

**Two Gray Hills**
Albuquerque, NM 87107
(505) 344-3668 or (800) 742-6193
(by appointment only, with Rick Richardson)

Rick Richardson deals Indian collectibles from his home in Albuquerque, so you need to call before you drop in. Rugs are not all he handles, but it is what impressed us the most. The ones we saw here were very old and very fine and very expensive, and of course very, very beautiful as well.

# NATIVE AMERICAN POTTERY AND BASKETS

**Adobe Gallery**
413 Romero NW
Albuquerque, NM 87104
(505) 243-8485

Many of the stores in Old Town are touristy-tacky; not so the Adobe Gallery. Everything this place sells is of excellent quality, especially the pots.

**Blue Lizard Traders**
15 West 39th Street
New York, NY 10018
(212) 840-5599

Proprietor Frank J. Gagne has a nice selection of handmade Indian pots at reasonable prices.

**Indian Territory**
5639 North Swan Road
Tucson, AZ 85718
(602) 577-7961

Connie and Neil Hicks run Indian Territory like a mini museum, except the good news is that everything is for sale. We saw some first-rate beadwork and some beautiful old concho belts, but were most impressed by their stock of Indian baskets.

**Jackalope**
2828 Cerrillos Road
Santa Fe, NM
(505) 471-8539

Billing itself as "the world's most incredible pottery store," and advertising "folk art by the truckload," Jackalope is *not* the place to find ancient treasures once used by cliff dwelling peoples. But it is a fun place to browse. They've got carved wooden howling coyotes in every shape and size, decorative skulls, and lots of well-priced pots. Also a nice mounted jackalope (not for sale) near the cash register.

**Kania-Ferrin Gallery**
622 Canyon Road
Santa Fe, NM 87501
(505) 982-8767

Kania-Ferrin has a little of this and a little of that. We once bought a nice old Hubbell bracelet, circa 1940, here, but it is in pots and baskets that this gallery really shows its stuff. Not cheap, but worth it.

## Miller Curio

100 West Elkhorn Avenue
Estes Park, CO 80517
(303) 586-3683
and
1724 East Speedway
Tucson, AZ 85719
(602) 325-6352

Miller Curio has been around since 1936, and although the Tucson store we visited seems modern enough, it did contain the kind of merchandise that only an experienced buyer knows to select. We especially like the miniature pueblo-style pottery, some no bigger than an inch across. There was also a nice selection of new Indian jewelry, and for shoppers on a budget some great canvas tote bags covered with stylized desert creatures.

## Mudhead Gallery

555 17th Street
Hyatt Regency Hotel
Denver, CO 80202
(303) 293-0007
and
321 17th Street
Brown Palace Hotel
Denver, CO 80202
(303) 293-9977
and
100 East Thomas Place #70
Hyatt Regency Hotel
Beaver Creek, CO 81620
(303) 949-1333

There are three locations on the Mudhead Gallery, and they all have a fine selection of Indianalia. Of particular interest are the lovely examples of basketry and the antique beaded Plains Indian goods.

## Old Territorial Shop

7220 East Main Street
Scottsdale, AZ 85251
(602) 945-5432

Rita Neal has run this handsome store for many years. Her specialties include Indian rugs, kachina dolls, beadwork, and some marvelous baskets and pots. The merchandise is museum-quality, and Ms. Neal is highly knowledgeable about what she sells.

# FIERY FOODS

## Carmen's of New Mexico

401 Mountain Road NW
Albuquerque, NM 87102
(505) 842-5119

Among the repertoire of this family-run mail-order source are coarsely ground chile pods from the Hatch Valley (New Mexico's main chile-growing region), white or blue posole (like hominy) for stews, blue corn flour and coarser-ground blue cornmeal for breads and cakes, nitrate-free beef jerky (use it like bacon bits, crumbled on a salad), and various degrees of hot chile jelly, from mild red and green to hot jalapeño. No store sales: catalogue only.

## Chili Pepper Emporium

328 San Felipe Road, NW (in Old Town)
Albuquerque, NM 87104
(505) 242-7538 or (800) 441-CHILI
and
140 Winrock Center
Albuquerque, NM 87110
(505) 881-9225
and
in the Hyatt-Regency Hotel
Albuquerque, NM
(505) 766-9119

"You sure do like chili, don't you?" is the rhetorical beginning of a Chili Pepper Emporium's newsletter/catalogue, which is subtitled, "WE'VE GOT THE HOTS FOR YOU!" Salsas, dried ground pepper, beans, blue cornmeal, pepper-pod jewelry, gift boxes, T-shirts, ceramic luminarias, and plenty of Southwest cookbooks.

## The Chile Shop

109 East Water Street
Santa Fe, NM 87501
(505) 983-6080

SuAnne Armstrong's pioneering chile-only shop carries *everything* for the devotee of the pod: a vast array of dried chiles and chile powder, salsa samplers and gift boxes, chile-shaped Christmas tree lights, and chile-themed kitchen implements and hostess gifts. Plus Cow Camp dinnerware, tin picture frames, and gorgeous handmade petroglyph pottery. Catalogue available.

### Coyote Café General Store
132 West Water Street
Santa Fe, NM 87501
(505) 982-2454

Probably the most in-depth selection of hot sauces and salsas to be found anywhere (well over a hundred at last count). Need some Jelly from Hell? Here it is (spiked with Habanero peppers), alongside Religious Experience hot sauce, Inner Beauty sauce, and prickly pear cactus salsa. The Coyote store also sells rare and odd beans, cornmeal, and all the requisite spices and flavorings to cook up a four-alarm Southwest feast. A mail-order catalogue is available.

### Hatch Chile Express
622 Franklin
Hatch, NM 87937
(505) 267-3226

Hatch calls itself the chile capital of the world, and if you need proof of its hegemony, browse this shop. Jo and Jimmy Lytle carry over two dozen different kinds of chile, from local "long greens" to imported Habaneros. Novelty items for sale include pod-shaped fishing lures and panties with pictures of chiles on them.

### Hot Stuff Spicy Food Store
227 Sullivan St.
New York, NY 10012
(212) 254-6120

The name of David Jenkins' store says it all. Here is a New York source of fiery foods from all around the U.S. and the world, including salsas, marinades, rijstaffel relishes, and ripe red pods straight from the New Mexico harvest in the fall. The inventory also includes hot-food cookbooks and such chile-lover's totems as ristras (wreaths made from real peppers) and pod-shaped Christmas tree lights (made of plastic).

### Mo Hotta—Mo Betta
P.O. Box 4136
San Luis Obispo, CA 93403
(800) 462-3220

A mail-order catalogue devoted exclusively to hot and spicy food. A huge selection from around the world, including dozens of salsas and barbecue sauces, Jamaican jerk marinade, curry pastes, pepper-filled chocolate bonbons, and pepper-flavored peanut butter. The catalogue contains many inspiring quotes about its ultra-hot merchandise, including, "Damn be him that first cries, 'Hold enough!'" from *Macbeth,* "Anybody that eats chili can't be all bad," which Pat Garrett allegedly said about Billy the Kid, and—on page one—"No crybabies!" which is attributed to *anon.*

### Pepper's
7128 East Fifth Avenue
Scottsdale, AZ 85251
(602) 990-8347

"The hottest little gift shop in Scottsdale" sells a good supply of four-alarm salsas and other Southwestern goods, as well as ristras for home decor, dinnerware, and cookbooks.

### Rivera's Chile Chop
109 ½ Concho Street
San Antonio, TX 78207
(512) 226-9106

For this tip, thanks to *The Food Lover's Handbook to the Southwest* (an indispensable source for chile heads). Rivera's carries fresh peppers, hot jellies, salsas galore, and cactus candy. Plus lots of fiery-foods cookbooks.

### Santa Cruz Chili & Spice Co.
P.O. Box 177
Tucson, AZ 85640
(602) 398-2591

Long before chiles became fashionable, this gift shop was selling great hot groceries to Tucson pepper-fanciers: salsas, chile powder, ristras for cooking and home decor.

### Stonewall Chili Pepper Co.
P.O. Box 241
Stonewall, TX 78671
(512) 644-2667

Stonewall grows its own chiles, tomatoes, and other vegetables; its catalogue warns that no one will answer the phone in the late winter and early spring when they are busy working in their greenhouses and their fields. Stonewall caters to restaurants and food companies, and their *minimum order* is $100, but if you are serious about hot food, they've got some doozies you won't find elsewhere: jalapeño salsa made with peppers smoked over mesquite; chile-spiked pear relish; Habanero lollipops ("WARNING: Extremely hot! Not for children"); and one salsa so hot that it is listed with the warning, "We don't even recommend using plastic spoons to get it out of the jar."

# COWBOY BOOTS

**Back at the Ranch**
235 Don Gaspar
Santa Fe, NM 87501
(505) 989-8110

Used or new, for work or dress-up, bargain-priced or collector's models, Back at the Ranch will likely have a pair of boots with your name on it. If they don't, they can custom-make a pair to fit, in whatever style you require.

**G. C. Blucher Boot Co.**
350 North Main
Fairfax, OK 74637
(918) 642-3205

One of the grand old (since 1915) names in cowboy boots, this custom shop is for those who are willing to wait six months, and to pay, for the very best. "They never lose a stirrup" is the company motto, and although Blucher's boots are indeed made for riding, they are fashion statements of supreme beauty equally at home on any boulevard. A catalogue is available for $2.00, and this lovely little document is guaranteed to set your mouth watering and inspire dreams of all the fine pairs you want and need. For aficionados of cowboy style, it's a must!

**P. T. Crow Trading Company**
114 Amherst SE
Albuquerque, NM 87106
(505) 256-1763 or (800) 657-0944

P. T. Crow's selection of new boots is unsurpassed—advertised as suitable "from boardroom to barroom"—and they will custom-design whatever your heart and feet desire; but what we like to gawk at in this shop are the owner's father's custom-made pair (not for sale): a leathern ode to Oldsmobiles.

**D. W. Frommer II**
308 N. 6th
Redmond, OR 97756
(503) 923-3808

Because so many people want a pair of boots by D. W. Frommer, you have to wait many months from the time you order to delivery. "Whatever design you choose, it is vitally important that concentration and care be brought to bear in measuring your own foot and leg," the company's ordering instructions advise. Frommer's precise fitting system includes a mock-up "fitters" boot, and ensures that your pair will feel as swell as they look.

**Bob McLean Custom Bootmaker**
P.O. Box 10234
Sedona, AZ 86336
(800) 845-7831

Mr. Mclean makes all styles of custom boots, both fancy and plain, for dress up and for hard riding.

**Billy Martin's Western Wear**
812 Madison Avenue
New York, NY 10021
(212) 861-3100 or (800) 888-8915

It sure is strange to buy cowboy clothing on the swankiest shopping strip in Gotham; instead of good old boys you will be served by chic salespeople who look like *Vogue* magazine material. Nevertheless, you can find a fantastic selection of boots—from plain to absolutely wild, including custom-made models that go for a thousand dollars a pair. Last time we browsed boots in the lower-level showroom, actor Bruce Willis was sitting in the next chair trying on a pair of golden suede models (size 10).

**J. L. Mercer**
224 South Chadbourne
San Angelo, TX 76903
(915) 658-7634

An old established firm (since 1923), known for well made and beautifully designed custom boots.

**R. J. Boot Company**
3321 Ella Boulevard
Houston, TX 77018
(713) 682-5520

A specialty store dealing fancy custom boots for Houston's well-heeled gentry.

**T. P. Saddle Blanket**
304 Main Street
Great Barrington, MA 01230
(413) 528-6500
and
Routes 11 & 30
Manchester Center, VT 05255
(802) 362-9888

The biggest selection of cowboy boots in the Northeast. Collectible vintage boots, wearable workhorse boots, and everything in between. Larry Mahans, Nacona, Rocket-busters, etc., etc.

**Santa Fe Boot Co.**
950 West Cordova Road
Santa Fe, NM 87501
(505) 983-8415

Store motto: "Slightly off the beaten path, but worth the search." It isn't really so remote, and the large inventory of boots, belts, and full complement of Western accessories is all reasonably priced.

**Jane Smith**
122 W. San Francisco
Santa Fe, NM 87501
(505) 988-9242
and
201 S. Galena
Suite B
Aspen, CO 81611
(303) 925-6105

See "Western Clothing," below, for a fuller description of Jane Smith's remarkable inventory, but let us take this opportunity to warn you that it is easy to be so dazzled by all the other things sold in this luxurious store that you miss the fact that Jane Smith also has ultra-fine and fashionable custom boots for sale, some available with silver inlay.

**Tom Taylor Boots**
La Fonda Hotel
Santa Fe, NM 87501
(505) 984-2231

In the market for serious custom work? Tom Taylor will fix you up with beautiful (not necessarily gaudy) handmade boots to last a lifetime.

# COWBOY HATS

**Az-Tex Hat Company**
15044 North Cave Creek Road
Phoenix, AZ 85032
(800) 972-2095

Call the 800 number and get a catalogue that will help you choose a cowboy hat to suit your needs. They carry their own brand and make them to fit head sizes ranging from 6⅜ to 8¼. We were especially struck by their 30X beaver platinum mink Rancher: It looks like something J. R. Ewing would have worn.

**Back at the Ranch**
235 Don Gaspar
Santa Fe, NM 87501
(505) 989-8110

(see "Cowboy Collectibles" and "Boots," above)

**Falconhead**
11911 San Vicente Boulevard
Los Angeles, CA 90049
(310) 471-7075

What "Life styles of the Rich and Famous" is to ordinary folks, Falconhead is to cowboy clothes. Scott Wayne Emmerich, founder and owner of the store, is the king of posh custom work, and will make you a cowboy hat out of chinchilla blend, or boots from exotic reptiles for approximately the cost of a small car. Such duds were never meant for the barn.

**Hatatorium Hat Shop**
25 North Chadbourne
San Angelo, TX 76903
(915) 655-9191

Like the name says, hats are the specialty of the house, along with all the requisite accessories, including hatbands, hat boxes, and hat brushes. They can reblock a limp brim or collapsing crown, thoroughly renovate a vintage hat, and help you select a style best suited to your personality.

**The Man's Hat Shop**
511 Central Avenue NW
Albuquerque, NM 87102
(505) 247-9605

Smack in the heart of Albuquerque, the Man's Hat Shop is run by pros who can tell you everything you need to know to keep your hat looking sharp for a lifetime. Hat etiquette lessons are given free of charge with any purchase. (See page 82.)

**Montecristi Custom Hat Works**
118 Galisteo Street
Santa Fe, NM 87501
(505) 983-9598

Montecristi specializes in handmade Panama hats, in three grades of woven straw. None are inexpensive, and the best cost about $1,000 per hat. In addition to traditional Panama hats (actually made from material handwoven in Ecuador, not Panama), this store sells some beautiful Western-style hats, as well as hatbands of Indian beads, porcupine quills, or silver conchas.

**Rand's Custom Hatters**
2205 1st Avenue North
Billings, MT 59101
(406) 259-4886 or (406) 248-7688

Rand's is world famous for their custom hats. In fact their products are so nice that when we were accidentally sent one by another company that sells Rand's hats, we kept it even though it didn't quite fit and wasn't what we had asked for. Rand's is also especially good at restoring old hats, putting in new silk liners, and replacing bands.

**Tonto Rim Trading Company**
P.O. Box 463
Salem, IN 47167
(812) 883-3023 or (800) 242-HATS

Tonto Rim sells hats via a catalogue and newsletter called the *Tonto Rim Times,* which also contains poetry, stories, and short essays about the cowboy way of life. Owner Denny Shewell is a mighty friendly guy who just loves to help his customers decide between a "High Country Bar 20" and a "Clint Black." He has more than 700 hats in stock, and custom-creasing is his pleasure.

# SADDLES AND TACK: MAKERS AND DEALERS

**J. M. Capriola Co.**
500 Commercial Street
Elko, NV 89801
(702) 738-5816

One of the most respected names in classic-look handcrafted spurs, spur straps and bits. Company motto: "If it doesn't say, 'Garcia, Elko, Nev.', it isn't an original."

**Continental Saddlery**
New Palestine, IN 46163
(317) 861-6871 or (800) 783-7996

If you are in the market for a saddle, do yourself a favor: spend $5.00 and get a Continental Saddlery catalogue. Makers of long-renowned Pullman saddles, these folks do everything the old-fashioned way, custom-building saddles from the tree you choose (Line Rider, Buckaroo, Top Hand, or Cheyenne), with the skirt you want (square or rounded), the seat that fits (hard, smooth padded, or suede padded), and the horn suited to your needs (sewn or rawhide bound), plus whatever carved leather tooling you desire. Also available: batwing chaps, shotgun chaps, vests, rifle scabbards, gun belts, and holsters.

**Dan's Frontier Store and Harness Shop**
Route 6
Woodbury, CT 06798
(203) 263-2284

Dan is a nice gent who once did riding and roping stunts for Gene Autry movies, and there are some eye-popping pictures of his skills on the wall of his tack shop. There is a large assortment of saddles for sale, plain and fancy, as well as boots, hats, jeans, H-Bar-C cowboy shirts, and everything you and your horse might need: a fine taste of the West in the Nutmeg State.

**R. Lloyd David & Sons Custom Saddlemakers**
3132 East Prince
Tucson, AZ 85716
(602) 323-2598

The high end of custom saddle work for true cognoscenti.

**Verlane Desgrange**
P.O. Box 1862
Cody, WY 82414
(307) 587-9078

Verlane is a leather artist; her specialty is classic-looking High Plains saddles crafted to fit modern horses and women riders (both of whom tend to be bigger than they used to be). Using tools she fashions herself, she makes gear that is widely known for its intricate patterns and flawless craftsmanship. She also makes other tack and leather goods: everything is on a custom-order basis.

**R. E. Donaho Saddle Shop**
8 East Concho Avenue
San Angelo, TX 76903
(915) 655-3270

Good old Texas saddles in classic designs.

**Franklin Saddle Co.**
135 West Main
John Day, OR 97845
(503) 575-0317

Bub Warren, who took over this respected business from founder Jerry Franklin, makes custom Western saddles that are of the highest quality. Although their specialty is good, sturdy saddles for everyday use, we couldn't help but dote on a Diamond Jubilee trophy saddle they made to commemorate seventy-five years of Oklahoma statehood. It features a hand-tooled state seal, state flag, state flower, state bird, state animal, and state motto, with a diamond set in the silver horn cap. Two hundred twenty-two plated nails were required, and 1,000 hours of work.

**Hamley's**
30 South East Court Avenue
Pendleton, OR 97801
(503) 276-2321

In the cowboy-outfitting business for more than a century, Hamley's continues to do some of the finest custom silverwork available for fancy saddles. They also sell gun rigs, boots, hats, and all manner of Western clothes.

**High Noon**
9929 Venice Boulevard
Los Angeles, CA 90034
(310) 202-9010

By appointment only, and don't even think of making an appointment unless you are a serious collector of vintage horse-and-cowboy artifacts. None of the spurs, chaps, and parade saddles sold by Linda Kohn and Joseph Sherwood are cheap. All are fine and important.

**J&S Western**
1038 East Main Street
Warsaw, MO 65355
(816) 438-2631 or (816) 438-6517

"Howdy . . . We love riding the old highbacks and appreciate the workmanship that was put into them," begins the mimeographed catalogue issued by J&S. If you, too, love old saddles—for riding or collecting—you need to know about this outfit, which has hundreds for sale, ranging from ultrafine Miles City Coggshells to side saddles and old "wall-hangers" for display only. Also available: horse-theme art work, spurs, bridles, bits, and breast collars, as well as vintage human apparel including gun belts, boots, hats, topcoats, and chaps. Last April, movie star and rodeo great Ben Johnson stopped by while in town for Warsaw's annual Celebrity Turkey Hunt.

**H. Kauffman & Sons Saddlery**
419 Park Avenue South
New York, NY 10010
(212) 684-6060

Horse-and-rider fittings have been the specialty of this shop for more than a century. A mail-order catalogue is available. Although Kauffman is well known for its Eastern-style riding gear, it is also a mother lode of Western clothes and tack; in fact, Sandra Kauffman wrote the eye-opening all-Western book *The Cowboy Catalogue,* in 1980.

## King Ranch Saddle Shop

201 East Kleberg
P.O. Box 1594
Kingsville, TX 78364
(800) 282-KING

The King Ranch Saddle Shop has a broad range of Western tack, but saddles are what they are best known for.

*Don King, Sheridan, Wyoming.*

## King's Saddlery and Ropes

184 North Main
Sheridan, WY 82801
(307) 443-8919

The High Plains has long been known for the high quality of its hand-tooled saddles. Don King created the Sheridan-style saddle, meaning one with finely detailed wildflowers in an elaborate scroll pattern—long a favorite among cowboy movie stars, and just about anyone who loves fine leather horse gear (and can afford to pay for it). King's Saddlery, in business since 1947, is considered among the best in the West; it is also famous for King Ropes, and it is a good source for almost any horse-related garb.

## Rusty May Saddlery

6239 West 34th
Loveland, CO 80538
(303) 663-4036

Rusty May makes saddles for everyone, from professional cowboys to physically challenged riders who need a special rig.

## Miller Saddlery

117 East 24th Street
New York, NY 10010
(212) 673-1400

Miller is a premier outfitter of Eastern-style riding clothes and tack, and their huge mail-order catalogue features mostly that. But the store in New York also has a good measure of Western clothes, saddles, and tack on display.

## Pitman's Treasures & Company

219 North San Marino Avenue
San Gabriel, CA 91775
(818) 281-6854

George Pitman is America's foremost collector of silver parade saddles and tack, in particular those made by the legendary craftsman Edward Bohlin. His saddles, as well as gun rigs, chaps, spurs, and bits, are museum quality and extremely costly. But to Mr. Pitman—and to a growing number of collectors—they are every bit as good an investment as diamonds or gold . . . and a whole lot more fun to own. If you are looking for the ultimate in horsewear, George Pitman is the man to meet. He has also reprinted several catalogues of the bygone master craftsmen, including Bohlin, Visalia, Morales, and Main-Winchester-Stone.

## Platte Valley Saddle Shop, Inc.

1908 Central Avenue
P.O. Box 1683
Kearney, NE 68848
(308) 234-4015

Platte Valley Saddle Shop has been making custom saddles since 1942. The saddle maker is Lyle E. Henderson, and if you cannot get to Nebraska, you can see his wares by sending $5.00 for a catalogue.

## Harry Thurston Saddlemaker

3144 East Bell Road
Phoenix, AZ 85032
(602) 992-4414

A well-respected saddle maker who sells his custom wares around the world.

# WESTERN CLOTHING

### Back at the Ranch
235 Don Gaspar
Santa Fe, NM 87501
(505) 989-8110

See "Cowboy Collectibles" and "Boots," above.

### Best of the West
8 Federal Road
Danbury, CT 06810
(203) 792-4743

There's a little something for everyone in this snug, super-friendly shop run by Western aficionados Ed and Lucy Prybylski: cowboy clothing, hats, Indian jewelry, and a saddle or two. Ed and Lucy host occasional open-house barn dances at their nearby Danbury ranch, where they keep a tiny herd of cattle to help their cutting horses stay sharp.

### Bridger Creek Outfitters
P.O. Box 3576
1280 Story Mill Road
Bozeman, MT 59715
(406) 586-7764

Bridger Creek Outfitters is an excellent all-purpose store selling everything from custom-made chaps to long rain slickers to saddles, spurs, and bits. They will send you a catalogue for $3.00 so you can shop in your easy chair.

### Creations in Leather
1031 12th Street
Cody, WY 82414
(307) 587-6461

A beautiful line of beaded and fringed vests and jackets out of elk or cow hide, guaranteed to have no holes or brands in it. The garments are made to order, so if you crave more beads or less fringe, or want to send a photo of a piece of Western clothing you saw on a favorite old-time cowboy, they can make it just the way you like.

### Dream Merchant
1658 Westheimer
Houston, TX 77006
(713) 520-0076

Some very nifty and unusual fashions for women and men. We especially like Dream Merchant's cowboy boots with the playing-card design, and the old-style (but new) shirts and bolero vests.

### Kallison's
### Western Wear Store
123 South Flores
San Antonio, TX 78204
(210) 222-1364
*and*
### Kallison's
### Farm & Ranch Store
1025 Nogalitos
San Antonio, TX 78204
(210) 222-8411

Kallison's western wear store has been outfitting working cowboys for nearly a century. They carry Brushpopper shirts, top-brand boots, hats, and some wonderful jackets, in buckskin fringe or brush-resistant denim. The farm and ranch store is where bull riders shop for their equipment: spurs, belts, gloves, and rope riggings with bells attached.

### Lariat Ranch Wear
1610 South Congress
Austin, TX 78704
(512) 444-2111

Well-priced, serious Western clothes you don't mind getting a little trail dust on. Lariat is the place University of Texas students go to get their hats creased and to buy their bright orange cowboy shirts.

### M. L. Leddy & Sons
2455 North Main
Fort Worth, TX 76106
(817) 624-3149

A Texas treasure. Leddy custom-makes everything for horse and rider, and has been doing so since 1922. In addition to ordinary tack, boots, et al., it is known for making some amazing Lone Star mementos, including hand-tooled briefcases and ice buckets. It has even been known to outfit cowboy boots with golf-shoe soles.

**Lorig's**
31 South Tejon Street
Colorado Springs, CO 80903
(719) 633-4695

This fine store in downtown Colorado Springs has been in business for fifty-five years. It has a wide selection of Stetson hats, boots by Lucchese, and Pendleton robes. The service is as old-fashioned and solid as the building.

**Manuel**
1922 Broadway
Nashville, TN 37203
(615) 321-5444

Manuel works by appointment only, although his ultra-fancy ready-to-wear clothes can be found at Jane Smith in Santa Fe and at better shops around the country. A personal visit for a custom fitting puts you in the same league with such sartorial legends as Hank Williams, Elvis, Porter Waggoner, Linda Ronstadt, Dolly Parton, and a host of other country kings and queens who knew their way around a sequin. Manuel apprenticed with Nudie of Hollywood, and *Vogue* recently defined his style as the epitome of cowboy couture.

**Billy Martin's Western Wear**
812 Madison Avenue
New York, NY 10021
(212) 861-3100 or (800) 888-8915

The complete Western apparel store for Manhattanites carries not only a major selection of boots (see above), but also fine Western shirts for work and play, jeans, hats, broomstick skirts, etc., etc.

**Vanessa Paukeigope Morgan**
P.O. Box 1101
Anadarko, OK 73005

Anadarko is Oklahoma's Indian capital, and the place Vanessa Morgan calls home. Ms. Morgan handmakes beaded buckskin dresses that are purely magnificent, hand sewn from brain-tanned hides and outfitted with German silver cones, glass tile beads, hawk bells, and the like. They can cost all the way up to $6,000 per dress, but they are rare and spectacular, favored by Native Americans who participate in festive dance events like Oklahoma's annual Red Earth Days.

**Nudie's Rodeo Tailors**
5015 Lankershim Boulevard
North Hollywood, CA 91601
(818) 762-3105 and (213) 877-9505

The most famous tailor in cowboy history (see page 70) has passed on, but Mrs. Nudie Cohn still minds the store. And what a store it is! Huge, filled with hats, boots, and everything in between, and plastered with 8 X 10 pictures of thousands of stars, past and present, who have availed themselves of the outrageous rhinestone cowboy fashions for which Nudie is known. You can buy good, fairly traditional stuff off the shelf, or Nudie's tailors can still custom-make whatever your—and their—imagination conjures.

**Ortega's Weaving Shop**
P.O. Box 325
Chimayo, NM 87522
(505) 351-4215

The handwoven woolen Chimayo coats and vests on sale here have been made by the same family for eight generations. They are top quality, reasonably priced, and the style is a Southwestern classic. The tiny picturesque town of Chimayo is reason enough to stop here.

**The Original Santa Fe Fiesta Fashions**
651 Cerrillos Road
Santa Fe, NM 87501
(505) 983-1632
and
118 Don Gaspar
Santa Fe, NM 87501
(505) 986-5078

These are the places to find the best Navajo-style broomstick skirts in Santa Fe. Fashion maven Lindee Shaw (see page 98) will show you how to put together the most elegant fiesta fashions for parties, grand occasions, or just eye-popping street wear.

**The Outfitters**
127 South Santa Fe Road
P.O. Box 1794
Taos, NM 87571
(505) 758-2966

A unique twist on Western wear, the Outfitters' field of concentration is mountain man gear. This includes many articles of clothing made of fur and pelts, as well as drums to beat, knives, flintlock rifles, and bench-made moccasins.

### PFI Western Store

2743 West Chestnut Expressway
Springfield, MO 65802
(800) 284-8191

We know "Missouri's Largest Western Store" only by its mail-order catalogue, which is jumbo. These are duds for modern Western-style folk, including purple jeans with concho-trimmed bows on a back yoke for the ladies, children's-size cowboy boots, and matching his-'n'-her pullover back-yoke shirts.

### Rancho

322 McKenzie Street
Santa Fe, NM 87501
(505) 986-1688

Propietors Chuck and Barbara Cooper—who are always so impeccably accoutered themselves—have recently supplemented their impressive inventory of one-of-a-kind cowboy collectibles with an array of classic-look Western wear that is practical as well as practically priced. If you are a real outdoors type, or just want to look like one, check out their dusters, oil-finish riding coats, and plaid Mackinaw jackets.

### Rancho Loco

830 Exposition #102
Dallas, TX 75226
(214) 827-1680

Rancho Loco owner Sharon Goldberg one day proved her mettle as a salesperson by giving us the world's most thorough description of an H-Bar-C replica shirt we were interested in buying. By the time she finished, we had embroidered roses and steer heads dancing in our heads, and couldn't resist the purchase. The store is a must for any serious connoisseur of cowboy clothing, with merchandise as good as you'll find this side of a vintage Nudie catalogue.

### Red River Frontier Outfitters

P.O. Box 241
Tujunga, CA 91043

It isn't easy to find bib-fronted shirts, full-length dusters like the ones in the movie *The Long Riders,* old-time cowboy trousers (not jeans) and sets of galluses (suspenders) to hold them up with. That is why the Red River catalogue is mighty handy.

### Ryon's

2601 North Main
Fort Worth, TX 76106
(817) 625-2391

"The Nation's Finest Western Wear Store" has everything a working cowboy (or a dreamer) could want, from custom-made saddles and tack to boots, hats, chaps, and spurs. A free catalogue is available.

### T. P. Saddle Blanket

304 Main Street
Great Barrington, MA 01230
(413) 528-6500
and
Routes 11 & 30
Manchester Center, VT 05255
(802) 362-9888

So you think you can't find great cowboy stuff in Pilgrim Country? If so, you are wrong, and if it wasn't for that tall Texan, Tyler Beard, who clued us in to T. P. Saddle Blanket, we might not have looked North ourselves. What a find these places are! We list them under clothing, because we especially love their vests inspired by Beacon blankets, made from cloth they have woven in Scotland, and also the vests they make inlaid with turquoise and coral, as well as all their other spectacular custom clothing. But the inventory goes way beyond things to wear, from cowboy furniture to Indian jewelry to hot chile powders and books about the West.

### Santa Fe Western Mercantile

6820 Cerrillos Road
Santa Fe, NM 87501
(505) 471-3655

A mammoth store with all sorts of gear for men, women, children, and their horses. From hats to boots, if you are shopping for functional Western gear, this is the place. We have found many handsome shirts here, at reasonable prices. There is a nice little supply of books about horsemanship and horse care, too.

**J. Seitz & Co.**
9 East Shore Road (Route 45)
New Preston, CT 06777
(203) 868-0119

When Joanna Seitz isn't in her shop in Connecticut, she is scouring the Southwest for merchandise to bring back. Among the treasures she finds are gorgeous broomstick skirts, fringed gloves and buckskin jackets, and shirts and sweaters with a Wild West motif. The shop also has handsome furniture for sale and impeccably chosen jewelry (see above), from fun and affordable earrings and pins to investment-level turquoise.

**Simply Santa Fe**
72 East San Francisco St.
Santa Fe, NM 87501
(505) 988-3100

An on-the-Plaza department store of high-end Santa Fe style at its most refined, including clothing, jewelry, home furnishings, and gifts. Recently featured: outfits made by Cathy Smith, who designed the costumes for *Dances with Wolves.*

**Jane Smith**
122 West San Francisco
Santa Fe, NM 87501
(505) 988-4775
and
201 South Galena
Suite B
Aspen, CO 81611
(303) 925-6105

Jane Smith is a swank store that sells clothing that most Western fashion fans only fantasize owning: hand-knitted custom-made sweaters with cowboy motifs, one-of-a-kind hand-tooled ladies' purses, and sumptuous buckskin jackets, some costing thousands of dollars. Shoppers' bonus: The people who work at Jane Smith, including Jane herself, are all fashionplates of super-model magnitude.

**Southwest Moccasin and Drum**
803 Pueblo Norte
Box 4904
Taos, NM 87571
(505) 758-9332 or (800) 447-3630

A 150-year-old adobe chapel just north of Taos with one of the best selections of moccasins anywhere, ready made or custom. In addition to footwear, there are magnificent "All One Tribe" drums handmade by artisans of the Taos Pueblo. "Each of us comes into the world having spent nine months listening to the beat of a heart-drum," explains the All One Tribe brochure, which recommends drumming as an activity that "increases intuition, shifts us out of our 'rational' minds, and centers us in our hearts." We especially like the drum chairs for children or adults; their seats serve as tom-toms when they are not occupied.

**Stelzig's**
3123 Post Oak Boulevard
Houston, TX 77056
(713) 629-7779
and
9511 Southwest Freeway
Houston, TX 77074
(713) 988-6530

For decades, the rearing stallion on the top of Stelzig's in Old Market Square was the sign of fine Western-style clothes for working ranch hands and dudes as well. From custom saddles to gaudy bolo ties, jeans and spurs, Stelzig's has always had what cowboys need. The old store is now closed, but the stallion has been relocated to the Post Oak location, and the range of merchandise is still fantastic.

**Tonto Rim**
2650 East Tipton
Seymour, IN 47274
(812) 522-7978

Denny Shewell is known to Western aficionados as publisher of the *Tonto Rim Times,* a great, fun-filled mail-order catalogue of cowboy gear. His newly opened retail store, housed in what was once a Hen House Restaurant, is filled with zillions of cowboy boots, ten-gallon hats, snap-button shirts, and Western-themed gifts. In this vast place, Indiana suddenly seems a lot like Montana!

## The Western Connection

374 Boston Street
Topsfield, MA 01983
(508) 887-8883

Deep in the heart of Massachusetts (actually way up north, near Gloucester), here's a store that will outfit you in full Western regalia, including championship buckles and boots made-to-order or off-the-shelf. They've got plain and fancy jeans, hats and belts, and deluxe tuxedo shirts trimmed with ultra suede. Glittering men's suits and ladies' dresses are a specialty.

## Western Corral

7734 Girard Avenue
La Jolla, CA 92037
(619) 551-9595

A hip, fashionable emporium of fine Western wear, including a big wall full of deluxe boots, stacks of jeans, shirts for work and show, and a selection of beautiful leather goods.

## Whiskey Dust

526 Hudson Street (between West 10th & Charles)
New York, NY 10014
(212) 691-5576

"A hoot & a holler" is how tipster Bill Luckey described this downtown Gotham haunt that bills itself as "The Place for Western Oddities." Proprietor Merv Bendewald, originally from Montana, has been collecting Westernalia for a lifetime, and he finally opened the store because he had amassed so much great stuff he had nowhere to keep it: stupendous gold and silver rodeo buckles and deluxe belts, vintage boots, Stetson hats already stained with cowboy sweat, and frontier knickknacks of all kinds and all levels of collectibility. Also for sale: worn jeans, plain and fancy shirts, and rugged buckskin jackets. Throughout the store, there are really nice old saddles to behold.

## Williams Western Tailors

1104 North West Twenty-Eighth Street
Fort Worth, TX 76106
(817) 625-2401

Shirts only: Custom-made with your brand or monogram, or a favorite critter or cactus, in styles named "The Hillsman," "The Cattleman," "The Westerner," "The Longhorn," "The Cowtowner," "The Plainsman," and "The Texan." Prices are reasonable (between $40 and $70), but be prepared to wait.

## The Wrangler

1518 Capitol Avenue
Cheyenne, WY 82001
(307) 634-3048

A beautiful big old Western-style red brick department store in the heart of Cheyenne, the Wrangler has everything you need if you arrive for Frontier Days without proper cowboy attire. You'll know the place by its moving sign at the corner: a mechanical cowboy on a horse that has been galloping perpetually for decades.

# BOOKS ON THE WEST

**Bookman's**
1930 East Grant Road
Tucson, AZ 85719
(602) 325-5767

A gigantic store with *all* sorts of books about *every* topic, from serious academic texts to more movie novelizations than you ever imagined have been published. In back, behind the shelves of used magazines and old records (wonderful stock!), the Collectibles Room features many unusual, rare, autographed, curious (and mostly reasonably priced) out-of-print books about the West. Also, *Arizona Highways* going back to the 1940s and assorted cowboy movie ephemera.

**Books West Southwest**
2452 North Campbell
Tucson, AZ 85719
(602) 326-3533

A precisely focused inventory of books about the West: state by state, topic by topic. There are new books, old books, kids' books, fiction, vintage and collectible editions. If you are looking for a particular volume, or a book about a certain Western subject, this is the place most likely to have what you want or need. It will also have dozens of other books you never knew you needed: heaven for the browser, and murder on the wallets of those of us who cannot resist. Proprietor W. David Laird also publishes a monthly newsletter, *Books of the Southwest,* including thumbnail reviews of current and recent nonfiction, fiction, poetry, children's books, mass market originals, and reissues. (By subscription, $24 per year: Box 40850, Tucson, AZ 85717.)

**Butler Publishing**
253 Grey Rock Road
LaPorte, CO 80535
(303) 221-2834

The only publisher we know that specializes in material about horseshoeing. These items are not for the dilettante; they include the book *Principles of Horseshoeing II* ($49.95) and *Shoeing the Sound Horse—the Video* ($49.95), as well as such tools as a portable shoe shaper for $219.95. The motto at Butler is "Guaranteed Tools to Ease the Farrier's Task."

**Case Trading Post**
Wheelwright Museum of the American Indian
704 Camino Lejo
Santa Fe, NM 87501
(505) 982-4636

A wide selection of new books about Western lore and history. Here is virtually everything in print about Indian collectibles, including jewelry, pots, rugs, and artifacts.

**The Collected Works Bookshop**
208-B West San Francisco
Santa Fe, NM 87501
(505) 988-4226

A superb selection of regional books as well as general interest stock. What we especially like about Collected Works is the staff: they read, they know what they sell, they can really help you select books if you have any questions.

**Hee Haw Book Service**
2901 North Elm
Denton, TX 76201
(817) 382-6845

Betsy and Paul Hutchins wrote the book on asses: *The Definitive Donkey.* They also run the American Donkey and Mule Society, which is the national club for people who like donkeys and mules, or just mules alone. Their Hee Haw publishing company puts out several books, including *The Modern Mule, The Mule* (reprint of a beguiling 1867 book), and their *The Definitive Donkey,* which includes chapters on *everything* an ass-lover could ever want to know, including: "Care of the Foot and Lower Leg," "Castration," and "Flapjackin'." (Flapjackin', by the way, is an annual party that takes place in Death Valley to honor the famous twenty-mule teams of times gone by.)

**Mesilla Book Center**
P.O. Box 96 (west side of the Plaza)
Mesilla, NM 88046
(505) 526-6220

We love shopping in this 132-year-old, four-room adobe store on the Plaza in the ancient village of Mesilla. The assortment of books about Western history, lore, and culture is tremendous—an estimated 12,000 volumes—and we never fail to find some obscure titles we never knew existed. The place is decorated with Apache baskets, Navajo rugs, and sand paintings, and there are lots of crafts and jewelry for sale in the front room. Another specialty of the house is children's books: shelves full of them, including many featuring Indian tales and cowboy stories.

## Parker Books of the West
142 West Palace Avenue
Santa Fe, NM 87501
(505) 988-1076

A large and eclectic selection of mostly old books (including some rare first editions) about the West: history, folklore, literature, Indian topics, and lots about Texas. Parker also has an ever-changing inventory of ephemera, postcards, brochures, catalogues, and art.

## Santa Fe Bookseller
203 West San Francisco
Santa Fe, NM 87501
(505) 983-5278

A big selection of regionalia, including autographed classics, locally published guides, and art books about the Southwest. If you like old books, this is the kind of store you could spend hours browsing.

## Taos Bookstore
122 East Kit Carson
Taos, NM 87571
(505) 758-3733

The oldest bookstore in New Mexico, with a selection of new books about the West and one of the finest inventories of out-of-print volumes and rare editions.

## The Tattered Cover
2955 East 1st Street
Denver, CO 80206
(303) 322-7727 or (800) 833-9327

A huge general-interest book store that bibliophiles know as one of the nation's finest, the Tattered Cover is also noteworthy for the depth and breadth of its Western section. Fiction, local history, gorgeous picture books: however you like to delve into the region, you will find your pleasure here.

# PLACES TO STAY

## Arizona Inn
2200 East Elm Street
Tucson, AZ 85719
(602) 325-1541

Pink stucco cottages surrounded by orange trees, date palms, and lush beds of poppies make the Arizona Inn an oasis in the city. The oldest resort hotel in Tucson and once the exclusive haunt of visiting royalty and well-behaved movie stars, this place has an aristocratic ambience that makes a guest feel pampered, private, and a little bit like a bon vivant from an Ernst Lubitsch drawing room comedy of the 1930s. In fact, the inn was built in 1930, and although it is thoroughly modern, its charm (including the dining room's relish tray) belongs to a gentler era.

## Goulding's Lodge
Monument Valley, UT 84536
(801) 727-3231

John Ford and his crew used to hole up here when they made Westerns in nearby Monument Valley; in fact, a building that appeared in *She Wore a Yellow Ribbon* (as John Wayne's cabin) is still standing. The rest of Goulding's has been thoroughly modernized and is now as contemporary as any pleasant roadside motel. There is a souvenir shop and a restaurant with a soggy salad bar. But none of that matters. Goulding's is the only lodging that puts you anywhere near the incredible field of rock monoliths in Navajo country. In the morning, when the sun rises above them, it is a magic place to be.

## The Hitching Post Best Western
1700 West Lincolnway
Cheyenne, WY 82001
(307) 638-3301

Most of the year, the Hitching Post is simply a nice, clean motel. Late in July when cowboys from around the nation come to Cheyenne to compete in the Frontier Days Rodeo, the Hitching Post is where those who are smart enough to book long in advance spend the week. Even if you cannot get a room here, it is a fun place to hang out. The scene in the lounge at night when the day's events are through is a wild, Wild West bristling with sexual energy. Cowboys with fresh bruises and contestant numbers still poking out of their jeans pockets crowd up to the bar among the "buckle bunnies" who adore them, and the party goes long into the night.

**Inn of the Anasazi**
113 Washington Avenue
Santa Fe, NM 87501
(800) 688-8100

The nicest-smelling hotel in America, fragrant with cedar and juniper, Inn of the Anasazi is the epitome of Santa Fe high style. It is our favorite place in town to spend the night, with an inventive regional-foods restaurant, too—especially at breakfast, when the chile-cheese grits are divine.

**Murray Hotel**
201 West Park
Livingston, MT 59047
(406) 222-1350

"The Murray is to Montana hostelries what the Chelsea is to the hotels of New York," the *New York Times* recently announced, declaring the nearly 100-year-old landmark "an antiquated classic" that epitomizes the rugged spirit of Big Sky country. The well-seasoned ambiance is deliciously Wild West; you can easily imagine Kerouac stopping here for all-night beers while "On the Road." In fact, many pop culture celebrities who have escaped to Montana (the last best place) in recent years have either stayed or visited (the *Times* lists Peter Fonda, Robert Redford, Donna Rice, Whoopi Goldberg, and Jack Palance, among others). The Holiday Inn it ain't . . . which is why its patrons love it so.

**Rancho Encantado**
Tesuque, NM 87501
(505) 982-3537

An idyllic place to get away from it all: an hospitable hotel sufficiently far from the bustle of the Plaza and downtown Santa Fe, but near enough to put you within striking distance. The free-standing casitas are rustic, but tastefully decorated, each with its own wood-burning fireplace. Rancho is surrounded by gorgeous riding trails and has a remuda of horses for guests.

**Sleep in a Wigwam**
811 West Hopi Drive
Holbrook, AZ 86025
(602) 524-6523

One of the classic motels along old Route 66. The wigwams were refurbished in 1988, and are tidy inside, with room enough for even a six-footer to move around without knocking up against the slanting walls. See page 239.

**Sundance Lodge**
RR-3, Box A-1
Sundance, UT 84604
(801) 225-4107

In the forests of the North Fork of Provo Canyon, Sundance Lodge is a Shangri-La with a 2,150-foot vertical drop ski slope, 14 kilometers of cross-country trails, and accommodations in cottages with rustic handmade wooden furniture, Native-American arts and crafts decor, and stone fireplaces. Time spent here can be an exhilarating experience found nowhere else but way out West.

**Thunderbird Lodge**
Box 548, Canyon de Chelly
Chinle, AZ 86503
(602) 674-5841

A vintage motel adjacent to some of the most riveting scenery on earth: the ancient cliff dwellings of the lost Anasazi tribes, cut into plunging red rock walls of immeasurable beauty. Thunderbird Lodge began nearly a hundred years ago as a trading post; now it is a modest motor court with rustic Native-American decor and rough-hewn beams in the ceiling of each room. The gift shop sells hordes of mementos and curios, and there is a cafeteria-style restaurant that features many colors of Jell-O: precisely the kind of old-time tourist facility we like to put us in a frame of mind for communing with the natural wonder of Canyon de Chelly.

# MUSEUMS

*If planning a visit, call ahead: many of these museums have limited hours, or close during hot summer months.*

### ¡Adevina!
333 Montezuma
Santa Fe, NM 87501
(505) 983-8799

We're not sure where to list ¡Adevina!, so let's call it a very lively museum. Billing itself as a "coffee cantina and gift store" off the Plaza (i.e., not for thundering hordes of tourists), ¡Adevina! is also an art gallery and literary center for local talent. Readings from works in progress are given in the evenings of the third Saturday of every month. If you are looking for the pulse of the real Santa Fe, this is a good place to find it.

### American Quarter Horse Heritage Center and Museum
2601 I-40 East at Quarter Horse Drive
Amarillo, TX 79104
(806) 376-5181

### Appaloosa Museum
5070 Highway 8 West
P.O. Box 8403
Moscow, ID 83843
(208) 882-5578

### Arizona-Sonora Desert Museum
2021 North Kinney Road
Tucson, AZ 85743
(602) 883-1380

Actually more a zoo than a museum, this wondrous environment amid the Saguaro National Monument is a good place for scaredy-cats to see Gila monsters, tarantulas, scorpions, buzzards, mountain lions, snakes, and lizards in the flesh. Also: a hummingbird aviary, an otter habitat, and a 140-species cactus garden. "Did you know?" asks the museum brochure, "A snake's skin feels like silk? [and] Tarantulas just want to be left alone?"

### Barbed Wire Museum
614 Main Street
La Crosse, KS 67548
(913) 222-3116

### Boot Hill Museum
Front Street
Dodge City, KS 67801
(316) 227-8188

### Buffalo Bill Cody Museum
Lookout Mountain Road
Route 5 Box 950
Golden, CO 80401
(303) 526-0747

### Buffalo Bill Historical Center
720 Sheridan Avenue
Cody, WY 82414
(307) 587-4771

One of the great, grand museums of the West, including a tremendous range of art, a major Plains Indians collection, and a collection of rifles and six-guns without equal. Whether you are a scholar of the frontier or just grazing through, this place is a must on your itinerary. Also, it has a big, wonderful gift shop.

### Buffalo Museum of America
10261 North Scottsdale Road
Scottsdale, AZ 85253
(602) 991-6162

Devoted to "the grandeur, grace, and power of these magnificent creatures," the Buffalo Museum has a roomful of Buffalo Bill artifacts (including one of his hunting rifles), a saddled buffalo you can sit on to have your picture taken, a full-size prop buffalo used in *Dances with Wolves*, memorabilia from the 1901 Pan American Expo held in Buffalo, New York, and a family of life-size buffalo that talk and sing.

### Coolidge Historical Society Museum
Central Avenue
Coolidge, AZ 85228
(602) 723-7186

Interesting historical artifacts on display in what was once the town's jail. Most relate to frontier history, but our favorite artifact is the X-ray shoe-fitting machine from the 1950s—the kind you could look into and see the bones of your feet (not operational).

**Cowboy Artists of America Museum**
1550 Bandera Highway
Kerrville, TX 78028
(512) 896-2553

**Gene Autry Western Heritage Museum**
4700 Zoo Drive (Griffith Park)
Los Angeles, CA 90027
(213) 667-2000

Wonderful memorabilia, including what may be perhaps the most deluxe saddle ever made (by Bohlin), this museum takes its role as a Western heritage center seriously. It's a must for anyone researching either the real West or the West of the imagination.

**Joe Gish's Old West Museum**
502 North Milam
Fredricksburg, TX 78624
(512) 997-2794

Included in the very personal, high-quality collection: screen actress Marion Davies's tan boots with red heart-shaped inlays and a beautiful silver parade saddle made by Keystone Brothers of San Francisco.

**The Heard Museum**
22 East Monte Vista Road
Phoenix, AZ 85004
(602) 252-8848

In addition to Barry Goldwater's kachina doll collection, the venerable Heard has Herman Schweizer's stuff. Mr. Schweizer was the man who bought the finest original Indian jewelry for the Fred Harvey company to use as models for the souvenirs they made around the turn of the century. He used to keep his things locked in an Albuquerque vault known as "the drool room" to envious collectors who understood the rarity and value of what he had accumulated.

**Institute of Texas Culture**
801 South Bowie at
Durango Boulevard
San Antonio TX 78294
(512) 226-7651

**J & S Old West Museum**
1038 East Main
Warsaw, MO 65355
(816) 438-2631

**King Ranch Museum**
405 North 6th Street
Kingsville, TX 78364
(512) 595-1881

**Lea County Cowboy Hall of Fame & Western Heritage Center**
New Mexico Junior College
5317 Lovington Highway
Hobbs, NM 88240

**Lost Dutchman Museum**
Goldfield Ghost Town
State Route 88
Apache Junction, AZ 85220
(602) 983-4888

The legendary claim of Jacob Waltz, the Dutchman prospector of the Superstition Mountains, inspired this museum devoted to gold fever, as well as Indian artifacts from the area. Exhibits include a videotape of the "Unsolved Mysteries" TV episode about the Lost Dutchman's Mine.

**Museum of the
Western Prairie**
1100 North Hightower
Altus, OK 73521
(405) 482-1044

**Museum of Western Art**
1727 Tremont Plaza
Denver, CO 80202
(303) 296-1880

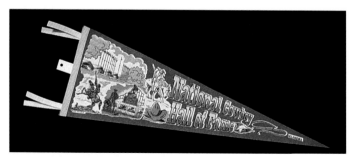

**National Cowboy Hall
of Fame and Western
Heritage Center**
1700 Northeast 63rd Street
Oklahoma City, OK 73111
(405) 478-2250

*The* museum of cowboy culture, including galleries full of fine art, cases full of sparkling rodeo memorabilia, Old West reproduction streets (indoors), and an outdoor walk with significant statues honoring cowboys as well as great rodeo animals. For serious study of the cowboy—in real life, rodeo, fine art, and movies—the archives here cannot be beat.

**National Cowgirl Hall of Fame and Western Heritage Center**
515 Avenue B
Hereford, TX 79045
(806) 364-5252

The Hall of Fame brochure sums up the cowgirl's life thusly: "Broncs before breakfast, babies after forty, life without pay, death without warning, God as her guide and a ballad on her wind-blistered lips, Woman in all her greatness gave flower to the great American West."

**National Museum of the American Indian**
3753 Broadway (at 155th Street)
New York, NY 10032
(212) 283-2420

**National Ranching Heritage Center**
4th Street and Indiana Avenue
P.O. Box 43201
Lubbock, TX 79409
(806) 742-2498

**North Fort Worth Historical Society**
131 E. Exchange Ave. #112
Fort Worth, TX 76106
(817) 625-5082

Fort Worth's cowtown museum: memorabilia, photos, and cowboy clothes from the glory days of the stockyards.

**Pro Rodeo Hall of Fame & Museum of the American Cowboy**
101 Pro Rodeo Drive
Colorado Springs, CO 80919
(719) 528-4761

Heaven-on-Earth for rodeo fans: memorabilia of all the greats, displays of saddles, ropes, cowboy clothing, etc.

**Rex Allen Arizona Cowboy Museum**
P.O. Box 995
Wilcox, AZ 85644
(602) 384-3059

**Robber's Roost Western Museum of the Pueblo Saddlemakers**
6001½ Boulder
Rye, CO 81069
(719) 489-3559

**Roy Rogers and Dale Evans Museum**
15650 Seneca Road
Victorville, CA 92392
(619) 243-4547

See page 235.

**Stradling Museum of the Horse**
350 McKeown Avenue
Patagonia, AZ 85624
(602) 394-2264

**Texas Ranger Hall of Fame and Museum**
Fort Fisher Park: Route 135 and the Brazos River
Waco, TX 76702
(817) 754-1433

**Tom Mix Museum**
721 North Delaware
Dewey, OK 74029
(918) 534-1555

**Tucson Rodeo Parade Museum**
4825 South Sixth Avenue
Tucson, AZ 85702
(602) 294-1280

See page 238.

THE CHAMP

# LIVESTOCK (ALIVE & DEAD) DEALERS AND ORGANIZATIONS

### American Bison Association
P.O. Box 16660
Denver, CO 80216
(303) 292-2833

The goal of the ABA is to promote and develop America's "buffalo" as an alternative to cattle. If you aren't interested in raising your own bison, you can nonetheless express your appreciation of the species by shopping the organization's gift catalogue (*The Trading Post*) for bison-themed mud flaps for your pickup or bison tote bags and hand puppets. Members of the ABA receive bimonthly *Bison World* magazine and *The Bison Breeders Handbook*.

### American Council of Spotted Asses Inc.
P.O. Box 121
New Melle, MO 63365
(314) 828-5430

A registry for rare spotted asses, which have a coat like a paint horse.

### The American Donkey and Mule Society
2901 North Elm
Denton, TX 76201
(817) 382-6845

When the ADMS was founded in 1967, it was a Dark Ages for donkeys and mules: "There was a minimally active Miniature Donkey Registry, and the Standard Jack and Jennet Registry . . . but no real activity was taking place," wrote Betsy and Paul Hutchins, who founded the society. "Contrast that to today's busy world of donkey fanciers! Countless people who thought donkeys were both stupid and stubborn have changed their minds."

### American Mustang and Burro Association, Inc.
P.O. Box 7
Benton City, WA 99320
1-800-US4-WILD
(509) 588-6336

The AMBA helps educate the public about wild equines, and is involved in the government's adoption and protection programs for them.

### American Quarter Horse Association
P.O. Box 200
Amarillo, TX 79168
(806) 376-4811

Cowboys love quarter horses, and the AQHA is an organization that sponsors some two thousand shows yearly for riders at all levels of skill. It also keeps the world's largest equine breed registry, produces "America's Horse" for broadcast on ESPN, maintains a Hall of Fame of great horses and great horse people, and stages a slam-bang weeklong convention and competition each year in November.

### The Bull Mart
HC 71-131 Turnout Road
Burns, OR 97720
(503) 573-7888

Shopping for an Angus, Shorthorn, or Beefmaster bull? Louie Molt and Larry Imbach of The Bull Mart have what you need.

### Cates Ranch
Wagon Mound, NM 87752
(505) 666-2360

Jack and Virginia Cates advertise that the Corriente cattle they sell are especially good for rodeos because they are "hardy and athletic and don't wear out."

### Desert West Skulls
P.O. Box 10334
Prescott, AZ 86304
(602) 772-4255

No living creatures are sold by this company, just the skulls of dead ones—cows in particular. Small steers to longhorns are available, priced by size and symmetry. Advertisements boast that the crania are "*ultra* clean" and sold with a money-back guarantee.

### Dickinson Cattle Co.
24001 Highway 94
Calhan, CO 80808
(719) 683-2655 or Fax: (719) 683-BULL

If you are in the market for breeding cows or frozen sperm to start your own herd of historic Texas Longhorns, Dickinson will fix you right up. They boast that their cattle are "hardy, colorful, big horned, and gentle." On occasion they also have some fantastic sets of horns and skulls for sale, and they publish a yearly "Texas Longhorn Celebrity Calendar" with glamour photos of some of the beefiest beefcake bulls and shapeliest longhorn cows you could imagine.

**The Grange**
Route 1 Box 57-B
Elkwood, VA 22718
(703) 399-1044

Larry and Nancy Terry raise Corriente cattle, the slim, agile animals used in rodeo roping contests and cutting horse contests. Bulls, cows, calves, and roping steers are available.

**National Cutting Horse Association**
4704 Highway 377S
Fort Worth, TX 76116
(817) 244-6188

Cutting horses keep a selected cow from rejoining the herd, and the fancy footwork involved in this activity is an animal skill unlike any other. Celebrities who ride cutting horses in competition include Tanya Tucker, Linda Blair, and Michael Keaton.

**Thundering Herd Buffalo Products**
Box 1051
Reno, NV 89504
(800) 525-9730

"Buffalo ranching makes good ecological sense for the American prairie," says the Thundering Herd company, and they sell a wide range of products made from buffalo, including a full-size robe (as seen in *Dances with Wolves*) complete with tail still attached, for $800.

**Twin Pines Ranch**
15970 Central Pike
Lebanon TN 37087
(615) 449-4719

The Twin Pines Ranch, in conjunction with the Cañon del Diablo Ranch in Mexico, has done a "genetic rescue" on Criollo cattle, the original stock that came to the New World starting in 1493 and became the ancestors of Texas longhorns. These lean, hardy critters are now available for breeding.

**Vela & Sons**
Route 3, Box 150
Edinburg, TX 78539
(512) 383-3697 or (512) 381-9375

One of the top suppliers of rodeo livestock. Vela's bucking bulls are notorious in the ring, but as Mr. Vela once told us, the secret of his success is careful training: "The gentler you are with them, the gentler they will be with you . . . and the higher they will buck when it's showtime." Mr. Vela defined an ideal bucking bull as one that spins and jumps like a hellion when the chute gate swings open, but trots like a gentleman back to its pen as soon as it leaves the ring.

# SCHOOLS

### Ann Mallett School of Dance
P.O. Box 564
Burlington, CO 80807
(719) 397-2447

The specialty here is Western dancing: the two step, line dances, cloggin', and much more in private or group situations.

### Casey and Son Horseshoeing
Route 3 Box 932
LaFayette, GA 30728
(404) 397-8909

The only horseshoeing academy in the country where you can earn full professional certification as a farrier.

### Marlene Eddleman Barrel Racing Clinics
1291 East F. Street
Oakdale, CA 95361
(209) 847-2217

Marlene has been a top barrel racer for more than a decade. Her two- and three-day clinics, given a few times each year, are for serious competitors: she promises that 80 percent of each eight-hour day will be spent in the saddle.

### D. W. Frommer II: Bootmaker
308 North 6th Street
Redmond, OR 97756
(503) 923-3808

Frommer, a custom bootmaker of note (see above), as well as author of a book on the history of Western boots, offers a video and textbook at-home course in how to make cowboy boots.

### Gary Leffew Bull Riding School
Box 5175
Santa Maria, CA 93456
(805) 929-4286

Leffew, one-time world champion rodeo bull rider, shows young cowpokes how to stay on a raging bull at his private arena on the grounds of his California ranch.

### Kentucky Horseshoeing School
P.O. Box 120
Mount Eden, KY 40046
(502) 738-5257

Courses last from two to twelve weeks and include classroom as well as hands-on forge training.

### The Ranching for Profit School
7719 Rio Grande Blvd NW
Albuquerque, NM 87107
(505) 898-7417

A program for western ranchers on everything from animal nutrition to drought management.

### Rodeo Announcing School
3504 English Road
Farmington, NM
(505) 327-3481

Once each year in March, veteran announcer Zoop Dove holds a three-day clinic for anyone who dreams of being the hypnotic voice on the P.A. system that thrills and inspires the crowds at rodeos. Mr. Dove, who was 1988 PRCA Announcer of the Year, teaches "everything from attitudes to responsibilities . . . with extra emphasis on motivation."

# MAIL-ORDER CATALOGUES

## Cattle Kate
P.O. Box 572
Wilson, WY 83014
(307) 733-7414 or (800) 332-KATE

If you want to look like you just stepped out of *Lonesome Dove,* this is the catalogue for you. Fringed gauntlet gloves, frock coats, Prairie Dancer bustle dresses, and silky brocade gambler vests abound. The original Cattle Kate, aka Ella Watson, was hanged for rustling in the Johnson County War in 1892. Today's Kate, aka Kathy Bressler, says she started her company because so many people admired the clothes she sewed for herself while working as a miner in Atlantic City, Wyoming (pop. 45).

## Cheyenne Outfitters
P.O. Box 12013
Cheyenne, WY 82003
(800) 234-0432

Here are clothes that real Westerners tend to favor these days—not vintage styles, but up-to-the-minute buckskin jackets, Roper boots, and flamboyant Western-styled dress shirts.

## The Cowboy Country General Store
P.O. Box 1464
La Porte, CO 80535
(800) 433-2247

"A Mail Order Emporium of Western Essentials" is how this juicy newsprint catalogue bills itself. Proprietor Kathy Lynn Wills has put together a broad selection of cowboy fashions including buckaroo neckerchiefs and "cowkid chinks" for little boys and girls, Western-themed dishware, classic reprints and modern books about cowboy topics, rare tapes of cowboy songs and poems, and Christmas gift baskets. The front page of the catalogue says, "Go West, Young Man . . . Or at Least Go Western with CCGS!"

## The Cowboys' Shopping List
Western Folklife Center
P.O. Box 888
Elko, NV 89801
(702) 738-7508

Elko is home to the original, biggest, and best cowboy poetry gathering each year. The Folklife Center issues a catalogue of video and audio tapes, as well as books of most of the major cowboy poets around today. Also available: Cowboy Poetry Gathering Neck Rags (scarves), "Sweetheart of the Rodeo" hat pins, and posters of ranch women and poets.

## Hitching Post Supply
10312 210th Street SE
Snohomish, WA 98290
(206) 668-2349

Need horsehair by the pound to braid into "stampede strings" to keep your cowboy hat on, or already-made horsehair earrings, friendship bracelets, belts, and suspenders? Here's a good place to find them, along with engraved silver bits, custom-made spurs and chaps, and starter kits for those interested in learning the craft of horsehair braiding.

## Indian Jewelers Supply Company
P.O. Box 1774 (601 East Coal Avenue)
Gallup, NM 87305
(505) 722-4451 or (800) 545-6540

A huge catalogue filled with silver conchas, turquoise stones, Zuni fetishes, bola tips, button shanks, buckle blanks, and bulk metals by the pound. Make your own Native American style jewelry!

## Kittelson Spurs
8832 West County Road 18E
Loveland, CO 80537
(303) 667-4098

Send for John B. Kittelson's catalogue and you get back a thick envelope filled with more designs for custom-made spurs then you ever imagined could exist. Big star-shaped rowels, fancy shanks with diamond shapes, others with stars and hearts. Mr. Kittelson also repairs antique spurs, and he has gift certificates if you want to give someone a pair but aren't sure what style they would like.

## Mark Allen Productions

3750 South Valley View #14
Las Vegas, NV 89103
(800) 858-5568

Want to learn fancy rope tricks, quick-draw, tomahawk throwing? Mark Allen carries books and videos about all such Western arts, as well as the requisite equipment.

## Mark Mfg.

Box 55
Deeth, NV 89823
(702) 752-3475

Mark E. Dahl makes custom bits, spurs, and buckles, and his work is gorgeous—all hand-tooled and laden with silver. He also makes conchas and saddle silver; you can have your initials or brand worked into the design if you wish. Mark does all the work himself in his one-man shop, and his craftsmanship is why customers keep sending in the orders.

## Marlene

13460 Landcaster
Oakland, CA 95361
(800) 542-8225

Marlene Eddleman, champion rodeo barrel racer, has put together an intriguing assortment of goods for horse and rider. Festive Western shirts, heavy on the glitter and glamour, are featured side-by-side with Marlene-designed saddles, hoof stimulant creams, and equine clothing, including full-body, head-to-tail coveralls that make a horse look rather like a grand piano about to be shipped.

## The Old Frontier Clothing Company

P.O. Box 691836
Los Angeles, CA 90069
(800) 422-9257 or (in California)
(213) 657-9257

Owner Larry Bitterman has what it takes to make his customers look authentically Old West. Both men and women can find fashions of a hundred years ago, retooled in today's (usually larger) sizes. We especially like the wide-placket shirts favored by Duke Wayne in all his Westerns.

## Old West Reproductions

446 Florence South Loop
Florence, MT 59833
(406) 273 2615

If you want a gun belt and holster that look like Wyatt Earp might have worn them, Rick Bachman's catalogue will help you realize your dream. He has made the gun belts for *Dances with Wolves, Gunsmoke II, The Young Riders,* and many other Western movies. The fine, old-style workmanship of these products will please even the most persnickety gunslinger. A catalogue is available, and it is a pleasure to browse—includes photos of the merchandise, as well as Mr. Bachman modeling some of his finest creations.

## Rodeo Video, Inc.

P.O. Box G
Snowflake, AZ 85937
(800) 331-1269 or (602) 536-7111

For anyone who resents all the other sports that crowd rodeo off television, here is a solution: *Rodeo Video* magazine, published on videotape each month with highlights of all the biggest contests around the country. The Rodeo Video catalogue also features blooper tapes, tapes devoted exclusively to bull riding, National Finals tapes going back to 1974, Indian Rodeo tapes, and how-to tapes for aspiring contestants.

## Ruby Montana's Pinto Pony

603 Second Avenue
Seattle, WA 98104
(800) 788-RUBY

Ruby calls her operation "Outfitters for the Cosmic Cowboy"; while not everything here is Western (there are pink flamingos, salt-and-peppers, and Elvis artifacts galore), the catalogue contains plenty of fine Westernalia such as bolo ties in the shape of steer skulls and china plates with bucking broncs on them. Ruby herself is from Oklahoma, and the window of her shop contains a license plate that proclaims the Sooner State "Land of Beautiful Women."

## Sheplers
6501 West Kellogg
P.O. Box 7702
Wichita, KS 67277
(800) 835-4004

Sheplers is the world's largest Western store, with nineteen branches throughout the region, and it produces the big kahuna of mail-order catalogues, filled with men's and women's wear from drover coats to lizardskin boots, including every type of Levi's made and a set of fifty silver-plated belt buckles to honor each of the United States. Extra-large sizes are a specialty, and everything is sold with a "handshake guarantee," promising satisfaction. "At Sheplers we take the timeless look of traditional Western fashions and give them to you in popular fabrics, designs, leathers and colors, to make 'dressing Western' the style you choose!"

## Sundance Catalog
1909 South, 4250 West
Salt Lake City, UT 84104
(800) 422-2770

Everything Robert Redford is connected with is special, and this catalogue, an offshoot of his Sundance Institute (founded in 1969), is a good example. It is filled with high-quality, well-chosen goods with a Western flair. We especially like the selection of mail-orderable furniture.

## Tim Bath Chaps, Inc.
1050 County Road 143
Burns, WY 82053
(307) 634-0242 or (307) 547-3640

If you ever wondered where rodeo champs like Skeeter Thurston, Robert Etbauer, et al., get their way-out chaps, here it is. Fringed, conchoed, and in flamboyant leather colors, these chaps are common in the arena; worn anywhere else, they are guaranteed to cause jaws to drop. "We are being copied," says the catalogue, "but never matched!"

## Wagman-Grenamyer, Inc.
10 Strawberry Street
Philadelphia, PA 19106
(215) 923-8090

Say you want to braid a nice hatband for yourself out of horsehair, but you don't have a horse handy to contribute to the endeavor? Wagman-Grenamyer supplies horsetail hair for braiding and hitching in three shades: white, black, and salt and pepper, in lengths from twenty-four to thirty inches.

# NEWSLETTERS AND PERIODICALS

### Arizona Highways
2039 West Lewis Avenue
Phoenix, AZ 85009
(800) 543-5432

One of the prettiest and most venerable of Western regional magazines, *Arizona Highways* is known for spectacular photography and coverage of the scenic wonders of the state. It originally took its name from the motto, "Civilization Follows the Improved Highway," and its enduring charm is as a record of the Arizona that remains pristine and natural. Of special interest are the collectors issues on turquoise and Indian jewelry.

### Art of the West
15612 Highway 7, Suite 235
Minnetonka, MN 55345
(612) 935-5850

A bimonthly journal filled with articles about the best-known Western artists working today. Also, listings of upcoming shows, and pages of advertisements for limited-edition prints and bronzes.

### Boots: The Magazine for Folks with Their Boots On
Box 766
Challis, ID 83226
(208) 879-4475

A magazine devoted to cowboy poetry, cowboy cookery, and other aspects of real Western life.

### Chile Pepper
P.O. Box 4278
Albuquerque, NM 87196
(800) 359-1483

The first and last word for pod people: recipes for peppers, articles about culinary history, listings of spicy food fairs, reviews of restaurants that serve chile-seasoned food, and advertisements from companies with pepper-related oddities to sell, including "sirloin in a shuck" hot tamales from Texas, a personal chile roaster, and chile pepper windsocks. One classified ad placed by a seed company in California with hot ones to sell begins, "Yeeeoooooowwwwwwwwwww!!!!!!"

### Country America
1716 Locust Street
Des Moines, IA 50336

Country life and country entertainment: profiles of top musicians and cowboy poets, listings of upcoming farm equipment shows and crafts fairs, and travel stories focusing on rural destinations.

### Country Sampler's West
707 Kautz Road
St. Charles, IL 60174
(708) 377-8000

Formerly *Southwest Sampler,* this thick, glossy magazine devoted to Western style celebrates "the spirit of the frontier home." Issues contain articles on cookery, basketry, Kachina carving, frontier furniture, antiques, and travel, and shopping guides to places throughout the West. In addition to the articles, there are lots and lots of ads for gifts and home decor.

### Country Woman
5400 South 60th Street
Greendale, WI 53129

"For farm and country women and those who have moved from the country in body, but not in heart." This folksy bimonthly isn't strictly about the West, but there are plenty of articles about such topics as spinning yarn from your sheep's wool, making a quilt from worn blue jeans, and cooking cowboy vittles. Regular features include "The View from My Kitchen" (photos taken by readers looking out their windows), "Notes from Nettie" ("While old tractor tires can serve nicely as sandboxes in some places, they require caution in snake country."), "Looking Back" (old-time farm photos), and "Grandma's Brag Page" (photos of adorable grandchildren). No advertising!

### The Cowboy Directory
Blue Roan Publishing
P.O. Box 314
Burns, OR 97720

No aficionado of the West should be without this wonderful resource guide. No frills: just plenty of meat-and-potatoes listings of Western-accented stores, museums, societies, events, personalities available for hire, veterinary supplies, and artists.

**Cowboy Magazine**
P.O. Box 126
La Veta, CO 81055
(719) 742-5250

"For People Who Value the Cowboy Lifestyle" is how *Cowboy* describes itself. It is among the best and most enlightening journals we have seen—filled with fascinating articles on everything from horse gear to old-time cowboy stars. If you are interested in the real West and/or the West of the imagination, you will find it invaluable.

**Cowboys & Indians**
P.O. Box 7260
San Carlos, CA 94070
(415) 361-8001

"A magazine for people who are inspired by the sharp scent of sagebrush, wide Western skies, and bunkhouse lore on a star-filled night." Sign us up! This magazine for Western enthusiasts includes stories about history, collectibles, real cowboys, and movie greats. The first issues, published in 1993, featured some gorgeous color photography, too.

**The Indian Trader**
Post Office Box 1421
Gallup, NM 87305
(505) 722-6694

A monthly tabloid that concerns itself with news of all sorts of recent Indian affairs, but especially anything having to do with trade and collecting. It serves also as a bulletin board for craftspeople, traders, dealers, and buyers of Indian-made goods. There are news of upcoming auctions, trading post activities, and swap meets, and a wonderful array of advertisements that clue you in about where to have Zuni jewelry repaired and when the next big powwow is.

**Ken's Rodeo Souvenirs**
P.O. Box 69
Black River Falls, WI 54615

A photocopied newsletter for serious rodeo devotees who want to express their affection for the sport by buying such mementos as a little yellow sign for their car window that says "Wrangler Butts Drive Me Nuts" or "Rodeo Mom on Board." Other items for sale: pro rodeo trading cards, lots of cassette tapes of rare cowboy songs, and Randy Schmutz's tribute tape to fallen rodeo hero Lane Frost.

**Native Peoples**
5333 North Seventh Street
Phoenix, AZ 85014

"Dedicated to the sensitive portrayal of the arts and lifeways of native peoples of the Americas," this handsome quarterly contains well-written and informative articles about what Native American artists are doing today, as well as historical essays.

**New Mexico**
1100 St. Francis Drive
Santa Fe, NM 87503
(505) 827-0220

Published for more than seventy years, *New Mexico* is always a treat to read, and monthly proof of the slogan, "Land of Enchantment." Here is complete coverage of people and events in this extraordinary place of hot chiles, magnificent mesas, and a trilogy of ethnic cultures like nowhere else on earth.

**Out West**
10522 Brunswick Road
Grass Valley, CA 95945

A "grass-routes" newspaper tip sheet to roadside pleasures that you won't find in most ordinary guidebooks: odd museums, mom-and-pop cafés, interesting places to stay.

**El Palacio**
P.O. Box 2087
Santa Fe, NM 87504-2087
(505) 827-6451

The magazine of the Museum of New Mexico is a treasury of well-written and beautifully illustrated articles about a wide range of Southwestern cultural topics: artist profiles, local archaeology, stories about current exhibits. One recent issue featured an interview with cartoonist Bill Mauldin, who calls himself "a hillbilly from New Mexico," pages of lovely old engravings from the Palace Print Shop on the Plaza, and a fascinating story by Wolf Schneider about Spanish Barbs, the hardy forebears of American Mustangs.

**Persimmon Hill**
The National Cowboy Hall of Fame
1700 N.E. 63rd Street
Oklahoma City, OK 73111

This beautiful quarterly publication is part of the package when you become a member of The National Cowboy

Hall of Fame, or you can buy it separately. *Persimmon Hill* contains modern cowboy poetry and stories as well as information about such topics as brands and branding and Western artists, past and present.

### The Plait

The Rawhide and Leather Braiders Association
Newsletter
c/o Robert Stewart
P.O. Box 25
Mountain Home, UT 84051

Rawhide braiding is an old Western skill. This newsletter contains information on how to do it in the form of questions and commentary written by readers to Dave Barrow, the editor, and Dave's replies.

### Rope Burns: Official Publication of the Working Cowboy

P.O. Box 35
Gene Autry, OK 73436

A bimonthly newspaper of cowboy-related events around the country. It reports on such activities as ranch rodeos, collectors' shows, chili cook-offs, horsehair hitching clinics, and auctions where you can buy one of Tom Mix's hats. A healthy dose of cowboy humor makes it always fun to read.

### Song of the West

136 Pearl Street
Fort Collins, CO 80521
(303) 484-3209

Issued three times yearly, this magazine is devoted to cowboy music and musicians. It includes stories about contemporary singers and cowboy music festivals, reviews of new recordings, and historical pieces about the greats of yesteryear.

### Texas Monthly

Box 1569
Austin, TX 78767

The biggest, fanciest, and most important of all regional magazines (as befits anything connected to Texas), *Texas Monthly* is always a treat to read, and it has entertaining and reliable listings of restaurants, clubs, and events all around the state. The articles go way beyond old-time cowboys and Indians (as does modern Texas); if you want to know what's going on in the Lone Star State, this is what you need to read.

### That's Country

1565 Scenic Ave., Suite C
Costa Mesa, CA 92626
(800) 432-9575

A magazine for people interested primarily in Western clothing. Stories, photos, and advertisements galore make *That's Country* a dream-come-true for hat aficionados and denim devotees. The premier issue features a profile of Dwight Yoakam ("Hillbilly High Style"), a story that tells where Roy Rogers bought his shirts, and an article about Manuel Cuevas, heir to Nudie's throne.

### Today's Old West Traveler

Box 2928
Costa Mesa, CA 92628
(800) 775-WEST

A journal "dedicated to keeping the spirit of the Old West alive." It fulfills its mission with stories about dude ranches, trail drives, pack trips, dance festivals, and other activities for adventurous travelers. Subscribers can avail themselves of a free Ranch/Match Service: "We'll find the right Old West trip for you."

### Western Horse Magazine

P.O. Box 2019
609 East Ross
Waxahachie, TX 75165
(214) 937-7666

Anything and everything related to Western horses and riding.

### Western Horseman

Box 7980
Colorado Springs, CO 80933-7980
(719) 633-5524

The "World's Leading Horse Magazine Since 1936" isn't only about riding, Western style. It is a magazine about horse people, too, as well as the great outdoors that is best enjoyed in the company of a good saddle horse.

### Western Styles

451 East 58th Ave., Suite 4781
Denver, CO 80216
(303) 293-0222

Volume 1, Number 1, published in the Spring of 1993 promised "40 Pages of Style-Smart Western Fashions." There are indeed plenty of beautiful—as well as practical—duds to look at; but this magazine's first issue contained a whole lot more: profiles of pioneer women, a fine National Finals rodeo report, stories about real Westerners today, and a fascinating column about Western art.

### Whispering Wind
8009 Wales Street
New Orleans, LA 70126

A high-quality bimonthly devoted to American Indian crafts, history, and culture—current and historical; 73 percent of the readership are practicing craftspeople, and over half attend five powwows per year.

### Wild West
602 South King Street
Suite 300
Leesburg, VA 22075

History, art, collectibles, literature: *Wild West* covers it all in a handsome bimonthly magazine that includes regular columns on "Warriors and Chiefs" and "Gunfighters and Lawmen," as well as book reviews and travel suggestions.

### Yippy-Yi-Yea Magazine
8393 East Holly Road
Holly, MI 48442

A newcomer to the newsstand, *Yippy-Yi-Yea* is spunky and loads of fun. Much attention is paid to Western style, with beautiful color photographs that will make you drool with envy at the interiors of some of the homes that are profiled. Also: stories about great Western shopping all around the country, contemporary and vintage cowboy art, chuck wagon recipes, and destinations for travelers.

# INDEX

# PICTURE CREDITS